An Introduction to Cognitive Linguistics

Learning About Language

General Editors:
Geoffrey Leech & Mick Short, Lancaster University

Already published:

Analysing Sentences (2nd edition) Noel Burton-Roberts

Words and Their Meaning Howard Jackson

An Introduction to Phonology Francis Katamba

Grammar and Meaning Howard Jackson

An Introduction to Sociolinguistics (2nd edition) Janet Holmes

Realms of Meaning: An Introduction to Semantics Th. R. Hofmann

An Introduction to Psycholinguistics (2nd edition) Danny D. Steinberg and Natalin V. Sciarini

An Introduction to Spoken Interaction Anna-Brita Stenström

Watching English Change Laurie Bauer

Meaning in Interaction: An Introduction to Pragmatics Jenny Thomas

An Introduction to Cognitive Linguistics (2nd edition) Friedrich Ungerer and Hans-Jörg Schmid

Exploring the Language of Poems, Plays and Prose Mick Short

Contemporary Linguistics: An Introduction William O'Grady, Michael Dobrovolsky and Francis Katamba

An Introduction to Natural Language Processing Through Prolog Clive Matthews

An Introduction to Child Language Development Susan Foster-Cohen

The Sounds of Language: An Introduction to Phonetics Henry Rogers

An Introduction to Foreign Language Learning and Teaching Keith Johnson

Varieties of Modern English Diane Davies

Patterns of Spoken English Gerald Knowles

The Earliest English Chris McCully and Sharon Hilles

An Introduction to Cognitive Linguistics

Second Edition

Friedrich Ungerer
Hans-Jörg Schmid

Harlow, England • London • New York • Boston • San Francisco • Toronto
Sydney • Tokyo • Singapore • Hong Kong • Seoul • Taipei • New Delhi
Cape Town • Madrid • Mexico City • Amsterdam • Munich • Paris • Milan

PEARSON EDUCATION LIMITED

Edinburgh Gate
Harlow CM20 2JE
United Kingdom
Tel: +44 (0)1279 623623
Fax: +44 (0)1279 431059
Website: www.pearsoned.co.uk

First published 1996
Second edition published in Great Britain in 2006

© Addison Wesley Longman Limited 1996
© Pearson Education Limited 2006

The rights of Friedrich Ungerer and Hans-Jörg Schmid to be identified as authors of this work
has been asserted by them in accordance with the Copyright, Designs and Patents Act 1988.

ISBN-13: 978-0-582-78496-3
ISBN-10: 0-582-78496-4

British Library Cataloguing in Publication Data
A CIP catalogue record for this book can be obtained from the British Library

Library of Congress Cataloging in Publication Data
An introduction to cognitive linguistics / Friedrich Ungerer & Hans-Jörg Schmid. -- 2nd ed.
    p. cm.
    Includes bibliographical references and index.
    ISBN-13: 978-0-582-78496-3 (pbk.)
    ISBN-10: 0-582-78496-4 (pbk.)
    1. Cognitive grammar. I. Ungerer, Friedrich. II. Schmid, Hans-Jörg.

    P165.159 2006
    415--dc22

                                                                              2006040863

10 9 8 7 6 5 4 3 2 1
10 09 08 07 06

Set by 71
Printed and bound in Malaysia

The Publisher's policy is to use paper manufactured from sustainable forests.

Contents

Publisher's acknowledgements   x

Preface to the second edition   vii

Typographical conventions   ix

Introduction   1

1 Prototypes and categories   7
  1.1 Colours, squares, birds and cups: early empirical research into lexical categories   7
  1.2 The internal structure of categories: prototypes, attributes, family resemblances and gestalt   24
  1.3 Context-dependence and cultural models   45

2 Levels of categorization   64
  2.1 Basic level categories of organisms and concrete objects   64
  2.2 Superordinate and subordinate categories   76
  2.3 Conceptual hierarchies   85
  2.4 Categorization and composite word forms   92
  2.5 Basic level categories and basic experiences: actions, events, properties, states and locations   101

3 Conceptual metaphors and metonymies   114
  3.1 Metaphors and metonymies: from figures of speech to conceptual systems   114
  3.2 Metaphors, metonymies and the structure of emotion categories   132
  3.3 Metaphors as a way of thinking: examples from science and politics   144
  3.4 Thinking in metonymies: potential and limitations   154

4 Figure and ground   163
  4.1 Figure and ground, trajector and landmark: early research into prepositions   163
  4.2 Figure, ground and two metaphors: a cognitive explanation of simple clause patterns   176
  4.3 Other types of prominence and cognitive processing   191

5 Frames and constructions   207
  5.1 Frames and scripts   207
  5.2 Event-frames and the windowing of attention   218
  5.3 Language-specific framing and its use in narrative texts   230
  5.4 Construction Grammar   244

6 Blending and relevance   257
  6.1 Metaphor, metonymy and conceptual blending   257
  6.2 Conceptual blending in linguistic analysis and description 268
  6.3 Conceptual blending in advertising texts, riddles and jokes 280
  6.4 Relevance: a cognitive-pragmatic phenomenon   288

7 Other issues in cognitive linguistics   300
  7.1 Iconicity   300
  7.2 Lexical change and prototypicality   312
  7.3 Cognitive aspects of grammaticalization   321
  7.4 Effects on foreign language teaching   328

  Conclusion   343

Preface to the second edition

This new edition of the book is more than the usual update of information and references. In response to recent developments in cognitive linguistics we have made some major changes and have introduced new topics extending the number of chapters from six to seven.

Our presentation of conceptual categorization has become more differentiated. With regard to individual categories, the notion of context-dependence has been strengthened. The presentation of cognitive models and cognitive hierarchies now emphasizes the importance of part-whole links as opposed to type-of relationships.

The third chapter now provides an innovative description of the role played by metaphors and metonymies based on the notion of 'mapping scope'. Generally metonymy has been given more prominence to accommodate recent research; the section on 'Metaphor as a way of thinking' has been complemented by an additional section 'Thinking in metonymies'c.

While Chapter 5 includes a section on 'Construction Grammar', a new Chapter 6 has been inserted providing a careful introduction of blending theory as an online processing strategy. The chapter includes many detailed analyses of lexical and grammatical phenomena, and also of ads, riddles and jokes. The last section of this chapter takes a look at 'Relevance Theory' exploring its potential to stimulate cognitive-linguistic approaches.

The final chapter of the book has almost doubled in size as two of the four sections, the sections on iconicity and on cognitive linguistics in foreign language learning, have been massively expanded and now contain a large amount of new material and original ideas.

The conclusion of the first edition has been reshaped into an 'Outlook' section which surveys some current attempts to put linguistic theorizing on a safer psychological and neurological footing.

We are indebted to Maura Bresnan-Enders, Kirsten Buchholz, Eva Drewelow, Sandra Handl, Susanne Handl, Nick Jacob-Flynn and Anne-Kristin

Siebenborn for their invaluable assistance in checking and proofreading manuscripts and generating the index. As the text of the first edition still makes up a substantial part of this book we want to renew our thanks to Ingrid Fandrych, Wolfgang Falkner, Nick Jacob-Flynn, Geoffrey Leech, Len Lipka, Andreas Mahler, Arthur Mettinger and Kieran O'Rourke for their contributions to the success of the first edition.

F. Ungerer and H.-J. Schmid

Rostock and Munich, Summer 2006

Typographical conventions

Cognitive categories, concepts, cognitive and cultural models	small capitals e.g. BIRD, VEHICLE, LOVE, ON THE BEACH
Attributes	single quotes e.g. 'juicy', 'has legs'
Members of categories	arrows and small capitals e.g. >ROBIN<, >PARROT<
Image schemas	single quotes e.g. 'in-out', 'part-whole'
Metaphors/metonymies	+ signs and small capitals e.g. +ANGER IS HEAT+, +PRODUCER FOR PRODUCT+
Basic correlations	single quotes and arrows e.g. 'cause<>effect', 'action<>motion'
Frames	small capitals in brackets e.g. [COMMERCIAL EVENT]

Publishers' acknowledgements

The publishers are grateful to the following for permission to reproduce copyright material:

Elsevier Science Publishers B.V. for the 'Smith brothers' illustration from page 269 of Sharon L. Armstrong, Lila R. Gleitman and Henry Gleitman (1983) 'What some concepts might not be' *Cognition* 13; Georgetown University Press for our Figures 1.4 (repeated as Figure 1.9), 1.5 and 1.6, being Figures 5 and 7 from William Labov 'The Boundaries of Words and Their Meanings', pp. 354 and 356 in Charles-James N. Bailey and Roger W. Shuy, Editors, *New Ways of Analyzing Variation in English* (1973); Linguistic Society of America and the author Ronald W. Langacker for our Figure 4.20, being an adaptation of a diagram on p. 69 of 'Nouns and Verbs' which appeared in *Language* 63 (1987); Pearson Education for two illustrations (our Figure 1.12) of a 'bungalow' and 'a typical English cottage' from the fourth edition of the Longman Dictionary of Contemporary English (LDOCE); Max Niemeyer Verlag GmbH & Co. KG for our Figure 1.10, being Figures 4.10, 4.11 and 4.9 (pp. 151 and 152) in H.-J. Schmid's *Cottage and Co., start vs. Begin. Die Kategorisierung als Grundprinzip einer differenzierten Bedeutungbeschreibung* (1993) and our Figure 1.17, being (12) on page 292 of Leonard Lipka's 'Prototype semantics or feature semantics: an alternative?' in W. Lorscher and R. Schulze's (eds) *Perspectives on language in performance. Studies in linguistics, literary criticism, and language teaching and learning. To honour Werner Hullen on the occasion of his sixtieth birthday* (1987); Stanford University Press for our Figure 4.21, being an adapted composite of Figures 3.11 (p. 144) and 7.1 and 7.2 (p. 245) from Ronald W. Langacker's *Foundations of Cognitive Grammar, Volume I: Theoretical Prerequisites* (1987).

Introduction

If someone says to you 'Our car has broken down', your reaction may simply be to feel sorry. For the linguist, though, even such a simple utterance calls for quite an elaborate explanation. As far as the meaning and the grammar of the sentence are concerned, a traditional description would try to paraphrase the meanings of the words used; it would analyze the clause pattern (here a simple combination of subject and verb or predicate), and would probably go on to discuss the use of the present perfect tense.

Another approach involves asking language users to describe what is going on in their minds when they produce and understand words and sentences. As experiments have shown, people will not only state that a car has a box-like shape, that it has wheels, doors, and windows, that it is driven by an engine and equipped with a steering wheel, an accelerator and brakes, and that it has seats for the driver and the passengers – more likely than not, they will also mention that a car is comfortable and fast, that it offers mobility, independence and perhaps social status. Some people may connect the notion of *car* with their first love affair, or with injury if they were once involved in an accident.

By adding these attributes, people include associations and impressions which are part of their experience. While the last two items ('first love affair', 'injury') point to a very personal, subjective experience, attributes like 'comfort', 'speed', 'mobility' and 'independence' seem to be part of our communal experience of cars. Taken together, the attributes collected from laypersons seem to reflect the way we perceive the world around us and interact with it. The wide and varied experience that we have of cars is also helpful when it comes to identifying and naming car-like objects that we encounter for the first time. For example, we do not hesitate to use the word *car* for vehicles with only three wheels or strange-looking safari jeeps, because we can compare them with the idea of a typical car we have stored in our minds. In other words, a description that takes account of our experience of the world – or more technically, an **experiential view** of words and other linguistic structures – seems to provide a rich and fairly natural description of their meanings, and this is one of the goals of the cognitive-linguistic approach presented in this book.

Experiential aspects of meaning do not only emerge in experiments and personal interviews. Our shared experience of the world is also stored in our everyday language and can thus be gleaned from the way we express our ideas. In order to open this mine, however, we have to go beyond the 'logic' of clause patterns and examine figurative language, especially metaphors. Looking again at our initial example *Our car has broken down*, it is evident that a car does not really break down just like a chair collapses so that its parts come apart. Nevertheless the conceptual background of this expression is clear enough. Since most of us do not know an awful lot about cars and how they work, we use our knowledge of chairs or other equally familiar objects collapsing to understand what happens when the car's engine suddenly stops working.

This transfer of our experience of well-known objects and events is even more important where abstract categories like emotions are involved. Imagine that someone describes the car owner's reaction to the breakdown of his car with the words *Dad exploded*. In order to get a full grasp of this utterance and the notion of *anger* expressed, we will call up our knowledge of actual explosions of gas stoves, fireworks and even bombs. This means that we will make use of our experience of the concrete world around us. Considering the wealth of observations, impressions and associations underlying metaphors, it is not surprising that they have joined tests and interviews as the second major basis of the experiential view of language.

Another important aspect of linguistic utterances concerns the selection and arrangement of the information that is expressed. For example, consider the sentence *The car crashed into the tree* which might be a description of the circumstances that led to the car's breakdown. Visualizing the accident situation sketched in this example, you will probably agree that the sentence seems to describe the situation in a fairly natural way. In comparison, other ways of relating the accident such as *The tree was hit by the car* seem somehow strange and unnatural. The reason is that the moving car is the most interesting and prominent aspect of the whole situation, and therefore we tend to begin the sentence with the noun phrase *the car*. What this explanation claims is that the selection of the clause subject is determined by the different degrees of prominence carried by the elements involved in a situation. This prominence is not just reflected in the selection of the subject as opposed to the object and the adverbials of a clause, but there are also many other applications of what may be called the **prominence view** of linguistic structures.

The prominence view provides one explanation of how the information in a clause is selected and arranged. An alternative approach is based on the assumption that what we actually express reflects which parts of an event attract our attention, and it can therefore be called the **attentional view**. Returning once more to the road accident, the sentence *The car crashed into the tree* selects only a small section of the event that we probably conjure up in our minds: how the car started to swerve, how it skidded across the road and rumbled onto the verge. Although all this happened before the car hit the tree, it is not mentioned because our attention is focused on the crucial point where the path of the car ended, i.e. when the vehicle collided with the tree, resulting in a severely damaged car and most likely causing injuries to its passengers. Analyzing the sentence in terms of attention allocation, the attentional view explains why one stage of the event is expressed in the sentence and why other stages are not.

The experiential, the prominence and the attentional view are three interlocking ways of approaching language via its relation to the world around us, which between them describe the core areas of cognitive linguistics. An additional aspect that has increasingly captured the attention of cognitive linguists is concerned with the **mental processing of cognitive input**, and in particular with the online processing of our conceptualizations. To add another example from the field of vehicles, consider the slogan of an advertising campaign for a well-known brand of cars: *Unleash a Jaguar.* Exploiting the origin of the brand name, this ad brings together ideas from the two conceptual domains of cars and wild animals; it amalgamates them into a powerful message suggesting an image of a car that is impatiently waiting for the customer, to be set free and allowed to act out its power, speed and ferocity. This happens although the relationships between the wild animal domain and the car domain are not really clarified, let alone permanently fixed. Technically speaking, the expression *Unleash a Jaguar* instructs the readers to simultaneously construct two 'mental spaces': a 'car' space containing associations like powerful engine, high maximum speed, attractive design, etc.; and a 'wild animal' space including associations normally attributed to jaguars, such as their ferocity, speed of running, litheness and elegance. To understand the message of the slogan, readers have to go through a process of **conceptually blending** the two mental spaces, a process resulting in a blended notion of 'car-as-a-wild-animal'. With regard to its meaning, this conceptual blend is somewhat vague and open-ended, and it is this quality that is exploited in ads and many other text-types.

If these examples and their analysis have provided you with a first impression of cognitive linguistics, you should perhaps now proceed to the individual chapters of the book to find out more about the issues raised. The remaining part of the introduction is primarily addressed to readers who are already more familiar with cognitive linguistics and want to get a concise overview of the topics dealt with in the book and their research background.

The first of the seven chapters will pursue the experiential view by looking at early psychological studies of cognitive categories (most of them conducted by Eleanor Rosch), which led to the prototype model of categorization. This will take us to a discussion of attributes, family resemblances and gestalts. Contrary to what one might assume, prototypes and cognitive categories are not static, but shift with the context in which a word is used and depend on the cognitive and cultural models stored in our mind.

The second chapter concentrates on the predominance of the 'middle' level of categorization, called basic level. It is argued that basic level categories for objects and organisms, such as DOG, RABBIT or KNIFE, are cognitively more important than either superordinate categories like ANIMAL or CUTLERY or subordinate categories like GREYHOUND or PENKNIFE, but it will also be shown that part–whole relationships like TABLE–KITCHEN–HOUSE–TOWN are just as important for the organization of our mental lexicon as the type-of hierarchies (GREYHOUND–DOG–ANIMAL) traditionally focused on. The notion of basic level categories can also be transferred from organisms and objects to the domain of actions. For the description of properties, it competes with another cognitive notion, the image schema, which is rooted in our bodily experiences.

Still within the framework of the experiential view, the third chapter starts out from the conceptual potential of metaphors (which was first pointed out by Lakoff and Johnson and has already been illustrated for the breakdown of the car). As a cognitive process it is understood as a mapping from a source to a target concept monitored by a conceptual mapping scope. Together with metonymies, conceptual metaphors make a significant contribution to the cognitive content and structure of abstract categories, especially emotion categories.

This view implies that metaphors and metonymies are no longer regarded as ornamental figures of speech (as in traditional stylistics), but are understood as important conceptual tools. The category-structuring power of metaphors is not restricted to lexical categories, but can also contribute to our understanding of complex scientific, political and social issues, and this is also true of metonymies, whose fundamental importance for human thinking has only been gradually realized.

The fourth chapter is devoted to the prominence view. At the heart of this approach lies the principle of figure/ground segregation, which has its origin in the work on visual perception by gestalt psychologists. This principle is first applied to locative relations underlying prepositions like *out* or *over*. Then it is extended to describe other syntactic relations, in particular the prominence of subject versus object. The chapter ends with a rough sketch of Langacker's view of cognitive processes, which is shown to be based on a multiple application of the figure–ground contrast.

In the fifth chapter the potential of the attentional view will be demonstrated. The chapter (which owes much to the ideas of Fillmore, Talmy and Slobin) starts out from the notion of 'frame'. Basically, a frame is an assemblage of the knowledge we have about a certain situation, e.g. buying and selling. Depending on where we direct our attention, we can select and highlight different aspects of the frame, thus arriving at different linguistic expressions. Although elementary types of frames, for instance the 'motion event-frame', are presumably shared by all human beings, they are expressed in different ways in different languages; this will be illustrated with English, German, French and Spanish examples. Closely related to event-frames is the notion of construction as a meaningful linguistic element, which, following mainly Fillmore and Goldberg, is exemplified for verbal and nominal constructions as well as syntactic idioms.

The sixth chapter deals with the analysis of online cognitive processing, as represented by Fauconnier and Turner's theory of conceptual blending. This approach is applied to a wide range of lexical, grammatical and pragmatic phenomena as well as to ads, riddles and jokes to test its versatility. For example, it explains how we bring together information expressed in the headline of a print ad with the message of the picture by linking and blending the mental spaces evoked by them. Finally, the blending theory and other cognitive principles are related to some of the tenets of Sperber and Wilson's Relevance Theory, which is characterized as a cognitive-pragmatic approach capable of stimulating cognitive-linguistic thinking.

The seventh chapter brings together a number of issues that have not originated in cognitive-linguistic research. Although three of them, iconicity, lexical change and grammaticalization, can look back on a long tradition in linguistics, they have benefited considerably from being put on a cognitive basis. The final section discusses the potential of a cognitive approach to foreign language learning, focusing on the potential of basic level, metaphor and metonymy, figure and ground as well as gestalt, to facilitate cognitive access to the language learning process.

To return to the general question of how 'cognitive linguistics' can be understood, the book will focus on the experiential aspects and the principles of prominence and attention allocation underlying language. By including cognitive online processing we want to emphasize the ties linking cognitive linguistics to psycholinguistic and pragmatic approaches.

CHAPTER 1

Prototypes and categories

1.1 Colours, squares, birds and cups: early empirical research into lexical categories

The world consists of an infinite variety of objects with different substances, shapes and colours. How do we translate this variety into manageable word meanings and why do we succeed even where no clear-cut distinctions seem to be available, such as between the colours 'red' and 'orange' or 'green' and 'blue'? Experimental psychology has shown that we use focal or prototypical colours as points of orientation, and comparable observations have also been made with categories denoting shapes, animals, plants and man-made objects.

Moving through the world we find ourselves surrounded by a variety of different phenomena. The most eye-catching among them are organisms and objects: people, animals, plants and all kinds of everyday artefacts such as books, chairs, cars and houses. In normal circumstances we have no difficulty in identifying and classifying any of them, and in attributing appropriate class names to them. However, it is not so easy to identify, classify and, as a consequence, to name other types of entities, for instance parts of organisms. Knees, ankles and feet of human beings and animals or the trunk, branches and twigs of a tree belong to this type. It may be fairly clear that one's kneecap belongs to one's knee and that the trunk of a tree includes the section which grows out of the ground. Yet at which point does one's knee end and where does one's thigh start? Where does a trunk turn into a treetop and where does a branch turn into a twig? Similar problems arise with landscape names, and words denoting weather phenomena. Who can tell at which particular spot a valley is no longer a valley but a slope or a mountain? Who can reliably identify the point where drizzle turns into rain, rain into snow, where mist or fog begins or ends?

When we compare the two types of entities mentioned, we find that they differ with respect to their boundaries. Books, tables, cars and houses are clearly delimited objects. In contrast, the boundaries of entities like knee, trunk, valley and mist are far from clear; they are vague. This vagueness has troubled philosophers and linguists interested in the relationship between word meanings and extra-linguistic reality, and has given rise to various theories of vagueness'.* Yet in spite of their vagueness, we have the impression that these boundaries exist in reality. A kneecap cannot be included in the thigh, and a mountain top will never be part of a valley. So classification seems to be forced upon us by the boundaries provided by reality.

However, there are phenomena in the world where this is not the case. Take physical properties such as length, width, height, temperature and colours, all of them uninterrupted scales extending between two extremes – how do we know where to draw the line between cold, warm and hot water? And how do we manage to distribute the major colour terms available in English across the 7,500,000 colour shades which we are apparently able to discriminate (see Brown and Lenneberg 1954: 457)? The temperature scale and the colour continuum do not provide natural divisions which could be compared with the boundaries of books, cars, and even knees or valleys.

Therefore the classification of temperature and colours can only be conceived as a mental process, and it is hardly surprising that physical properties, and colours especially, have served as the starting point for the psychological and conceptual view of word meanings which is at the heart of cognitive linguistics. This mental process of classification (whose complex nature will become clearer as we go on) is commonly called **categorization**, and its product are the **cognitive categories**, e.g. the colour categories RED, YELLOW, GREEN and BLUE, etc. (another widely used term is 'concept').

What are the principles guiding the mental process of categorization and, more specifically, of colour categorization? One explanation is that colour categories are totally arbitrary. For a long time this was what most researchers in the field believed. In the 1950s and 1960s, anthropologists investigated cross-linguistic differences in colour naming and found that colour terms differed enormously between languages (Brown and Lenneberg 1954; Lenneberg 1967). This was interpreted as a proof of the arbitrary nature of colour categories. More generally, it was thought to support the relativist view of languages, which, in its strongest version as advocated by Whorf, assumes that different languages carve up reality in totally different ways.[2]

A second explanation might be that the colour continuum is structured by a system of reference points for orientation. And indeed, the anthropologists Brent Berlin and Paul Kay (1969) found evidence that we rely on

*Suggestions for further reading are given at the end of each chapter.

so-called **focal colours** for colour categorization. Berlin and Kay's main target was to refute the relativist hypothesis by establishing a hierarchy of focal colours which could be regarded as universal. To support the universalist claim they investigated 98 languages, 20 in oral tests and the rest based on grammars and other written materials. In retrospect, their typological findings, which in fact have not remained uncriticized, have lost some of their glamour. However, the notion of focal colours, which emerged from the experiments, now appears as one of the most important steps on the way to the prototype model of categorization. We will therefore confine our account of Berlin and Kay's work to aspects relevant for the prototype model, at the expense of typological details.[3]

Focal colours

Like other researchers before them, Berlin and Kay worked with so-called Munsell colour chips provided by a company of the same name. These chips are standardized for the three dimensions which are relevant for our perception of different colours, namely hue, brightness and saturation, of which mainly the first two were tested. The advantage of using such standardized colour samples rather than pieces of dyed cloth is that anthropological and psychological tests become more objective, since they can be repeated by other researchers and the findings of different tests can be compared. The set of chips used by Berlin and Kay was composed of 329 colour chips, 320 of which represented 40 different colours, or, more precisely, 40 hues, each divided up into eight different levels of brightness. The remaining nine chips were white, black, and seven levels of grey. The chips were set out on a card in the manner shown in Figure 1.1. The vertical axis in the figure displays the various shades of brightness of one identical hue. On the horizontal axis the chips are ordered in such a way that starting from red the hues move through yellow-red to yellow through green-yellow to green and so on.

With the help of the colour card Berlin and Kay set about testing how speakers of the 20 selected languages categorized colours. In doing so, they were not so much interested in the colour vocabulary in general, but rather in a particular set of colour terms which met the following criteria: the terms should consist of just one word of native origin (as opposed to *greenish-blue* and *turquoise*); their application should not be restricted to a narrow class of objects (as opposed, e.g., to English and German *blond*); the words should come to mind readily and should be familiar to all or at least to most speakers of a language (as opposed to, say, *vermilion, magenta* or *indigo*).

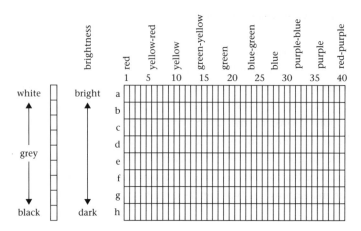

Figure 1.1   Arrangement of Munsell colour chips used by Berlin and Kay (numbers and letters added)

Colour terms which fulfilled these criteria were called **basic colour terms**. In the first stage of the experiments, Berlin and Kay collected the basic colour terms of the 20 languages. This was achieved by means of a 'verbal elicitation test', which is just a more complicated way of saying that speakers of the respective languages were asked to name them. In the second stage, these speakers were shown the colour card and asked to point out

1. all those chips which [they] would under any conditions call *x*
2. the best, most typical examples of *x*.

(Berlin and Kay 1969: 7)

The questions show that, unlike Lenneberg and other anthropologists before them, Berlin and Kay were not only interested in the extension of colour categories, but also in their best examples. One might even say that what was later called 'prototype' is anticipated in the wording of their second question.

What were Berlin and Kay's findings? In categorizing colours, people rely on certain points in the colour space for orientation. For example, when speakers of English were asked for the best example of the colour 'red', they consistently pointed to colour chips in the lower, i.e. darker, regions under the label 'red' (f3 and g3 in Figure 1.1; of course, in the tests no colour terms were given on the card). For yellow, informants consistently selected chips with the second degree of brightness under the label 'yellow' (b9 in Figure 1.1). These chips (or regions in the colour space), which were thought of as best examples by all or by most speakers of English, were called 'foci' by Berlin and Kay.

Foci or focal colours were also found for the other 19 languages. When the focal colours were compared, the result was amazing. Focal colours are not only shared by the speakers of one and the same language but they are also very consistent across different languages. Whenever a language has colour terms roughly corresponding to the English colour terms, their focal points will be in the same area. And even in languages with a smaller number of basic colour terms than English, the best examples of these fewer categories will agree with the respective focal colours of 'richer' languages like English.

In sum, there is compelling evidence that instead of being arbitrary, colour categorization is anchored in focal colours. While the boundaries of colour categories vary between languages and even between speakers of one language, focal colours are shared by different speakers and even different language communities.

As is often the case with important scientific findings, the discovery of focal colours not only helped to solve one problem but also raised a number of new questions. Are focal colours to be treated as a phenomenon which is a matter of language or of the mind? What, assuming the latter, is their psychological status? And finally, are 'foci' (focal points) restricted to colours or can they be found in other areas as well? These questions will be taken up in the following sections.

The psychological background of focal colours

From a psychological standpoint the categorization of natural phenomena is a rather complex task involving the following processes:[4]

1. *Selection of stimuli* Of the wealth of stimuli which are perceived by our sensory systems (visual, auditory, tactile, olfactory), only very few are selected for cognitive processing, i.e. they attract our attention.
2. *Identification and classification* This is achieved by comparing selected stimuli to relevant knowledge stored in memory.
3. *Naming* Most cognitive categories are given names though some remain unlabelled, e.g. 'things to eat on a diet', 'things to pack in a suitcase'.

(Barsalou 1987: 102)

Most of these aspects were investigated by Eleanor Rosch, who in the early 1970s set out to explore the psychological background of focal colours.[5] As a psychologist, her primary aim was to find out whether focal colours were rooted in language or in pre-linguistic cognition. Her idea was that a cognitive status might be claimed for focal colours if they could be proved to be prominent in the cognitive processes involved in categorization.

Starting out from the most basic of the three cognitive processes, Rosch first examined whether focal colours are perceptually salient. To eliminate the influence of purely language-based categorization, she required informants who had stored as little knowledge of colour names and related colour categories as possible. So she decided to work with pre-school children and with members of a non-Westernized culture in Papua New Guinea, the Dani. Earlier research had shown that Dugum Dani, the language spoken by the Dani, contained only two basic colour terms, in contrast to the 11 basic colour terms available to speakers of English (Heider 1971). Like children, the Dani were therefore particularly well suited as uncorrupted informants for colour-categorizing experiments. English-speaking adults, who were supposed to have the full system of basic colour terms at their disposal, were only used as control groups in some of the tests.

Rosch's first experiment (Heider 1971), which was to test the arousal of attention (or stimulus selection), was dressed up as a 'show me a colour' game. She gave 3-year-old children arrays of colour chips consisting of one focal colour, as found by Berlin and Kay, and seven other chips of the same hue, but other levels of brightness. The children were told that they were to show the experimenter any colour they liked. The reasoning behind this game was that young children's attention would be attracted more readily by focal colours than by other colours. In fact, it turned out that the children did pick out focal chips more frequently than non-focal chips. The preponderance of the focal chips was particularly strong for the colours yellow, orange and green, where 22, 21 and 11 respectively out of the total of 24 children selected the focal chip from the array. For the other five hues, the numbers were smaller, but still statistically significant.

The second experiment which Rosch conducted with children was a colour-matching task. The children, this time 4-year-olds, were given focal and non-focal chips one at a time in random order and asked to point to the same colour in an array of colour chips which were identical to those used in the earlier experiment. As predicted by the test hypothesis, focal colour chips were matched more accurately than non-focal chips, and this again supports the perceptual salience of focal colours. In terms of cognitive processes, this second test involves identification and classification; both the test chip and one or several possible target chips have to be identified and classified so that they can be compared. Comparison in turn presupposes that the data collected about the chips are temporarily stored somewhere, and this is where memory comes into play.

Matching situations where both the test item and the target items are simultaneously present are rather the exception. Normally we are confronted with an item (i.e. a colour which has to be identified and classified) but have to rely fully on data stored in memory for comparison. This raises the question whether focal colours are salient in memory as well, whether they are recognized more accurately, learned more easily and recalled more readily than other colours. Investigating these aspects Rosch used specific memory tests: recognition tasks to test the short-term memory and learning tasks aimed at the long-term memory (Heider 1972).

The recognition task was similar to the matching task discussed above, but demanded more concentration from the informants. As this proved too difficult for children, Rosch used Dani informants who, as already mentioned, have only two basic colour terms. The same test was conducted with a control group of Americans. Both the Dani and the English-speaking informants were shown eight focal and eight non-focal colour cards in random order each for five seconds. Each single presentation was followed by an interval of 30 seconds, after which the subjects were asked to point out the matching colour chip on a colour card of the Berlin and Kay type. For both groups the matching accuracy for focal colours was significantly higher than for non-focal ones. The conclusion one may draw is that focal colours are remembered more accurately in short-term memory than non-focal ones. Another result was that the English-speaking control group surpassed the Dani in matching accuracy both for focal and non-focal colours. This may be due to the fact that the larger set of basic colour terms available to speakers of English facilitates colour recognition.

The second experiment consisted of a learning task testing retention of previously unknown colour names in long-term memory. This experiment exploited the fact that, because of their limitation to two basic colour terms, the Dani could be taught additional ones under controlled conditions. Before the test began, the Dani informants were told that the experimenter would teach them a new language. When learning was completed, they were paid for their help. At the start, the 16 colour cards (again eight focal colours and eight non-focal colours) were laid out in random order and the Dani were told the name for each card. (The names used were the names of Dani clans.) After their first display the cards were gathered into a pack, shuffled and presented one by one to the Dani, who were asked to produce the name of each colour. They were praised for every correct response and told the correct name when they were wrong. This procedure was repeated five times a day until the Dani managed to get all 16 answers right and the learning process was considered completed. A detailed record was kept of the whole learning process, which took three and a half days on average. This record supplied the means of measuring the ease of retention of focal and non-focal colours because it allowed a computation of all the correct and incorrect answers. Whereas, on average, the Dani gave 9.9 incorrect answers per colour for non-focal colours before they produced their first completely correct run, the mean number of errors per colour for focal colours was only 7.3. Even without previous knowledge of the colour names, the Dani associated focal colours more rapidly with their names than non-focal colours.

As well as perception and memory work, naming was mentioned as the third component of categorization. Given the salience of focal colours we would expect the following results: first, names should be produced more rapidly for focal colours than for non-focal ones; second, children should acquire the names of focal colours earlier than the names of non-focal colours. Empirical evidence, again provided by Rosch, suggests that both assumptions are correct.

Let us now review Rosch's findings:

- Focal colours are perceptually more salient than non-focal colours. The attention of 3-year-olds is more often attracted by focal than by non-focal colours, and 4-year-olds match focal colours more accurately to a given display of other colours than non-focal colours.
- Focal colours are more accurately remembered in short-term memory and more easily retained in long-term memory.
- The names of focal colours are more rapidly produced in colour-naming tasks and are acquired earlier by children.

All in all, focal colours appear to possess a particular perceptual–cognitive salience, which is probably independent of language and seems to reflect certain physiological aspects of man's perceptive mechanisms (Kay and McDaniel 1978). These results encouraged Rosch to extend the notion of foci – or **prototypes**, as she now called them – beyond colour categories, e.g. into the domains of shapes, organisms and objects.

Prototypical shapes

Let us start our discussion of shapes with a little experiment based on the drawings in the top row of Figure 1.2 (set 1). Imagine you were asked to describe what you see in this figure to someone who is not allowed to inspect it. Presumably you would proceed more or less like this: 'There is a row of little drawings depicting a square and a number of variations of it. The first drawing is a proper square. The second square has a gap in the right-hand side. The right-hand side of the third square has an indentation. The fourth square . . . .'

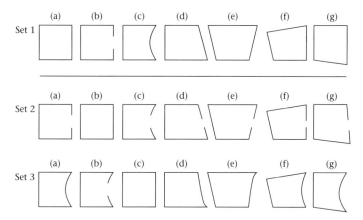

Figure 1.2 Shapes used by Rosch in prototype experiments (Rosch 1973) (Sets 2 and 3 reconstructed from Rosch's description, letters added)

Such a description would be in full agreement with the notion of 'good forms' as proposed by gestalt psychology (a school of psychology discussed in more detail in Section 1.2). These good forms, i.e. squares, circles and equilateral triangles, are assumed to be perceptually salient among geometrical shapes.

Thus it is only natural that in a situation like the one described above people will single out the square as a reference point for characterizing the other drawings. Squares and the other good forms are therefore prime candidates for 'natural' prototypes in the domain of geometrical shapes, similar to the focal colours in colour space.

Using the kind of line drawings shown in Figure 1.2, Rosch (1973) sought confirmation for the notion of prototypes in the domain of shapes. Prior to the actual tests, she had to make sure that, as with colours, the Dani had no category names or even conventional paraphrases at their disposal which could bias them towards the supposed prototypes. This was verified in a pilot study, which used the description method demonstrated above: one test subject explaining the line drawings to another subject who was sitting behind a screen and could not see them. Unlike educated Western speakers, the Dani did not talk of squares and variations, but used expressions like 'It's a pig' or 'It's a broken fence' for their description of the drawings.

For the actual experiment, Rosch contrasted set 1 (the set with the prototype) with other sets which were derived from the variations of set 1. Sets 2 and 3 in Figure 1.2 show two of the possible six alternative sets. Set 2 is based on the principle of gapping (gap on the right-hand side). Considering this principle, the prototype which appears as (b) in set 2 is indeed a very extreme case because it represents the absence of the gap. Set 3 is based on the principle of indenture, and again the square is just a marginal member of the set.

As in the earlier colour-learning experiments, the Dani had to learn names which were again borrowed from Dani clans. This means they had to associate sets of drawings with names. The result fully confirmed Rosch's assumption that the prototype is associated with a name and also judged best example, no matter whether it is presented in a natural category (set 1) or as a marginal realization of the principle underlying one of the other sets.

Combined with the findings from the earlier colour experiments, these results suggest that prototypes have a crucial function in the various stages involved in the formation and learning of categories.

Prototypical organisms and objects

It could still be argued at this point that prototypes ultimately depend on the perceptual nature of the categories examined so far (colours, shapes) and are therefore a very limited if not exceptional phenomenon. The question is whether the notion of prototype can be extended to entities which are less obviously perceptual. Granted there are good and bad examples of reds and squares. Are there also good and bad examples of dogs, cars and houses? According to Rosch and her informants there are. In a series of experiments (Rosch 1973, improved version 1975) she confronted informants, this time American college students, with the following test instructions:

> This study has to do with what we have in mind when we use words which refer to categories. Let's take the word *red* as an example. Close your eyes and imagine a true red. Now imagine an orangish red . . . imagine a purple red. Although you might still name the orange red or the purple red with the term *red*, they are not as good examples of red (as clear cases of what *red* refers to) as the clear 'true' red. In short, some reds are redder than others. The same is true for other kinds of categories. Think of dogs. You all have some notion of what a 'real dog', a 'doggy dog' is. To me a retriever or a German shepherd is a very doggy dog while a Pekinese is a less doggy dog. Notice that this kind of judgment has nothing to do with how well you like the thing. [. . .]
>
> (Rosch 1975: 198)

In the remainder of the instructions the students were asked to judge the **goodness** (or **typicality**) of category members, i.e. to decide how good an example of the category BIRD a sparrow, a parrot, a penguin and about 50 other candidates were. Rating was based on a 7-point scale of goodness (one point for very good, seven points for very poor examples). Altogether ten categories were tested: in addition to BIRD, the categories were FRUIT, VEHICLE, VEGETABLE, SPORT, TOOL, TOY, FURNITURE, WEAPON and CLOTHING.

Admittedly, Rosch's test instructions show a certain bias towards the notion of prototypicality ('. . . some reds are redder than others. The same is true for other kinds of categories'). Yet this should not have distorted the test results too much. As Rosch stresses, the rating test was readily accepted by the student informants and there was a high level of agreement among them as to what were good and bad examples of the categories. To give an impression of what the results were like, the best, some intermediate and the poorest examples of five out of the ten categories are assembled in Figure 1.3.

rank	category				
	BIRD	FRUIT	VEHICLE	FURNITURE	WEAPON
top eight					
1	robin	orange	automobile	chair	gun
2	sparrow	apple	station wagon	sofa	pistol
3	bluejay	banana	truck	couch	revolver
4	bluebird	peach	car	table	machine gun
5	canary	pear	bus	easy chair	rifle
6	blackbird	apricot	taxi	dresser	switchblade
7	dove	tangerine	jeep	rocking chair	knife
8	lark	plum	ambulance	coffee table	dagger
.....	.....	.....	.....	.....	.....
middle ranks					
26*	hawk	tangelo	subway	lamp	whip
27	raven	papaya	trailer	stool	ice pick
28	goldfinch	honeydew	cart	hassock	slingshot
29	parrot	fig	wheelchair	drawers	fists
30	sandpiper	mango	yacht	piano	axe
.....	.....	.....	.....	.....	.....
last five					
51*	ostrich	nut	ski	picture	foot
52	titmouse	gourd	skateboard	closet	car
53	emu	olive	wheelbarrow	vase	glass
54	penguin	pickle	surfboard	fan	screwdriver
55	bat	squash	elevator	telephone	shoes

* Since the total number of listed items varied between 50 and 60, the numbers of middle and bottom ranks are not identical with the original ranks for all categories.

Figure 1.3 A selection of examples from Rosch's goodness-of-example rating tests (Rosch 1975)

The goodness ratings were also confirmed in matching experiments in which the 'priming' technique was used (Rosch 1975). In one of these tests, subjects were shown pairs of names or pictures on a screen. The subjects had to press a 'same' key when pairs of identical names or pictures of items appeared on a screen (e.g. a word sequence like *eagle–eagle* or two identical pictures of an eagle); the time between the presentation and the reaction was measured (it was in the range of 500 to 1000 milliseconds). Two seconds before the presentation, subjects were given the category name (in this case BIRD) as advance information, so they were 'primed' with the category name. (There was also a control group that performed the test unprimed.) The hypothesis was that advance knowledge of the category name would influence the speed with which the matching task was performed and that it might influence the matching of good and poor examples in different ways. Indeed, priming had a twofold effect which nicely supported the goodness ratings. Primed informants were faster in reacting to identical pairs of items that had been rated as good examples (both words and pictures). Conversely, reaction was slowed down by priming where poor examples were involved. Reaction to pairs of intermediate examples was not noticeably affected by priming. Without getting lost in speculations about the cognitive representations of categories at this point, we can still support Rosch's claim that the advance information which is called up by the primed category name is most readily applied to good examples; sparrows, oranges or cars (*automobiles* in American English) simply fit the expectations called up by the names of the categories BIRD, FRUIT and VEHICLE. However, this advance information is not helpful with poor examples. In fact, priming with the category name tends to confuse test subjects when they are confronted with pairs of penguins, olives or wheelbarrows, which can at best be placed at the periphery of the BIRD, the FRUIT or the VEHICLE category.

Good examples, bad examples and category boundaries

As the categorization of colours, shapes, birds and vehicles suggests, category membership is not, as was for a long time assumed by philosophers and linguists, a yes-or-no distinction. Rather it involves different degrees of typicality, as is supported by goodness-of-example ratings, recognition, matching and learning tasks.

Rosch's main concern was to prove that categories are formed around prototypes, which function as cognitive reference points. As far as the boundaries of categories are concerned, she leaves us with the impression that at some unspecified point or area beyond their periphery the categories somehow fade into nowhere. This is not the idea we have when we talk about categories in a naive way. Normally, we tend to imagine them as boxes, drawers or some sort of fenced compound – certainly as something which has boundaries. With regard to the category BIRD, the allocation of boundaries seems to be easy enough, even though a little knowledge of zoology might be required.

Yet our confidence will be undermined when we follow the philosopher Max Black and consider the imaginary 'chair museum' he invented. According to Black it consists of

> a series of 'chairs' differing in quality by least noticeable amounts. At one end of a long line, containing perhaps thousands of exhibits, might be a Chippendale chair: at the other, a small nondescript lump of wood. Any 'normal' observer inspecting the series finds extreme difficulty in 'drawing the line' between chair and non-chair.   (Black 1949: 32)

What Black's interpretation of his chair museum suggests is that the collection of chairs could and should be regarded as a continuum with a kind of transition zone between chairs and non-chairs but no clear-cut boundaries. This view seems to be in conflict with what we observed at the beginning of the chapter: that concrete objects like houses, books and also chairs are clearly delimited and easy to identify, and that vague boundaries and transition zones are restricted to items like knees, fog and valleys and to scales like length, temperature and colour.

Here one must be careful not to confuse two different types of boundaries and transition zones. One type of transition zone arises from the observation that some concrete entities do not have clear-cut boundaries in reality – this is the case with knee and other body parts; it applies to fog, snow and similar weather phenomena and to landscape forms like valley or mountain. In Black's chair museum, however, the visitor is confronted with a different type of transition zone, since each exhibit in the museum is an entity with absolutely clear boundaries. In the chair museum, it is not entities that merge into each other, but categories of entities, and these categories are the product of cognitive classification. Consequently, it is not the boundaries of entities that are vague, but the boundaries of these cognitive categories (here: chairs and non-chairs). To distinguish the two types of vagueness we will restrict the terms 'vague entity' and 'vagueness' to the first type (knee, fog, valley) and use 'fuzzy category boundaries' or **fuzziness** for the second, i.e. for the category boundaries of CHAIR etc.

The issue is, however, even more complicated because there are in fact cases where vagueness and fuzziness coincide. This is true of the second type of entities, as already observed by the philosopher Willard Quine, who found that the category MOUNTAIN is

> vague on the score of how much terrain to reckon into each of the indisputable mountains, and it is vague on the score of what lesser eminences to count as mountains at all.   (Quine 1960: 126)

In other words, entities like mountains are vague because they are not clearly delimited as individual entities; the cognitive category MOUNTAIN (or KNEE or FOG) is fuzzy because it does not have clear boundaries either.

Summing up, we can say that our deeper understanding of the cognitive background of categorization has considerably changed our original idea about the threefold classification of entities into clearly delimited organisms and objects, into entities with vague boundaries and into scales – a view which is based on a kind of 'naive realism'.[6] From a cognitive perspective these distinctions and the discussion of vagueness arising from them are of minor importance. What is important is that all types of concrete entities and natural phenomena like colours are conceptually organized in terms of prototype categories, whose boundaries do not seem to be clear-cut, but fuzzy.

How can the fuzzy nature of category boundaries, which intuitively seems to be a convincing notion, be investigated empirically? This was the task which William Labov set himself in a series of experiments involving cups and cup-like containers (Labov 1973, 1978).[7] Starting from Black's interpretation of the chair museum, Labov drew the following conclusion:

> The subjective aspect of vagueness [i.e. fuzziness in our terminology] may be thought of as the lack of certainty as to whether the term does or does not denote; and this may be transformed into the consistency with which a given sample of speakers does in fact apply the term.   (Labov 1973: 353)

If all informants in a test call an object *chair*, the consistency is 100 per cent. If half the informants have doubts whether a certain object is still a chair and therefore do not call it *chair*, the consistency value will drop to 50 per cent. If hardly any of the informants regard an object as a chair and refuse to call it a chair, the consistency value will approach zero. The actual test procedure of Labov's experiments was very simple: informants were shown line drawings of cups and other vessels, as collected in Figure 1.4. The drawings were presented one by one and the informants were asked to name them (additional descriptive details supplied by the informants were neglected in the analysis).

Figure 1.4   A selection of the drawings of cup-like objects used by Labov (1973: 354); (no. 5 reconstructed; alternative drawings without a handle or with two handles were also used in the tests)

The results of the naming task were analyzed in terms of consistency and presented as 'consistency profiles'. Figure 1.5 presents the consistency profile for the vessels shown in the top row of Figure 1.4. As the graph for the use of *cup* indicates, consistency is 100 per cent for vessel no. 1 but decreases as we proceed towards vessel no. 5. In addition, Figure 1.5 also contains the complementary graph for the use of *bowl*. This graph demonstrates that Black's chair museum was rather unrealistic in that he only compared 'chairs' with 'non-chairs'. In contrast, Labov's test shows that in experimental and everyday categorizing situations, we normally do not just make a division between the two categories 'X' and 'not X', but that we have two or several names at our disposal which allow us to choose between neighbouring categories, in this case between CUP, BOWL, MUG and VASE, etc. Therefore, it is more realistic to think of fuzzy category boundaries as fringe areas between adjacent categories than as transitions to a conceptual vacuum. Figure 1.5 shows that as the consistency value for *cup* drops dramatically for vessels 4 and 5, the use of *bowl* slowly begins to pick up. It is for these fringe

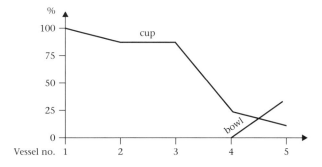

Figure 1.5   Consistency profile for neutral context
(Adapted from Labov 1973)

areas between the two categories that the term 'fuzzy boundaries' seems to
be particularly appropriate. Labov's tests can therefore be taken as a first experimental proof of the fuzziness of category boundaries.

However, this fuzziness assumes a new dimension when one considers
the full range of Labov's experiments. In the first test (the one discussed
so far) the informants were only confronted with the drawings, but not
given any background information (this was called 'neutral context' by
Labov). In the subsequent three tests they were asked to imagine one of
three different scenes: (a) a coffee-drinking situation, (b) a dinner table situation with the object filled with mashed potatoes ('food context') and (c)
a scene where the objects were standing on a shelf with cut flowers in them.
In later experiments different materials like china and glass were introduced
as well.

The result of including these variables was a massive shift of category boundaries. To give just one example, in a food context, vessel no. 3 was no longer
a *cup* for the majority of the informants. As indicated in Figure 1.6, half the
informants called it *bowl* in spite of its unchanged shape, and this switch
towards *bowl* was even more pronounced for vessel no. 4. In this way Labov's
experiments show that the fuzziness of category boundaries has many facets,
of which context-dependence is one of the most important. (This issue will
be taken up in Section 1.3; another aspect of Labov's tests, his carefully controlled use of scalar properties like width, depth and shape, will be discussed
in the next section.)

Let us now relate Labov's findings to what has already emerged about
the nature of cognitive categories in the preceding sections:

• Categories do not represent arbitrary divisions of the phenomena of the
  world, but should be seen as based on the cognitive capacities of the
  human mind.

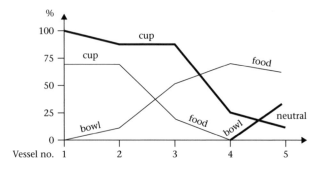

Figure 1.6 Consistency profile for neutral and food contexts (Labov 1973)

- Cognitive categories of colours, shapes, but also of organisms and concrete objects, are anchored in conceptually salient prototypes, which play a crucial part in the formation of categories.
- The boundaries of cognitive categories are fuzzy, i.e. neighbouring categories are not separated by rigid boundaries, but merge into each other.
- Between prototypes and boundaries, cognitive categories contain members which can be rated on a typicality scale ranging from good to bad examples.

If we accept that cognitive categories consist of prototype, good examples and bad examples, and have fuzzy boundaries, this suggests that the internal structure of categories is indeed rather complex and that it deserves a more detailed examination.

To conclude this section a word of caution is in order. Cognitive categories, as we have discussed them, are stored in our mind as mental concepts and signalled by the words of a language, so one might come to think that they are equivalent with the meanings of these words. Yet if we consider that colour terms do not just denote colours, but can also stand for political parties, that *bird* does not only refer to a creature with wings but, at least occasionally, also to a pretty girl, that *chair* can denote the president of a meeting and that cups and bowls can be trophies in sport, it is clear that there is no one-to-one relation between categories (or concepts) and words. In fact it is quite normal that one word denotes several categories, or in conventional linguistic terminology, that words are polysemous.[8] As the later chapters will show (especially Chapters 3 and 4), cognitive linguistics is not only concerned with the exploration of individual categories, but also has something to say about the relationship between the categories which are signalled by one and the same word.

Exercises

1. List basic colour terms in English (or your native language) by checking which colour terms consist of only one short word and are freely applicable to different kinds of objects and organisms. Describe the colour of sweaters, T-shirts, etc., using basic colour terms as points of reference.

2. Select typical examples of the categories T-SHIRT, LONG-SLEEVE (T-SHIRT), SWEATER and JUMPER. Can you think of items of clothing which illustrate the fuzziness of the boundaries between these neighbouring categories?

3. Draw pictures of prototypical examples and of objects on the border-line between the categories BOTTLE, GLASS, VASE and BOWL, and use them as stimuli for a naming task with your friends or family.

4. As we have found, the vagueness of objects and the fuzziness of categories must be kept apart. Look at the following examples and discuss which of them involve fuzziness or vagueness or both aspects:

> *mountain, hill, summit, plateau, valley;*
>
> *tree, shrub, flower;* — a Holly plant can be all 3
>
> *hedge, bush, forest, park;*
>
> *street, road, avenue, drive, highway;*
>
> *river, stream, brook, torrent, firth, estuary, spring.*

5. The names of category prototypes tend to come to mind before those of peripheral examples. Check this hypothesis with two informal tests: ask one group of friends to name as quickly as they can five types of dogs, birds, trees and cars. List the items mentioned by the informants, add other suitable items and present this extended list to a second group for a goodness-of-example rating. Compare the results and discuss reasons for discrepancies between the two tests.

1.2 The internal structure of categories: prototypes, attributes, family resemblances and gestalt

If cognitive categories are made up of prototypes and periphery, of good and bad examples, how do these differ and how are they related to each other? The listing and the analysis of attributes seem to provide a good approach to these aspects of internal category structure, while the notion of family resemblances is helpful as a theoretical explanation. A fascinating though less well explored factor in categorization is the 'gestalt' of organisms and concrete objects, which will also come up for discussion.

Cognitive categories are, as we have just seen, labelled by words, and words are listed in dictionaries. It is therefore only natural to look for information about the contents of categories in dictionary entries. Here are some examples of dictionary definitions for types of birds:

robin   A small brown European bird with a red breast. (OALD)

| **parrot** | A tropical bird with a curved beak and brightly coloured feathers that can be taught to copy human speech. (LDOCE4) |
| **ostrich** | An ostrich is a large African bird that cannot fly. It has long legs, a long neck, a small head and large soft feathers. (COBUILD) |

In terms of categorization, these dictionary definitions yield two types of information. To start with, they supply the name of the category to which the robin, the parrot and the ostrich belong (in this case BIRD). This category name in turn suggests the properties which are shared by most birds: that they have feathers, two legs, two wings and a beak, and that they lay eggs. The main body of the dictionary entries lists properties which are specific to the item in question. Thus the robin is characterized by small size, brownish colour and red breast-feathers. These properties clearly set the robin apart from other members of the category BIRD, such as parrots and ostriches. So robins, parrots and ostriches have properties which serve to tie them to a common category as well as properties which distinguish them from each other. Collecting both the shared and the distinctive properties seems to provide a feasible way of describing the internal structure of categories.

However, there are some problems. Dictionary definitions are written for a practical purpose and not with a systematic linguistic and cognitive analysis in mind. Lexicographers can afford to skip some properties that are to be taken for granted, or they can modify their definitions by limiting expressions or 'hedges', like *usually* (parrots 'usually' have brightly coloured feathers). A more systematic linguistic approach not only has to fill in gaps, e.g. by adding to the definition of *robin* that it chirps and to the definition of *ostrich* that it can run very fast. A linguistic analysis will also have to clarify the notion of property or **attribute** (to use the more technical term).

Regarding the attributes used in dictionary entries, it may be quite sufficient to understand them in the rather vague sense of 'characteristics' or 'typical aspects'. From a more theoretical stance, an additional question must be asked: are attributes to be regarded as obligatory or not? This distinction was first suggested by Aristotle, who contrasted the 'essence' of things with the 'accidence'. The notion of essence gave rise to what has been called the 'categorical view' or 'classical view', a position which was vigorously defended by structuralist and transformationalist linguists.[9] According to this view, a category is defined by a limited set of necessary and sufficient conditions. These conditions are conceived as clear-cut, 'discrete' features (or **essential features**, as they will be called here), which can be either present or absent. In the case of the category BIRD, this means that a creature is only a bird if it has two wings and two legs, a beak, feathers and lays eggs (these are the necessary conditions). If, on the other hand, a creature has all these essential features, this is also sufficient for classifying it as a bird.

Such a rigid view of attributes and categorization is bound to run into difficulties when it is applied to cognitive categories consisting of good and bad examples and equipped with fuzzy boundaries, as introduced in Section 1.1. To cope with these experiential prototype categories we need a much more differentiated notion of attributes than is supplied by the classical view. The following discussion of attributes for birds will exemplify the problems.

Attributes, good birds and bad birds: an example

Our starting point is a list of attributes collected for >ROBIN<, which was rated best example of the category BIRD in Rosch (1975; see Figure 1.3). The idea is that this list is the closest approximation available of the 'prototypical' attribute list for BIRD and that it would be very suitable for comparisons with lesser category members:

1. 'lays eggs'
2. 'has two wings and two legs'
3. 'has a beak'
4. 'has feathers'
5. 'can fly'
6. 'has thin, short legs'
7. 'is small and lightweight'
8. 'has a short tail'
9. 'chirps/sings'
10. 'has a red breast'

The list is based on dictionary definitions of *robin* and *bird*, but is also supported by attributes collected from informants (Hampton 1979). More precisely, it assembles what dictionary makers and ordinary people (the informants) find worth mentioning about robins. Such a list will never be complete (for example, our description does not mention what kind of food a robin eats) and the items will tend to overlap (in our case this applies to nos 2 and 6, which both refer to the bird's legs, and to nos 4 and 10, which are both concerned with the bird's plumage). Yet while these deficiencies may be confusing to the linguist raised in the classical tradition, they still seem, for the time being, to provide the best empirical way of describing the properties that can be used in categorizing a robin.

When trying to apply the attributes collected for robins to other examples of the category BIRD which scored high in Rosch's rating test, e.g. >SPARROW<,

>CANARY< and >DOVE<, one will find that, with the exception of the red breast, sparrows and canaries share all the attributes assembled for robins. Doves do not chirp or sing and surpass the other three types of birds in size and weight; otherwise they share the attributes listed. It seems, therefore, that at least the attributes 'lays eggs', 'has a beak', 'chirps/sings', all the attributes concerning wings, feathers and the ability to fly, and, finally, the 'thin, short legs' and the 'short tail' are somehow related to a central position within the category BIRD.

Now take a less good example of a bird, say >PARROT<. Going through our list again, you will find that a parrot resembles a robin in that it lays eggs, has a beak, two wings, two legs and feathers and can fly. However, compared to a robin a parrot has rather strong legs, most parrots are much larger than robins and have quite long tails. And a parrot certainly does not chirp or sing.

Finally, when considering the attributes of >OSTRICH< (which was, of course, rated a poor example of the category BIRD), the result will be that the only attributes an ostrich shares with our short list are that it lays eggs, has two legs and feathers, and that it has some kind of beak.

All in all, there seems to be a bundle of attributes that represent important aspects of 'birdiness'. These attributes tend to correlate in nature, i.e. they appear together. A creature that has wings and feathers is more likely to be able to fly than one that has fur and four legs. Types of birds qualifying for these attributes have a particularly prominent position in the category. Intermediate and bad examples of the category BIRD differ from these prototypical examples in two ways: either they deviate to a moderate degree with regard to one or more attributes (think of the parrot's legs and tail) or some attributes are missing altogether (e.g. ostriches cannot fly).

This distribution is illustrated in matrix form in Figure 1.7, where a plus sign stands for an attribute which is present, a minus sign for a missing attribute, and a plus/minus combination for a greater or lesser deviation from the expected form of the attribute. The matrix thus reflects the fact that a yes/no representation of attributes (which would correspond to the classical view) cannot adequately render the attributes of birds and has to be modified to include intermediate judgements.

Though this may not be obvious at first glance, 'deviant' and 'missing' attributes can be seen as different problems and have been addressed in different ways in cognitive research. Since the absence of attributes (as in the case of >OSTRICH<) seems to be the more serious problem, it will be tackled first, while the deviant attributes (as observed with >PARROT<) will be taken up later.

Attributes	Category members				
	>ROBIN<	>SPARROW<	>DOVE<	>PARROT<	>OSTRICH<
lays eggs	+	+	+	+	+
beak	+	+	+	+	+
two wings & two legs	+	+	+	+	+/−
feathers	+	+	+	+	+
small & lightweight	+	+	+/−	+/−	−
can fly	+	+	+	+	−
chirps/sings	+	+	+	+/−	−
thin/short legs	+	+	+	+/−	−
short tail	+	+	+	+/−	−
red breast	+	−	−	−	−

Figure 1.7 Goodness-of-example and distribution of attributes in the category BIRD

The principle of family resemblances

The paradox in the case of the ostrich is that we are quite prepared to call it a *bird* though it shares only few attributes with prototypical birds like the robin. Yet as the above dictionary definition suggests, there is no lack of attributes to describe >OSTRICH<, and while some of these attributes ('is very tall', 'runs very fast') seem incompatible with our idea of a bird, some are less so. Take the attribute 'long neck' and you will find that this applies to birds as far apart from ostriches as are flamingoes and storks (though not to robins). Or take the attribute 'large soft feathers' and it may remind you of swans, while the alternative version offered by other dictionaries for this attribute, i.e. 'decorative feathers', suggests links with peacocks and perhaps even with parrots (though not with sparrows).

However, in other categories the items are even more dissimilar, as the philosopher Ludwig Wittgenstein showed in his much-quoted passage about the category GAME:

> Consider for example the proceedings that we call 'games'. I mean board-games, card-games, ball-games, Olympic games, and so on. What is common to them all? – Don't say: 'There must be something common, or they would not be called "games" ' – but look and see whether there is anything common to all. – For if you look at them you will not see something that is common
> to all, but similarities, relationships, and a whole series of them at that. To repeat: don't think, but look! – For example at board-games, with their multifarious relationships. Now pass to card-games; here you find many correspondences with the first group, but many common features drop out, and

others appear. When we pass next to ball-games, much that is common is retained, but much is lost. – Are they all 'amusing'? Compare chess with noughts and crosses. Or is there always winning and losing, or competition between players? Think of patience. In ball-games there is winning and losing; but when a child throws his ball at the wall and catches it again, this feature has disappeared. Look at the parts played by skill and luck; and at the difference between skill in chess and skill in tennis. Think now of games like ring-a-ring-a-roses; here is the element of amusement, but how many other characteristic features have disappeared! And we can go through the many, many other groups of games in the same way; we see how similarities crop up and disappear.

(Wittgenstein 1958: 66f)

Wittgenstein's conclusion was that games are connected by a network of overlapping similarities, which he called **family resemblances**. On a somewhat more abstract level, the principle of family resemblances has been defined as a set of items displaying the following kind of distribution:

Item	Attributes	Overlapping similarities
1	AB	A B
2	BC	B C
3	CD	C D
4	DE	D E

In the words of Rosch and Mervis (1975: 575), 'each item has at least one, and probably several, elements in common with one or more other items, but no, or few, elements are common to all items'.

Wittgenstein's explanation and the definition supplied by Rosch and Mervis both pursue the same aim: to show that the principle of family resemblances opens up an alternative to the classical view that attributes must be common to all category members, that they must be 'category-wide'. This could be most impressively demonstrated with the analysis of 'superordinate categories' like GAME (Wittgenstein's example) and FURNITURE, VEHICLE, FRUIT, etc., which were investigated by Rosch and Mervis (1975). As will be shown later in Section 2.2, it is not surprising that superordinate categories largely depend on family resemblances.

The picture changes when one considers categories like BIRD or other more concrete categories like CAR, TRUCK, AIRPLANE, CHAIR, TABLE and LAMP. As observed in the case of BIRD, even very bad examples of the category like >OSTRICH< (and we might add >PENGUIN<) have some important attributes in common with all the other category members. And, of course, the good examples such

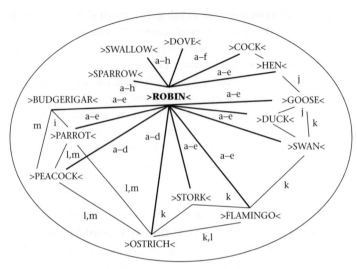

Selected category-wide attributes
(a) lays eggs
(b) has a beak
(c) has two wings and two legs
(d) has feathers

Selected family resemblance attributes
(e) can fly
(f) is small and lightweight
(g) chirps/sings
(h) legs are thin/short
(i) kept in a cage
(j) reared for the use of its meat, eggs and feathers
(k) has long neck
(l) has decorative feathers
(m) has exotic colours

Figure 1.8 Selected common attributes and family resemblances of the
category BIRD

as >ROBIN< and >SPARROW< all share whole bundles of attributes, so that only
a few of their attributes rely on the family resemblance principle. This situation is illustrated in Figure 1.8, where attributes are indicated by lines.

Just as with birds, members of categories like CAR and CHAIR (i.e. different types of cars and chairs) share many more attributes than the members
of the superordinate categories VEHICLE and FURNITURE (i.e. different types of
vehicles and different items of furniture). Here Section 2.1 will provide an
explanation.

Yet however much the significance of family resemblances may vary for
individual categories, this does not affect the explanatory potential of the
underlying principle. What is decisive is that family resemblances can
explain why attributes contribute to the internal structure of the category
even if they are not common to all category members, i.e. if they are not
essential features according to the classical view. An ostrich is a bird not
only because it has feathers and lays eggs, like a robin (indicated by bold

lines in Figure 1.8); category membership is also supported by the fact that the ostrich has a long neck like a flamingo, and decorative feathers like a peacock (see thin lines in Figure 1.8). In defining the position of a category member in its category, we are thus justified in considering any sensible attribute proposed for this item. This is the theoretical background of the attribute-listing experiments carried out by Rosch and her associates and the typicality ratings that were based on them.

Attribute listing and attribute-based typicality ratings

Given the ease with which we seem to be able to call up the attributes for familiar objects and organisms, attributes can be collected in a fairly simple test procedure that can be easily administered to a large number of subjects. In the attribute-listing experiments conducted by Rosch and Mervis (1975), each of the subjects (400 American psychology students) was given six sheets of paper with the test item written on the top of the page. The subjects had a minute and a half to write down all the attributes that they could think of. To eliminate answers that were obviously false or wrongly attributed to an item or too general in meaning, the attribute lists were checked by two judges.

The test items used were selected from the lists obtained in the goodness-of-example ratings described in Figure 1.3 and consisted of sets of 20 graded category members, one set for each of the categories FURNITURE, VEHICLE, FRUIT, WEAPON, VEGETABLE and CLOTHING. Altogether, 120 items from >CHAIR< to >TELEPHONE< (for FURNITURE), >CAR< to >ELEVATOR< (for VEHICLE) and from >ORANGE< to >OLIVE< (for FRUIT) were tested.

The experiment had two aims: to demonstrate the notion of family resemblance (see above) and, more important for Rosch and Mervis, to supply attribute-based typicality ratings (this neutral term seems preferable to Rosch and Mervis's own term 'measure of family resemblance'). These typicality ratings could then be used to verify the earlier goodness-of-example ratings.

How were the attribute-based ratings calculated? Leaving aside mathematical details, two stages can be distinguished. First, the attributes were 'weighted', that is, it was established for how many of the 20 tested category members each attribute had been listed. The top score of 20 was given if an attribute was shared by all category members ('means of transport' in the case of vehicles). An attribute listed for only one category member (think of 'installed in buildings', which would only fit >LIFT< or >ELEVATOR<) received the score 1; attributes applying to several but not all category members were assigned intermediate scores. The result was a list of weighted attributes.

In the second stage the weights of all the attributes listed for each category member were added up and rank-ordered (the actual procedure was somewhat more complex).[10] Category members with many shared and therefore highly weighted attributes, such as >ORANGE< or >APPLE< in the FRUIT category, achieved high overall ratings; category members like >OLIVE<, which shared only few, if any, attributes with other category members, scored low. When this attribute-based rank order was compared with the goodness-of-example ratings, the two types of ratings showed a high degree of correlation.

This correlation could be used to support the notion of prototype categories in two ways. On the one hand, the hypothesis that these categories consist of good and bad members was no longer solely dependent on the intuitive judgements of the goodness-of-example ratings, but could now be related to a large range of attributes. On the other hand, the notion of good and bad examples could be used to explain why attributes are so unevenly distributed among category members. While good examples have many attributes in common with other members of the same category, bad or marginal examples share only few attributes with members of the same category.

Yet as we know from the dictionary entries discussed at the beginning of this section, the intra-categorial links of attributes represent only one side of the coin. Equally important is the question of distinctive attributes, i.e. whether the members of a category, both good and bad examples, share attributes with members of neighbouring categories. This was tested in a further attribute-listing experiment in which good and bad examples of the category CAR were contrasted with members of the categories TRUCK, BUS and MOTORCYCLE. As it turned out, the overlap of attributes is smallest between the good examples of the different categories, but is much larger in the case of bad or marginal examples. In other words, a prototypical car, say a saloon, has fewer attributes in common with a prototypical truck than an estate car does; the saloon also shares fewer attributes with a prototypical motorcycle than a three-wheeler does.

Looking now at both sides of the coin we can summarize the attribute structure of prototype categories as follows:

- Prototypical members of cognitive categories have the largest number of attributes in common with other members of the category and the smallest number of attributes which also occur with members of neighbouring categories. This means that in terms of attributes, prototypical members are maximally distinct from the prototypical members of other categories.

- Bad examples (or marginal category members) share only a small number of attributes with other members of their category, but have several attributes which belong to other categories as well, which is, of course, just another way of saying that category boundaries are fuzzy.

Attributes and dimensions

Returning to the matrix of bird attributes in Figure 1.7, it is clear that Rosch and Mervis have indeed solved the problem of 'missing' attributes as observed with >OSTRICH< and other bad examples of the BIRD category. This still leaves the 'deviant' cases, that is category members whose attributes do not comply with the expected norm. Most of these 'deviant cases' involve attributes related to **dimensions**, such as 'size' and 'weight', 'length (of tail)' and 'thickness (of legs)'. This takes us back to Labov's cups and bowls, which were already discussed in the context of fuzzy category boundaries in Section 1.1. In choosing cups and cup-like containers for his experiments Labov could rely on 'width', 'height/depth' and 'shape', i.e. on generally accepted 'logical' properties of the dimension type, and did not have to expose himself to the vagaries of empirical attribute listing. In this respect he is more in line with traditional linguists than Rosch and Mervis are. The dimensions had the advantage that they could be varied under controlled conditions, and these variations could be easily and unequivocally represented in line drawings. This was illustrated in Figure 1.4, which is here repeated for convenience as Figure 1.9.

In this figure the variation of the dimensions is based on the 'prototypical' cup no. 1. In the top row the height (or depth) of the vessels is kept constant while the width is extended systematically from vessel to vessel. Conversely, in the second row the width of vessels is identical, but from left to right the vessels become deeper and deeper. Other scalar variations used by Labov (and not illustrated in Figure 1.9) concerned the shape of the vessels and involved cylinders, truncated cones, etc. In addition, he used

Figure 1.9 A selection of the drawings of cup-like objects used by Labov (1973: 354, no. 5 reconstructed)

attributes like 'context' or 'function' ('neutral/coffee/food/flower context'), 'material' (glass, china) and 'presence/absence of handle(s)', all of them 'non-scalar' attributes at first sight.

To bring these diverse attributes in line with dimensions, Labov defined the specific width/height ratios of his test vessels as discrete values on the width and height dimensions. In the same way the attributes involving context, material and handles were interpreted as values on a dimension: the neutral, coffee, food and flower contexts as values on the 'context' dimension; glass and china as values on the 'material' dimension; presence and absence of handles as two values on the 'handle' dimension.

How did these attribute values show up in the actual test results, i.e. the use of *cup* or *bowl* or *mug* for certain vessels? According to Labov, the use of these words reflected the 'weighted' acceptability judgements of test subjects. These judgements were weighted in the sense that the different values of the attributes involved led the subjects to choose different names for the test vessels. If the 'prototypical' cup (vessel no. 1) was called *cup* by all test subjects, this judgement could be related to the fact that vessel no. 1 represented the favourite width/height ratio in a neutral context. Vessel no. 2 was still overwhelmingly called *cup* because it represented a very similar width/height ratio. In contrast, vessel no. 4 was assessed as a borderline case of *cup* because its width/height ratio differed markedly from the favoured value. If the use of *cup* was extended by the test subjects in a coffee context and reduced in a food context, this was due to the interaction of the width/height ratio with the respective values on the 'context' dimension.

While such three-variable constellations could still be documented in consistency profiles (as shown in Figure 1.5 and 1.6), the more complex interactions could only be mastered by mathematical formulas and probability calculation which are beyond the scope of this introduction (see reading note 7).

Nevertheless, the aims and the methods employed by Labov should have become clear. Starting out from attributes which could, at least theoretically, be regarded as values on dimensions, he overcomes the limitations implicit in the discrete attributes of the logical view, and this is where he seems to go further than Rosch and Mervis. The scalar values are then related to each other in a weighting process, and here his method comes closest to Rosch and Mervis's procedure.

Internal category structure and gestalt

When comparing attribute-based typicality ratings with the goodness-of-example ratings (i.e. direct typicality ratings), we suggested that the latter are based on intuition. The question is, however, what this intuition might be derived from. Does it perhaps rely on some internal attribute-based rating? From a 'naive' point of view, this seems unlikely. When we encounter an animal we will hardly begin categorizing by evaluating specific attributes, unless we are struck by a very salient one like the stripes of a zebra or the trunk of an elephant. With most organisms and concrete objects, especially those that are familiar to us, we seem to proceed in a different way. We simply take in an overall picture of the whole and use it for a first assessment of its goodness. The consideration of specific attributes can then be left until later.

The problem with this quite plausible conception is that it seems impossible to investigate it in controlled test situations or, to put it more pointedly, to exclude experimentally that people categorize and evaluate the goodness of items on an attribute-by-attribute basis. To return once more to Labov's naming tests, it does indeed make sense to assume that informants' judgements are based on the overall impression of a cup or bowl rather than on an internal computation of the width/height ratio, material and context, but this alternative cannot be ruled out. For the time being, we have to be content with results of more informal test interviews.

A series of such interviews was conducted in the context of the categorization of houses (Schmid 1993: 121ff). The starting point was Labov's method of eliciting category names for the drawings of objects, which was applied to the buildings shown in Figure 1.10. The aim of the interview

Figure 1.10 Examples of houses used for a categorization task (Schmid 1993: 151f)

part of the test was to collect information about how the categorization process was carried out and how it was experienced by the informants.

After a first glance at the drawings (which were presented one by one with other pictures interspersed) the informants named the buildings. At this stage, pictures (a) and (b) were quite readily categorized as cottages, while picture (c) was assigned to adjacent categories which were labelled *house in the country* or *villa*. Just as with Labov's cups and bowls there was no total agreement among the informants. While 10 of the 12 informants did not call picture (c) *cottage*, two were prepared to do so. When asked to give the reasons for their categorizing decision, the informants explained they had judged on the basis of a general impression of the drawings. This can be taken as an indication that an internal goodness-of-example scale was already established on the basis of the first overall impression. Only on second thoughts were the informants able to pinpoint certain individual properties that might have led them to select the name they did. The choice of *cottage* seems to have been influenced by the material ('made of stone') and the simple but sturdy construction in the case of picture (a), and by the thatched roof for picture (b). The deviant width/height relation ('too big') and the numerous extensions of building (c) may have helped to rule out *cottage* as an appropriate name for the majority of the informants.

As far as these interviews go, they support the initial assumption that categorization and goodness ratings may indeed involve two stages: the perception of an object as a whole as the first step (the so-called **holistic perception**), and a kind of decomposition of the perceived whole into individual properties or attributes as a second (optional) step.[11]

The idea of 'perceived whole' comes close to the notion of **gestalt** as advocated by gestalt psychologists,[12] so it may be helpful to look at some of their findings. Their major claim is that gestalt perception can be traced back to 'gestalt laws of perceptual organization', or 'gestalt principles', which are usually demonstrated with line drawings and dot patterns. The most important of these principles are:

- 'principle of proximity': individual elements with a small distance between them will be perceived as being somehow related to each other;
- 'principle of similarity': individual elements that are similar tend to be perceived as one common segment;
- 'principle of closure': perceptual organization tends to be anchored in closed figures;
- 'principle of continuation': elements will be perceived as wholes if they only have few interruptions.

The more a configuration of individual elements adheres to these principles, the more it will tend towards a clear-cut and cogent organization (called *Prägnanz* by the gestalt psychologists), which lends itself to gestalt perception. Examples which show a high degree of *Prägnanz* are called 'good gestalts' or 'good forms'. Among them are circle, square and equilateral triangle, which we already encountered in our discussion of shapes in Section 1.1, where they appeared as prototypes of shape categories.

However, shape is just one aspect of the gestalt of organisms and objects, although such an important one that it is sometimes, inaccurately, treated as equivalent with gestalt. The question is whether the gestalt principles are not only valid for dot patterns and geometrical shapes, but can also be applied to the much more complex configurations of organisms and objects.

As it seems, a central role in providing an object with a gestalt is played by its constituent parts.[13] Consider once more the cottages (a) and (b) in Figure 1.10. It is obvious that they consist of walls, windows, a door, a roof and a chimney. Yet when we look at these drawings for the first time, the cottages are not visually 'deconstructed' into these parts, but are perceived as an integral whole. This holistic visual perception is possible because the parts are organized according to the gestalt principles of proximity (all the parts are close together), of similarity (identical windows), of closure (all the parts are included in one overall outline) and continuation (all the lines are uninterrupted).

Similarly, if you look at some everyday object that is in your view at the moment, maybe a chair, a table or a bookshelf, you will realize that the salient parts make an important contribution to the whole without at first being noticed as individual parts. Other perceptual aspects such as the overall proportions, the material and the colour of objects interact with the overall shape and the parts to complete the holistic impression of a gestalt.

Having established that objects are perceived as integral wholes, we can go on to ask ourselves what makes one gestalt more prototypical for a category than another. Here one enters new ground, because apart from the good forms among geometrical shapes, this question was not really the concern of gestalt psychology. We would like to argue that it is again the parts of an object that play an important role in establishing a prototypical gestalt. Parts do not only contribute to the overall shape of an object, but are also related to its function, which for most artefacts is the *raison d'être* of the object. Likewise, the existence of most parts of an object is motivated by the particular purpose the object serves.

Consider a chair, for example. The functionally relevant parts of a chair are the legs, the seat and the back. Our assumption now is that the prototypical

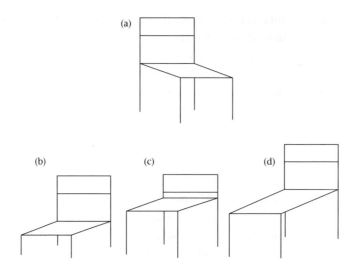

Figure 1.11   A prototypical chair gestalt and other chairs

gestalt of a chair relies predominantly on the presence of these three functional parts in optimally functional proportions. Looking at the drawings
of chairs shown in Figure 1.11, the prototypical chair gestalt is best represented by picture (a).

   An analogous explanation can be attempted for the gestalts of organisms
such as birds if we understand the 'function' of a bird to mean the enactment of a certain form of organic life. This prototypical mode of life would
be characterized by the ability to live on trees and shrubs, to fly, and to pick
nuts, seeds, worms, etc., for food. Assuming a functional design of the parts,
we would expect from a prototype gestalt that parts like the beak, the legs,
and especially the wings, have the appropriate form: the legs should have
claws which allow the bird to cling to branches, the beak should be protruding
and sharp to facilitate food picking, wings should be shaped aerodynamically.
Even more important, the parts would have to have the right proportions
(large wings in comparison to the remaining part of the body etc.). This may
read like a replica of the attributes listed in the matrix at the beginning of
this section (see Figure 1.7). The decisive difference is that these functionally
balanced parts are all integrated into one gestalt, and are perceived as a whole.

   All this might suggest that for concrete objects as well as for organisms
the prototype gestalt should be conceived as a kind of reduction to the relevant and mainly visual essentials, though perceived as a whole. Such a notion
is supported by the experience of how easy it is to grasp and categorize
reduced illustrations, as have been increasingly used in dictionaries over the

last few years.[14] (The case of pictograms, as used in traffic signs, is more complex because here the drawings are used as a vehicle for instructions and will therefore be neglected.)

We would hold the position that the effectiveness of reduced drawings is not a general phenomenon even with concrete objects and organisms, but depends on the kind of lexical category to be illustrated. Just look at the drawings of a bungalow and a cottage in Figure 1.12, which are both taken from the same dictionary (LDOCE2, 1987). The bungalow is reduced to the functional parts (one-storey building with walls, roof, windows, door), and can still be readily identified. In contrast, the illustration of the cottage contains a wealth of detail, and this seems to be necessary for easy recognition, so it is in fact more easily categorized than some of the plainer drawings of cottages in Figure 1.10.

From this it can be deduced that the prototype gestalt of a cottage comprises more than the complete and well-proportioned parts of a house, important as all this may be. The function of a cottage includes notions like creating warmth and cosiness and being embedded in natural rural surroundings. In other words, all sorts of emotional and attitudinal properties are involved. Similarly it is difficult to imagine a line drawing of an English pub (and, incidentally, none of the major dictionaries provides one); the wealth of gestalt properties applying to a pub is simply too great.

Or take another simple case, the teddy bear. To approximate the prototype gestalt of a teddy bear it is certainly not enough to give the outline drawing of a teddy that coincides with its natural model, the brown bear. What is also needed is an indication of its softness (something that takes us beyond the visual to the tactile properties of the gestalt), and, perhaps most important, the teddy should be hugged by a child to round off the general impression of its function.

This shows that even in the domain of concrete objects we are not just confronted with a single kind of gestalt prototype (the 'reduced type') but

Figure 1.12 Bungalow and cottage: examples of reduced and 'rich' dictionary illustrations (from LDOCE2, 1987)

have to take into account that certain lexical categories require richer visual representations, which in turn suggest richer underlying gestalt prototypes. The situation becomes even more complex when we consider that for many lexical categories – those loosely called 'abstract' categories – gestalt perception is largely excluded.

Summing up at this point, our discussion of gestalt has shown mainly two things:

- Gestalt perception seems indeed to play an important part in categorization and goodness ratings. For the categories discussed it seems to be as essential as the possibility of studying attributes and family resemblances and computing attribute-based typicality ratings.
- The role of gestalt in the categorization of objects and organisms need not be completely left to intuition; it can be studied by making selective use of the principles of gestalt psychology and by considering additional aspects like parts and function.

Any research into gestalt properties, and even the preliminary sketch attempted here, is intimately bound up with questions of mental representation and processing, just as the notions of good and bad examples, of attributes, and of prototypicality in general cannot be isolated from their cognitive background. So it seems appropriate to conclude this section with a few more general remarks about the cognitive status of categories and of the notions involved in categorization.

The cognitive status of categories, prototypes, attributes and gestalt

For the linguist, categorization is an important issue because it underlies the use of words and the use of language in general. Since producing and understanding language undoubtedly involve cognitive processes, categorization is necessarily something that takes place in our minds, and the categories resulting from it can be understood as mental concepts stored in our mind. Taken together they make up what has been called the 'mental lexicon'.[15] Unfortunately, we do not have direct access to cognitive phenomena, so everything that is said about the categories of the mental lexicon can only have the status of a more or less well-founded hypothesis. Such a hypothesis can be supported by philosophical argument, by physiological research into the human sensory apparatus and by experimental evidence based on linguistic and other human behaviour.

To avoid misunderstandings, two things should be kept in mind. First, the number of hypotheses about cognitive categorization is theoretically unlimited; it is definitely not restricted to the two paradigms which will be discussed in this section. Second, the postulated category paradigms need not apply indiscriminately to the whole domain of human categorization, but may be restricted to certain areas and perspectives.

Let us start with the 'classical' model of categorization, a hypothesis with a very long tradition. This hypothesis claims that categories come as homogeneous units with clear-cut borderlines and that all members are characterized by a limited number of essential features (a set of necessary and sufficient conditions, as discussed above). This beautifully simple model is often accompanied by the philosophical speculation that this type of category mirrors, or is even predetermined by, the constitution of the organisms and objects in the 'real' world. The problem is that this hypothesis is not in accordance with the evidence collected by physiologists and psychologists. *purely theoretical.*

In contrast with the classical model, the experiential prototype hypothesis of categorization claims that categories are not homogeneous, but have a prototype, good and bad members, and have fuzzy boundaries. Category members do not all share the same discrete attributes, but may be linked by family resemblances. In the case of colours and shapes, prototype theory is supported by both physiological and psychological evidence. As suggested in Section 1.1, colour categories and focal colours seem to be based on the nature of the human perceptual apparatus. Their prototype structure was also confirmed by psychological tests. In the case of organisms and concrete objects only this second type of evidence is available. As this short survey of the classical and the prototype paradigms has shown, it does indeed help to take the strictly cognitive view, the view that categorization is something that underlies the mental processes of language comprehension and language production. This view provides us with a vantage point from which we can now delve deeper and examine the main elements of the prototype hypothesis: the notions of prototype, category membership and typicality, attributes, family resemblances and gestalt.

Prototype

Basically, there are two ways to understand the notion of prototype. It can be deduced from categorization experiments. For instance, some members of a category first come to mind in association experiments and are recognized more rapidly as category members in verification tasks. If one takes these members as prototypes of the respective categories, this leads to definitions like 'best example of a category', 'salient examples', 'clearest cases of category membership', 'most representative of things included in a class' or 'central and typical members' (see Rosch 1978; Lakoff 1986; Brown 1990; Tversky 1990).

But this is not the conception of prototype that we would advocate. Instead we would claim that if one takes the cognitive view of categories seriously, one is justified in defining the prototype as a mental representation, as some sort of cognitive reference point. Thinking of prototypes in this genuinely cognitive way still leaves open the nature of the mental representation, so that definitions may range from the more concrete notion of 'image' or 'schema' to the more abstract 'representation of a category' or 'ideal' according to the categories to which they are applied (definitions from Rosch and Mervis 1975; Coleman and Kay 1981; Lakoff 1986).

Category membership and typicality

Unlike the homogeneous categories postulated by the classical hypothesis, cognitive prototype categories always consist of good and bad members and include marginal examples whose category membership is doubtful.[16] This not only applies to attested cases of prototype categories, such as colour categories or CUP, BOWL, MUG and CHAIR, but also to categories like BIRD, where category membership seems to be safely based on discrete attributes such as 'laying eggs'. But do ordinary language users have the encyclopaedic knowledge to decide whether a penguin lays eggs or not? If they do not, the issue whether the penguin is a bird will remain undecided, and >PENGUIN< will be a doubtful member of the prototype category BIRD.

Even for prime cases of apparently discrete homogeneous categories, such as ODD NUMBER, SQUARE and kinship categories (MOTHER, UNCLE, etc.), a prototype structure cannot be completely excluded. As experiments have shown (Armstrong *et al.* 1983; Fehr and Russell 1984), informants do in fact distinguish between good and bad examples of odd numbers and squares, and similar reactions can be assumed for MOTHER (Lakoff 1987) and other kinship terms.

However, this only applies to 'everyday' categorization. In a mathematical or scientific context the classical view comes into its own. In such a context ODD NUMBER, SQUARE, kinship categories and even BIRD can be established as clear-cut and homogeneous categories by an act of definition. In other words, the classical paradigm of categorization has a wide field of application wherever there is a need for precise and rigid definitions as in the domain of scientific categorization or in the legal field. And there is no reason why the discrete categories of science and the everyday prototype categories should not coexist in the mental lexicon and even influence each other.

Attributes and family resemblances

Attributes as collected from informants by Rosch and others are statements which provide information about the members of a category. In this sense attributes are part and parcel of the empirical investigation of category structures.

When the attribute lists for individual category members are compared, this is assumed to reflect the similarity relations between category members. Such similarity relations may encompass all category members ('category-wide attributes') or they may establish links only between some of the members. In the latter case, category coherence is produced by family resemblances.

Since similarity relations between good and bad members of a category are part of the hypothesis of prototype structure, this implies that they are also part of the mental representation of a category. This is not necessarily so for the empirically collected attributes which are elicited from informants and which may be fragmentary and overlapping. So attributes are best considered as a descriptive tool and not as part of the mental representation of the category. Such a cautious position is even more advisable when attributes are treated as values on dimensions. For such dimensions as 'size', 'width' and 'shape' may be imposed on the attributes by the logically minded researcher and are not necessarily a reflection of our natural way of thinking about the objects in the world around us.

Gestalt

As originally conceived by gestalt psychologists, the notion of gestalt was intended as an explanation of holistic perception. We have suggested a link between gestalt and the notion of prototype categories. If a gestalt is organized according to the gestalt principles and includes the functional parts of an item in functionally balanced proportions, it may be regarded as a 'prototype gestalt'. This ties in with the definition of prototype as an 'image', which was quoted above. In fact, in the case of organisms and concrete objects where visual perception seems to be important, the prototype gestalt contributes considerably to the ability of the prototype to function as a model or cognitive reference point.

This is where we think we should leave the psychological issues of categorization, moving on in the following section to look at some sociological, or, more broadly, cultural factors that influence the formation of prototypes and prototype categories.

Exercises

1. Collect attributes for the following categories and try to distinguish between objective properties and subjective associations:

   MAN, WOMAN, BOY, GIRL;

   MANSION, PALACE, COTTAGE, CASTLE;

BICYCLE, MOTORBIKE, CAR, VAN, LORRY;

JEANS, LEGGINGS, TUXEDO, TAILCOAT, MINISKIRT.

2. Look at the picture of the 'Smith brothers' devised by Armstrong *et al.* (1983: 269).

All 'brothers' have hair and beards
The majority have large noses

In what way is the principle of family resemblances illustrated by this drawing? Which attributes are shared by all the brothers?

3. Have a look at how Wierzbicka (1985: 19–36) explains the difference between CUP and MUG and discuss whether you find her arguments plausible. Wierzbicka claims that the difference in meaning boils down to the difference in the intended use of the respective objects; apply this idea to the categories VASE, BOWL and PLATE.

4. Discuss the attributes 'fun', 'no purpose other than the game itself', 'uncertain outcome' and 'governed by rules' as candidates for the status of category-wide attributes for the category GAME. Try to come up with other possibilities and discuss possible counterexamples.

5. Pictograms are more than simple line drawings. Look at some traffic signs and some of the signs in railway stations, bus terminals or airports and explain whether they make use of gestalt perception. What additional information do they convey?

6. Ask a friend or two to draw simple pictures of a car, a bus, a telephone, a book, a bottle, a tree, a house and a church. Discuss to what extent the principles of gestalt psychology can be applied to their drawings. Does the perspective or vantage point from which the objects are viewed play a role?

7. Discuss the difference between the classical view of categorization and the prototype model with reference to legal categories like MURDER, MANSLAUGHTER; VANDALISM, LOOTING; ASSAULT, ASSAULT AND BATTERY; NEGLIGENCE, GROSS NEGLIGENCE. What are the problems a judge faces when he has to deal with unclear cases?

8. In the context of the acquisition of the meaning of words Aitchison (2003: 193) writes about a child's use of the word *qua* ('quack') as discussed by the Russian psychologist Vygotsky:

> The child began with *qua* as a duck on a pond. Then the liquid element caught the youngster's attention and the word was generalized to a cup of milk. But the duck had not been forgotten, and this surfaced in *qua* used to refer to a coin with an eagle on it. But then the child appeared to ignore the bird-like portion of the meaning and focus only on the roundness of the coin, so reapplied the word *qua* to a teddy-bear's eye.

Discuss how the strange assembly collected by the child in the category QUA can be explained with the principle of family resemblances.

The 'bits' were treated as one; duck + pond = qua
pond + liquid + milk = qua   duck + bird + coin = qua
coin + round = qua

1.3 Context-dependence and cultural models

The prototypes of cognitive categories are not fixed, but may change when a particular context is introduced, and the same is true for category boundaries. More generally, the whole internal structure of a category seems to depend on the context and, in a wider sense, on our social and cultural knowledge, which is thought to be organized in cognitive and cultural models.

Reading the sentence *He opened the door to face a pretty young woman with a dog in her arms*, what kind of dog would first spring to your mind? Would it be an Alsatian or a collie, which would presumably turn out to be prototypical dogs in a goodness-of-example rating? Or would you not rather think of a Pekinese or some other kind of small lapdog? The chances are that you would. Though this may look like a rather trivial example, it has far-reaching implications for the theory of prototypes. What it suggests is that prototypes are not after all the fixed reference points for cognitive categories that we have assumed them to be, but that they are liable to keep shifting as the context changes.

The context-dependence of prototypes and of the whole internal category structure

Let us first expand the lapdog example and, by way of a little experiment, compare it to other examples involving references to dogs. Read the following four sentences one by one, pausing for a second after each example to check what kind of dog is suggested to you:

1. The hunter took his gun, left the lodge and called his dog. *Golden Retriever*
2. Right from the start of the race the dogs began chasing the rabbit. *Greyhound whippet*

3. She took her dog to the salon to have its curls reset. *Poodle*
4. The policemen lined up with the dogs to face the rioters. *Alsatian*

We can safely assume that for each of the four sentences you will have formed a different image of the kind of dog that is denoted. In a hunting context like example (1), the most likely dog would probably be some kind of retriever; in the dog racing context of example (2), it would certainly be a greyhound that would first come to mind. In examples (3) and (4), you will presumably have imagined a poodle and an Alsatian respectively. These examples suggest that what turns out the most likely member of a certain category depends on the context. Since we may expect the prototype to be our first choice, the result of our little experiment indicates that, depending on the context, the prototype shifts. The 'context-dependent' categories thus evoked may be completely different from the non-contextualized prototypes elicited in goodness-of-example experiments.

However, more than a shift of prototypes is at stake in these examples. Let us assume that in a goodness-of-example test >ALSATIAN< would be rated as a prototypical dog, with >GREYHOUND<, >SETTER< and >POODLE< being just slightly less prototypical. >PEKINESE< would presumably be a rather peripheral dog because of its small size, flat face and somewhat 'undoggy' behaviour. Taking this category structure as a starting point, it seems clear that the sentences above do more than just shift the prototype. In some cases the category structure of the context-dependent category is much leaner than that of the non-contextualized category. For example in sentences (2) and (3) the context-dependent prototypes are >GREYHOUND< and >POODLE< respectively; virtually all other types of dogs are so unlikely that, for all practical purposes, they are highly peripheral members of the context-dependent category.

In contrast, in sentence (1) the internal category structure of DOG is retained to a larger extent. One could certainly imagine an Alsatian or a setter being used as a hunting dog. Nevertheless they are clearly less typical members of the context-dependent category (HUNTING) DOG than retrievers. Thus the principle of different degrees of goodness-of-example is still valid in this case, and the same is true for examples (3) and (4). The main point, however, is that the context-dependent category structure is different from the structure that was obtained in non-contextualized goodness-of-example ratings. Altogether, it seems that the context not only determines the choice of the category prototype, but that it also leads to an adjustment of the position of other category members. How can this be explained?[17]

One way is to use attributes as an explanatory tool. As shown in Section 1.2, weighted attributes can be employed to explain the typicality structure of a category. When viewed in terms of attributes, context seems to have a twofold effect: first, the context can change the weight of attributes that seem to be relevant for a certain category. Attributes of the category DOG that seem to be decisive in the goodness-of-example ratings and attribute-based typicality ratings (e.g. 'barks', 'has four legs', 'wags tail when happy', 'likes to chase cats', etc.) apparently lose weight in specific contexts; second, the context can emphasize attributes that are not prominent and even introduce new attributes which would not be mentioned at all in non-contextualized attribute-listing experiments. In the hunting-dog context, attributes like 'brings back the kill' or 'points out the position of animals for shooting' increase in importance. In the dog-racing context, 'has long, thin legs', 'can run fast', 'is enduring' and others become crucial. With the introduction of new attributes and the re-evaluation of the weights of existing ones the attribute list for a member of a category changes completely. The result is that previously peripheral examples are equipped with large bundles of heavily weighted attributes and turned into good examples or even prototypes, while well-established good examples are reduced to the status of marginal members.

Context, situation and cognitive models

Once we have acknowledged that the context can completely reshuffle the positions of members within the category structure, we must ask ourselves what the context is. How can we grasp this rather elusive notion, which is nevertheless one of the most widely used terms in linguistics?

'Context' has been defined in many ways by scholars with different backgrounds and various aims in mind. From a purely linguistic point of view the context has been regarded as the linguistic material preceding and following a word or sentence. Language philosophers and pragmalinguists, most notably Searle (1979: 125), have defined context as the set of background assumptions that are necessary for an utterance to be intelligible. In discourse-oriented approaches to language the context has been related to the situation in which an utterance is embedded. Originating in the work of the anthropologist Malinowski, the term 'context' has been extended still further to include the so-called 'context of culture'. Malinowski had argued as early as 1923 that both the 'context of situation' and the 'context of culture' were necessary for a proper understanding of an utterance or text (Halliday and Hasan 1989: 5ff).

For cognitive linguists it is important that the notion of 'context' should be considered a mental phenomenon. This requirement is stressed by Langacker, for example, who defines his central notion of domain 'as a context for the characterization of a semantic unit' (1987a: 147).[18] This very general interpretation of 'context' will be discussed in Chapter 4 alongside other basic tenets of Langacker's theory. In this section we will try to present a more tangible, but still cognitive, view of the notion of 'context'.

To do this it will be helpful to distinguish 'context' from 'situation' and a few other related terms. Figure 1.13 illustrates our suggestion for a meaningful terminological distinction between the notions 'context' and 'situation' with reference to the example sentence *The boy was building a sandcastle with his bucket and his spade*. The figure shows that we will treat the 'context' as belonging to the field of mental phenomena, while the 'situation' refers to some state of affairs in the 'real world'. (The quotation marks around *real world* are necessary in view of the age-old debate among philosophers as to whether there is such a thing as a 'real world' at all; see reading note 6).

As Figure 1.13 indicates, we define the term **situation** as the interaction between objects in the real world. In the exemplary situation described by the sentence above, the situation is made up by four objects, namely a boy, a sandcastle, a bucket and a spade, which interact through the activities of the boy. When the sentence is being processed by the hearer or reader, the words call up the corresponding cognitive categories, or to put it more simply, the mental concept we have of the objects in the real world. In addition, a cognitive representation of the interaction between the concepts

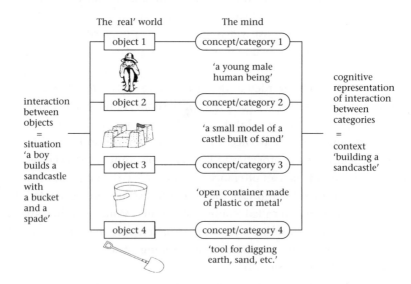

Figure 1.13 'Situation' and 'context' illustrated with reference to the sentence *The boy was building a sandcastle with his bucket and his spade*

is formed, and it is for this cognitive representation that the term **context** will be used. In Figure 1.13, we have characterized the context for the example sentence roughly as 'building a sandcastle'. It should be emphasized that in contrast to most pragmatic and/or sociolinguistic approaches to *context,* our notion does not focus on the speech event in which an utterance is made, but on the cognitive representation of the situation depicted by the utterance.[19]

Of course, this cognitive representation, or context, does not remain an isolated mental experience, but is immediately associated in at least two ways with related knowledge stored in long-term memory. On the one hand, context-specific knowledge about the categories involved is retrieved.[20] This leads to the selection of >PLASTIC BUCKET< as the most typical member of the context-dependent category BUCKET and of >CHILDREN'S SPADE< as the most typical member of the context-dependent category SPADE.

On the other hand, the currently active context calls up other contexts from long-term memory that are somehow related to it. In our example, experiences about other aspects of sand and sandcastles, besides those expressed in the sentence above, might be evoked. Related categories like WATER, HANDS, SHELLS, TURRET or MOAT, and frequent interactions between all these categories like 'digging sand' or 'shaping turrets' are good candidates for such associated contexts.

It stands to reason that for all kinds of phenomena that we come across in everyday life, we have experienced and stored a large number of interrelated contexts. Cognitive categories are not just dependent on the immediate context in which they are embedded, but also on this whole bundle of contexts that are associated with it. Therefore, it seems quite useful to have a term which covers all the stored cognitive representations that belong to a certain field. We will use the term **cognitive model** for these knowledge bases; other related terms like 'frame' or 'script' will be taken up again in Chapter 5.[21]

Figure 1.14 shows one of the two cognitive models (ON THE BEACH and IN THE SANDPIT) in which the context 'building a sandcastle' could possibly be embedded. When we consider this example, two important properties of cognitive models become immediately apparent. First, as indicated by the reference to 'other contexts' in Figure 1.14, cognitive models are basically open-ended. A practical consequence of this property is that it is very hard to describe the cognitive model of a domain and that descriptions of cognitive models are never exhaustive, but always highly selective.

Second, just like the contexts that build the basis for cognitive models, cognitive models themselves are not isolated cognitive entities, but interrelated.

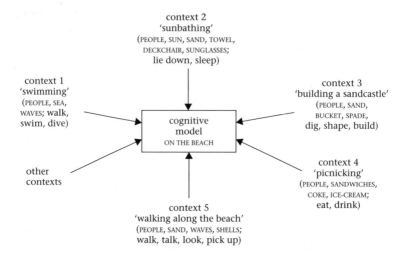

Figure 1.14 Schematic illustration of the cognitive model ON THE BEACH (the major categories and the way they interact are indicated in brackets)

In our example, it can be seen that the categories PEOPLE, SEA, SAND and others keep occurring in various contexts that make up the model ON THE BEACH. Consequently, the cognitive models of PEOPLE, SEA and SAND are closely related to the model ON THE BEACH. In line with theories of the mind which emphasize its so-called 'connectionist' architecture, one can argue that cognitive models combine to build networks.[22] This tendency can probably best be explained using a visual representation. Figure 1.15 gives an idea of a network which consists of various cognitive models that are interrelated through multiple connections.

So far, two aspects of cognitive models have emerged from the exemplary representations that we have provided: their incompleteness and their tendency to build networks. There is a third, although not so obvious, property of cognitive models that should not be neglected, namely the

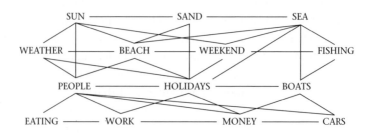

Figure 1.15 Exemplary network of cognitive models

fact that cognitive models are omnipresent. In every act of categorization we are more or less consciously referring to one or several cognitive models that we have stored. Only in the very rare case when we encounter a totally unfamiliar object or situation will no appropriate cognitive model be available, but even then we will presumably try to call up similar experiences and immediately form a cognitive model. Imagine the case of a foreign visitor to Britain who goes to watch a cricket game for the first time in his life. Having no cognitive model of the situation at his disposal he will have no idea what is going on on the field. Nevertheless the visitor will try to relate what he sees to similar cognitive models perhaps about games in general or about his knowledge of baseball.

Clearly, then, we can neither avoid the influence of cognitive models nor function without them. Even in the rather artificial situation of goodness-of-example ratings, the cognitive model of the field that the subjects are being asked to rate is at work. Therefore, it would be misleading to say that such experiments take place in an uncontextualized vacuum. What these experimental situations generate is a very neutral or zero-context which can be compared to sentences like *When she looked out of the window she saw a* . . . or *She thought of the* . . . . Uncontextualized language in the sense of 'language without cognitive models' is apparently unthinkable.

Cultural models

Cognitive models, as the term suggests, represent a cognitive, basically psychological, view of the stored knowledge about a certain field. Since psychological states are always private and individual experiences, descriptions of such cognitive models necessarily involve a considerable degree of idealization. In other words, descriptions of cognitive models are based on the assumption that many people have roughly the same basic knowledge about things like sandcastles and beaches.

However, as the cricket example has shown, this is only part of the story. Cognitive models are of course not universal, but depend on the culture in which a person grows up and lives. The culture provides the background for all the situations that we have to experience in order to be able to form a cognitive model. A Russian or German may not have formed a cognitive model of cricket simply because it is not part of the culture of his own country to play that game. So, cognitive models for particular domains ultimately depend on so-called **cultural models**. In reverse, cultural models can be seen as cognitive models that are shared by people belonging to a social group or subgroup.

Essentially, cognitive models and cultural models are thus just two sides of the same coin. While the term 'cognitive model' stresses the psychological nature of these cognitive entities and allows for inter-individual differences, the term 'cultural model' emphasizes the uniting aspect of its being collectively shared by many people. Although 'cognitive models' are related to cognitive linguistics and psycholinguistics while 'cultural models' belong to sociolinguistics and anthropological linguistics, researchers in all of these fields should be, and usually are, aware of both dimensions of their object of study.

Our earlier reference to Malinowski's 'context of culture' has already shown that to include cultural aspects in linguistic considerations is not really a recent invention. Yet although the cultural background has long been part and parcel of investigations in sociolinguistics and anthropological linguistics, only few semanticists have bothered to deal with such matters.[23] In the following we will discuss three examples of categories where cultural models are highly relevant for a proper understanding of cognitive categories and their structure.

The English and French prototypes of the category FIRST MEAL OF THE DAY can serve as first illustrations. The prototypical attributes of the meal in the two countries are listed in Figure 1.16. The two lists in Figure 1.16 show how different the French and the English prototype of the category are. While the French >PETIT DÉJEUNER< is a rather frugal affair consisting of a large bowl of coffee and a croissant, the >ENGLISH BREAKFAST< includes a whole array of things to eat and drink. Since the French breakfast needs much less crockery, cutlery and atmosphere, French hotels often do not provide a breakfast room, but serve breakfast on a tray in the bedroom or ask you to have your coffee and croissant in a nearby café or bar. In contrast, the English breakfast is never served in the bedroom, but in a breakfast room. The reasons why the two types of breakfast are so different, and this is our point here,

>PETIT DÉJEUNER<	>ENGLISH BREAKFAST<
Components:	Components:
coffee	cereal and milk
croissant	tea or coffee, orange juice
	toast, butter, marmalade
	bacon, eggs, baked beans, sausages,
	tomatoes
served at bedside	served in breakfast room
or local café or bar	
not included in room rate	included in room rate

Figure 1.16   Prototypical attributes of the category FIRST MEAL OF THE DAY in Britain and France

is that they reflect different cultural models concerning the function and relevance of the meals of the day. According to the French MEALS OF THE DAY model, breakfast is of minor importance because the midday meal is supposed to be rather solid and will be followed by another substantial evening meal. In contrast, the English cultural model is based on a substantial first and last meal, while the midday meal or lunch is a rather slender affair.

What this example also illustrates is that cultural models are not static but changing. In fact, what we have described as the English prototype may still be practised in hotels and bed and breakfast places, but can no longer be regarded as standard routine in families. Conversely, many continental hotels which used to serve a 'Continental breakfast' modelled on the French prototype (though normally replacing croissants by something else) are now offering 'buffet breakfasts', which have many of the attributes of an English breakfast.

The differences between cultural models and their effects on the structure of a category become more obvious when cultures of countries as far apart as Europe and Japan or China are compared. Consider the objects depicted in Figure 1.17. The desks illustrated in (a) and (b) represent traditional European desks at which people used to work either standing or seated on a chair. In contrast, in China and Japan writing was traditionally performed sitting cross-legged or on one's heels on the floor. Within

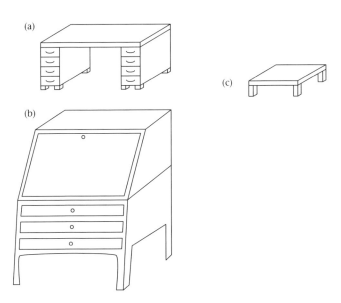

Figure 1.17 Illustration of European and traditional Japanese prototypes of the DESK category (idea based on Lipka 1987: 292, but extended)

this traditional cultural model of writing, object (c) in Figure 1.17 is proto-typical while objects (a) and (b) would have been rather peripheral members of the desk category. Yet this cultural model is also changing under the influence of modern communication; computer and telecommunication equipment are erasing the traditional Japanese and Chinese cultural writing model in favour of 'international' business standards for categories like DESK.

Our last example is perhaps more intriguing because it documents that different cultural models must be assumed even where the same language and the same words are used. This is quite common in languages that are spoken in many parts of the world such as English. Employing Rosch's methods of goodness-of-example ratings (see Sections 1.1 and 1.2), Schmid and Kopatsch (forthcoming) show that the conceptual structures underlying everyday words in the English spoken by students in Northern Nigeria differed significantly from those elicited at two universities in the USA. English is an official language in Nigeria, which is spoken as a second or third language by all people with tertiary education. One of the categories investigated was FOOD. The experiment was based on interviews with 75 Nigerian students at the University of Maiduguri, Northern Nigeria, and 74 students from two American universities in Santa Barbara, California and Lexington, Massachusetts. The informants were asked to give typicality ratings based on a list of 48 food items which included not only *meat*, *bread*, *beans* or *pizza* and *chips*, but also items such as *millet*, *yam* (a tuber similar to potatoes), *cassava* (a flour made from a tropical plant) and *colanut* (seeds of the cola tree containing caffeine which play an important cultural role in celebrations). A selection of the results is presented in Figure 1.18.

Although some correspondences can be observed – cf. e.g. the similar ratings for *chicken* and *meat* – each of the two lists is characteristic of the disparate cognitive models of FOOD prevalent in the respective culture. The prototypical items heading the lists read like plans for the week's dishes, with *chicken, fish, bread, pizza, salad* and *meat* featuring most prominently on the American table, and *beans, rice, yam, chicken, meat* and *cassava* on the Nigerian. Common Western items like *apple, orange* and *sausage* with good rankings by the American students have their places much lower down in the Nigerian list, while Nigerian staple food, especially basic foodstuff like *millet, maize* – admittedly not a very common term in American English – and *wheat* are trailing behind in the American list and illustrate the differences between the disparate living conditions in the USA and Nigeria.

In sum, these examples indicate that the cognitive models shared by the members of a culture are similar and distinct from the cognitive models

Rank	Nigeria	Rank	USA	Rank	Nigeria	Rank	USA
1	beans	1	chicken	15	millet	15	pie
2	rice	2	fish	16	bread	16	cheese
3	yam	3	bread	17	salad	17	beans
4	chicken	4	pizza	18	apple	18	chips
5	meat	5	salad	19	porridge	19	toast
6	cassava	6	meat	20	groundnut	20	tomato
7	macaroni	7	apple	...		...	
8	maize	8	orange	27	orange	26	yam
9	egg	9	banana	...		...	
10	fish	10	potato	35	sausage	33	maize
11	banana	11	rice	36	tomato	...	
12	wheat	12	biscuit	37	toast	39	wheat
13	chips	13	sausage	...		40	cassava
14	potato	14	egg	41	pizza	...	
						47	millet

Figure 1.18 Selected results of goodness-of-example ratings for the category FOOD by Nigerian and US-American students (from Schmid and Kopatsch, forthcoming)

stored in the minds of people from other cultures. They also show that cultural models have an enormous influence on the conceptual structures of categories. This is not only true when one compares distant cultures like the (traditional) Japanese or Chinese cultures and European cultures, it also applies to the relationship between native varieties of English (like American English) and New Englishes (like Nigerian English). In fact even different native varieties of English are affected: an internet-based attribute-listing test fully endorsed the assumption that the category BUS elicits attributes like 'yellow', 'school' and 'kids/children' in the US, while in Britain the attributes 'red', 'public transport' and 'work' are more prominent and yield a different conceptualization of BUS.[†]

Naive models and expert models

As they are based on our everyday experiences of the phenomena around us, cultural models may include assumptions that, from a strictly scientific point of view, may be questionable or even inaccurate. For example, it is part of our cultural model of 'dogs' that wagging their tails means 'I am happy'

[†] We are indebted for these results to Elisabeth Friedrich, Bayreuth.

and growling means 'I am angry'. When cats are purring they are said to be enjoying themselves. For an ethologist or biologist, all these beliefs are highly dubious, because it is by no means clear that animals have emotions at all in the sense that humans do. In their expert models which are based on hard scientific facts and the rules of logic, these types of assumptions would have no place. Naive cultural models, on the other hand, are based on informal observations, traditional beliefs, and even superstitions, and have therefore also been called 'folk models'.

For obvious reasons, the discrepancy between the scientifically founded models of experts and the naive models of laypersons is particularly noticeable in scientific and technical domains. Consider for example the case of the naive model of the physical phenomenon of motion. McCloskey (1983) carried out experiments and interviews to elicit the cultural model of motion prevalent in America. He asked his informants to imagine an airplane flying at constant speed and altitude. In addition, the informants should assume that at one point during the journey a large metal ball is dropped from the plane, which continues flying at the same speed and altitude and in the same direction. The task was to draw the path the ball will follow until it hits the ground, ignoring wind and air resistance. Its final position in relation to the plane should also be indicated. Before you read on, you should perhaps try to solve the task yourself, i.e. make your own drawing of the paths followed by the plane and the metal ball.

Now compare your drawing with the scientifically correct answer to the problem. As physicists tell us, the ball will fall in a kind of parabolic arc and hit the ground directly below the point the plane has reached in the meantime. The ball will take this kind of path because it will continue to travel horizontally at the same speed as the plane while acquiring constantly increasing vertical velocity.

If your drawing does not agree with the scientific explanation, you are in good company, with 60 per cent of the informants, because no more than 40 per cent of McCloskey's informants gave the scientifically correct response. The majority of the subjects thought that the ball would take a different course (for instance that it would drop in a straight line or would fall in a diagonal), revealing a 'naive' cultural model of motion that differs from the expert model current in physics.

What this experiment shows is that the cultural models held by the majority of the people need not be, and often are not, in line with the objectively verifiable, scientific knowledge available to experts. If we consider that cultural models are based on the collective experience of a society or social group this does not come as a surprise. To get through everyday life, laypersons do not need scientifically correct models, but functionally effective ones. This means that as long as a model is in line with what we perceive and enables us to make functionally correct predictions, it can have widespread currency although it may be technically inaccurate.

Another illuminating example is provided by Kempton (1987). When she studied the American cultural model of home heat controls or thermostats by means of interviews and behavioural records, she found two competing theories.

> One, the feedback theory, holds that the thermostat senses temperature and turns the furnace on and off to maintain an even temperature. The other, which I call the valve theory, holds that the thermostat controls the amount of heat. That is, like a gas burner or a water valve, a higher setting causes a higher rate of flow.
>
> (Kempton 1987: 224)

The feedback theory is technically correct, while the valve theory is wrong. What is of special interest about the two theories is that even though the valve theory is wrong, it also enables us to make the right predictions for the control of temperature in a house and therefore there is no reason why laypersons should not espouse it.

It seems, then, that many naive cultural models, especially in the scientific and technological domain, are inaccurate from a scientific point of view, but usually correct as far as their functional predictions are concerned. In other domains of everyday life the question of the accuracy of a model does not seem to be as relevant. For example, for the cultural models of SANDCASTLE, BEACH, DESKS and BREAKFAST which have been singled out in this section for illustrative purposes, it would not be appropriate to speak of correct or inaccurate models, although experts with particularly refined cognitive models could certainly be found for all spheres. What counts is that 'ordinary' everyday experiences do not follow the doctrines laid down for scientific research and the rules of formal logic, but have other, more genuinely cognitive, principles behind them, some of which will be discussed below in Chapters 3 and 4.

To conclude this section, here is a summary of the main issues that have been addressed:

- Cognitive categories interact with and influence each other and this can cause a shift of category prototypes, of boundaries and of the whole category structure.
- Over and above the actual context in which the use of categories is embedded, the internal structure of categories depends on cognitive and cultural models which are always present when language is processed.

- A number of terminological distinctions seem necessary for a differentiated view of the context-dependence of categories. Thus we have defined
  - *situation* as the interaction of objects in the real world;
  - *context* as the cognitive representation of the interaction between cognitive categories (or concepts);
  - *cognitive model* as the sum of the experienced and stored contexts for a certain field by an individual;
  - *cultural model* as a view of cognitive models highlighting the fact that they are intersubjectively shared by the members of a society or social group.

- 'Naive' cultural models, especially those for technical domains, need not be in line with the scientifically accurate knowledge of experts, but may be based on what is communal experience, and strictly speaking even 'wrong' assumptions. Nevertheless these naive cultural models can be shared by most laypersons in a society as long as the functional predictions they make are correct.

Exercises

1. In pragmatics and sociolinguistics the participants of a speech event are often seen as part of the wider 'situational context'. Discuss this notion of 'context' in relation to the one put forward in this chapter.
2. Object categories like CAR are characterized by attributes relating to their form, size, material, parts, functions, and the associations and emotions they call up. Discuss which of these attributes are more likely to change their 'weight' when the context changes, let us say from ordinary traffic to a car race context.
3. Repeat the two-stage test in exercise 5 of Section 1.1 with special contexts like *The estate agent climbed out of his . . . (Jaguar, Rolls-Royce, BMW, Mercedes,* etc.) or *The children loved to climb the . . . (apple tree, pear tree, cherry tree,* etc.) *in the orchard* given before the association and the goodness-of-example rating task.
4. Eskimos have many words for different types of snow, Aborigines for different types of sand, and in Arabic one must choose from a whole range of words which are subsumed under the Western category CAMEL (cf. Lyons 1981: 67). Can you explain these phenomena with the help of the notion of 'cultural model'?
5. Compare the cultural model BACHELOR with that of its apparent counterpart SPINSTER. Discuss the parallel examples GENTLEMAN–LADY, MASTER–MISTRESS and BOY–GIRL.

6. When Nigerian and US-American students were asked to list attributes for TOMATO, the survey yielded the following results (Schmid and Kopatsch, forthcoming):

> Nigerian informants: 'used for making stew/soup' 61%; 'red (when ripe)' 54%; 'planted/grows on farm/in garden' 50%; 'round' 29%; 'leaves' 29%; 'fruit' 25%; 'root' 18%, 'kind of vegetable' 18%.
>
> American informants: 'red' 88%; 'fruit' 72%; 'vegetable' 60%, 'salad' 55%; 'green (when not ripe)' 49%; 'seeds' 49%; 'sauce' 45%; 'juicy' 45%; 'round' 45%; 'pasta/spaghetti' 28%; 'pizza' 19%, 'soup' 17%; 'plant' 17%; 'sandwiches' 15%; 'sliced' 15%.

What conclusions would you draw from these results with regard to the prevailing cultural models?

7. Ask your friends and family how they imagine the various processes are carried out by the components of a personal computer and extract the naive cultural model from their answers. If you happen to be a specialist in the field, compare the naive model to the expert model.

8. It can be claimed that naive cultural models are regarded as valid as long as they make the right predictions. Look for linguistic examples that reflect either wrong or outdated naive models like *the sun rises in the east* (of course the earth revolves) or *the apple fell to the ground* (it is attracted by the force of gravitation). Discuss examples of so-called folk etymologies like *sparrow-grass* for *asparagus*, *causeway* for *chausée*, *cowcumber* for *cucumber*, and the compounds *crayfish*, *starfish* and *jellyfish*.

Suggestions for further reading

Section 1.1

For an overview of the early development of research into categorization see Lakoff (1987, ch. 2) and Taylor (2003, ch. 3.2). Kleiber (1998) provides a discussion of the development of prototype theory, though on a fairly abstract level. The shortest description of Rosch's important contributions to the field is available in Rosch (1978). Rosch (1988) is an informal retrospect of the early stages of prototype theory from her own point of view, which is definitely worth reading. Recent concise accounts of categorization accompanied by critical comments of prototype theory are provided by Cruse (2000: 130–40) and Croft and Cruse (2004: 74–91). Geeraerts (1997) surveys the implications of prototype theory for the explanation of diachronic changes in meaning.

1. Ullmann (1962: 116–28) discusses the sources of vagueness with many examples from different languages. Quine (1960: 125f) puts

forward some interesting thoughts on vagueness from a philosophical perspective. More recent publications on the topic from a cognitive perspective are Geeraerts (1993) and Tuggy (1993). For critical comments on the notion of fuzziness see Croft and Cruse (2004: 93–5).

2. Lakoff (1987, ch. 18) discusses Whorf and relativism in some detail. Wider philosophical implications of relativist theories can be found in Putnam (1981: 103–26, esp. 119–24). The continuing interest of cognitive linguists in Whorf's theories is documented in collections edited by Niemeier and Dirven (2000) and Pütz (2000).

3. The introductory section of Berlin and Kay (1969: 1–5, 14ff; republished several times) certainly makes good reading. A concise survey of various reactions to Berlin and Kay (1969) is provided by Taylor (2003: 9ff). Kay and McDaniel (1978) present neurophysiological data which support part of Berlin and Kay's claims. See also Kay (1999) on the evolution of basic colour lexicons.

4. Smith and Medin (1981) provide a survey of various theories of categorization. Though not the most recent psycholinguistic textbook, Clark and Clark (1977) is still helpful for the basic psychological and psycholinguistic aspects of categorization. Medin, Ross and Markman (2001, ch. 10) take a critical stance towards prototype theory, which is presented in our chapter. Aitchison (2003) focuses on the storage of categories in the 'mental lexicon'.

5. Up to 1972, E. Rosch published under her earlier name Heider. So Heider (1971, 1972) and Heider and Oliver (1972) are written by the same author as the publications in the bibliography under the name of Rosch.

6. Lyons (1977: 109ff) is helpful to get a first idea of realism, nominalism and conceptualism, i.e. theories of status of the world. Discussions of the realist–conceptualist model that provides the basis for much thinking in the paradigm of cognitive linguistics can be found in Johnson (1987, ch. 8), Lakoff (1987, ch. 16) and Lakoff and Johnson (1999, chs. 6 and 7). An important source for these chapters is Putnam (1981, esp. ch. 3), which makes some fascinating but not very easy reading.

7. Being the later article, Labov (1978) is more comprehensive; however, the developments mainly concern the mathematical technicalities involved in formalizing fuzziness.

8. For discussions of polysemy and the problem of keeping it apart from homonymy in the structuralist tradition see Lyons (1977: 550ff), Leech (1981: 227ff), Lipka (2002: 152–7). For the lexicographical treatment of polysemy from a prototype perspective see Geeraerts (1990).

Section 1.2

9. For a psychologically oriented account of the classical view of categories see Smith and Medin (1981, ch. 3); for a description from a linguistic and philosophical point of view, Lakoff (1987, ch. 11). Lakoff (1987) also has a chapter (ch. 9) on 'Defenders of the classical view', which in fact has the function of defending his own prototypical view of categories. As regards the notion of 'essential features', the classic is Katz and Postal (1964, ch. 2). Wierzbicka (1985) considerably extends the notion of essential features and gives interesting, but very detailed, feature definitions for organisms and everyday objects. Lipka (2002: 114–34) gives a concise introduction, which also integrates non-necessary features. See also Croft and Cruse for a short survey (2004: 76–82).

10. For details on the statistical method used see Rosch and Mervis (1975) and Rosch et al. (1976). These articles are also interesting because the statistical notion of 'cue validity' is introduced to measure what we call attribute-based ratings. Explanatory remarks are provided in Smith and Medin (1981: 78ff) and Geeraerts (1988a).

11. For a similar view of categorization illustrated with the category UNCLE see Langacker (1987a: 19ff).

12. Most books of the major proponents of gestalt psychology, Wertheimer, Köhler and Koffka, are still available in reprints. For original sources of 'gestalt', 'Prägnanz' and 'gestalt principles' see Koffka (1935; republished 2002); Köhler was republished in the 1990s (Köhler 1992), while Wertheimer is the subject of a recent book (King and Wertheimer 2005). For recent surveys of the more theoretical aspects of gestalt psychology see Gordon (2004, ch. 2).

13. Other cognitive implications of the part–whole relationship will be discussed in Section 2.3 and Section 3.1. See Chapter 2, reading note 11 and Chapter 3, reading note 9 for references to the literature.

14. Illustrations in dictionaries are discussed by Stein (1991) and Lipka (1995), though from a lexicographic rather than a cognitive point of view. For an account of psychological research into the perception of shapes using 'templates' see Smith and Medin (1981, ch. 6) and Medin, Ross and Markman (2001: 104–8).

15. Aitchison (2003) is a very palatable survey of empirical and theoretical approaches to the mental lexicon, which is predominantly based on linguistic and psycholinguistic work. A critical discussion from a psychological point of view can be found in Smith (1978).

16. Opinions about how to interpret typicality effects have changed with the development of the prototype model. For Rosch's later position see Rosch (1978) and (1988). For more extensive discussions of the issue see Lakoff (1987: 40ff and ch. 9) and Kleiber (1998). These texts, as well as Croft and Cruse (2004: 79f), include discussions of the distinction between goodness-of-example and degree of category membership, which is irrelevant in our framework, since we rely on cognitive categories based on everyday folk models rather than scientific classifications. Geeraerts argues that prototypicality itself should be regarded as a prototypical notion (1988a) and discusses potential sources of prototypicality (1988b).

Section 1.3

As mentioned in the text, the notion of context has a long research tradition in diverse disciplines. See Schmid (2003) for a very brief survey. Two recent interdisciplinary collections on context are Bouquet *et al.* (1999) and Akman *et al.* (2001).

17. For an empirical examination of the context-dependence of prototypes and the category structure see Roth and Shoben (1983), who investigated the effects of sentences like *The bird walked across the barnyard* on the internal structure of the category BIRD.

18. See Langacker (2001: 144) for an alternative view of context as a part of 'current discourse space'.

19. The closest approximation to our conception of the terms 'context' and 'situation' that we know of is van Dijk (1981: 222, 269 *passim*) who emphasizes the selective or 'abstractive' nature of the cognitive context. See van Dijk (1999: 142) for his more recent cognitivist and subjectivist notion of context.

20. An attempt to provide experimental support for a distinction between context-dependent and context-independent information in categories can be found in Barsalou (1982).

21. Dirven, Frank and Pütz (2003) is a recent collection of articles on cognitive models in language and thought and their relations to ideologies. For notions which largely correspond to our conception of 'cognitive models' see Johnson (1987: esp. 28f, 101ff) on 'image-schemata'; Lakoff (1987: 68ff, 118ff) on 'idealized cognitive models'; Gentner and Stevens (1983) and Johnson-Laird (1983) on 'mental models'; and Holland and Quinn (1987) on 'cultural' and 'folk models'. Langacker's notion of 'domains' is discussed in Section 4.3, and the notion of 'frames' in Section 5.1.

22. A good introduction to the connectionist theory of the mind is provided by Bechtel and Abrahamsen (2002).

23. For German-speaking readers interested in differences between cultural models current in Britain and on the Continent, a very interesting and readable source is Leisi (1985: 87ff). He discusses the British models for such spheres as the ACADEMIC FIELD, HOUSEHOLD ITEMS, FOOD and SPORTS.

CHAPTER 2

Levels of categorization

2.1 Basic level categories of organisms and concrete objects

Scientific classifications may be fascinating in their complexity and rigidity, but are they really suitable for human categorization? So-called folk taxonomies suggest that we approach hierarchies from the centre, that we concentrate on basic level categories such as DOG *and* CAR *and that our hierarchies are anchored in these basic level categories.*

Let us return for a minute to the naive view of the world sketched at the beginning of Chapter 1. This view suggests that we are on the whole surrounded by readily identifiable organisms and objects such as dogs, trees, houses and cars. Yet when it comes to categorizing these entities, we normally have a choice between categories on different levels of generality. Thus, we can think of the creature comfortably stretched out on the hearth rug as a 'dog', a 'terrier', a 'Scotch terrier' or, more theoretically, as a 'mammal' or an 'animal'. Obviously all these cognitive categories are connected with each other in a kind of hierarchical relationship. Dogs are regarded as superordinate to terriers, and terriers as superordinate to Scotch terriers and bull terriers; looking in the other direction, dogs are seen as subordinate to mammals, and mammals as subordinate to animals.

The principle underlying this hierarchical structure is the notion of **class inclusion**, i.e. the view that the superordinate class includes all items on the subordinate level. The class 'animal' includes not only mammals, but birds and reptiles as well. On the next level, the class 'mammal' comprises not only dogs, but cats, cows, lions, elephants and mice. Still further down, the class 'dog' includes terriers, bulldogs, Alsatians, poodles, and various other kinds of dogs. If viewed from below, class inclusion appears as a **type-of relationship**: a terrier is a type of dog, a dog a type of mammal, a mammal a type of animal. Similar hierarchies exist for man-made objects like vehicles, which embrace cars, vans, bicycles, sledges, etc., and their respective subdivisions. All in all, it seems that the whole range of concrete entities in the world can be hierarchically ordered according to the principle of class inclusion. Starting from this notion of hierarchy, the detailed type-of classifications (or **taxonomies**) which have been developed in many scientific fields may simply appear to be an extension of the basic human faculty of categorization.

Scientific classifications

The prime example of scientific taxonomies is the classification of plants and animals based on the proposals made by the Swedish botanist Linnaeus (Carl von Linné) in the middle of the eighteenth century. Linnaeus's original conception has been considerably expanded and has grown into a very complex system which today contains 13 major levels of generality (see the list in Figure 2.2).[1]

More general in scope and closer to our linguistic concerns is the classification proposed by Mark Roget in his still widely used *Thesaurus of English Words and Phrases*, which was first published in 1852. Roget, a physician with wide-ranging scientific interests and a writer as well, approaches the age-old dream of organizing human knowledge with a claim to scientific rigidity. The knowledge of the world is divided up in six 'classes' which are rigorously subcategorized into sections, heads and further subdivisions. Part of his system is illustrated in Figure 2.1, which gives an impression of the monumentality of his conception.[2]

What these classifications have in common is that, apart from their claim to class inclusion, they do not seem to be tailored to the human mind in at least two respects. First of all, scientific taxonomies simply consist of too many levels. Normally the sole aim of setting up such a taxonomy is to classify all the 'objects' on hand, e.g. the two million or so kinds of plants and animals which have been discovered around the world, or the hundred thousands of words of a language. If in the process of classifying it seems necessary to expand the taxonomic grid, new levels and sublevels of classification are introduced no matter how bulky and complex the taxonomy will grow.

In addition to being too complex, scientific classifications do not consider the fact that we are in constant contact and involvement with the organisms and objects of the world around us. As a consequence of this interaction, organisms and objects are evaluated and assume different degrees of importance in our eyes. In contrast with these subjective judgements, scientific classifications

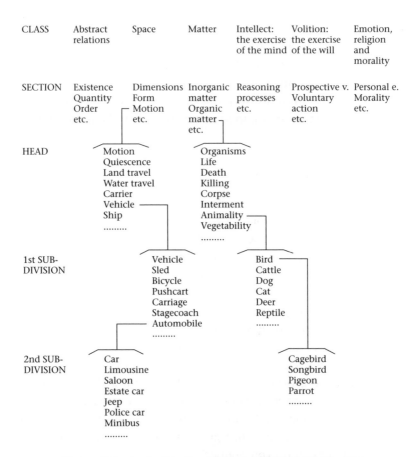

Figure 2.1 A selection from Roget's system of classification
(based on the edition by Betty Kirkpatrick 1987)

aim to be as objective as possible; they do not favour any one of the items classified or a certain taxonomic level. Another look at Figure 2.1 will show how the automobile is more or less hidden somewhere on the fourth level in the company of pushcart and sled. As for animals, all major kinds are subordinated to 'animality', which ranks together with 'corpse' and 'interment'. If any of the levels attract more attention than the others, it is probably the top level and the lowest level because they occupy the salient positions on the borders of the hierarchy.

However, observations about the use and acquisition of cognitive categories and their names seem to indicate that intermediate levels are just as important, if not more so. After all, the cognitive category most naturally selected for the creature on the hearth rug would be DOG rather than SCOTCH TERRIER or ANIMAL, not to mention MAMMAL. Describing a traffic accident one would probably start by saying: 'two cars crashed into each other' rather than referring to 'two vehicles' or 'an estate car and a jeep'. This shows that speakers prefer category names like *dog* and *car* in neutral contexts or when they introduce new items into the conversation. Category names on a middle level like *dog, cat, car* or *truck* are also the ones that are first learned by children; they tend to be the shortest names in hierarchies and they are used most frequently (Brown 1958, 1965). All this lexical evidence appears to invalidate the idea that classification should be objective.

In conclusion, it seems that scientific taxonomies are neither mind-sized nor mind-oriented. The question is what a more subject-related alternative of organizing our knowledge of the world would look like. Such an alternative would have to take account of the mental capacities and limitations of ordinary human beings, and would have to be geared to their experience, their essential needs and interests. Yet so powerful has been the impact of logical taxonomies on modern Western thinking that it is difficult for anyone who has been educated in the Western tradition to imagine such an alternative. This is why, for a fair cognitive evaluation of 'natural' hierarchic structures, we must again (as in the case of focal colours and prototypes in Chapter 1) leave the domain of Western culture and study the taxonomies of 'prescientific' societies.

Tzeltal plant classification: a case study in folk taxonomies

The most detailed account of a non-scientific taxonomy available is the description of the plant classification of the Tzeltal people, a Mayan-speaking community in southern Mexico, which was provided by Brent Berlin and the botanists Dennis Breedlove and Peter Raven.[3] The aim of their research project (Berlin *et al.* 1974) was to analyze the 'folk taxonomy' used by Tzeltal speakers for classifying and naming the plants in their environment, and to discuss how this folk taxonomy is related to scientific Western classifications. Figure 2.2 presents some of their results. Apart from the obvious reduction in taxonomic complexity (of the 13 major levels of the scientific classification a mere five are left in the Tzeltal plant classification), the major insight to be gained from Figure 2.2 is the numerical superiority of what is called the **generic level**, which attracts no less than 471 categories in all. In contrast, the number of superordinate terms, called 'life forms' (level 2), is exceedingly small; it contains no more than four plant names. Of the lower levels, the level of 'species' (level 4) is comparatively well represented, though membership is more restricted than on the generic level, while subclassification on the level of variety (level 5) is again negligible.

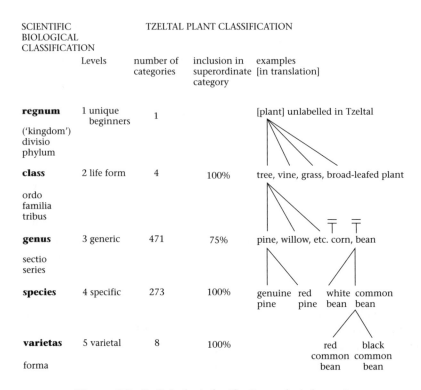

SCIENTIFIC BIOLOGICAL CLASSIFICATION	Levels	number of categories	inclusion in superordinate category	examples [in translation]
regnum ('kingdom') divisio phylum	1 unique beginners	1		[plant] unlabelled in Tzeltal
class ordo familia tribus	2 life form	4	100%	tree, vine, grass, broad-leafed plant
genus sectio series	3 generic	471	75%	pine, willow, etc. corn, bean
species	4 specific	273	100%	genuine pine, red pine, white bean, common bean
varietas forma	5 varietal	8	100%	red common bean, black common bean

Figure 2.2 Tzeltal plant classification: selected aspects

The numerical superiority of generic level categories is supported by their linguistic and cultural significance. Cognitive categories on the generic level are not only the most numerous, but also the ones most commonly chosen by Tzeltal speakers even where higher or lower level categories are available, which means that their names first come to mind. Thus a certain type of pine would more likely be called 'pine' than either 'tree' or 'red pine' (in the case of pines this is true for Tzeltal, not necessarily for English, as we will see). In addition, Tzeltal names for generic categories are often short, unanalyzable lexemes, while lower level names typically consist of adjective + generic name, and this is also true of our English translations. Compare *pine* vs *red pine*, or the more elaborate example of *bean* (genus) vs *common bean* (species) and *black common bean* (variety). All these findings substantiate to a large degree what was said earlier about the extraordinary status of the middle level in hierarchies in Western culture. Therefore the linguistic evidence both from English and Tzeltal testifies to the special status of the generic or middle level in taxonomies.

Investigating the cultural significance of the generic level in Tzeltal plant classification helps to examine how the taxonomy handles the principle of class inclusion (or type-of relationship), which seems to embody the very essence of the scientific notion of hierarchy. As shown in Figure 2.2, the degree of inclusion of categories in their respective superordinate categories is 100 per cent, with the notable exception of the generic level, where the figure is 75 per cent. This means that three-quarters of the generic Tzeltal terms can be clearly related to life forms. For Berlin *et al.* this is proof that the principle of class inclusion holds for folk taxonomies as well, and this judgement has since been tacitly accepted by many researchers. However, the remaining 25 per cent of 'aberrant cases' do not only consist of borderline cases between two possible life forms. Ninety-seven, or 20 per cent, of the generic level categories were found to be 'unaffiliated generics', which means that they are not related to any superordinate life form in the eyes of the Tzeltal people. These 'exceptions' in fact make up the most interesting portion of the taxonomy because of their 'economic importance' and their 'cultural significance' (Berlin *et al.* 1974: 24, 96). Included among them are corn and beans, for example, certainly two basic ingredients of the Tzeltal diet.

The conclusion that can be drawn from these observations adds a fairly important point to our collection of characteristics of the generic level. As illustrated by categories like CORN and BEAN, the salience of the generic level seems above all to be due to its cultural significance; sometimes it is even rooted in basic biological needs. In other words, generic level categories represent the preferred cognitive perspective. They seem to meet 'basic' cognitive needs because they pinpoint where the focus of human interest lies. Regarding their position within hierarchies, generic categories are characterized by 'taxonomic centrality' (which is not to be confused with the intracategorial centrality of prototypes).

To sum up, anthropological research into one folk taxonomy has yielded a number of interesting cultural and linguistic findings which suggest the experiential primacy and centrality of the generic level:

- Folk taxonomies focus on the generic level, because it is often culturally salient and sometimes directly rooted in basic biological needs.
- The names for generic categories are readily available for human interaction: they first come to mind in naming situations, and their morphological structure is simple.
- Non-generic levels seem to have a subsidiary status, because they are not fully developed where there is no need for additional categorization.

Basic level categories: psychological factors

How can we support the claim that the centrality of the generic level meets 'our basic cognitive needs'? Berlin *et al.*'s anthropological evidence, thorough and informative as it may be, is after all taken from the case study of a single folk taxonomy. Therefore it is worth reviewing what is known about the psychological background of the generic level (or **basic level**, as it is called in psychology) and examining the relevant experimental findings.

Summarizing early interpretations by Roger Brown and Paul Kay, the primacy and centrality of the basic level can be traced back to mainly three factors (Brown 1958, 1965; Kay 1971).

First, the generic or basic level is where we perceive the most obvious differences between the organisms and objects of the world. This becomes clearer when lower and higher levels of categorization are taken into account. The subordinate level categories ALSATIAN, COLLIE and GREYHOUND each contain category items which closely resemble the items in the neighbouring categories. For instance, all specimens of Alsatians, collies and greyhounds have a tail, they wag when they are happy, they all bark, all of them like to chase cats and postmen. Making distinctions between these categories may therefore seem almost pedantic. The superordinate category ANIMAL, on the other hand, embraces such a disparate variety of items (elephants, mice, whales, etc.) that the similarities are very small indeed. Against this background, basic level categories like DOG seem to strike a balance. Each kind of dog shows a great deal of similarity with other kinds of dog, yet all dogs are distinguished from cats, lions, etc., by what seem to be the characteristics of 'dogginess' (barking, tail wagging, etc.). In other words, the cognitive category DOG, and the basic level in general, normally 'correspond to the most obvious discontinuities in nature' (Kay 1971: 878).

A more technical explanation is possible in terms of attributes, which, as shown in Section 1.2, can be understood as representing similarity relations. Taking this into account, the claim that basic level categories achieve an ideal balance between internal similarity and external distinctiveness can now be rephrased in terms of attributes: the basic level is the level on which the largest bundles of naturally correlated attributes are available for categorization (e.g. all the attributes expressing 'dogginess' or 'chairiness'). These bundles of attributes are as it were earmarked for the members of a certain cognitive category (e.g. DOG or CHAIR) and will be accorded to dog-like beings or chair-like objects in the real world according to their goodness-of-example status; at the same time these attribute bundles distinguish these categories from other

CONCRETE OBJECTS
IN THE 'REAL' WORLD

COGNITIVE
CATEGORIES

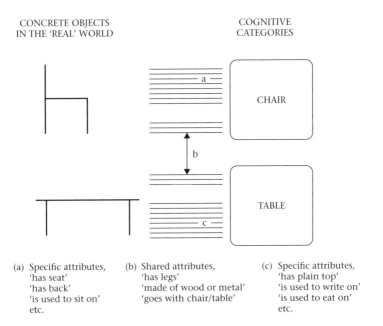

(a) Specific attributes,
'has seat'
'has back'
'is used to sit on'
etc.

(b) Shared attributes,
'has legs'
'made of wood or metal'
'goes with chair/table'

(c) Specific attributes,
'has plain top'
'is used to write on'
'is used to eat on'
etc.

Figure 2.3 Schematic representation of attributes for the basic level categories
CHAIR and TABLE

categories. Compare Figure 2.3, where the attributes available for the basic level categories CHAIR and TABLE are schematically represented by lines.

As the figure shows, each of the two cognitive categories commands a large bundle of attributes that would apply to most chairs or tables respectively. Thus all kinds of chairs (kitchen chairs, living room chairs, garden chairs) would agree with the attributes 'has a seat', 'has a back', 'is used to sit on'. Only some of the attributes will be shared by both categories, e.g. 'has legs', 'made of wood' (in the figure these attributes are linked by an arrow), while most of them are not, and this reflects the ease with which we distinguish between chairs and tables.

Since attributes convey information, yet another view seems possible. As the notion of correlation implies, the bundles of attributes available on the basic level are already presorted, they have been conveniently linked up and are therefore more easily digestible. This is why it can be claimed that the basic level is where the largest amount of information about an item can be obtained with the least cognitive effort. This principle is called **cognitive economy**, and it probably explains best why the basic level is particularly well suited to meet our cognitive needs.[4]

The other two factors that are thought to be responsible for the primacy of the basic level can be dealt with more briefly. One is the common over-all shape, which is perceived holistically and can be seen as an important indicator of gestalt perception (see Section 1.2). If organisms and objects are categorized on the basic level, it is obvious that all category members (e.g. all members of the category DOG) have a characteristic shape. This shape not only unites all kinds of dogs, but also distinguishes them from the members of other basic level categories, such as ELEPHANT, MOUSE and WHALE. If we approach organisms and objects on the superordinate level, the level of MAMMAL, REPTILE or INSECT, there is no common shape for the category which, to take the case of MAMMAL, applies to dogs, elephants, mice and whales. Since a common shape does not exist, it cannot, of course, be used to dis-tinguish mammals from reptiles and insects. In contrast, categories on the subordinate level, the level of species like ALSATIAN and TERRIER, do have a com-mon characteristic shape, just like basic level categories, and this shape is shared by all kinds of Alsatians or by all kinds of terriers. However, this shape is less helpful in distinguishing Alsatians from terriers because, both being dogs, the differences in shape are much smaller than between dogs and elephants or whales.

The third relevant factor is concerned with the actions or, more precisely, the motor movements we perform when we interact with objects and organ-isms. As Brown suggested, it is only on the basic level that organisms and objects are marked by really characteristic actions. Cats can be stroked, flow-ers can be sniffed, balls can be rolled and bounced, while it is difficult to imagine that different kinds of cats are stroked in different ways or that all animals are stroked like cats.

Experimental evidence for basic level categories

The experimental investigation of these psychological assumptions was again carried out by Rosch and her associates (Rosch *et al.* 1976), and the significance of all three factors for basic level categories was confirmed.

The first aspect, the balance between similarity and distinctiveness achieved in basic level categories, was tested in an attribute-listing task. The experiment was similar to the one employed in prototype research (see Section 1.2), but the perspective was a different one. This time the aim was to measure the size of the correlated bundles of attributes (which were taken to reflect both similarity and distinctiveness; see above) and to show that the size of the bundles was different from those on other levels of cate-gorization. Informants were asked to list attributes for basic level categories, like APPLE, PEACH, GRAPE, for superordinate categories (in this case FRUIT) and for subordinate categories (e.g. DELICIOUS APPLE, MACINTOSH APPLE). The basic level categories (APPLE, PEACH, etc.) had an average total of eight attributes in common, while for the superordinate category FRUIT the number was three. The total for CAR, BUS, TRUCK (basic level) was 12 against only one common attribute for VEHICLE (superordinate). Similar scores were obtained for the other artefact categories tested (TOOL, FURNITURE, CLOTHING and MUSICAL INSTRUMENT). Attribute totals for subordinate categories (DELICIOUS APPLE, JEEP, etc.) were somewhat higher than for basic level categories, a result which will be put in perspective in Section 2.2.

The results did, however, deviate for the biological categories where, following Berlin *et al.*, TREE, FISH and BIRD had been chosen as superordinate categories. As it turned out, the total numbers of attributes for these categories were as high as the average totals for MAPLE, BIRCH, BASS, TROUT, EAGLE, SPARROW, etc., the assumed basic level categories, so TREE, FISH and BIRD had to be regarded as the real basic level categories. After what has been said about cultural models (see Section 1.3), this is not surprising. It simply shows that cultural models do not only influence the selection of prototypes, but are equally important for the choice of the basic level perspective. Urbanized American psychology students, who are neither foresters nor otherwise dependent on the distinctions between maples, birches, oaks, pines, etc., will have a different perspective from the Tzeltal people who live agricultural lives and are much more bound up in their natural surroundings.

The second factor, the common overall shape, was addressed in two ways. One experiment was based on a comparison of outline drawings of category members. For the basic level category CAR these were the outlines of >SPORTS CAR<, >SALOON< and >ESTATE CAR<, etc., while the superordinate category VEHICLE was represented by the outlines of >CAR<, >BUS< and >MOTORCYCLE<. These outline drawings were derived from randomly selected pictures, which had been normalized for size and canonical orientation (side view for cars etc.). When these normalized outlines were juxtaposed, overlaps between the shapes of the various types of car were naturally much greater than between the outlines of a car, a bus and a motorcycle. This proves that it is easy enough to produce an average overall shape for basic level categories and to assume an underlying common gestalt, while this is not the case for superordinate categories. As for subordinate categories, like SPORTS CAR, the overlap between the outlines of category members, e.g. a >JAGUAR< and a >PORSCHE<, is even greater, and this was again in line with the test hypothesis (see also Section 2.2).

In a related experiment, an identification task, subjects were shown the overlapped outlines of basic level categories (e.g. a shape computed from the outlines of a sports car and an estate car for CAR) as well as similar combinations for superordinate categories (e.g. a shape combining the outlines of a car and a motorcycle for VEHICLE). Again the overlapped shapes of basic level categories were readily identified, and the combined shapes of superordinate categories were not.

To investigate the third factor, the motor movements, subjects were asked to imagine and describe the muscle movements they tend to produce when interacting with certain objects and organisms. Figure 2.4 provides two examples that show that motor movements are most diversified on the basic level, the level of CHAIR and PANTS, where the movements of sitting down and of putting on pants could be extracted from the informants in great detail. In contrast, the only human reactions which were considered to be stimulated by all types of furniture and all types of clothing, i.e. 'eyes scan' for FURNITURE and 'eyes scan' as well as 'hands grasp' for CLOTHING, are among the most general form of contact imaginable. On the subordinate level, little was added

Movement for	FURNITURE		CLOTHING	
superordinate	Eyes:	scan	Eyes:	scan
categories			Hands:	grasp
Additional	CHAIR		PANTS	
movements	Head:	turn	Hands:	grasp
for basic level	Body:	turn, move	Arms:	extend
categories		back position	Back:	bend
	Knees:	bend	Feet:	position
	Arm:	extend–touch	Knee:	bend
	Waist:	bend	Leg:	raise, extend
	Butt:	touch	Foot:	raise, extend
	Body–legs:	release weight	Hands:	raise, extend
	Back–torso:	straighten,	Knee:	bend
		lean back	Leg:	raise, extend
			Hands:	extend, raise
			Fingers:	grasp
			Elbows:	bend
			Arms:	pull up
Additional	LIVING ROOM CHAIR		LEVIS	
movements	+body:	sink	+toes:	extend
for subordinate			+butt:	rotate
categories				

Figure 2.4 Typical motor movements for selected object categories
(after Rosch *et al.* 1976, Appendix II)

to descriptions for the basic level categories, although it is interesting to note that the movements listed for LIVING ROOM CHAIR or LEVIS are exactly those that would be highlighted in advertisements for these items.

The symbiosis of basic level and prototype categories

As we have seen, some of the tests used in the investigation of the basic level were very similar to the experiments of prototype research. At first the two lines of investigation were pursued side by side, often with divergent aims, and it took some time before the relationship between the prototype structure and the basic level notion was sorted out and recognized for what it was, a perfect kind of symbiosis based on the following two interdependent principles:[5]

1. Prototype categories are most fully developed on the basic level.
2. Basic level categories only function as they do because they are structured as prototype categories.

To explain the first principle, it should be sufficient to recall two of the aspects of basic level categories which have just been discussed:

- The basic level provides the largest amount of relevant and digestible information about the objects and organisms of the world (e.g. information about bird-like animals) or, to put it more technically, it offers the largest bundles of correlated attributes. These attributes are accumulated in their most complete form in the prototype (>ROBIN< in the case of BIRD) and expressed by the category name (e.g. *bird*).
- The basic level is where the overlap of shapes is so great that it permits reliable gestalt perception, which is particularly easy for prototypical examples (like the >ROBIN<).

The second principle is best explained by claiming that prototypes maximize the efficiency of basic level categories (Rosch 1977, 1978). In more detail, this means:

- Prototypes maximize the distinctiveness of basic level categories because they attract not only the largest number of attributes shared inside the category, but also the largest number of attributes not shared with members of other categories (e.g. of all birds, the robin shares the smallest number of attributes with other kinds of animals).
- Prototypes maximize holistic perception because their gestalts integrate all functionally important parts.

All in all, basic level categories with prototypes seem to be just the kind of tools needed for the difficult task of categorizing the concrete objects and organisms of the world around us. Seen in the wider context of categorization which will unfold in the course of the book, basic level categories contribute a decisive share to the **basic experiences** that govern our interaction with the world around us.

Exercises

1. In Tzeltal plant and animal classification PINE, WILLOW, CORN and BEAN, and RABBIT, SQUIRREL, SKUNK and POCKET GOPHER represent the basic or generic level. Is this also true for your dialect of English or your native language (if this is not English)?

2. Compare the plan of Section A (*Life and Living Things*) and Section M (*Movement, Location, Travel, Transport*) in the *Longman Lexicon* (LLCE, 1981) with the respective sections in *Roget's Thesaurus* and discuss them in terms of everyday (or folk) taxonomies.

3. As Rosch showed for chairs and pants (see Figure 2.4), we can name the largest number of typical movements when we categorize these objects on the basic level. Find out whether this is also true of bicycles, racing bikes, mopeds and vehicles, and of drills, hammers, saws, circular saws and tools.

4. When Rosch carried out her experiments of the basic level she found that for a former airplane mechanic the basic level had shifted from the category PLANE to more specific categories. Discuss the influence of the language user's personal, geographical and social background on his choice of basic level categories for plants, animals and technical appliances. Make use of the information about context, cognitive and cultural models in Section 1.3.

5. Discuss whether in your opinion the notion of cognitive economy is only important for everyday categorization (or folk taxonomies) as opposed to scientific classifications and information processing in computers.

2.2 Superordinate and subordinate categories

If basic level categories are exceptional in many ways, how do other types of cognitive categories differ from them? Are other categories just to be regarded as poor relations or do they have specific functions for which they are uniquely equipped and which determine their category structure?

When choosing the cognitive categories for their investigation of prototypes, early researchers did not consciously distinguish between basic level categories and other kinds of categories. Quite naturally, they selected the categories that promised the best results for the demonstration of the individual effects of the prototype structure they had in mind. As shown in Chapter 1, gestalt characteristics of categories and the fuzziness of category boundaries could best be illustrated with basic level categories like CUP and BOWL. Goodness-of-example ratings and attribute listings involving family resemblances worked well with cognitive categories such as FRUIT, FURNITURE and VEHICLE, which are commonly placed on a superordinate level. Yet when basic level categories were contrasted with the superordinate (and subordinate) categories in the last section, it became clear that an ideal prototype structure can only be found on the basic level and that, seen from this angle, superordinate categories are deficient in many ways.[6]

The structure of superordinate categories and the notion of parasitic categorization

To start with the most obvious deficiency of superordinate categories, there is no common overall shape and, consequently, no common underlying gestalt that applies to all category members. However, this does not mean that the objects categorized as FRUIT or FURNITURE or VEHICLE cannot be approached holistically. Consider what you would do if you were asked to provide a picture of these categories. You would probably draw an orange, a banana, etc. to illustrate FRUIT, or a chair, a table and a bed for FURNITURE, or a car, a bus and a motorbike for VEHICLE. In other words, you would 'borrow' the gestalt properties of the superordinate category from the basic level categories involved – a first case of what will be called **parasitic categorization**.[7]

This principle of parasitic categorization is also reflected in the way in which attributes are used in categorizing experiments. As already discussed in Sections 1.2 and 2.1, informants tend to list few category-wide attributes for superordinate categories. Indeed, in the case of FURNITURE, Rosch's informants did not suggest a single common attribute. The most likely reason is that the common attributes available for FURNITURE are so general and unobtrusive that informants do not find them worth mentioning – think of 'large movable objects' or 'things that make a house or flat suitable for living in'. Apart from category-wide attributes, informants offer the names of basic level categories which are members of the superordinate category and, in addition, attributes of these basic level categories. In the case of FURNITURE this means that informants will name the basic level categories CHAIR, TABLE, BED,

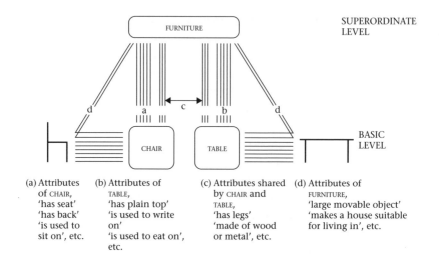

Figure 2.5 Schematic representation of attributes for the superordinate category FURNITURE

etc. and add a number of attributes from the attribute inventory of these cognitive categories, e.g. 'has legs', 'has a back', 'used to sit on' for CHAIR, etc. This situation is schematically represented in Figure 2.5.

If one compares the superordinate category FURNITURE with the basic level categories CHAIR and TABLE, the difference in terms of attributes and categorization is indeed striking. While both CHAIR and TABLE are largely self-sufficient in terms of categorizing attributes (as was already illustrated by Figure 2.3), there are only few attributes that emanate directly from the superordinate category FURNITURE (e.g. 'movable objects', 'make a room suitable for living in'), and even these attributes are shared by CHAIR and TABLE, as indicated by the converging attribute lines in Figure 2.5. The bulk of the attributes are borrowed from the rich attribute inventories of the basic level categories CHAIR and TABLE – a clear case of parasitic categorization.

Yet why is it that we normally do not realize that we draw the attributes for the superordinate category FURNITURE from basic level categories, and in fact from quite diverse basic level categories, such as CHAIR, TABLE, SOFA, BED, SHELF and CUPBOARD? This seems to be mainly due to the family resemblances which can be observed between category members. When the notion of family resemblance was introduced in Section 1.2, it was used to justify the category membership of poor examples, e.g. to explain why penguins and ostriches can be called *birds* or laptops and coffee machines can be seen as (rather marginal) items of furniture. Starting from superordinate categories such as FURNITURE, family resemblances appear in a different light.

Looking at the attributes of FURNITURE that are borrowed from the member categories once more, we find that there is indeed quite a lot of overlap. Both CHAIR and TABLE seem to have attributes like 'has legs' and 'made of wood, metal or plastic' in common (this is indicated in Figure 2.5 by the two vertical bundles of attributes in the centre linked by the double arrow). Other attributes available for FURNITURE will be shared by CHAIR and SOFA, by SOFA and BED, by TABLE and SHELF, by SHELF and CUPBOARD. The effect of these overlaps is that in describing FURNITURE we never think that we are just borrowing isolated attributes from the respective basic level categories like CHAIR, TABLE or BED. Rather we have the impression that each of the borrowed attributes is relevant for a large section of the FURNITURE category, though it may in fact only apply to two or three member categories.

This effect of the family resemblance principle is even more important in the case of superordinate categories like TOY, for which we can find only a single category-wide attribute (our proposal for TOY is 'used to play with'), not to mention Wittgenstein's extreme case of the category GAME, where it is difficult to extract even a single category-wide attribute. (Frequent associations are 'spending time in a basically pleasant way', 'leisure activity', 'fun' and others.) Here it is quite obvious that the attributes available for the description of the superordinate category are overwhelmingly based on family resemblances between various types of toys or games, all of them basic level categories, and that these basic level categories are activated by parasitic categorization.

To round off the picture, one might point out that the non-basic status of superordinate categories is also reflected linguistically. Many words for superordinate categories do not belong to the simple one-syllable type which is dominant among basic level terms; this is true of FURNITURE, VEHICLES, MUSICAL INSTRUMENTS, for instance. In addition, superordinate terms do not normally come to mind first, i.e. before the respective basic level terms, and they are learned by children only after basic level words have been acquired.

Subordinate categories: characteristics of category structure

The most frequent type of lexical category apart from basic level categories are not superordinate, but subordinate categories. There are many kinds of dogs, of flowers, of cars and boats, of beds and tables, and all of them can be understood in terms of cognitive categories. In some cases, the structure of these subordinate categories is very similar to the structure of basic level categories. Categories like POODLE, TERRIER or ROSE have identifiable gestalts, they are constructed round prototypes, have good and bad members, can muster substantial lists of attributes and are expressed by simple words. However, when we follow Brown (1990) and turn to more extreme examples of subordinate categories, the differences become more marked.

Sticking to flowers, but replacing ROSE with DANDELION or DAISY, we still have a fairly clear gestalt perception, including the holistic impression of the overall shape, the jagged leaves, the yellow blossom of dandelions or the distinction between the yellow disc and the white rays typical of daisies. The difference between these categories and a category such as ROSE becomes obvious when we start looking for prototypes of dandelions or daisies. How does an ordinary language user, someone who is neither a botanist nor a lexicologist, single out a perfect dandelion or daisy? How does he or she describe the difference between this perfect specimen and a poor one? Indeed, the average language user will hardly attempt to distinguish prototypical dandelions and daisies from less typical category members, both in terms of individual examples and varieties. Moving from natural kinds to man-made objects, such as coins, we find that subordinate categories like DIME or QUARTER also do not yield prototypes that can be easily distinguished from more marginal examples. All dimes and quarters are very much alike, and can be regarded as equally good examples of the category. The reason is not that real-life examples of dandelions, daisies, dimes or quarters are in fact identical, the differences in shape or colour (in the case of dandelions and daisies) or in newness and gloss (for dimes and quarters) which might emerge in a thorough scrutiny are simply irrelevant for everyday categorization and do not influence our holistic perception.

The question is how this obvious indifference towards the details of subordinate categories squares with Rosch's findings that informants have no difficulty in compiling lengthy attribute lists for these categories, lists that are even more detailed than those provided for basic level categories.

As Rosch herself observed, only some of these attributes are specific to the subordinate category in question, while the majority are identical with the attributes of the respective basic level category. Applied to our flower categories this means that the jagged shape of the dandelion's leaves and the distinction between the daisy's yellow disc and white rays would rank among the small number of specific attributes. Everything else that can be said about the bloom, the stem and the leaves, i.e. all the other attributes of DANDELION and DAISY, will be borrowed from the basic level category FLOWER; this can again be regarded as a case of parasitic categorization. Compare Figure 2.6.

This figure should be seen in conjunction with Figure 2.5, which illustrates the categorization of superordinate categories. In both cases the bulk

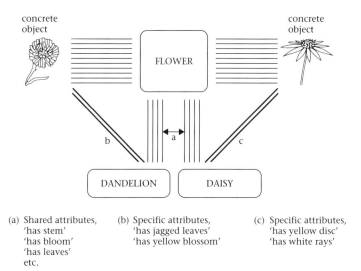

(a) Shared attributes,
    'has stem'
    'has bloom'
    'has leaves'
    etc.

(b) Specific attributes,
    'has jagged leaves'
    'has yellow blossom'

(c) Specific attributes,
    'has yellow disc'
    'has white rays'

Figure 2.6   Schematic representation of attributes for the subordinate categories
DANDELION and DAISY

of the categorization is carried out through basic level categories while direct categorization (indicated by bold lines) is limited to a few attributes. Yet there is a crucial difference which concerns the quality of the attributes available for direct categorization. In the case of superordinates this is a set of **general** attributes that are also shared by all the basic level categories (e.g. the attributes 'large movable object' and 'makes a house suitable for living in', which are shared by chairs, tables and many other items of furniture). In contrast, the attributes available for direct categorization of subordinate categories are **specific**, i.e. they specify the category in question; they are not normally shared by other categories: jagged leaves are a characteristic property of dandelions and not part of the attribute lists of DAISY, ROSE or TULIP.

The functions of non-basic categories

Specific and general attributes of subordinate and superordinate categories respectively are a good starting point to explain the cognitive function of non-basic categories. The reason why we use subordinate categories is that we want to stress or '**highlight**' the specific attributes they feature. If we want to distinguish a flower with jagged leaves and a yellow blossom from other types of flowers, we choose the relevant subcategory and communicate this by using its label, the word *dandelion*. If botanists want to go further and point out a specific colour of the blossom they may use a term such as *white-flowering Japanese dandelion* to indicate a more finely graded subcategorization. Whether the highlighting function of the subordinate category refers to colour (as in our example) or to shape, material or the use to which an item is put (e.g. use of dandelions in salads and soups) does not make any difference. It can be shown that, for different items, all these aspects are eligible for highlighting.

For superordinate categories, successful highlighting cannot be so easily deduced from the generality of an attribute, which is shared by a set of basic level items, e.g. by chairs, tables, beds, etc. or by cars, buses, vans and trucks. Obviously, only certain of these 'general' attributes are judged **salient** enough to be highlighted, while others are not. Trying to assemble the attributes for BUS, one would not just want to mention that it is used to move people and things around; one would probably like to add that a bus has a box-like shape, that it has wheels, doors and windows and also seats, and that it holds a large number of people. Or one may even want to stress that, given the right size, a bus is used by children to play with. If we survey the linguistic evidence we find that all these attributes can be easily expressed as sentences or clauses (as has just been done in fact), yet only some of them have actually sparked off specific superordinate lexical items that can be used freely. Compare Figure 2.7, where the selected attributes are indicated by single quotes, the superordinate categories that might be based on them are indicated by capitals, and the actual linguistic realizations are printed in italics.

As it emerges from Figure 2.7, only the two attributes 'moves people and things around' and 'used to play with' have generated freely usable lexemes, namely *vehicle* and *toy*. The words *seater* and *wheeler* can only be used in

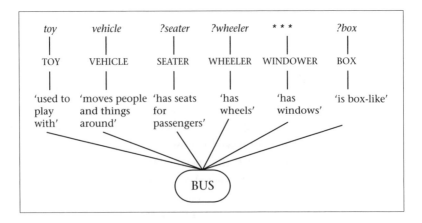

Figure 2.7 Highlighting attributes of the basic level category BUS

certain collocations, such as a *50-seater* or a *6-wheeler* (which is more likely to be used of a lorry or truck), while **windower* is not acceptable as a lexical item, and *box* would not be readily understood as a superordinate of *bus*. The reason why only *vehicle* and *toy* (and in numerical compounds *seater*) have been established as lexical items seems to be that their underlying cognitive categories are supported by attributes referring to what may be regarded as the most salient quality of artefacts: their function or purpose. Calling a bus *vehicle*, we automatically stress its function of moving persons or things around: calling it *50-seater* we emphasize that a bus is capable of carrying a large number of people. Referring to a bus as *toy*, we again stress a specific though very different function. Other attributes apart from function which seem to be so salient that they support names for superordinate cognitive categories include 'material' (for TEXTILES, MINERALS and EARTHENWARE), 'origin' (for ANCESTORS), 'relatedness' (for RELATIVES, IN-LAWS).

Highlighting attributes, however, is not the only function of superordinate categories. Closely linked with it is a second function, and this becomes more obvious when we look at Figure 2.8, which shows the attribute links between superordinate categories like VEHICLE and TOY and related basic level categories. While it seems quite natural that VEHICLE is related to CAR, BUS, MOTORBIKE, etc., through the attribute 'moves people and things around'(and that, conversely, CAR, BUS, MOTORBIKE can be seen as types of vehicles), the wide range of links emanating from TOY may be surprising at first sight: relevant basic level categories include not only CAR and BUS, but also BALL and SWING, and the list could be extended almost indefinitely; nevertheless, CAR, BUS, SWING and BALL can all be seen in a type-of relationship to the superordinate TOY.

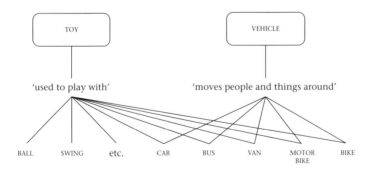

Figure 2.8 The collecting function of the superordinate categories TOY and VEHICLE

It is with categories like TOY that the enormous potential of what we will call the **collecting function** of superordinate categories becomes really obvious: the faculty to subsume a large number of categories under one label which makes the whole set of categories available for easy handling. It is not surprising that this potential has been used for scientific purposes and that collecting items under a common heading has become a crucial aspect of scientific work. The extension of the type-of relationship across ever more levels has led to the establishment of extensive scientific taxonomies. The detailed biological classifications or Roget's attempt to organize lexical categories as a multi-level taxonomy are cases in point. When these scientific taxonomies were introduced in Section 2.1, we found that they differ widely from folk taxonomies as used by the Tzeltal people for plants. These differences can now be explained in terms of the highlighting and collecting functions of superordinate categories.

Exercises

1. Ask your fellow-students to list attributes for the following categories:

    CHAIR, BED, LAMP;

    KNIFE, FORK, SPOON;

    RING, BRACELET, NECKLACE;

    FURNITURE; CUTLERY; JEWELLERY;

    KITCHEN CHAIR, DINING ROOM CHAIR, ARMCHAIR, WICKER CHAIR;

    BREAD KNIFE, POCKET KNIFE, JACK KNIFE, PAPER KNIFE, CARVING KNIFE;

    EARRING, NOSE RING, WEDDING RING, DIAMOND RING, SIGNET RING.

    Test whether your lists support Rosch's findings about the attribute inventories of basic level, superordinate and subordinate categories.

2. Considering BOOK, JOURNAL, NEWSPAPER, E-MAIL and WEBSITE as basic level categories, suggest subordinate and superordinate categories related to these categories. Which of the possible superordinate categories have given rise to lexical items in English? Which dimensions (shape, colour, material, origin, function) are highlighted?

3. Compare the ratio of basic level, superordinate and subordinate level words in a sample of scientific text to that in a sample of a fairytale or children's story.

4. The notion of 'parasitic categorization' is based on the view that superordinate categories 'borrow' attributes from basic level categories.

Alternatively, one might say that basic level categories supply the attributes which are then 'transferred' to the respective superordinate categories. Which view do you find more convincing?

5. How is the notion of parasitic categorization reflected in pictograms for fruit, vegetables, toiletries, stationary, electrical appliances, luggage, motorized vehicles and pedestrians?

2.3 Conceptual hierarchies

Basic, subordinate and superordinate categories are the building material
of type-of hierarchies. However, there is competition from part–whole relationships.
The latter gain in importance if we do not focus on scientific hierarchies, but on the
folk hierarchies observed in ordinary language use.

Scientific and folk taxonomies revisited

Discussing the Tzeltal plant taxonomy in Section 2.1, we found that while there is a superordinate category TREE for the basic level categories PINE, WILLOW and other kinds of trees, there is no such category for CORN and BEAN. Obviously it is convenient for the Tzeltal people to highlight one or several salient properties common to all the kinds of trees they know, e.g. 'consist of a trunk, branches and leaves or needles', 'provide shade' or 'used as fire wood'. In contrast, the fact that both CORN and BEAN are grown in fields and used as food is so self-evident that within the cultural model of the non-Westernized agricultural Tzeltal community they need not be highlighted. And since there are only few items involved, there is no reason to collect them in a special superordinate category.

The picture changes when we return to industrialized societies and the cultural model based on them, and when we survey the almost infinite variety of food items available. In such a context various superordinates such as VEGETABLES, FRUIT, CEREAL and even FOOD seem to be very useful indeed. Imagine the chaos that would be created in supermarkets if the food items were not arranged with respect to these superordinate categories. The same applies to non-food categories such as STATIONERY, TOILETRIES, CLOTHING and ELECTRICAL APPLIANCES. How could anybody find their way around one of the larger department stores if it were not for the signs carrying these linguistic labels? While this illustrates the collecting function of superordinates, their highlighting function is exploited in the labelling of individual goods, especially with new products. Whether it is a newly introduced kind of exotic fruit or a new type of precooked dish, it will often be necessary to clarify their purpose or function, and this is where the superordinate category label will at least provide a first clue.

However, although a large number of superordinate categories may be necessary to cope with the ever-expanding range of goods and services, this does not mean that ordinary language users are in any way as consistent in their use of superordinates as scientists are. This is particularly true when it comes to establishing multi-level hierarchies. While it is the aim of scientific classifications to provide a complete system of taxonomic levels, experiential everyday categorization may very well be prepared to skip some levels, even if, from a logical point of view, they make sense and have been lexicalized.

A good example is the superordinate category MAMMAL, which undoubtedly highlights the important attributes 'born from the mother's womb' and 'fed by milk from the mother's body'. Admittedly *mammal* is not only used in scientific discourse, but also in ordinary conversation when these attributes are focused. Yet as a rule, language users will regard ANIMAL rather than MAMMAL as the direct superordinate of DOG and CAT. Similarly, INSECT is not generally seen as a natural superordinate category for BEETLE though it may be more readily accepted as superordinate for FLY, MOSQUITO, WASP and BEE. The issue becomes more complex when we consider that for many language users BIRD and FISH are not subordinated to ANIMAL, so if we look for a superordinate category we have to opt for CREATURE, and this raises another problem. For CREATURE has biblical associations for many language users ('God's creatures'), or at least it highlights the aspect of creation at the expense of other aspects of 'animality'. Looking for a more comprehensive superordinate we have to go as far as LIVING BEING, and this is obviously a category which includes plants as well. From this we may conclude that there is no satisfactory superordinate for MAMMAL, BIRD, FISH, REPTILE and INSECT or, to put it differently, that English does not have a comprehensive labelled category that can be used for 'animals' as opposed to plants.[8]

Yet this wider sense of *animal* becomes available when we use the composite terms *higher animal* and *lower animal* and consider the respective categories. HIGHER ANIMAL is largely equivalent with the restricted conception of ANIMAL suggested above and mainly refers to mammals, while LOWER ANIMAL embraces INSECT and REPTILE. This still leaves us with BIRD and FISH, which cannot be safely related to either HIGHER ANIMAL or LOWER ANIMAL. Figure 2.9 is an attempt to sketch this rather confused situation. In this figure the superordinate categories of neutral everyday categorization are printed in bold letters and linked to basic level categories by bold lines. Other superordinate

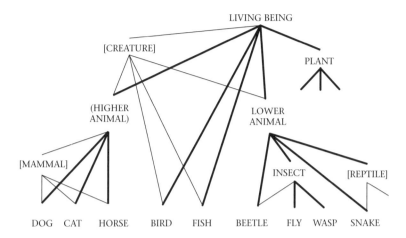

Figure 2.9 A cognitive view of superordinate categories of living beings in English

categories are given in brackets and linked to the respective categories by normal lines.

Looking at the diagram one might easily get the impression that this classification is indeed most unsatisfactory. This may be true if the matter is approached from a purely logical point of view. Considering the cognitive needs of the ordinary language user, however, one will come to understand that it may be helpful to have the superordinate category ANIMAL (or HIGHER ANIMAL) to refer to the living beings that seem most relevant to human beings, such as dogs, cats and horses, and it may also be useful if insects and reptiles can be treated in a rather summary fashion under the label LOWER ANIMAL. Birds and fish may indeed hold an intermediate position between the larger domestic animals and the lower animals, which does not call for an immediate superordinate category as the other animals do.

Summarizing this cognitive view of lexical hierarchies as employed by ordinary language users one might say that these 'folk taxonomies' are characterized by gaps, inconsistencies and alternative paths (i.e. offering both MAMMAL and ANIMAL as superordinates for DOG and CAT). What is reassuring is that this picture is fully supported by the experiences of practically minded lexicographers, both in the definitions of superordinate terms and in the hierarchical framework of Thesaurus-type dictionaries.[9] Lexicologists and linguists in general who have been reared in the tradition of rigid classification will be more sceptical, but even they should be appeased by the fact that in spite of the obvious differences between lexical folk taxonomies and logical hierarchies both can be accommodated in a wider cognitive framework.

Type-of hierarchies vs part–whole hierarchies

The notion of conceptual hierarchy becomes even more complex when we consider a relationship that is pervasive in the world around us, but was somewhat neglected in earlier cognitive studies: the part–whole relationship.[10] Nobody will deny that there is a close connection between finger and hand, hand and arm, arm and body, and this applies to other body parts as well. Similarly, the link between tyre and wheel, wheel and car (and other components of cars) is just one of many examples of part–whole relationships for artefacts. This suggests that part–whole relationships are directly based on observable links between things; they can be described in terms of the spatial contiguity (i.e. nearness) and continuity of individual objects in the real world, and this is why they seem to be closer to concrete reality than type-of relationships (Cruse 1986: 178). A cognitive-linguistic view of part–whole relations will emphasize that they are based on our familiarity with our own body and its parts, which is clearly one type of basic experience.[11] Like other kinds of basic experiences, among them basic level categories, part–whole relationships may thus have a high cognitive accessibility, and this is reflected in a short processing time and the immediacy of gestalt perception, in which the idea of wholes and their parts (body and limbs or chair, legs, seat and back, etc.) plays a central role (see Section 1.1).

Unlike many taxonomic superordinates such as VEHICLE or MUSICAL INSTRUMENT, part–whole 'superordinates' like BODY, CAR or HOUSE are not superordinates per se, but basic level categories that can be activated as superordinates if needed. If one thinks of LIVING ROOM, BEDROOM and KITCHEN, it makes sense to relate these part categories to their common 'whole', the category HOUSE. With regard to its cognitive function, the superordinate category HOUSE does not highlight a single or a few attributes of its 'members', as is typical of type-of superordinates (ROOM for LIVING ROOM, BEDROOM, KITCHEN, etc.). Its strength is its assembling function, the notion that the category HOUSE is thought of as being composed of LIVING ROOM, BEDROOM, etc., and the same assembling function is fulfilled by KITCHEN with regard to COOKER, FRIDGE and KITCHEN TABLE or by TOWN with regard to HOUSE, SHOP and STREET. While type-of superordinates *collect* things on the basis of conceptualized similarities, part-whole superordinates *assemble* things on the basis of their conceptualized co-presence in time and space. It is in this sense that we talk of part–whole hierarchies or **partonomies**.[12*] As the prime example of BODY

---

* We avoid the term 'meronomy', as it is easily confused with 'metonymy', which is discussed in Chapter 3. 'Partonomy' is used to refer to hierarchies while the relationship between individual parts and wholes is called 'partonymic'.

shows, we have no difficulty in extending segmental part–whole relationships like FINGER – HAND into longer 'chains' (FINGER – HAND – ARM – BODY), as
these combinations have been called (Croft and Cruse 2004: 154), to stress
the fact that the links of the chain do not automatically belong to different taxonomic levels of categorization.

Part–whole and type-of relationships are not mutually exclusive ways of
categorizing things in conceptual hierarchies. Rather they are alternatives
from which speakers can choose according to their needs in specific speech
situations. Figure 2.10 illustrates this conceptual interaction for KITCHEN, HOUSE,
TOWN and related categories. Depending on the speech situation, the category KITCHEN, for example, can be conceptualized both as a type of ROOM and
as a part of HOUSE. Even with the small selection of items illustrated, the figure shows how a complex network of interrelated categories emerges. The
type-of links are indicated by dotted lines in Figure 2.10, because they seem
to be less basic than the part–whole links. Indeed there are many examples
where the type-of relationships are based on similarities between categories
that may be more difficult to fathom: just think of the hidden similarity
that joins elephants, mice and whales in the category MAMMAL. It is therefore hardly astonishing that children have difficulties understanding the type-
of relationship and long refuse to accept the idea that, for example, a horse

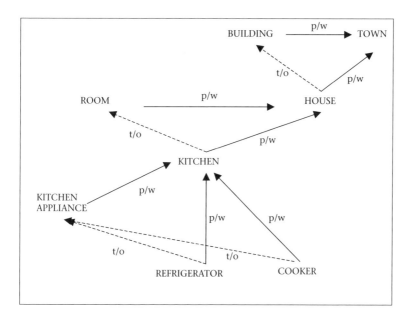

Figure 2.10 Type-of (t/o) and part–whole (p/w) relationships involving the
categories KITCHEN, HOUSE and TOWN

can be both a horse and an animal at the same time (Aitchison 2003: 196f); in contrast, children, at least those with a rural background, have no difficulty in enumerating, and thus mentally assembling, the animals found on a farmyard.

Given the grounding of partonomies in basic experiences, it is not surprising that the part–whole relationship also seems to motivate our understanding of many less tangible relations. These range from quasi-partonymic locative links illustrated above (e.g. TOWN – HOUSE/SHOP/STREET) to much looser associations (as illustrated in Figure 2.11), where the notion of 'being a part of' has a more or less figurative meaning. Compared with BODY, CAR or HOUSE, only the SHOPPING partonomy offers an array of predominantly concrete categories (SHOP, BUYER, GOODS, COUNTER, CASH, DESK, etc.). In contrast, the categories assembled in the TRAFFIC and DEMOCRACY partonomies are quite abstract and only few of them permit immediate gestalt perception. Nevertheless, categories like TRAFFIC or PUBLIC TRANSPORT, DEMOCRACY or ELECTION, whose structures are arguably based on the part–whole experience, seem to play a more important role in everyday conceptualization than the somewhat technical categories MOTION or ACTIVITY and HUMAN RIGHTS or POLITICAL SYSTEM, which might be introduced as type-of superordinates for the domains of TRAFFIC and DEMOCRACY respectively. This is due to the assembling potential of partonymic superordinates, which is often outwardly mirrored in their grammatical status as uncountables. Although they do not allow the quantification of instances of a certain category, uncountable terms like TRAFFIC, DEMOCRACY (or TELEVISION, SPORTS, RECREATION, etc.) are well suited to absorb everything that we connect with these categories. In this way, partonymic links contribute an important share to the construction of cognitive models and the networks in which they are assembled (see Section 1.3).

Finally, as will be shown in Section 3.1, partonymic links are the indispensable foundation of metonymies. A metonymic expression like *the*

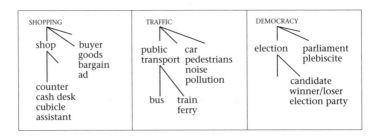

Figure 2.11 From part–whole links to loose associations: the categories SHOPPING, TRAFFIC, DEMOCRACY

university needs more clever heads is obviously based on the relation of the head being a part of the whole person; here the part comes as it were 'to stand for' the whole.

To sum up, we have distinguished two ways of establishing conceptual hierarchies, one based on the type-of relationship of class inclusion, the other on the part–whole principle and similar relationships. They can be characterized in the following way:

- Type-of relationships can take the form of extensive and rigid scientific classifications, which are strictly based on one or several salient attributes.

- Closer to the concerns of cognitive linguistics are experiential type-of hierarchies emerging from everyday categorization (i.e. the folk taxonomies), which also rely on salient attributes, but are neither complete nor fully consistent, and therefore tolerate gaps and alternative hierarchical paths.

- Part–whole hierarchies (or partonomies) are based on a relationship of continuity and connectivity between entities in the real world, which can be arguably traced back to our own basic bodily experiences. The links may range from genuine connections between parts and wholes to a loose association of elements. Partonomies seem to provide one of the major structuring principles for the construction of cognitive models (see Section 1.3) and play a key role in the explanation of metonymy.

Exercises

1. Check in the Yellow Pages how the goods and services that are offered are categorized in terms of hierarchies. Check in one of your big local department stores whether the goods are arranged according to a strict logical order.

2. Draw a conceptual hierarchy for the following food categories and check it for hierarchical gaps: SAUSAGE, HAM, BEEF, PORK, CHICKEN, TURKEY, SALMON, TROUT, MEAT, POULTRY, FISH, FOOD, and MILK, YOGHURT, ORANGE JUICE, MINERAL WATER, SOFT DRINK, DRINK.

3. Many scientific books and research papers use a decimal system comprising four or five digits in their table of contents to achieve a strictly logical taxonomy. Take one of these publications and check whether such a system is in fact helpful for the reader and how it could be rendered more 'digestible' in the light of our findings.

4. Decide which of the following items should be regarded as type-of and which items as part–whole superordinates: CLOTHES, HOLIDAY, HOUSE, MEALS, PARTY, SPORTS, TELEVISION, TOOLS. Suggest subordinated categories. Explain why ROOM, MEAL and SPORTS can be seen as both type-of and part–whole superordinates. Find other superordinates showing this ambiguity.

5. Sketch some of the cognitive models mentioned in Section 1.3 (e.g. WEATHER, HOLIDAYS, FOOD, MEALS OF THE DAY) by assembling the major categories they are based on (SUN, WIND, RAIN, SNOW for WEATHER, etc.). Decide which categories are connected by partonymic links and where the links are more difficult to define. Create a network containing the cognitive models mentioned above (and other suitable cognitive models) and comment on the conceptual links between them.

2.4 Categorization and composite word forms

If both type-of and part–whole relationships are decisive for our conceptualization of the world, it is not surprising to find them reflected in composite word forms even if a formal analysis of these items suggests a uniform modifier-head structure.

Type-of and part–whole relationships in compounds

Looking at composite word forms like *blackbird*, *black bean* or *black hair*, it seems plausible to assume a conceptual type-of relationship for these items and to claim the status of subordinates for them. In each case the 'nominal' category (BIRD, BEAN or HAIR) can be regarded as a basic level item, commanding a rich category structure, i.e. a prototype, good and bad examples and a sizeable number of attributes, which are also available for the conceptualization of the subordinate category. In contrast, the contribution of the adjectival element to the composite item seems to be restricted to the attribute 'black colour'.[13] If the category structure of BLACK is to be defended at all (see Section 2.5 below), it is definitely much leaner than in the case of BIRD or BEAN or HAIR. These findings are also fully compatible with the accepted word-formation analysis, which sees compounds like *blackbird* as modifier-head constructions, with the first element modifying the second.[14]

Turning to noun–noun compounds such as *apple juice*, word-formation analysis is the same, but the cognitive set-up is somewhat different. Here we have reason to assume that two fully developed basic level categories are

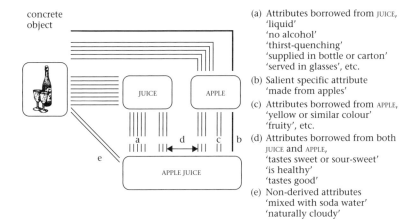

(a) Attributes borrowed from JUICE,
    'liquid'
    'no alcohol'
    'thirst-quenching'
    'supplied in bottle or carton'
    'served in glasses', etc.

(b) Salient specific attribute
    'made from apples'

(c) Attributes borrowed from APPLE,
    'yellow or similar colour'
    'fruity', etc.

(d) Attributes borrowed from both
    JUICE and APPLE,
    'tastes sweet or sour-sweet'
    'is healthy'
    'tastes good'

(e) Non-derived attributes
    'mixed with soda water'
    'naturally cloudy'

Figure 2.12   The attributes of the subordinate category APPLE JUICE
(schematic representation)

involved in this type-of relationship, i.e. JUICE and APPLE. Compare Figure 2.12, which illustrates the categorization for the subordinate category APPLE JUICE and is a simplified version of the findings of an attribute-listing experiment (Ungerer and Schmid 1998).[15]

As shown in the figure, most of the attributes listed by informants for APPLE JUICE are also named for the head category JUICE, among them 'liquid', 'no alcohol', 'thirst-quenching', 'supplied in bottle or carton' and 'served in glasses' (see (a) in Figure 2.12). This supports the impression that APPLE JUICE borrows these attributes from JUICE and largely depends on JUICE for its categorization. Also in line with our expectations, the link with the category APPLE is first of all established by the specific attribute 'made from apples' (represented by the line in bold print; see (b)).

However, this is not the only attribute that links APPLE JUICE with the category APPLE, but informants also put the attributes 'yellow or similar colour' and 'fruity' on their lists (see (c)) for both APPLE JUICE and for APPLE. In addition, there are three attributes, 'tastes sweet or sour-sweet', 'is healthy' and 'tastes good' (d) which occur on the lists for all three categories so that it cannot be decided whether APPLE JUICE has taken over these attributes from JUICE or APPLE. Thus as many as five attributes of the subordinate APPLE JUICE could be derived from the category APPLE. What this seems to indicate is that in categorizing APPLE JUICE we make much wider use of the first basic level category APPLE than is assumed by the traditional analysis, and this should throw first doubts on the rigidity of the modifier-head arrangement.

These doubts are reinforced when we turn to compounds like *coat collar* or *shoelace*. Here the point is reached where the traditionally assumed parallelism between type-of relationship and modifier-head structure is no longer maintained. Most items in the attribute lists supplied for COAT COLLAR establish links with COAT (i.e. the modifier category) and not with COLLAR (the head category). Apart from the salient specifying attribute 'part of a coat' (see (a) in Figure 2.13), a coat collar is made of cloth (this attribute is also shared with COLLAR), it keeps warm, it protects against wind, rain and snow and is worn in winter (see (b)) – all these attributes could be regarded as essential properties of both coats and coat collars. Compared with them, the links between COAT COLLAR and COLLAR add little beyond the reference to the material (c), and this is of course also shared by COAT; most prominent is the fact that collars tend to get dirty and greasy (d). This distribution of attribute links is illustrated in Figure 2.13.

Applying the same method to SHOELACE, one may expect to get similar results. Again more attributes will be derived from the source category SHOE than from LACE, and there are many other subordinate categories with a similar attribute distribution, like SHIRTSLEEVE, CHAIRLEG or LAMPSHADE. After what has been said about the role of part–whole relationships in conceptualization these findings are not difficult to explain. What the attribute lists for *coat collar, shoelace, shirtsleeve*, etc. mirror is simply the fact that these categories are conceived as parts or accessories of the wholes represented by the first element of the compound (COAT, SHOE, SHIRT), whose conceptual weight overrides the type-of relationship (a type of collar, lace, sleeve) in the minds of the ordinary language user. The result is what from a cognitive perspective may be called **part–whole compounds** (as opposed to **type-of compounds**).

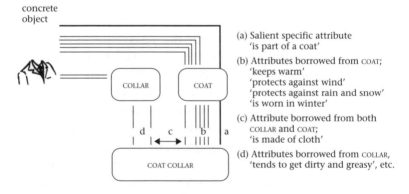

concrete
object

COLLAR   COAT

d   c   b   a

COAT COLLAR

(a) Salient specific attribute
'is part of a coat'

(b) Attributes borrowed from COAT;
'keeps warm'
'protects against wind'
'protects against rain and snow'
'is worn in winter'

(c) Attribute borrowed from both
COLLAR and COAT;
'is made of cloth'

(d) Attributes borrowed from COLLAR,
'tends to get dirty and greasy', etc.

Figure 2.13   Attribute links for the subordinate category COAT COLLAR
(schematic representation)

In fact this conceptual overriding effect of the first element can also be observed with compounds which from a logical point of view do not represent a part–whole relationship, but would be assigned to a type-of taxonomy even by the layman. In this vein, the compound *raincoat* would be understood as a coat that is additionally specified by an attribute such as 'protects against rain'. However, when informants were asked to name attributes for RAIN, COAT and RAINCOAT (each category name was given to a different group), it turned out that RAINCOAT and RAIN have much more in common than RAINCOAT and COAT. As it emerged from the attribute listings, both raincoats and rain are linked with wetness and water, with thunderstorms and gales, with cold and bad weather in general. As far as numbers go, the overlap of attributes between RAINCOAT and the 'modifier' category RAIN was far greater than between RAINCOAT and the 'head' category COAT. Some of the attributes quoted for RAINCOAT and RAIN may not belong to a sober 'objective' description of the essential properties of a raincoat, its shape or material (these attributes are mostly borrowed from the head category COAT). Yet if we accept the cognitive view that category descriptions include associative and experiential attributes, the idea that for the ordinary language user RAINCOAT is part of a comprehensive cognitive model RAIN rather than a type of coat (besides other types of coats) cannot be dismissed.

The emergence of new basic level categories from compounds

Apart from the findings discussed, the analysis of the category APPLE JUICE yielded another interesting result: the category APPLE JUICE was credited with two attributes that were listed neither for JUICE nor for APPLE ('naturally cloudy' and 'mixed with soda water'; see (e) in Figure 2.12).[16] Even if these 'non-derived' attributes may be rather marginal for APPLE JUICE, there are many other compounds where this is not the case. For an item like WHEELCHAIR, for example, informants do not just list a few, but in fact a large number of attributes that are not borrowed from either of the two source categories WHEEL and CHAIR.

Where do these attributes come from? A widely accepted, basically cognitive answer is that we rely on our 'knowledge of the world'. Indisputable as it is, this explanation is not really satisfactory because the notion of world knowledge is very general indeed. Looking at the example again, we find that most of the attributes are fairly concrete in nature. Some have to do with being an invalid, others with hospital, still others relate wheelchairs to engines and brakes. Obviously, the areas just mentioned can also be understood in terms of cognitive categories (INVALID, HOSPITAL, ENGINE, BRAKE, etc.); so we may assume that for the categorization of wheelchairs these categories (and other categories as well) are tapped in addition to WHEEL and CHAIR. In other words, the cognitive categories underlying compound terms like *wheelchair* do not only rely on the two categories suggested by the linguistic form, but draw on a large number of other cognitive categories. This is indicated in Figure 2.14, where the attributes emanating from these additional source categories are represented by broken lines.

As a closer look shows, most of these categories are not just plain person or object categories. Just think of HOSPITAL and the wealth of persons, objects and actions involved in its categorization. As suggested in Section 1.3, we should regard HOSPITAL (and also to a lesser extent INVALID and ENGINE) as complex cognitive structures or cognitive models, and this makes it much easier to link them with the general notion of world knowledge.

If we accept, as an interim result, the special role played by additional source categories (or cognitive models), we may take our explanation one step further. It seems plausible that the more source categories are involved in the structuring of a *composite* category, the smaller the contribution of the individual cognitive category becomes. In the course of this process it gets increasingly troublesome to go back to all these diverse categories for parasitic categorization. More and more attributes are no longer felt to be related to the source categories but are linked only with the compound category WHEELCHAIR (this is indicated by the normal lines connecting WHEELCHAIR with the real-world object in Figure 2.14), and there is no reason why in the final stage of this process such a category should be denied basic level status. This final stage may not quite have been reached in the case of WHEELCHAIR. Yet

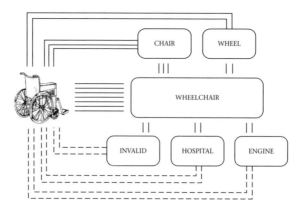

Figure 2.14 Attribute links of the subordinate category WHEELCHAIR

there are other compounds where this has happened, such as NEWSPAPER and AIRPLANE, both of which are generally recognized as basic level categories today, and this is indicated by the ease with which informants supply a substantial number of attributes, obviously without thinking of other categories. As a linguistic reflection of this change from subordinate to basic level status, *newspaper* and *airplane* tend to drop the first element, thus assimilating to the simple form of basic level categories as *paper* and *plane*, a stage which has long been reached by (*motor*) *car*.

Another well-known effect of this process is that the linguistic form of a compound may preserve the reference to a source category which has already been superseded by conflicting 'non-derived' attributes. A famous case is *holiday* (from *holy* + *day*), which is, of course, also used for non-religious workfree days. Similarly, *blackboard* refers to an object that is more often green today than black, as suggested by the modifier component. Incidentally *blackboard* also illustrates the tendency of new basic level compounds to drop the first element, as in *Could you write these words on the board*?

Summing up at this point, we can say that the description of compounds in terms of cognitive categories and informant-based attributes seems to have several advantages over both traditional word-formation analysis and a rigid logical view of subordination. The major points are:

- The standard view which posits a basic head item and a strictly specifying modifier element is far too rigid. With many compounds, even with model cases like *apple juice*, the modifier category supplies more than just the specifying attribute; these additional attributes may not all be 'objective' properties, but are often associative and 'experiential'.

- The basic item, i.e. the conceptually dominant source category, is not necessarily expressed by the second element of a compound. Depending on the salience of the categories involved, the cognitive category corresponding to the first element may be equally important (as illustrated by *raincoat*) or even dominant, especially if a compound is based on a part–whole rather than a type-of relationship (as in *coat collar* and *shoelace*). This means that from a cognitive perspective we may distinguish type-of compounds and part–whole compounds.

- To some extent, almost all compounds attract additional attributes. Many of them can be traced back to additional source categories (or cognitive models). The larger the overall number of source categories gets, the less important the cognitive categories which are expressed by the linguistic form of the compound becomes. If the number of source categories reaches a level that makes it difficult to handle them all, parasitic categorization becomes irrelevant, the attributes are thought to be attached to the compound category itself and a new, self-supporting basic level item has been created. The component categories as well as the additional source categories serve, to use Langacker's metaphor, as a kind of scaffolding which is disposed of when it is no longer needed.[17] This process can be studied in its various stages starting with items like *apple juice* and *wheelchair* and finishing with (*motor*) *car* and (*air*)*plane*; it gives a tangible view of what has traditionally been called lexicalization.[18]

Perhaps we should add a final remark which throws some light on how cognitive structures are expressed in language. From a cognitive perspective, what happens in compounding would be best reflected in blends such as *motel* or *heliport* because here the intersection of two cognitive categories involving various attributes can be expressed iconically (Ungerer 1999: 313f). However, compounds are much more frequent than blends because, more than blends, they are safe indicators of the source categories. This is why they are the first choice when it comes to expressing subordinate categories. As an acceptable second choice we would expect at least one of the cognitive categories to be expressed linguistically, and this alternative will be explored in the next section.

The myth of the 'simple' subordinates

In Section 2.2 we described simple or seemingly unanalyzable subordinates such as *daisy, dandelion, poodle, terrier, quarter* or *dime* as relying on the basic level categories FLOWER, DOG or COIN respectively, but adding one or several specifying attributes. Considering the fact that compounds and many other composite forms are based on two source categories (neglecting ties with additional source categories for the moment) it is strange that *daisy* and the other examples should not have this background.

Here a short excursion into the etymology of these words will be helpful. *Daisy*, it turns out, is derived from 'day's eye' which refers to its sun-like disc, while *dandelion* is French for 'lion's tooth', an obvious reference to the jagged shape of its leaves. In other words, though blurred by their historical development, the two words denote specific attributes of the respective subordinate categories. They do not do this by directly tapping a modifier category, but by providing a metaphorical bridge which links the subordinate category to several source categories (DAY and EYE in the case of *daisy*, LION and TOOTH with *dandelion*), and this is typical of many flower subcategories. To mention just two more examples, the word *buttercup* expresses metaphorical links with *cup* (indicating its shape) and with *butter* (indicating its yellow colour), and *tulip* is derived from a Persian word for 'turban' (again a reference to shape).

Turning to *quarter* and *dime*, we find that they both denote fractions of a dollar (*dime* is derived from Latin *decimus*, 'the tenth'), so the dollar-related value 'stands for' the coin, establishing a metonymic relationship. With *poodle* and *terrier* the metonymy is less obvious, but dictionaries tell us that *poodle* has something to do with puddles of water, and *terrier* is linked to Latin *terra* ('earth') because in hunting a terrier would pursue foxes or badgers into their burrows. Thus most of the examples make use of metaphorical or metonymic links, whose general eminence in cognitive linguistics will be discussed in Chapter 3.

But this is only half the story. What is equally noticeable is that the basic source categories, i.e. FLOWER, DOG and COIN, are not signalled in the linguistic expression. This is the more surprising since they are, as we have seen, indispensable for the cognitive identification and categorization of DAISY, DANDELION, etc. A possible explanation is that basic level categories like FLOWER, DOG or COIN are such a self-evident part of our cognitive models of nature and money that they need not be expressed explicitly. The dependence on cognitive, and more precisely, cultural models becomes clearer when we move to a more specific context, i.e. the restaurant context, where subordinate categories like APPLE JUICE or LIGHT BEER are signalled as *two apples* or *two lights*, and this is widespread in all kinds of specialist contexts, e.g. among craftsmen, athletes, students or teachers, and makes up an essential part of their group slang.

Summarizing we may conclude that most simple or unanalyzable subordinates are in fact not simple in terms of underlying cognitive categories, but are based on an expressed modifier category and an unexpressed implicit head category. However, there are exceptions. Take the category ROSE: it has been a simple word right from its assumed Greek origins; it has an easily identifiable gestalt and a rich attribute inventory, so we might be tempted to claim basic level status for this cognitive category, even if logically it is subordinate to FLOWER.

To resolve these inconsistencies we have to remind ourselves of two basic tenets of the cognitive approach. The first is that cognitive units are not discrete. Just as there are no clear-cut boundaries between categories, the transition between levels of conceptualization is better regarded as gradual. This is particularly obvious in the case of part–whole hierarchies, which cannot be easily attributed to different levels, but it also applies to type-of folk taxonomies. While QUARTER or DANDELION (or composite terms like BLACK BEAN or BLACKBIRD) are clearly seen as subordinate to their basic level categories, POODLE, TERRIER and DAISY are probably less so, but are still judged to be more subordinate than categories like ROSE which border on or actually belong to the basic level.

The second tenet takes us back to the discussion of conceptual hierarchies in Section 2.3. Unlike scientific hierarchies, we found, these cognitive or folk taxonomies can be inconsistent by admitting competing superordinates, such as ANIMAL and PET for DOG. This principle can be applied to the basic level as well. Ordinary language users seem to be perfectly capable of using several competing basic level categories side by side. While relying on FLOWER as a source category for DANDELION and perhaps DAISY, roses may be categorized independently (and may serve as a source category for the various types of roses and rose-like flowers). A similar coexistence between basic level categories can be observed in other fields, e.g. between BUILDING and HOUSE, between JEANS and TROUSERS or between PLANE and JET.[19] In some cases the newer category (JEANS, JET) may eventually replace the other category as basic level category illustrating the principle of lexical change by substitution. But other categories will go on being used simultaneously, as they have been for a long time, e.g. FLOWER and ROSE, if this promises a more economic form of categorization than strictly logical subordination.

Exercises

1. Look at the following items containing the element *shoe* and decide in each case whether the compound is based on a type-of relationship (with a dominant second element) or a part–whole relationship (with a dominant first element):

ballet shoe	shoe hammer	shoe-shop
canvas shoe	shoe heel	shoe-tip
patent-leather shoe	shoe leather	shoemaker
peep-toe shoe	shoe-boy	
sling-back shoe		
town shoe		
walking shoe		

   Do any of the type-of compounds suggest that – as with RAINCOAT – the dominance of the second element is overridden in conceptualization?

2. Traditional word-formation analysis distinguishes between modifier-head compounds and copulative compounds like *actor–manager* (also called

dvandva compounds). Comment on this distinction in terms of the cognitive analysis put forward in this chapter.

3. Just like WHEELCHAIR the following compound categories cannot be characterized by only relying on the labelled source categories: ASHTRAY, BEER MAT, TEA POT, NUMBER PLATE, WALLPAPER, HORSE SHOE, SPARK PLUG. Which additional attributes would you suggest for them and to which other categories or cognitive models can they be related? Discuss whether these compounds are already approaching the status of basic level categories.

4. The text suggested that flower names are linked to several source categories, normally via metaphor or metonymy (e.g. *daisy* < *day's eye*). Look up the etymological origin of the following flower names and discuss the cognitive processes that are involved: *bugloss, coltsfoot, bluebell, harebell, pink* and *groundsel*.

2.5 Basic level categories and basic experiences: actions, events, properties, states and locations

So far the discussion of the basic level and other levels of categorization has been restricted to objects and organisms. Yet in Chapter 1 the notion of basicness was introduced in connection with basic colour terms, which usually take the form of adjectives. This is why it seems natural to ask the question whether other 'adjectival' properties such as tallness and strength and especially many 'verbal' activities are equally basic for human categorization.

Intuitively, most people would probably think that frequently recurring activities like eating, drinking, sleeping, walking and talking are just as essential and show as much variation as familiar objects like apples, dogs or cars. Assuming, as we have done, that apples, dogs and cars are mentally represented by basic level categories with prototype structures, why shouldn't we claim the same kind of cognitive categories for these activities as well?

Surprisingly, cognitive linguists have been slow to support this intuition. The first attempts to provide evidence for a prototype structure of action categories were not concerned with eating or sleeping, but with the mental activity of lying. Coleman and Kay (1981), the authors of this study, took up Labov's method of using a limited number of given dimensions for the description of cups and bowls (see Sections 1.1 and 1.2). The dimensions they chose for the cognitive category LIE were:

(a) factual falsehood (an utterance or proposition is false)
(b) falsity of belief (the speaker believes that the utterance is false)

(c) intention to deceive (in making the utterance, the speaker intends to deceive the addressee).

Instead of Labov's line diagrams of cups and bowls, Coleman and Kay used fictitious stories describing various combinations of these three criteria. One story was about a boring dinner party. At the end of the party someone says to the hostess 'Thanks, it was a terrific party' just in order to be polite, a statement which is obviously false (criterion (a)) and believed to be false by the speaker (b), but probably not delivered with the intention to deceive (c). In another story, a nurse had mixed up the diseases of two patients who were ready to be wheeled into the operating room and therefore gave the doctor the wrong information. Even though her utterance was again factually false (criterion (a)), she did not mean to say something that was not true (b) and had no intention to deceive the doctor (c). These stories were contrasted with the prototype case in which all three criteria applied, a child's blatant denial that she had eaten the cake (which she had).

The stories were presented to informants who were asked to rate on a 7-point scale whether they were sure/not so sure/etc. that the story was a lie. All in all, Coleman and Kay argue that the meanings of the verb *lie* can be understood as a cognitive category with prototypical instances which satisfy all three criteria and less prototypical instances that do not.

A second study, Verschueren's (1985) investigation of linguistic actions, is closer to our intuitive suggestions, but not necessarily convincing as a list of basic actions, since it comprises not only suitable candidates such as *speak* and *write*, but also more problematic items like *answer, apologize, ask, congratulate, name, tell* and *thank*. The reason is that Verschueren mainly adapts the criteria which Berlin and Kay had established for basic colour terms (simple linguistic form, cannot be defined in terms of another basic item, wide range of applicability, psychologically salient and known to most speakers of the language; see Section 1.1). Though he also mentions Rosch's investigation of basic level terms, he does not make much use of her findings, which, as we have seen in Section 2.1, have added at least three important criteria to the definition of basic level categories: 'large bundles of correlated attributes', 'structured as prototype categories' and 'high potential for gestalt perception'.

Even if these criteria cannot be easily applied to most of the activities with which Verschueren is concerned, it seems quite feasible to use them with the action categories from which we started out, i.e. eating, drinking, sleeping and walking.

Action categories

Starting with the category EAT, we may take it for granted that it has a simple linguistic form which is known by speakers of English and is learned at a very early stage by children. We also have no difficulty in calling up a number of attributes which are quite unique to this cognitive category: 'picking food up from a plate', 'opening one's mouth', 'putting the food into one's mouth', 'biting', 'chewing', 'swallowing', etc. Note that since the category refers to an activity, the attributes tend to denote actions rather than objects or properties. However, the principle that the part–whole relationship is essential for our conceptualization of categories also holds true for action categories. For example, stages like 'biting', 'chewing' and 'swallowing' can be regarded as parts of the more complex action of eating.[20] As for prototypicality, it is possible to distinguish the more prototypical instances >EATING A SANDWICH< or >EATING AN APPLE< from the less prototypical instance >BEING SPOONFED BY ANOTHER PERSON< and the rather peripheral one >SIPPING SOUP WITH A STRAW< (e.g. after dental surgery). Finally, it is perfectly plausible that the action of eating can be perceived, and indeed categorized and conceptualized, as one integrated whole, i.e. as a gestalt.

Taking KILL as a second example,[21] again all three criteria seem to be met: in the media-dependent Western societies, the prototypical instance of the category is probably >SHOOTING DEAD (WITH A GUN)<, which can also serve as the basis for a gestalt image of the action. Attributes of KILL that could be expected from informants include major action stages: the raising and aiming of a gun or similar weapon, the firing of a gun and other stages of the process which are familiar from movies such as fighting, hitting, falling, tumbling and shedding blood.

Given the unpleasant nature of the example KILL the reader may perhaps wonder why it was chosen in the first place. The reason is that KILL was already established as a classic in the linguistic literature in the 1960s when it was analyzed as consisting of the semantic primitives CAUSE, BECOME and NOT ALIVE.[22] This kind of analysis is very interesting from a cognitive point of view because of the divergent nature of the three components. While the attribute 'not alive' would certainly crop up in some form or other in informants' attribute lists, probably in the form 'dead', we would think that the attributes 'cause' and 'become' are too abstract to be named. However, what these attributes remind us of are very general attributes such as 'used to play with' or 'means of transport' which can be extracted from basic level object categories (e.g. DOLL or BUS) and used to conceptualize the superordinate categories TOY and VEHICLE. In other words, what we suggest is that verbs like *cause* or *become* can be regarded as representing superordinate action categories because their main function is to highlight one very general attribute which is part of a whole range of basic level action categories. As a consequence we assume that in line with the principle of parasitic categorization informants would revert to basic level actions like KILL, THROW, PUT in order to conceptualize the more abstract cognitive category CAUSE. This view is supported by Lakoff and Johnson's (1980/2003: 70) observation that direct causation is expressed by verbs like *kill* and *throw*, and it is in accordance with the hypothesis that little children learn about causation by intentionally throwing bottles and dropping toys. Other candidates for superordinate action categories with a salient general attribute are HAPPEN, BECOME, BEGIN and STOP.

It thus seems plausible that both basic level and superordinate categories can be found in the field of actions. What is more difficult to decide is whether there are subordinate categories expressing a type-of (and not a stage-of or part-of) relationship. Along the lines established in the last chapter, assuming a type-of subordinate would mean that we are looking for action categories that are distinguished from basic level categories by one or several specific attributes (like the attribute 'jagged leaves' for DANDELION). We would also expect to find it quite difficult to distinguish prototypical examples from lesser ones (all dandelions look pretty much alike, we found). Finally we would assume that many subordinate categories are linguistically expressed by compound or composite terms in which one element signals the specification and the other one the respective basic level term (e.g. APPLE JUICE with APPLE indicating the specification and JUICE referring to the basic level category).

To test these assumptions, Figure 2.15 gives a selection of words denoting kinds of walking, which is taken from the *Longman Lexicon* (LLCE, 1981).[23]

walk ...	
	Specific characteristics
limp	'lamely, unevenly, usually because one leg has been hurt'
hobble	'in an awkward way, like rocking from one side to the other'
amble	'at an easy gentle rate, in a way suggested by an ambling horse'
stroll	'slowly and leisurely'
wander	'around without a fixed course'
stride	'with long steps'
strut	'in a proud way, with pompous, erect gait'
march	'with a regular, esp. forceful step'
pace	'with even steps'
stamp	'pushing (one's foot) down heavily'

Figure 2.15   Some potential subordinates of the action category WALK

(The descriptions of the specific characteristics are partly taken from the *Concise Oxford Dictionary,* COD 1999.) To start with the linguistic form, there is not a single compound form in the list, which reflects the fact that verbal compounds are extremely rare in English. So we get no linguistic clue which category might serve as the source category for the specification. Indeed, the attributes that can be extracted from the paraphrases are either complex (walk 'in a proud way, with a pompous, erect gait' for STRUT) or fairly vague (walk 'around without a fixed course' for WANDER). Gestalt perception is another problem. Good and bad examples of limping, striding or strutting are probably more difficult to distinguish than different kinds of walking; indeed, a uniform gestalt of the actions of limping or strutting, which we found to be typical of subordinate categories, is more difficult to imagine than a uniform gestalt for dandelions.[24] The result is that the subordinate status of these action categories is less certain than in the case of object and organism subordinates. Many of the action categories like LIMP, AMBLE, WANDER seem to have a status comparable to that of ROSE, which puts them closer to the basic level than we would expect from proper subordinates.

What is the consequence for hierarchy building? Of course, it is possible to assemble a hierarchy of actions, by arranging categories like STRIDE, WALK, MOVE or MUNCH, EAT, CONSUME on the subordinate, basic and superordinate levels respectively, but these hierarchies will more likely than not be scientific constructs and will not necessarily reflect the cognitive framework of the ordinary language user. In addition, these action hierarchies seem to be even more patchy than their counterparts in the domain of objects and organisms.

So we leave action categories with a feeling that they include a number of basic activities which are probably perceived in terms of prototype categories, but that the analysis becomes less conclusive as we turn to superordinates and subordinates and, more generally, to lexical hierarchies of action categories.

Between actions, objects and organisms: event categories

When comparing action categories like EAT or DRINK with related object categories like BREAD, SOUP or TEA one is struck by the amount of overlap between the respective attribute lists. The names of some basic level food categories will be found in the attribute list of EAT, and conversely, the names of basic level action categories like EAT will certainly rank among the more important of the attributes of the basic level food categories. So it seems that there is a strong cognitive interdependence between action and object basic level categories.

However, action and object (or organism) categories are not just related via the mutual give-and-take of attributes, but they can also be fused into categories of a secondary, but still very basic, nature. A good example of such an **event category** is the category BREAKFAST which was already mentioned in the context of the cultural model of MEALS in Section 1.3. Here we are not interested in the cultural background of the category but in its internal structure. From this perspective the category BREAKFAST combines basic level object categories (e.g. BREAD, BUTTER, KNIFE, SPOON, CUP, TABLE and CHAIR) with basic level action categories (e.g. EAT, DRINK, CUT, SPREAD), and has therefore been seen as a complex basic level category. This was claimed by Rifkin (1985) (who, incidentally, starts out from the notion of frame which will be discussed in Chapter 5).[25] Using an attribute-listing test Rifkin was able to show that informants could produce large numbers of attributes for basic level event categories such as BREAKFAST, LUNCH, DINNER, PARTY, SEEING A MOVIE, TAKING A BATH, BRUSHING ONE'S TEETH, TAKING A SHOWER and THEFT, RAPE, MURDER. For the related (type-of) superordinates MEAL, ENTERTAINMENT, HYGIENIC ACTIVITY and CRIME the category structure was much leaner, while subordinates such as QUICK BREAKFAST, BIRTHDAY PARTY, SHAMPOOING and PICKPOCKETING yielded about the same number of attributes as basic level categories.

However, this taxonomic set-up is put into perspective when we approach event categories from the angle of partonomies. If actions are subdivided into parts or stages (as we have claimed for verbal actions), and if we consider that action categories form integral constituents of event categories, the relationship between whole and parts, between MEAL and STARTER, MAIN COURSE and DESSERT, or between PARTY and WELCOMING, SMALL TALK, BUFFET MEAL, DRINKING, DANCING and FAREWELL appear more relevant for categorization than any type-of relationship. In fact what we have already indicated in Section 2.3 is particularly true of event categories: it is these partonymic links that seem to provide the texture for event categories (or the cognitive models underlying them).

Properties: basic level categories or basic experiences?

Leaving the 'nominal' domain of objects and the 'verbal' domain of actions and turning to 'adjectival' properties and especially colour terms, we are faced with a dilemma. On the one hand there is a strong tradition which holds that an adjective denotes a single property of an object or organism and does not have the attribute inventory of a basic level category. On the other hand, informants are capable of selecting focal or prototypical colours and of distinguishing them from more marginal ones – indeed this was the starting point of the cognitive notion of prototype categories (see Section 1.1).

What is also important for linguists is that the varying typicality of colour terms cannot only be experienced intuitively or described with abstract scientific terms like hue, brightness and saturation, it is also reflected linguistically in the variety of colour terms available. Words like *crimson, purple, scarlet, vermilion* all denote recognizable shades of RED; other examples are *cherry* or the compound *brick-red*. As the last two colour words show, types of RED are often identified as properties of certain objects, e.g. of cherries or bricks, and this use is widespread across the colour spectrum – compare *chestnut, olive* or *lilac*, not to mention the numerous colour terms derived from precious stones such as *amber, aquamarine* and *turquoise*. This suggests that colours are not categorized in isolation, but are experienced as attributes of categories denoting objects and organisms.

The extent to which the category structure of properties depends on these object and organism categories becomes even more obvious in the case of TALL, which has been investigated by Dirven and Taylor (1988). As the authors see it, the structure of TALL is a matter of collocations with certain nouns, and it is on the basis of collocations that Rosch's procedure of goodness ratings can be applied to adjectival properties like tallness. By asking informants to judge how well TALLNESS applies to a certain noun, Dirven and Taylor get the information needed to compile their lists of goodness ratings, as illustrated in Figure 2.16.[26]

There can be no doubt that these goodness ratings of collocations with *tall* are very helpful for the understanding of collocational possibilities and restrictions of the adjective. What is less certain is whether they can be regarded as sufficient proof for Dirven and Taylor's claim that TALLNESS is a

Good examples	a sky-scraper the Eiffel Tower a block of flats a spire a telegraph pole a tower a pylon	Less good or doubtful examples	a pyramid people a church ..... a book-case a bridge a dog	Bad examples	a door a room a cloud ..... a bird hair a baby

Figure 2.16 Goodness ratings for objects and organisms in terms of TALLNESS (excerpts from Dirven and Taylor (1988: 397, Table 3)).

cognitive category with a prototype and a rich cognitive structure. Indeed, one might argue that when informants are asked to rate the fit between the noun phrases *a skyscraper* or *a baby* and the adjective *tall*, what they have in mind are not specific instances of the category TALL, but instances of the categories SKYSCRAPER and BABY. Or to put it in a different way: what would be left if the collocational links with the noun phrases were no longer considered? It is equally difficult to imagine how, without invoking related objects, we should be able to call up large numbers of attributes for colours, dimensional properties like *tall*, *long*, *small* or physical properties such as *smooth*, *hot* or *sweet*. And likewise, how might we pinpoint good or bad instances of these properties? And how should we envisage properties like tallness as gestalts?

The question then is whether properties like 'tall' or 'smooth' or 'hot' should be regarded as cognitive categories comparable to object, organism and action categories, or whether they represent a different kind of cognitive experience. Such an alternative interpretation would be based on the assumption that properties consist either of single attributes, or at most of small clusters of attributes, and this strongly reminds us of the traditional explanation. What is important in the cognitive context is that these properties must be understood as representing cognitive phenomena which are based on sensory events derived from our most immediate interaction with objects, other people and our own bodies. To take some of the more obvious cases, one could establish a relationship between the properties 'sweet', 'sour', 'bitter' and 'salty' and the respective physiological receptors on our tongue or between 'warm' and 'cold' and the receptors registering temperature in our skin, not to mention the links observed between basic colour terms and physiological colour perception (see Section 1.1). Even if the relationship with sensory events will be less direct in other cases, e.g. with dimensional properties, the evidence suggests that these adjectival properties might also reflect basic experiences, which can be seen on a par with the bodily experiences of wholes and parts, on which our idea of partonomy seems to be grounded.

Static and locative relations

Closely linked as it is with the domain of adjectival properties, this is another area in which an interpretation in terms of both categories and basic experiences seems feasible. Apart from verbs with a 'static' meaning like *be*, *exist*, *resemble* or *contain*, the most common way of expressing these relationships in language is by means of prepositions and preposition-based adverbs. Since prepositions like *in*, *up*, *out* or *off* show a strong tendency towards a pro-liferation of meanings, it is not surprising that they became the favourite objects of study when cognitive linguists started transferring the prototype model to fields other than organisms and objects. Especially, the family resemblance notion could be particularly well illustrated by the relation-ship between the various senses of *up* or *over* for example. (For a detailed discussion see Section 4.1.)

However, faced with the inherently relational nature of prepositions, we cannot be sure whether it is necessary to stick to the interpretation in terms of prototype categories. When viewed in isolation from object cate-gories, prepositions do not really invite us to think in terms of attribute lists, typicality gradients and gestalts. Rather we have the feeling that loca-tive relations like 'up–down', 'in–out', 'front–back', 'left–right', reflect basic experiences as we have suggested them for important adjectival properties. This interpretation is in accordance with Lakoff's view that these locative relations should be regarded as basic **image schemas** that are directly derived from everyday bodily experience (Lakoff 1987: 267; see also Section 4.1).

To sum up what we have discussed in the present chapter, attention should again be drawn to the following points:

- For our categorization of actions, much of the descriptive apparatus devel-oped for categories of objects and organisms seems to be available:

    – actions are processed as prototypical categories;
    – there is a psychologically prominent basic level of action cat-egories within this hierarchy;
    – other hierarchical levels (superordinate and subordinate cate-gories) exist, but are less fully developed; subordinate categories often express stages or parts of the action rather than subtypes.

- Although events are secondary in the sense that they represent fusions of object, organism and action categories, many of them show the fea-tures of basic level categories. Type-of hierarchies are possible, but quite often relationships between parts (or stages) and wholes seem to be more essential for the conceptualization of events.

- For properties, locative and static relations ('tall', 'under/over', 'belong', etc.), the analysis in terms of prototype categories is only one possibil-ity. An alternative interpretation of these properties and relations is based on the notion of image schemas, which are regarded as a different but related type of basic experience (see Sections 3.1 and 4.1).

Exercises

1. Find possible subordinates of the basic action categories EAT, DRINK, CLEAN, COOK, READ and DRIVE in the *Longman Lexicon* and *Roget's Thesaurus*. Consider items expressing stages or subtypes of the action.

2. Ask fellow-students for their personal gestalt image and for attributes of basic event categories like LECTURE, TRAFFIC ACCIDENT, CONCERT, AUDITION, INTERVIEW, CHURCH SERVICE and EXAMINATION.

3. Consider the following collocations with *strong* and *weak*:

   a strong drink, a strong beer, a strong man

   a strong scent, a strong anaesthetic

   a weak heart, a weak point, weak eye-sight

   a weak dosis, a weak stomach, a weak man

   Is it possible to see these uses as members of prototype categories for STRONG and WEAK? Or should they all be derived from a single dimension, for example 'strength' or 'intensity', which represents a basic experience?

4. Compile a list of English prepositions from a grammar book and discuss why some of them seem to be more basic than others.

Suggestions for further reading

Section 2.1

Lakoff (1987: 46ff) and Taylor (2003, ch. 3.3) supply reasonable but rather short summaries of the major issues discussed in this section. On the whole they neglect the basic level notion in comparison with the notion of prototypes. Kleiber (1998, ch. II.II) gives a more comprehensive survey of the basic level and Schmid (forthcoming) looks at the basic level in the context of the notions of salience and entrenchment. Brown (1990) takes a more differentiated view of types of cognitive categories, which is further developed by Ungerer (1994).

1. Cain (1958) addresses the question of how psychological considerations have influenced Linnaeus's classification. Stuessy (1990) provides a very comprehensive discussion of the principles underlying modern plant taxonomies.

2. An informative account of the history of *Roget's Thesaurus* and other attempts to map the world into thematic reference books can be found in McArthur (1986, ch. 18).

3. The gist of the book by Berlin *et al.* (1974) on Tzeltal plant classification is more easily accessible in an earlier article (Berlin *et al.* 1973). Their account of Tzeltal plant names is complemented by Hunn's (1977) study of Tzeltal folk zoology. There is again a shorter version (Hunn 1975), which includes a more general discussion of the relationship between folk and scientific classifications.

4. Rosch (1978) introduces the notion of cognitive economy into theories of categorization and is well worth reading. This issue is taken up in Geeraerts (1988a). See also our remarks on cognitive economy in Section 6.4.

5. For more background concerning the relation between the basic level and prototypes see Rosch *et al.* (1976), Mervis and Rosch (1981) and Kleiber (1998, ch. 3.2) . Geeraerts *et al.* (1994) present the results of a detailed empirical study of Dutch words denoting items of clothing, in which they define the notions of basic level and prototypicality in terms of 'onomasiological' and 'semasiological variation'.

Section 2.2

For a concise summary of the main ideas in this section see Croft and Cruse (2004: 84–7). Wierzbicka (1985, ch. 4) gives a wide-ranging and very detailed discussion of different types of superordinate categories including the part–whole superordinates discussed in Section 2.3 below.

6. Early references to the special status of superordinates can be found in Rosch (1977) and (1978). Cecil Brown (1990) provides good, though somewhat technical, background reading for both this chapter and the opening section of the next.

7. For a concise description of the notion of parasitic categorization see Ungerer (1994).

Section 2.3

8. For comparison see more traditional views of hyponymy in Lyons (1977: 291ff), Cruse (1986: 145ff), Lipka (2002: 167ff). Both Lipka and Cruse stress the limited range of ANIMAL but accept CREATURE as an unproblematic superordinate category. This position is also taken by Taylor (2002, ch. 7), who integrates hierarchies into the concept of schema and instance.

9. See McArthur's (1981) *Longman Lexicon of Contemporary English*, section A30ff.

10. This is true of Rosch and her collaborators, but see Tversky and Hemenway (1984) and Tversky (1990), who report on interesting studies revealing the importance of attributes describing parts of objects for basic level categorization. For an up-to-date treatment of part–whole hierarchies see Croft and Cruse (2004: 150–63).

11. On image schemas see Johnson (1987: 28f) and Lakoff (1987: 267ff), Turner (1993) and Lakoff and Johnson (1999: 30–6). On the psychological reality of image schemas see Gibbs and Colston (1995).

12. The notion of partonomy is also used by Seto (1999), who discusses in detail the relationship between partonomy, taxonomy and metaphor and also clarifies the relationship between part–whole metonymy and the classical notion of *synecdoche*.

Section 2.4

13. This approach is more closely investigated by Smith *et al.* (1988), who propose a 'selective modification model' for the cognitive explanation of composite forms. For critiques of compositionality from the perspective of conceptual-blending theory (discussed in Sections 6.1 to 6.3), see Sweetser (1999), and Coulson (2001: 38ff).

14. For reasons of space the analysis of word-formation processes is here restricted to compounds. For a cognitive analysis of derivation (suffixation and prefixation) see Ungerer (2002), for an overview of other research in the field see Ungerer (forthcoming (a)), and for an overall cognitive treatment see Schmid (2005).

15. Ungerer and Schmid (1998) is a more detailed account of attribute-listing experiments for compounds, which provide empirical support for the cognitive view of lexicalization that is put forward here.

16. A good introduction to the problem of non-derived attributes is provided by Murphy (1988), whose position is supported by psychological experiments reported in Springer and Murphy (1992).

17. For Langacker's comprehensive discussion of composition, see Langacker (1987a, ch. 12). His use of the scaffolding vs the building-block metaphor will be taken up in Section 3.3.

18. For a discussion of the notion of lexicalization, see Bauer (1983: 42ff), Lipka (2002: 110ff) and Schmid (2005: 73ff). Leech (1981: 225) invokes the metaphor of the 'petrification' of lexical meanings and discusses the related examples *wheelchair* and *pushchair*.

19. Compare Geeraerts *et al.*'s (1994) investigation of Dutch items of clothing as well as Schmid's (1996c) comments on *jeans* and *trousers*.

Section 2.5

20. Compare the discussion of parts of activities and processes in Cruse (1986: 174).

21. For a cognitive discussion of the category KILL see Lakoff (1987: 54f). See also Fillmore's (1982) short discussion of the prototype category CLIMB, which is taken up by Taylor (2003: 108ff), who proposes a (problematic) structure with several prototypes.

22. For an overview of semantic primitives of verbs, see Lipka (2002: 116ff).

23. See also Aitchison (2003: 107f) on *walk* and some other verbs.

24. The possibility of using the uniform gestalt attributed to subordinates as a criterion is explored by Ungerer (1994) for momentary verbs like *tap*.

25. The article by Rifkin (1985) includes a lot of experimental material on superordinate and basic level event categories.

26. To get an idea which properties should be considered in this context, see Dixon's (1977) account of elementary adjectives and Langacker (1987a: 147ff) on basic domains.

CHAPTER 3

Conceptual metaphors and metonymies

3.1 Metaphors and metonymies: from figures of speech to conceptual systems

Traditionally, metaphors and metonymies have been regarded as figures of speech, i.e. as more or less ornamental devices used in rhetorical style. However, expressions like the foot of the mountain *or* talks between Washington and Paris *indicate that the two phenomena also play an important part in everyday language. Moreover, philosophers and cognitive linguists have shown that metaphors and metonymies are powerful cognitive tools for our conceptualization of the world.*

Metaphor and metonymy as figures of speech

It is common knowledge that words are often used in figurative senses. Even very young children are adept at using figurative language.[1] Nevertheless, the study of this linguistic phenomenon was for a long time the exclusive domain of literary scholars and the odd linguist who was interested in rhetoric or stylistics.[2] In view of this it is perhaps appropriate to begin the discussion of figurative language with some literary examples. Consider the following five instances of the word *eye* extracted from Shakespeare's sonnets (Kerrigan, 1986):

(1) So long as men can breathe or eyes can see,

So long lives this, and this gives life to thee. (18, 13–14)

(2) Is it for fear to wet a widow's eye

That thou consum'st thyself in single life? (9, 1–2)

(3) Sometimes too hot the eye of heaven shines,

And often is his gold complexion dimmed. (18, 5–6)

(4) Lo, in the orient when the gracious light
     Lifts up his burning head, each under* eye
     Doth homage to his new-appearing sight
     Serving with looks his sacred majesty. (7, 1–4)

(5) Mine eye and heart are at a mortal war
     How to divide the conquest of thy sight. (46, 1–2)

If we take for granted that the attribute list of the concept EYE includes properties like 'part of the body of people and animals', 'located in the head',
'organ of sight', 'locus for production of tears', we have no difficulty in interpreting the first two instances of the word *eye* as quite prototypical instances
of this concept. However, the same can certainly not be said of the other
three examples, because they involve figurative uses of the word *eye*.

Looking at the other examples we will gather that the expression *the eye of
heaven* in (3) is meant to refer to the sun. In example (4) we will presumably
interpret the image that eyes 'do homage' by assuming that the eye stands for
the whole person which behaves in a particularly deferential way. These two
examples are fairly typical of what has traditionally been called 'metaphor' and
'metonymy' respectively. Example (5) involves both types of figurative use at
the same time: the word *eye* is used as referring to the whole visual capacity
of a person which is contrasted with the field of affections symbolized by the
heart (both are fairly conventional instances of metonymy); in addition, the
visual and the affective domain are treated as persons or parties engaged in a
war (i.e. personification, a frequent and conventional type of metaphor).

How can these two major types of figurative uses of words, metaphor and
metonymy,† be characterized in more general terms and how can they be distinguished from each other? To take the latter first, it has been argued that
metonymy involves a **relation of 'contiguity'** (i.e. nearness or neighbour-
hood) between what is denoted by the literal meaning of a word and its figurative counterpart and that one constituent of the metonymic link **stands for**
the other. Typical examples of such stand-for relations are given in Figure 3.1.[3]

In contrast, metaphor has traditionally been based on the notions **'similarity'** *or* **'comparison'** between the literal and the figurative meaning of
an expression. More specifically, metaphor has been seen as a three-item pattern involving the elements 'tenor', 'vehicle' and 'ground' (Leech 1969: 148),

---

* According to the Penguin commentary, *under* in this context can mean both 'below
  (on the ground)' and 'socially inferior'.
† Note that both metaphors and metonymies will be indicated by small capitals between
  '+' signs throughout this book.

+PART FOR WHOLE+ (*all hands on deck*)
+WHOLE FOR PART+ (*to fill up the car*)
+CONTAINER FOR CONTENT+ (*I'll have a glass*)
+MATERIAL FOR OBJECT+ (*a glass, an iron*)
+PRODUCER FOR PRODUCT+ (*have a Löwenbräu, buy a Ford*)
+PLACE FOR INSTITUTION+ (*talks between Washington and Moscow*)
+PLACE FOR EVENT+ (*Watergate changed our politics*)
+CONTROLLED FOR CONTROLLER+ (*the buses are on strike*)
+CAUSE FOR EFFECT+ (*his native tongue is German*)

Figure 3.1   Types of stand-for relations in metonymies

or to use less technical language, of 'explained element', 'explaining element' and 'base of comparison'. This is illustrated in Figure 3.2 for the eye-of-heaven metaphor in example (3).

Setting out from such a 'comparison' or 'substitution' view of metaphor, I.A. Richards (1936) and Max Black (1962, 1993) developed the so-called 'interaction theory' of metaphor. They maintained that the essence of metaphor lies in an interaction between a metaphorical expression and the context in which it is used. In our example, the interaction can be described as a semantic clash or tension between the metaphorically used concept *eye* and the context *of heaven*, and this results in the interpretation of the expression *eye of heaven* as 'sun'.[4]

Conventionalized metaphors

As the examples of metonymic expressions in Figure 3.1 have shown, metonymy is not restricted to literary language, and the same is true of metaphor. Indeed, everyday language is rife with metaphorical expressions. Staying within the field that has already been opened up with the example *eye*, we find that most words denoting body parts are used in a multitude of metaphorical extensions. Figure 3.3 gives a list of examples of words denoting body parts in the upper half of the human body (some of which also involve metonymic components).[5]

The sun	is	the eye of heaven	(*in respect of*	*shape, radiation, domination of face or sky, etc.*)
X	is like	Y	in respect of	Z
TENOR		VEHICLE		GROUND
'explained element'		'explaining element'		'base of comparison'

Figure 3.2   The traditional explanation of metaphor
(after Leech 1969, explanatory paraphrases added)

head	of department, of state, of government, of a page, of a queue, of a flower, of a beer, of stairs, of a bed, of a tape recorder, of a syntactic construction
face	of a mountain, of a building, of a watch
eye	of a potato, of a needle, of a hurricane, of a butterfly, in a flower, hooks and eyes
mouth	of a hole, of a tunnel, of a cave, of a river
lips	of a cup, of a jug, of a crater, of a plate
nose	of an aircraft, of a tool, of a gun
neck	of land, of the woods, of a shirt, bottle-neck
shoulder	of a hill or mountain, of a bottle, of a road, of a jacket
arm	of a chair, of the sea, of a tree, of a coat or jacket, of a record player
hands	of a watch, of an altimeter/speedometer

Figure 3.3 Conventionalized metaphors of body parts
(collected from Wilkinson 1993 and LDOCE4)

Examples from many other fields could easily be provided and some will be given as this chapter unfolds. What all these examples show is that metaphor and metonymy are not just figures of speech in literature but also pervasive in everyday language. To capture the difference between the more inventive, expressive and unexpected metaphors devised by poets and the *head-of-department* type, which is usually not even recognized as being metaphorical by language users, the latter type has been called conventionalized, lexicalized or 'dead' metaphor. The logic behind these labels is that through its frequent association with a certain linguistic form, the figurative meaning of a word has become so established in the speech community (i.e. conventionalized) that it is entered in the lexicon as one sense of the word in its own right (i.e. lexicalized). From a cognitive point of view, however, this is highly misleading. In the words of Lakoff and Turner (1989: 129)

> the mistake derives from a basic confusion: it assumes that those things in our cognition that are most alive and most active are those that are conscious. On the contrary, those that are most alive and most deeply entrenched, efficient, and powerful are those that are so automatic as to be unconscious and effortless.

The conclusion from a cognitive perspective is that the metaphors that have unconsciously been built into the language by long-established conventions are indeed the most important ones.

Metaphors as cognitive instruments

In tracing the development from the traditional to a cognitive conception of metaphor and metonymy, we have now arrived at a crucial point. As already recognized by Black in a precognitive context, metaphors act as 'cognitive instruments' (1962: 37). This means that metaphors are not just a stylistically attractive way of expressing ideas by means of language, but **a way of thinking** about things. In the same vein Lakoff and Johnson (1980/2003: 7f) argue that we do not just exploit the metaphor +TIME IS MONEY+ linguistically, but we actually think of, or conceptualize, what they call the **target** concept TIME via the **source** concept MONEY. In other words, when we use the following English phrases we establish links between two concepts that do not seem to belong together by their very nature.

> You're *wasting* my time.
>
> Can you *give* me a few minutes.
>
> How do you *spend* your time?
>
> We are *running out of* time.
>
> Is that *worth* your while?

The source and target concepts are not conceived in isolation, however, but are felt to be embedded in 'cognitive models' and 'cultural models' (see Section 1.3). What is transferred, then, by a metaphor is not only the properties inherent in the individual concepts, but the structure, the internal relations or the logic of a whole cognitive model. Using a metaphor originating in cartography later taken over by mathematicians, cognitive linguists have called the transfer a 'mapping' from a source to a target. This means that from a cognitive perspective a metaphor is a mapping of the structure of a source model onto a target model. As the distinction between concept and cognitive model is often vague, we will use the more neutral terms 'source concept' and 'target concept' in what follows.*

Let us look at another example to illustrate this conception of metaphor (Lakoff and Turner 1989: 1ff). The human life cycle is conventionally conceptualized as starting with *arriving in* the world, *going through life* and *leaving* or *departing* at the time of one's death. This means that we think of our life in terms of three journeys: when we are born we arrive from our first journey, our entire life is the second journey in the world, and when we die we set out on our last journey. The first and the last journeys are reflected in language by **metaphorical expressions** such as *the baby is on the way, the baby has arrived, we bring babies into the world,* and *he is still with us, they brought him back, he is gone, he has departed, he has passed away.* What we

---

*The term 'domain', which is used in the cognitive literature in this context, is also established as a technical term in Langacker's *Cognitive Grammar* and we would therefore like to reserve its use for Chapter 4.

are really interested in, however, is the middle journey, our journey through life, which may be described for instance by the following metaphorical expressions (Lakoff and Turner 1989: 3f): *she went through life with a good heart, he knows where he is going in life, I don't know which path to take, he made his way in life, he works his way round many obstacles.*

Returning to the traditional explanation of metaphor (the three-element system presented in Figure 3.2), one finds that the cognitive approach, as presented so far, focuses on two of its three elements: the tenor (or 'explained element'), which is now seen as **target concept**, and the vehicle (or 'explaining element'), now regarded as the **source concept** of the metaphor. To integrate the third element of the traditional system (the ground or 'base of comparison') into the cognitive view, we extend the descriptive apparatus by introducing the notion of **mapping scope**, as shown in Figure 3.4.[6]

As we see it, the mapping scope of a metaphor is best understood as a set of constraints regulating which correspondences are eligible for mapping from a source concept onto a chosen target concept. These constraints not only help to avoid just any kind of feature that is transferred from the source to the target concept but also motivate the range of possible correspondences. Essentially, the mapping scopes of metaphors reflect our conceptual experiences in dealing with the world around us. More specifically, we can distinguish three major components of mapping scopes:

- **image schemas**, which are firmly grounded in our bodily experiences. They include orientational schemas like 'in–out', 'inside–outside', 'front–back' as well as the 'inside–outside' (or 'container–contained) schema, the 'part–whole' (or 'whole–part') and the 'path' schema; image schemas are most probably shared by all human beings (see also Section 2.5).

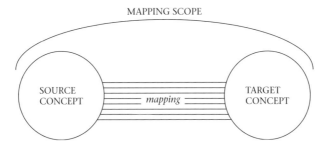

Figure 3.4   Basic components of metaphorical mapping: source concept, target concept, mapping and mapping scope

- **basic correlations**,[7] which we do not experience bodily like image schemas, but which guide us in understanding the events and actions in the world around us. Examples are relations of presumably universal significance like 'action/change correlates with motion' (or short 'action/change<>motion'[†]), 'cause<>effect', 'purpose<>goal' and 'presence<>existence'; it is likely that they also have a universal status like image schemas.

- **culture-dependent evaluations**, which are restricted to the members of a specific culture. In the Western culture they include for example evaluative attributes like 'rich', 'young', 'stupid' or 'beautiful' (attributed to persons); 'strong', 'majestic', 'aggressive' or 'dirty' (for animals), and 'valuable', 'durable', 'useful' or 'fragile' (for objects).

Applying this conception to the metaphors already discussed, the +LIFE IS A JOURNEY+ metaphor is best activated within a mapping scope that relies on the image schema of 'path' and is supported by the correlations 'change <>motion' and 'purposes<>goals'; in contrast a mapping scope based on the 'inside-outside' or the 'up-down' image schemas or on the correlation 'cause<>result' would be less suitable. The +TIME IS MONEY+ metaphor as expressed in *You're wasting my time* or *We are running out of time* requires a mapping scope incorporating the widespread evaluation that money is a valuable commodity; here the moralist attribute that money is evil would be less helpful. And to add an example illustrating distinct cultural differences, the Western culture-specific attributes of pigs as 'dirty' and as 'greedy' establish that the metaphorical phrase *John is a pig* is understood as meaning 'he is untidy' or 'he does not eat with good manners', while in other cultures pigs may be associated with different attributes. In modern China, for example, the lexeme *pig* can have connotations similar to the Western ones, but it is also used as a term of endearment for a lover and carries associations of a somewhat straightforward and silly kind of loveliness. In this culture the metaphor +A PERSON IS A PIG+ has an interpretation entirely different from the Western one, because attributes like 'dirty' and 'greedy' are not suggested as part of the mapping scope.

This shows that for the effortless conceptualization of a metaphor the mapping scope must be well entrenched in the minds of the members of a given culture. For an innovative literary metaphor, however, such as the fabricated example +WINTER IS FOOD+, the mapping scope available to the average (Western) reader will be very hazy indeed. Even with better-known literary metaphors, as the example quoted from Shakespeare above (+SUN IS

[†]The sign <> stands for 'correlates with'.

THE EYE OF HEAVEN+), novices may have their problems because the mapping scope is still less well entrenched than it is for consolidated 'everyday' metaphors like +TIME IS MONEY+ or +LIFE IS A JOURNEY+. In other words, the entrenchment of the mapping scope may vary widely, and this is reflected from a sociopragmatic angle in the **degree of conventionalization** (or social sanctioning) a metaphor has achieved in a speech community.

After this first overview of the cognitive-linguistic conception of metaphor it seems reasonable to ask what the typical target concepts and the typical source concepts of conceptual metaphors are. See Figure 3.5, which assembles a selection of major source and target concepts discussed in the literature. Comparing the two lists we find that the concepts in the left-hand column are rather abstract in nature, while those in the right-hand column are more concrete. What this seems to demonstrate is that we rely on concepts of the concrete world to conceptualize abstract phenomena. To substantiate this claim, the abstract concepts ARGUMENT and IDEA, which both command a whole range of metaphors, will be examined in more detail.

The structuring power of metaphors I: argument

How do we conceptualize the concept ARGUMENT? In traditional semantic terms we can distinguish three meanings of the word *argument*. Apart from 'line of thought', an argument can be a 'disagreement or quarrel', and finally a 'reason given to support or undermine something'. However, these paraphrases do not capture in any way the wealth of information that we have stored

Target concepts	Source concepts
life	journey
death	departure
lifetime	day
time	money
anger	dangerous animal, container
love	war, valuable object
argument	journey, war, building, container
ideas	plants, building, container
understanding	seeing
communication	packing, sending, unpacking
world	theatre

Figure 3.5   Major source and target concepts of metaphorical mappings

in relation to the concept ARGUMENT: the stages through which arguments usually go; the characteristic pattern of exchanges between the participants; the purposes pursued by the participants; the force of the reason given. These aspects of the concept may not be very helpful in distinguishing between different meanings of *argument*. In fact, they illustrate how closely the various meanings are linked by a shared conceptual structure, and it is this structure that cognitive linguists have been interested in. According to Lakoff and Johnson (1980/2003) our conceptualization of the concept ARGUMENT is based on the following four related metaphors:

> +AN ARGUMENT IS A JOURNEY+
>
> +AN ARGUMENT IS A BATTLE+
>
> +AN ARGUMENT IS A BUILDING+
>
> +AN ARGUMENT IS A CONTAINER+

These metaphors will now be considered in some detail.

+AN ARGUMENT IS A JOURNEY+

The first metaphor mainly serves to conceptualize the progress of an argument. Expressions based on this metaphor are (Lakoff and Johnson 1980/2003: 90):

> We have *set out* to prove that bats are birds.
>
> *When we get to the next point*, we shall see that philosophy is dead.
>
> *So far*, we've seen that no current theory will work.
>
> This observation *points the way* to an elegant solution.
>
> We have *arrived at* a disturbing conclusion.

As the examples show, we understand the progress of an argument by creating a structural analogy with the detailed knowledge that we have of the progress of journeys, which is as it were 'monitored' by a mapping scope based on the image schema 'path'. Nominal concepts like (STARTING) POINT, LANDMARK, WAY, PATH and GOAL, and action concepts like SETTING OUT, MOVING ON, COVERING GROUND, FOLLOWING A PATH and ARRIVING, which play a major role in supplying a structure for the concept JOURNEY, are mapped onto the concept ARGUMENT. Compare the following expressions:

> He *strayed* from the line of argument.
>
> Do you *follow* my argument?
>
> Now we've *gone off* in the wrong direction again.
>
> I'm *lost*.

You're *going around* in circles.

+AN ARGUMENT IS A BATTLE+

A second concept, which is particularly useful for the conceptualization of the structural sequence, but also for the strength or force of an argument, is the concept BATTLE (Lakoff and Johnson prefer the more general label WAR). Like a battle, an argument can be divided up into several stages, notably the initial positions of the opponents, followed by the stages of attack, retreat and counterattack, and finally the victory of one side or, more rarely, a truce. Figure 3.6 shows how these structural analogies between BATTLE and ARGUMENT are reflected in linguistic expressions.

+AN ARGUMENT IS A BUILDING+

The third metaphor can put the content, the progress and the quality of arguments into perspective by drawing on attributes which the superordinate concept BUILDING inherits from basic level concepts such as HOUSE, TOWN HALL and CASTLE.

We've got *a framework* for a *solid* argument.

If you don't *support* your argument with *solid* facts, its whole *structure will collapse.*

He is trying to *buttress* his argument with a lot of irrelevant facts, but it is still so *shaky* that it will easily *fall apart* under criticism.

We will show his argument to be without *foundation.*

With the *groundwork* you've got, you can *construct* a pretty *solid* argument.

Initial positions of the opponents	*They drew up their battle lines.* *I braced myself for the onslaught.*
Attack	*She attacked every weak point in my argument.*
	He shot down all my arguments.
Defence	*They defended their position ferociously.*
	She produced several illustrations to buttress her argument.
Retreat	*He withdrew his offensive remarks.*
Counterattack	*I hit back at his criticism.*
Victory/defeat/truce	*OK, you win.* *He had to succumb to the force of her arguments.* *Let's call it a truce.*

Figure 3.6 Structural analogies of the concepts BATTLE and ARGUMENT and their linguistic realizations (some examples from Lakoff and Johnson 1980/2003)

+AN ARGUMENT IS A CONTAINER+

Finally, to conceptualize the content dimension of arguments we make use of the +CONTAINER+ metaphor, which functions within a mapping scope based on the image schema 'inside–outside'. From this perspective, which is mainly focused on the last sense of the word *argument* ('reason to support or undermine something'), arguments are seen as containers holding a substance:

> Your argument doesn't have much *content*.
>
> That argument has *holes in it*.
>
> Your argument is *vacuous*.
>
> I'm tired of your *empty* arguments.

The structuring power of metaphors II: idea

The examples that Lakoff and Johnson give have shown that they are not concerned with providing a definition of the meaning or category structure of ARGUMENT. Instead, their starting point is the concept ARGUMENT and their explicit aim is to elucidate how people conceptualize it via metaphor. In the analysis of the concept IDEA (Schmid 1993: 165ff; 1996a: 111ff), a complementary, inductive approach was chosen. Setting out from real occurrences of the word *idea* extracted from corpora and the OED, the metaphorical expressions were examined with the aim of analyzing the structure of the concept IDEA. This yielded the following main metaphors:

> +THE MIND IS A CONTAINER FOR IDEAS+
>
> +IDEAS ARE OBJECTS+
>
> +IDEAS ARE ANIMATE BEINGS OR PERSONS+

The first metaphor that is very important for our understanding of the concept IDEA is again a variant of the +CONTAINER+ metaphor. The collected data clearly reveal that we think of our minds as containers for ideas. This metaphor is often combined with the second metaphor which treats ideas as objects, or, more specifically, as goods. In a large proportion of the metaphorical expressions ideas are conceptualized as goods transferred. We talk about *having, getting, borrowing* or even *selling ideas*; something or someone can *give us ideas*, we can *put ideas* somewhere, e.g. *into other people's heads*.

The second metaphor, +IDEAS ARE OBJECTS+, also becomes manifest when properties of objects like extension and form in space, material or substance are expressed. Ideas can be

> big, little, slender, broad or sharp;
>
> rigid, strong or faint;

bright, clear or hazy;

supported, dropped, thrown out, shelved or fixed.

The third metaphor establishes a link between IDEAS and ANIMATE BEINGS or PERSONS. Based on these two fields people say that ideas can be *impoverished* or *wild*; they can *be adopted, conceived* and *killed*; they *get about*; ideas can be conceptualized as *offspring* or as *combatants*. As has already become apparent in the discussion of +AN ARGUMENT IS A BATTLE+, ideas can also be *attacked* and *surrendered*.

Types of concepts, rich and lean mapping

Let us recapitulate what the study of the two examples ARGUMENT and IDEA has revealed. The evidence strongly suggests that abstract concepts are indeed based on or 'grounded' in more concrete source concepts, in particular in basic level concepts. Metaphorical mapping may take place directly between basic level and target concept. Alternatively, the link is established through superordinate concepts like BUILDING. Looking at the metaphor +AN ARGUMENT IS A BUILDING+ again, it is easy to see how the salient attributes of individual basic level concepts like HOUSE, TOWN HALL and CASTLE are used to structure the abstract concept ARGUMENT. Quite frequently the source concept of such **specific metaphors** is an event concept that is in itself composed of several other basic object and basic action concepts. For example, the source concept BATTLE of the metaphor +AN ARGUMENT IS A BATTLE+ is a combination of basic level object concepts (GUN, TANK, BOMB, etc.) and action concepts (FIGHT, ATTACK, SHOOT, DRIVE).

However, there are also metaphors such as +IDEAS ARE OBJECTS+, +IDEAS ARE PERSONS+ and +IDEAS ARE CONTAINERS+ whose source concepts are not specific basic level concepts or their superordinates. Rather the source concepts of these metaphors are an assembly of more general conceptual experiences that we have collected about the objects, living organisms and human beings that we encounter in the world around us, and this is why we call them **generic metaphors** (not to be confused with the use of *generic level* in biological taxonomies). Among these generic experiences are for instance that objects can be obtained, given away, shelved or dropped, that containers can be empty, filled with liquid and overflow, that living organisms can be nurtured or killed, that persons can be adopted, embraced or attacked. Because these general concepts are extremely familiar to us, they quite naturally offer themselves as the source of metaphorical mappings onto abstract target concepts, as the discussion of the concept IDEA has shown.

What has been sketched so far is the metaphorical structuring of abstract target concepts through a combination of specific and generic metaphors. In this process a large number of metaphorical correspondences are established, especially between a concrete source concept and a target concept, perhaps less so between a generic source concept and a target concept. It is this **rich mapping** that fascinated the authors of early cognitive studies of metaphor to the extent that other types of metaphor were neglected. Yet as Ruiz de Mendoza Ibañez (2000: 111–13) has rightly pointed out, there are many metaphorical links, in particular links with **concrete target concepts**, which focus on a single property of a concrete source concept.[8] This applies for instance to the example *John is a pig*, where, as shown above, the metaphorical mapping is restricted to a few correspondences by a mapping scope focusing on 'dirtiness', with aspects like 'greediness' playing an additional but subordinate role. With other well-known examples, for instance the animal metaphor underlying the use of *crane* for a piece of construction equipment, the number of correspondences is also much smaller than is assumed in the theoretical discussion, because the mapping scope is restricted by the correlations 'shape<>object' and 'action<>motion'. This **lean mapping** is sufficient because the target concept is well equipped with attributes of its own to guarantee successful conceptualization and the metaphor is used to **highlight** one or a few additional attributes (such as the bad manners of John in *John is a pig*, the shape and movements of the crane). Lean mapping may also occur between a generic source concept (e.g. the PERSON concept) and a concrete target concept. These cases – traditionally called *personification* – are not only found in fairytales and children's books, where animals and objects think, talk and act like persons, but also in everyday life when we talk about (and to) computers or cars as if they were human beings.

Metaphorical mapping: a summary

Although diagrams tend to oversimplify matters, Figure 3.7 should provide a final overview of the essentials of cognitive metaphor analysis. It shows that what metaphors basically do is establish a conceptual link between a source and a target concept. The diagram also illustrates – visually and in writing – how the various aspects of metaphor are interrelated: specific source concepts contribute to both concrete target concepts and abstract target concepts. Yet in the former case (e.g. +A PERSON IS A PIG+) the metaphorical transfer is restricted to basically one single correspondence ('lean mapping') while abstract target concepts, such as ARGUMENT, IDEA or ANGER, draw a large number of attributes from concrete concepts like BUILDING or JOURNEY. These abstract target concepts

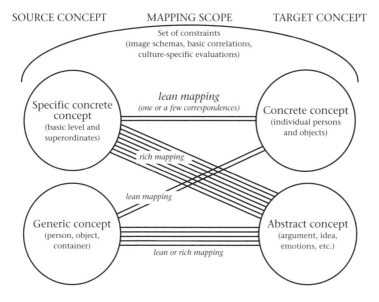

Figure 3.7 Metaphorical mapping: an overview

are also supported by links with more general source concepts, e.g. the generic OBJECT concept, as in *Ideas can be sold* (*like objects*) or the generic CONTAINER concept as in *Anger welled up in his body* (*like a liquid in a container*); these metaphors may vary between lean and rich mapping. To complete the picture, concrete target concepts (e.g. animals concepts, objects concepts like TREE, RIVER or CAR) may achieve personification by drawing on the generic source concept PERSON, again a case of lean rather than rich mapping.

The different mapping scopes also explain why conceptual metaphors fulfil different cognitive functions:

- Lean mapping between specific concrete source concepts and concrete target concepts is primarily used to **highlight** individual aspects of the target concept (e.g. the dirtiness attributed to John in *John is a pig*).
- Rich mapping between specific concrete source concepts and abstract target concepts, plus additional mapping from generic concepts, is primarily used to **supply a tangible conceptual structure** for abstract target concepts (e.g. ARGUMENT, IDEA, emotion concepts).

Metonymies as cognitive instruments

When we turned to a cognitive view of figurative language we somehow lost sight of the role played by metonymy in our conceptualization of the world. To redress the balance this section will focus on how metonymies parallel and differ from metaphors as cognitive instruments.

To begin with, it should be emphasized that two major claims made by cognitive linguists in the description of metaphor also apply to metonymy (Lakoff and Turner 1989: 103): both are seen as being conceptual in nature and both can be understood as mapping processes. This means that the set-up chosen for metaphor (source concept, target concept, mapping scope) is applicable to metonymies as well. The source concept and the target concept are cognitive equivalents of the entities linked through a contiguity relation (part–whole, whole–part, place for person, material for object etc.; see Figure 3.1). In order to see how the third aspect of mapping processes, the notion of mapping scope, must be understood in the case of metonymies consider the following sentence pairs:

(1a) All hands on deck.
(1b) All heads on deck.

(2a) The university needs more clever heads.
(2b) The university needs more hands.

(3a) The White House has launched a tax-cutting campaign.
(3b) The greenhouse has launched a tax-cutting campaign.

The examples illustrate how the mapping scope determines the appropriateness of a metonymic mapping by providing a suitable context for its interpretation. (Recall that the mapping scope was introduced for metaphor as a set of constraints regulating the correspondences between source and target concepts.) In the first two pairs (1a/b and 2a/b) the prototypical part–whole relation of body parts vs. the whole body or person is applied, yet it is only in the (a) versions that the metonymy is successful. In sentence (1a) this is due to the fact that the context of shipping suggested by the key word *deck* is socially sanctioned and situationally relevant. Since it includes the idea of physical work required on a ship, 'shipping' provides a suitable mapping scope for a part–whole link between HAND and BODY/PERSON. It seems natural that the concept HAND is used to stand for physical labour; a metonymic link between HEAD and PERSON, as suggested in (1b), does not fit the shipping context equally well. In (2a/b) the situation is reversed: the mapping scope 'university' invites a link between HEAD and BODY/PERSON (2a), which concentrates on the intellectual capacity of human beings, while the link based on HAND and its physical strength (2b) would carry little conviction.

This analysis can also be transferred to other types of metonymy, as illustrated by example (3a/b), where only (3a) calls up 'US administration' as a suitable mapping scope. Within this mapping scope, which also includes the notion of tax-cutting, the place concept WHITE HOUSE quite naturally suggests a spatial link with PRESIDENT. The concept GREENHOUSE would probably be seen in the context of gardening, which does not really embrace the notion of tax-cutting, and this would make it difficult to establish a convincing mapping scope sanctioning the metonymic link.

Reviewing what has been offered as mapping scope for the metonymies expressed by the (a) version of (1)–(3), it is obvious that the number of correspondences between source and target concept is not decisive here – this link is uniformly reduced to a contiguity relation, often a part–whole relationship, or some other basic relation, e.g. place for institution or cause for effect. What is more important and at the same time more variable is the amount of encyclopaedic knowledge accepted by the community of speakers as mapping scope.[9] In the case of 'shipping', 'gardening', 'university' and 'US administration' the mapping scope seems to be largely equivalent in status with the concepts (or cognitive models) discussed in Section 1.3 and in previous sections of this chapter – think of BEACH, MONEY, JOURNEY, BATTLE or ARGUMENT. All three aspects of the metonymy (source concept, target concept and mapping scope) are thus part of one cognitive model, and this explains why cognitive linguists have claimed that metonymies are prototypically restricted to a single cognitive model, unlike metaphors, which are mappings from one model to another.

However, the notion of mapping scope is more flexible than that. Instead of being tied to a single clearly delineated cognitive model, the mapping scope may also be constituted as a loose assembly of encyclopaedic cues that can be associated with different, though related, cognitive models. For example, when the concept TABLE is the source concept for the target concept PEOPLE SEATED AROUND THE TABLE, as in *the whole table was roaring with laughter*, the mapping scope can oscillate between the fairly concrete cognitive model DINNER PARTY and the more general model SOCIAL EVENT. The reason is that both models supply the necessary cues about the convivial companionship that may develop among people sitting round a table. Similarly, the metonymic use of the source concept HOUSE in *the house of Windsor* thrives on mapping scopes linked with a range of cognitive models such as ROYAL FAMILY, MONARCHY or even ENGLISH HISTORY. Frustrating as this can be for linguists bent on the neat assignment of cognitive models, ordinary language users seem to have little difficulty in dealing with this vaguer type of mapping scope (which can be compared with the 'folk approach' to conceptual taxonomies; see Section 2.2).

To round off this discussion of metonymy, one could raise the issue of conventionalization, which was tied to the entrenchment of the mapping scope in the case of metaphors. Indeed, examples of non-conventionalized metonymies are feasible, as shown by example (4) (both examples from Barcelona 2003: 244):

(4) We ate an excellent *Mary* yesterday.

(5) I have just bought a *Picasso*.

Compared with (5) it is quite obvious why sentence (4) is doomed as a metonymy. The mapping scope of 'pie baking' is only available for a small family circle, but not socially sanctioned by the larger community of speakers, so the source concept MARY is not felt to stand for the target concept EXCELLENT PIES; in contrast the mapping scope 'famous painters' fully supports the +AUTHOR FOR WORK+ metonymy for Picasso. More importantly, there is little chance that Mary's pie-baking will become famous enough to justify the metonymy. This is different from the fate of innovative metaphors, especially those used first in literature and the media, where the prospects of conventionalization are much brighter.

Metonymic mapping: a summary

The diagram containing the final overview of metonymic mapping (Figure 3.8) is designed along the same lines as the summary of metaphorical mapping (Figure 3.7). As shown in the diagram, metonymy is also understood as a relationship between a source concept and a target concept. This relationship develops within a socially accepted mapping scope that prototypically corresponds to a cognitive model. Compared with metaphor, the range of source and target concepts in metonymies is normally restricted to concrete concepts. Metonymic correspondences are directly grounded in image schemas or basic

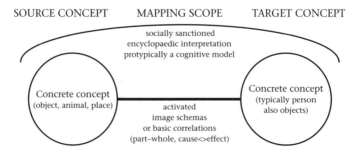

Figure 3.8 The mapping of conceptual metonymies: overview

correlations ('part–whole', 'inside–outside', 'cause<>result'), which are only indirectly involved in metaphors as part of the mapping scope. In this sense metonymies are more elementary than metaphors.

In addition, metonymies are also more straightforward than metaphors: their major goal is to refer to an entity, prototypically a person, denoted by the target concept by means of the source concept. This **referential function** of metonymies is quite well represented by the simple stand-for notion (the White House 'stands for' or 'gives mental access' to the President, the table 'stands for' or 'gives access' to the people sitting round it, etc.). Yet there are metonymies where the referential goal gives way to a **highlighting function** based on a predicative use, as in *I'm all ears* (highlighting as it does one attribute of a person) and it is not difficult to see that this type of metonymy is quite close to lean-mapping metaphors like +A PERSON IS AN ANIMAL+. This has led to suggestions that metaphor and metonymy should be seen as a cline of cognitive operations (Ruiz de Mendoza Ibañez 2000: 115).

Apart from these transitional phenomena there are many other ways in which metonymies interact with metaphors.[10] This is particularly true of emotion concepts, which will be discussed in the next section.

Exercises

1. Collect conventionalized metaphors that have body parts in the lower half of the body (*leg*, *foot*, *toe*, etc.) as their source concepts. Find out which parts of the human body are particularly productive as source concepts and try to explain why this is so.

2. According to Quinn (1987) the main metaphors with which Americans conceptualize MARRIAGE are:

   +MARRIAGE IS A MANUFACTURED PRODUCT+,

   e.g. *we want to work hard at making our marriage strong*

   +MARRIAGE IS AN ONGOING JOURNEY+,

   e.g. *we went in a common direction*

   +MARRIAGE IS A DURABLE BOND BETWEEN TWO PEOPLE+,

   e.g. *they are tied to each other*.

   Find other linguistic expressions which reflect these metaphors.

3. Find linguistic expressions in English and another language you know which illustrate the metaphor +A WORD IS A COIN+.

4. Discuss how the abstract concept TIME is conceptualized via metaphors in some of Shakespeare's sonnets (e.g. 12, 15, 16, 19, 104 and 115).

What are the prevalent source concepts and which mapping scopes can be assumed for these metaphors?

5. Collect animal metaphors like *He is a real pig* or *She is a bitch* from a dictionary and explain them with the notions 'source' and 'target concept'.

6. Assemble as many metonymies with basic colour concepts as sources as you can (e.g. *feel blue* or *green with envy*). Try to find metonymies with non-basic colour concepts as sources such as *crimson, scarlet, turquoise, ochre* or *olive*. Why do the results support the basicness of basic colour terms? For additional examples and classification proposals see Niemeier (1998).

7. Aitchison (2003: 169f) writes of a child who, when asked to describe an Afro hairstyle, said: 'Lots of snakes are coming out of his head.' Make up similar inventive metaphors and discuss the source and target concepts as well as the mapping scopes involved.

8. Look at the following idiomatic expressions using the source concept HOUSE and their meanings. Analyze the metaphorical and metonymic mappings licensing these expressions and discuss plausible mapping scopes:

to keep open house	'to be at home to visitors all the time; to offer them hospitality regardless of who they are'
a rough house	'a fight, a violent disturbance'
a full house	'a theatre that is fully attended'
a drink on the house	'a drink that is paid for by the landlord of the public house'
in the best houses	'in the best society'
a house of cards	'an idea that has no foundation in fact, a wildly impracticable idea'

3.2 Metaphors, metonymies and the structure of emotion concepts

We all know what anger is like: how people get red faces, how they begin to shake, how they clench their fists, how anger seems to build up inside them until they explode. With fear, the picture is totally different: the blood leaves the face, the body is paralyzed, people feel tormented, tortured and overwhelmed. For the cognitive linguist, all these aspects of anger and fear are reflected in metonymic and metaphorical expressions.

Trying to describe what emotion terms mean is anything but an easy task. This is mirrored in dictionaries where definitions of emotion words tend to show a considerable degree of vagueness and circularity. Thus *anger* is paraphrased as a strong or violent feeling of displeasure and hostility. *Love* is defined in terms of fondness while *fondness* is described as liking or love.

A similar situation of frustration has prevailed among psychologists who have tried to grapple with the elusiveness of emotions for generations. The only tangible foothold they were able to find in empirical research was the impact emotions have on the body. When informants in psychological tests were asked to describe what they feel when they are angry, sad or happy they always included physiological experiences, like increase of body temperature, change of pulse rate, palpitations of the heart or the production of sweat and tears. In other words, they establish a link between emotions and physiological symptoms, which are regarded as the cause, or more often, as the effect of the emotions in question.[11]

Emotions and physiological metonymies

Returning to the framework of conceptual metaphors and metonymies introduced in Section 3.1, we find that the link between emotions and physiological symptoms reminds us of certain metonymic mappings, especially the cause–effect relationship observed in metonymies like +THE TONGUE STANDS FOR SPEECH+ or +THE HAND STANDS FOR WRITING+. These similarities make it understandable why Kövecses and Lakoff (Lakoff 1987: 382) have postulated a general metonymy: +THE PHYSIOLOGICAL EFFECTS OF AN EMOTION STAND FOR THE EMOTION+. Figure 3.9 gives an idea of the kinds of bodily symptom that are related to emotions in linguistic expressions in English. The examples collected are taken from dictionaries and from informants' statements in the psychological tests mentioned above. As a result they reflect the naive view or 'folk theory' of the physiological effects of emotions, but not necessarily objective scientific observations.

Going through Figure 3.9, we can single out three aspects that between them illustrate both the potential and the limitations of physiological metonymies. First we find that there are indeed bodily symptoms which seem to be helpful for a description of the conceptual structure of emotions because they are peculiar to one particular emotion: drop in temperature, sweat, dryness in the mouth, blood leaves face for FEAR, erect posture for PRIDE, drooping posture for SADNESS, jumping up and down for JOY. Obviously these physiological phenomena help us in conceptualizing the emotions in question, especially where they are contrasted with opposites as in the case

Physiological effect (source)	*Emotion* (target)	*Example*
Increase in body temperature	ANGER, JOY, LOVE	*Don't get hot under the collar.*
Drop in body temperature	FEAR	*I was chilled to the bone.*
Redness in face and neck area	ANGER, JOY	*She was flushed with anger.*
Blood leaves face	FEAR	*She turned pale/white as a sheet.*
Crying and tears	ANGER, SADNESS, FEAR, JOY	*Tears welled up in her.* *She cried with joy.*
Sweat	FEAR	*There were sweat beads on his*
Dryness of mouth	FEAR	*forehead, his hands were damp, his mouth was dry.*
Increased pulse rate and blood pressure, palpitations	ANGER, DISGUST, FEAR, LOVE	*His heart pounded.* *He almost burst a blood vessel.*
Lapses of heartbeat	FEAR	*You made my heart miss a beat.*
Erect posture, chest out	PRIDE	*He swelled with pride.*
Drooping posture	SADNESS	*My heart sank.*
Inability to move	FEAR	*She was paralyzed with fear.*
Flight	FEAR	*He ran for his life.*
Jumping up and down	JOY	*He was jumping for joy.*
Hugging	JOY, LOVE	*I could hug you all.*
General physical agitation	ANGER, DISGUST, FEAR, JOY, LOVE	*She was quivering/excited/keyed up/overstimulated.*

Figure 3.9 A selection of physiological metonymies for emotions (based on various publications by Kövecses, Davitz 1969 and Shaver *et al.* 1987)

of erect vs drooping posture. Other examples are the drop of body temperature (for FEAR), which is juxtaposed with its increase (for ANGER, JOY, LOVE), or the paleness of the face (again typical of FEAR), which contrasts with a red or even scarlet face and neck area (for ANGER).

The other two points we would like to draw attention to are less straightforward. As the example FEAR shows, an emotion concept can attract conflicting metonymies, and this raises the question: which of them is more reliable and representative? Do we connect FEAR with paralysis of the body or with flight? It might be that our preference depends on the situation, perhaps on the individual person, or it could also be a matter of sequence, with a state of paralysis functioning as a preface to flight. In any case this could mean that both metonymies may play a part in the conceptualization of FEAR.

The last, and probably the most serious, problem is that many metonymies apply not just to one or a few closely related emotions, but to a range of quite different emotions. ANGER, JOY and LOVE can cause an increase in body temperature (though with ANGER this would be irritating heat, while with

JOY it takes the form of comfortable warmth, and with LOVE both forms are possible); all three emotions may flush one's face. ANGER and JOY, but also SADNESS and FEAR can result in tears, an accelerated heartbeat and palpitations can be due to ANGER, FEAR, DISGUST and again LOVE, and general physical agitation seems to underlie all the major emotions listed in Figure 3.9. This means that though they may be helpful, metonymies cannot provide the conceptual structure of emotions all by themselves. To achieve this goal, metonymies have to be supported by the conceptual potential supplied by metaphors.

The interaction of metonymies and metaphors

The classic case of this interaction is the link between the metonymy based on body heat, and heat metaphors, as described by Kövecses and Lakoff (Lakoff 1987: 382ff).[12] This is illustrated in a simplified way in Figure 3.10.

The basic metaphor which is triggered off by the physiological metonymy is +ANGER IS HEAT+, but this rather abstract principle is made much more accessible if we imagine the heat in the forms of a fire and a hot fluid. Figure 3.10 makes it quite clear that the first of these two metaphorical applications (+ANGER IS FIRE+) is less developed than the second one (+ANGER IS THE HEAT OF A FLUID IN A CONTAINER+). Although FIRE is an important basic level event concept combining a number of action and object concepts, the various stages of kindling, maintaining and extinguishing a fire and the fuels involved in an ordinary fire (wood, coal, oil, gas) do not seem to provide a very rich concept structure which could be mapped onto the ANGER concept.[13]

In contrast, the second +HEAT+ metaphor, +ANGER IS THE HEAT OF A FLUID IN A CONTAINER+, has a much richer conceptual background. One reason is that many more source concepts are involved, especially highly suggestive basic level concepts like BOIL, RISE, STEAM, FUME, BURST, EXPLODE, for which most informants would be able to call up substantial attribute lists. More important still, this metaphor relies on one of the most important generic metaphors, the +CONTAINER+ metaphor, here in the guise of +THE BODY IS A CONTAINER FOR EMOTIONS+.

The result of this powerful metaphorical potential is the large number of derived metaphors listed in Figure 3.10. In combination with the metonymies we have discussed in the last section the concept ANGER thus acquires a very rich conceptual structure. In the case of ANGER the contributions of metaphors on the one hand and metonymies on the other are quite balanced. The physiological effects mentioned above are counterbalanced by the heat metaphors and a series of other metaphors, such as +ANGER IS AN

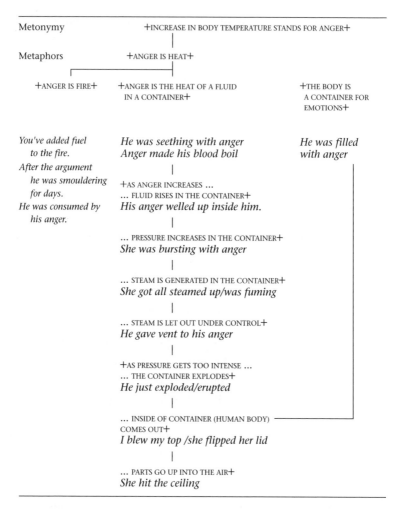

Figure 3.10   The link between the heat metonymy and heat metaphors for
ANGER (selected from Lakoff 1987: 381ff)

ACTIVE ENEMY+ (you *fight, struggle, wrestle* with it), +ANGER IS A DANGEROUS AGGRES-
SIVE ANIMAL+ (anger can be *ferocious* and *fierce*) and finally +ANGER IS A NATURAL
FORCE+ (anger *overwhelms you, engulfs you* and *sweeps over you*).

However, there are also cases where the balance between metaphors and
metonymies is lopsided. The concept FEAR, which commands a large number of metonymies (by far the largest number of any emotion listed in Figure
3.9), does not seem to attract many conceptual metaphors. Apart from the
+NATURAL FORCE+ metaphor just mentioned for ANGER, Kövecses lists +FEAR IS A
VICIOUS OPPONENT OR TORMENTER+ (fear *preys* and *creeps up on you*) and +FEAR IS
A TRICKSTER+ (*fear may deceive you*).

The opposite extreme is represented by JOY. There are few bodily phe-nomena that specifically indicate JOY, and, consequently, few physiological metonymies, but this deficit is made up by a wealth of conceptual metaphors. JOY can be experienced as a valuable commodity (that is *received* or *bought*), as a hidden object (which one *searches* or *strives for*), as an animal that lives well and has pleasurable sensations (*purring with delight, wallowing in delight*). JOY is compared to light (*you radiate with joy*), JOY is vitality (*it is spry, lively, puts pep into your life*). To put it in more technical terms, these metaphors map a large range of basic level source concepts involving events, actions and objects onto the abstract emotion JOY. In addition, JOY also makes use of the +CONTAINER+ metaphor, but with the important difference that the container does not explode, as is typical of ANGER metaphors, but simply over-flows. Finally the 'up–down' image schema is exploited in the metaphor +JOY IS BEING LIFTED UP+ (*I'm six foot off the ground, I'm on cloud nine, she's walking on air*).

The concept LOVE is an even more extraordinary case. Again the number of metonymies is relatively small (prominent, of course, is the metonymy based on sexual desire), but with regard to the number of conceptual metaphors LOVE surpasses all other emotions. Many of these metaphors are shared with JOY. In addition there is, quite naturally, a range of metaphors that is based on the metonymic relationship with sexual desire (+LOVE IS A NUTRIENT+, +LOVE IS APPETIZING FOOD+), and there are flattering comparisons with magic and deity (+LOVE IS MAGIC+, +THE OBJECT OF LOVE IS A GODDESS+), where the poetic source is still particularly noticeable. What is unusual in comparison with JOY is that LOVE is not only structured by 'positive' metaphors, but that it also seems to attract a full range of 'negative' conceptual metaphors, among them +LOVE IS WAR+, +LOVE IS HUNTING+, +LOVE IS A DISEASE+. This also applies to the +CONTAINER+ metaphors, where LOVE is characterized not only as a fluid over-flowing from the container, but alternatively by the explosion of the con-tainer, which is also typical of the ANGER concept. While it is easy to see how these negative metaphors might be (and have in fact often been) used in poetry to embellish the topic of love, their integration into the conceptual structure of a single concept is less feasible. The question is whether the con-cept LOVE consists of several independent categories (e.g. 'GENTLE' ROMANTIC LOVE and PASSIONATE LOVE), or whether we should assume that there is one (perhaps prototypical) concept with several variations.

What can be said at this point concerning the interaction of metaphors and metonymies is that there seems to be a principle of compensation at work which trades off metaphors and metonymies against each other. While ANGER strikes a balance between the two cognitive processes, FEAR largely depends on metonymies, and JOY and LOVE rely much more on metaphors for their conceptual structure.

However, in spite of the wealth of metaphors available for LOVE and JOY, these metaphors alone do not provide a tidy conceptual structure for either of these emotion concepts, so they do not really compensate for the lack of metonymies observed for JOY and LOVE. Taken together, metaphors and metonymies may supply a certain conceptual substance to these emotion concepts, but they cannot be used as a hard-and-fast distinction between them in the same way that attributes can help to distinguish between object concepts like CHAIR and TABLE.

Similar reservations must be expressed for many of the other emotion concepts we have discussed so far. The problem becomes even more serious when we consider that English has a huge number of emotion words and that there is probably an equivalent number of emotion categories to be taken into account.

Emotion words and basic emotion concepts

When Johnson-Laird and Oatley (1989) collected the emotion words in English from various dictionaries, their corpus amounted to no less than 590 items. To give an idea of the variety of English emotion terms, here is a list of items related to FEAR, which were collected and analyzed by Wierzbicka (1986, 1988).

> fear: afraid, scared, fright, frightened, terrified, petrified, horrified, dread, alarmed, panic, anguish, anxiety, worried, concerned, apprehension, shame, embarrassment

In order to cope with this mass of emotion words and underlying emotions, philosophers and psychologists have long tried to distinguish between essential and more marginal emotion terms and to set up a system of basic emotions, perhaps stimulated by a tradition that is already reflected in the medieval theory of the four tempers (Geeraerts and Grondelaers 1995). While eighteenth-century proposals, e.g. by Descartes, were based on philosophical argument, more recent attempts have tried to deduce basic emotions from neural agitation patterns, from facial expressions, and, closer to our concerns, from the emotion vocabulary, to mention only a few approaches.[14]

This linguistic approach was pursued by Johnson-Laird and Oatley (1989), whose list of emotion words has already been mentioned. Their hypothesis was that certain emotion terms are basic and unanalyzable in the sense that they cannot be broken down into attributes or other even more basic emotions (a view also supported by Langacker 1987a: 149). This means that basic emotion concepts like JOY or ANGER will normally be used as points of reference to describe non-basic ones like EUPHORIA, EXUBERANCE, FURY or RAGE and not vice versa. Consequently, a good way to identify basic emotions is to look at the emotion vocabulary of a language and to try to describe its emotion words in terms of attributes. This would filter out all analyzable emotion terms, so the residue of this process would have to be regarded as unanalyzable or basic. The result of this procedure was no surprise. The set of basic emotions that evolved was very similar to other recent proposals and comprised (in its improved version; Johnson-Laird and Oatley 1992) all the basic emotions assembled in Figure 3.11.

Plausible as this list of basic emotions may seem, Johnson-Laird and Oatley's claim that they are in fact unanalyzable cannot be left uncommented. This claim may be true as far as discrete, abstract attributes are involved, and it is exactly this kind of attribute, such as intensity, causation and goal-orientation, that Johnson-Laird and Oatley use to filter out the non-basic emotion terms. Yet if we consider the conceptual potential of metonymies and metaphors, we cannot really regard basic emotion terms as unanalyzable. As we have seen in the previous sections, which were almost exclusively concerned with examples of basic emotions, these concepts are linked with vital bodily functions by way of metonymy and, in addition, with a wide range of basic level concepts by way of metaphor. This means that a wealth of bodily sensations and basic level concepts are mapped onto basic emotion concepts, or seen from the other end, basic emotion concepts borrow heavily from basic experiences by way of parasitic categorization. The problem is that if in a cognitive context we reject conceptual unanalyzability as a yardstick for the basicness of emotions, how do we define their basic status? At this point it may be helpful to review once more the set of criteria that has emerged for basic level categories of objects and organisms (Section 2.1). One of these criteria, gestalt perception, will have to be rejected for

negative emotions	SADNESS		positive emotions
		JOY/HAPPINESS	
	ANGER		
	DISGUST/HATE	DESIRE/LOVE	
	FEAR		

Figure 3.11 A proposal for basic emotion terms in English (Double labels like DISGUST/HATE indicate that basic emotions can be viewed as short-lived states (DISGUST) or dispositions (HATE); see Ungerer 1995: 187)

emotion concepts, if we disregard cartoon-like images of jumping up and down for JOY, exploding for ANGER or a drooping posture for SADNESS. The second criterion, the existence of large correlated bundles of attributes, cannot be applied in the same way as with concrete objects such as apples or cars. The reason is that, as we have seen, observable properties of emotions are rare and often vague. So we are more or less left with three criteria: goodness-of-example ratings, the morphological simplicity of basic level words and the observation that they come to mind first and are acquired by children before they learn related words.

Starting with the last two criteria, we can easily gather from Figure 3.11 that most of the basic emotion terms have a simple linguistic form either as nouns (*anger, hate, fear, joy, love*) or as adjectives (*sad, happy*), while nonbasic emotion terms often have not – compare *frightened, terrified, petrified, horrified, alarmed, anxiety, apprehension* and *embarrassment* in the list given above. It is also well known that the basic terms first come to mind and are learned first by children. As for the goodness-of-example ratings, psychological tests confirm our intuition at least indirectly (because some of these tests were not aimed at basic emotions but the superordinate concept EMOTION; Fehr and Russell 1984). The result is indeed that our candidates for basic emotions have many of the qualities that we have found typical of concrete basic level concepts: they are recognized as prototypical category members while other emotions, e.g. the additional variants listed for FEAR above, are regarded as more marginal. Basic emotions do not necessarily command observable attributes, but they do attract a large range of conceptual metonymies and metaphors: in sum, they can be regarded as reference points that guide us through the elusive domain of emotion concepts.

Granted there are basic emotion concepts, it seems quite natural to regard the more general concept EMOTION as their superordinate concept. Pursuing the analogy with concrete objects a little further the claim would then be that the primary function of the concept EMOTION is to single out and highlight salient attributes shared by the related basic level concepts, or, viewed from the other end, to 'collect' basic level concepts with respect to these attributes.

In trying to validate this claim we will have to look for properties that are shared by all major emotions and which are so salient that they are expressed by the word *emotion*. Now as we already know, there is no inventory of observable properties for emotion concepts, but rather an array of metonymies and conceptual metaphors. Sifting this material for items that are shared by most emotions and might be regarded as equivalent to salient attributes, we arrive at the list assembled in Figure 3.12. One of the interesting aspects for the cognitive linguist in looking at this figure is that the +CONTAINER+ metaphor is among the shared properties. However, it is only the more general aspects of the CONTAINER (in itself already understood as 'generic' concept; see above) that seem to be common to all emotions. If we consider the actions that are carried out in the container, the individual basic emotions differ markedly: as has been shown, the container may explode to indicate ANGER, it may gently overflow with JOY, and we may add that it may be drained in the case of SADNESS. So in order to conceptualize more than a very vague sensation that the emotion is something that fills us up we have to go back to one of the basic emotion concepts, and this is again an instance of parasitic categorization, this time between the superordinate concept EMOTION and the basic emotion concepts.

Surveying the metonymy and metaphors of Figure 3.12 as a whole, we could say that they are all concerned with the development of the emotion, which includes the external source, the onset, which is often overwhelming, the grip it has on us while it is present and (more tentatively) its termination. This suggests that what emotions have in common is a sequence of several phases, and this finding has encouraged both psychologists and cognitive linguists to develop so-called emotion scenarios.

Emotion scenarios and prototypicality

The idea that cognitive categories should not be seen as isolated static units has been with us from the first chapter of this book. Categories, we found,

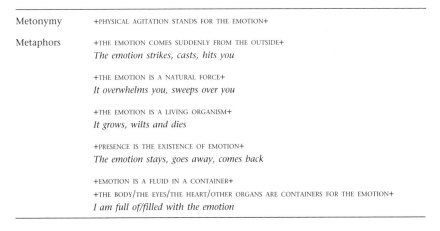

Metonymy	+PHYSICAL AGITATION STANDS FOR THE EMOTION+
Metaphors	+THE EMOTION COMES SUDDENLY FROM THE OUTSIDE+
	The emotion strikes, casts, hits you
	+THE EMOTION IS A NATURAL FORCE+
	It overwhelms you, sweeps over you
	+THE EMOTION IS A LIVING ORGANISM+
	It grows, wilts and dies
	+PRESENCE IS THE EXISTENCE OF EMOTION+
	The emotion stays, goes away, comes back
	+EMOTION IS A FLUID IN A CONTAINER+
	+THE BODY/THE EYES/THE HEART/OTHER ORGANS ARE CONTAINERS FOR THE EMOTION+
	I am full of/filled with the emotion

Figure 3.12 Major metonymy and metaphors supporting the concept EMOTION
(collected from publications by Kövecses)

must be seen in their conceptual context, against the background of larger cognitive models, and it is obvious that these models will at some point have to include sequencing in time (see Section 1.3). This line of investigation has also been pursued by linguists and artificial intelligence researchers and has led them to postulate notions like 'frames', 'scripts', 'stories' and 'scenarios', which will be discussed in detail in Chapter 5. For the time being we will simply look at some of the scenarios developed for emotions, and this will round off our survey of emotion concepts.

Figure 3.13 presents, in a condensed form, the emotion scenarios Kövecses and Lakoff offer for ANGER and FEAR. As the figure shows, the principle underlying the scenarios is to embed the emotion concept in a larger sequence including the cause of the emotion (stage 1) as well as its consequences (stage 5). Though these extensions are supported by psychological emotion theories, the majority of metonymies and metaphors refer to what Kövecses (1991: 40) has called 'the essentials' of the emotion, i.e. stage 2. Control and loss of control (stages 3 and 4) are more closely connected with the central stage 2 and can claim a number of conceptual metaphors, at least in the case of ANGER. Indeed, if we again go through the list of ANGER metaphors presented in Figure 3.10, we find that their sequence neatly reflects the development from stage 2 to stage 3 and stage 4 of the scenario: ANGER heats up the fluid in the container, the fluid rises, pressure is increased, steam is generated (all these metaphors refer to stage 2), then

	ANGER	FEAR
Stage 1: Cause	Wrongdoer offends Self	Dangerous situation, involving death, physical or mental pain
	Offending event displeases Self	Self is aware of the danger
Stage 2: Emotion	Anger exists	Fear exists
	Self experiences physiological and behavioural effects	Self experiences physiological and behavioural effects
Stage 3: Attempt at control	Self exerts a counterforce in an attempt to control anger	Self makes effort not to display fear and/or not to flee
Stage 4: Loss of control	The intensity of anger goes beyond the limit	The intensity of fear goes beyond the limit
	Anger takes control of Self	Self loses control over fear
Stage 5: Action	Retribution: Self performs act against Wrongdoer	Flight: Self flees from danger

Figure 3.13 Scenarios for ANGER and FEAR
(based on Lakoff 1987: 377ff and Kövecses 1990)

steam is let out under control (stage 3), and if this fails, the container explodes and parts go up into the air (stage 4). All in all, one may well claim some plausibility for the view that the concept ANGER can be described in the format of a sequential scenario in which the central stages are well supported by metaphors.[15]

The problem with this view, however, is that this scenario is only really convincing for ANGER and perhaps for other negative emotions like DISGUST/HATE, for which similar metaphors apply. In the case of FEAR the scenario only works smoothly if we concentrate on flight as the resulting action and forget about the alternative that we may feel paralyzed by fear. More problematic still are positive emotion concepts like JOY. Here Kövecses argues that control is motivated by social constraints, which keep us from exhibiting JOY. With regard to LOVE even Kövecses admits that ROMANTIC LOVE, which he propagates as the 'ideal model', lacks a cause and also the aspect of control because loss of control is immediate and unexplainable. To save the blueprint of the emotion scenario, he establishes the 'typical model' (LOVE LEADING TO MARRIAGE) as an alternative to ROMANTIC LOVE, claiming that it includes control and that love is channelled into the action of marriage. It seems, then, that the scenario idea is a quite powerful descriptive tool in the case of ANGER and other negative emotions (though with limitations). For positive emotions like JOY and LOVE, however, it is much more difficult to cast the structure of the categories into this format. An additional problem with the scenarios offered by Kövecses and Lakoff is that they do not account for all the metonymies or metaphors available for the various emotion concepts.

Finally, taking a more general view of the issue, this discussion of emotion scenarios and prototypicality has made it obvious that the structure of emotion concepts is far from clear. Nevertheless, cognitive linguistics has opened up new avenues of investigation which have so far led to the following observations:

- Emotion concepts are structured by metonymic links with physiological effects.
- Triggered off by these metonymies, metaphorical links are established with concrete basic level concepts, which also contribute heavily to the conceptual structure of emotions.
- The contribution of metaphors is essential with emotion concepts such as JOY and LOVE, which are supported by fewer physiological metonymies.
- Some emotion concepts, especially concepts of negative emotions like ANGER and FEAR, can be understood as scenarios involving the stages of cause, actual emotion, control, loss of control and resulting action. For

positive emotions like JOY and LOVE this type of cognitive model is less convincing.

- There is linguistic and empirical psychological evidence that a set of about six emotions concepts (SADNESS, ANGER, DISGUST/HATE, FEAR, JOY/HAPPINESS and DESIRE/LOVE) may be regarded as basic, and that there are certain parallels between this basic status and concrete basic level concepts.

Exercises

1. The introductory passage of this chapter gives a rough sketch of ANGER and FEAR in terms of metonymies and metaphors. Give a similar account of SADNESS and DISGUST/HATE. Does your description fit the scenario developed in Figure 3.13?

2. In Exercise 1 in Section 3.1 you were asked to point out which parts of the body are favoured as source concepts for metaphors and metonymies. Focusing now on emotions, analyze the list of metonymies in Figure 3.9 in terms of source concepts. Try to find reasons why certain parts and aspects of the body are preferred as source concepts for emotions.

3. If your native language is not English, try to find out what the basic emotion terms in your language and culture are and compare them with the English terms discussed here.

4. Examine the following emotion concepts: PRIDE, ADMIRATION, GRATITUDE, PITY, EMBARRASSMENT, SHAME, GUILT. Can you see a close relationship between these concepts and any of the basic emotion concepts? Find reasons why they are less basic.

5. Look up definitions of emotion terms like *anger, rage, hate, disgust, fear, panic, love, affection* in several dictionaries and decide whether they are helpful as descriptions of these emotions. Do these definitions make use of metonymies and metaphors?

3.3 Metaphors as a way of thinking: examples from science and politics

If metaphors are not just stylistic ornaments, but a way of thinking, there is no reason why this potential should only be used to structure concepts underlying certain abstract words, and why it should not show up in the way we approach the complex scientific, political and social issues of our world. So cognitive linguists have joined philosophers in investigating these more general effects of conceptual metaphors.

Metaphors are rich in the sense that they do not just link up two isolated items but rather connect multi-faceted categories or cognitive models. To pick up just one of the simpler examples we have discussed (see Section 3.1), the metaphor +AN ARGUMENT IS A BUILDING+ is based on a source concept (BUILDING) which provides a tangible gestalt and a wealth of attributes. A building has foundations, it consists of walls, windows and a roof, it is normally constructed solidly and will then provide safe protection, yet it may be assembled sloppily, and in this case the walls may come apart and the whole structure is likely to collapse. All these characteristics of buildings can be mapped onto the target concept and may help us to conceptualize – and also to explain – the abstract notion 'argument'.

This second aspect, the explanatory potential of metaphors, has not escaped the attention of linguists, who are always looking for explanatory tools.

Metaphors and the description of linguistic phenomena

A striking example of how metaphors are employed in linguistic description is Langacker's (1987a: 452ff) use of the +BUILDING BLOCK+ and +SCAFFOLDING+ metaphors, which are part of his analysis of compounds and composite expressions (a topic discussed in Section 2.3). His starting point is a harsh criticism of the +BUILDING BLOCK+ metaphor, which, according to Langacker, 'sees the meaning of a composite expression as being constructed out of the meanings of its parts simply by stacking them together in some appropriate fashion' (1987a: 452). Applied to compounds like *apple juice* or *wheelchair* (our examples in Section 2.3), the +BUILDING BLOCK+ metaphor suggests that we regard the words *apple* and *juice* or *wheel* and *chair* as the building materials from which we construct the compounds just as we use bricks or concrete or wooden blocks in constructing a house (or perhaps a toy house). The blocks may be large or small, they may be placed side by side or on top of each other, they may be linked by a layer of mortar or nailed or screwed together, but whichever variant we prefer, the essential explanatory message is that these two words and their underlying concepts constitute the compound. Since, as we have seen, this is not at all convincing in the case of *wheelchair*, it is understandable that Langacker is not prepared to accept the +BUILDING BLOCK+ metaphor as a reliable explanation of composition.

However, being a cognitive linguist, he realizes that this metaphor is a powerful explanatory tool which cannot be defeated by only offering an abstract alternative explanation in terms of compositionality and analyzability, which is Langacker's real goal. This is why he offers an alternative metaphor, the +SCAFFOLDING+ metaphor, which suggests that the constituents of the compound (e.g. *wheel* and *chair*) and their concepts are to a large extent mere scaffolding for the construction job at hand. As we know, the concept WHEELCHAIR has derived so many attributes from other source concepts that the contribution of WHEEL and CHAIR has become less and less important. In the case of NEWSPAPER or AIRPLANE this process has reached a stage where the scaffolding is superfluous and can be removed. Needless to say, the SCAFFOLDING concept is also rich in detail and well suited to counter and supersede the building block explanation.

Word-formation aside, Langacker has also provided important metaphors for syntactic processes, which will be discussed in Section 4.2. Here we will have a look at another metaphorical explanation that was crucial in our description of lexical categories and was then called the principle of family resemblance (Section 1.2). It is not difficult to see that this 'principle' is based on the metaphor +THE MEMBERS OF A CATEGORY ARE A FAMILY+, and this explains both its power and its vagueness. The family resemblance principle is so powerful because FAMILY is a very rich source concept and also one that is salient as far as the categorization of persons goes. The FAMILY concept suggests all sorts of resemblances – those concerning the outward appearance of face or body, similar behaviour and similar speech habits, but it also allows for larger or smaller differences between individual family members. This makes it easy to see the +FAMILY+ metaphor as a flexible alternative to a rigid definition of category membership.

A possible disadvantage is that family resemblance can mean several things. It may refer to the fact that the members of some categories apparently do not share a single attribute (this is Wittgenstein's notion), or it may refer to the rich overall relationship between family members that includes category-wide attributes (this underlies the interpretation of Rosch and Mervis's 'measure of family resemblance'). If we want to be more precise, we will have to distinguish between the definition of family resemblance as a relationship of the AB BC CD type (with A, B, C, and D designating attributes) and an alternative interpretation as Σatt_{cat} (i.e. the sum of all attributes of the category).

Leaving the area of cognitive linguistics we find that many other linguistic approaches make use of explanatory metaphors. The structuralist notions of 'distribution' and 'immediacy' are both based on spatial metaphors

(+ELEMENTS DISTRIBUTED ARE OBJECTS SPREAD OUT+, +IMMEDIATE CONSTITUENTS ARE OBJECTS CLOSE TOGETHER+), transformational grammar has the metaphorical notions of embedding, nesting and transformation, to mention just a few. Valency grammar has borrowed the metaphor +THE VALENCY OF AN ELEMENT IS THE STRENGTH OF AN OBJECT+ from an earlier adaptation of this metaphor to chemistry. As with our examples from cognitive linguistics, the explanation contained in the metaphors can still be given in an alternative, usually more abstract, way.

This is no longer certain when we turn to what may be regarded as the most powerful metaphor that has sprung from the description of language, the +PREDICATE+ metaphor. This metaphor transfers an age-old source concept (*predicate* means 'that which is said about the subject', OED) from grammatical description to related disciplines like logic and artificial intelligence. In its simplest version this metaphor exploits the fact that in a sentence like *Peter is working*, the predicate *is working* makes a statement about the subject *Peter*. The concepts PREDICATE and SUBJECT and the relation between them are so well known that they can certainly be considered as being part of a naive folk model of grammar as it is taught in schools. The familiarity and richness of the link between PREDICATE and SUBJECT make it possible that the two concepts can act as source concepts when it comes to describing the more abstract relationship which is assumed to exist between the target concepts (LOGICAL) PREDICATE and (LOGICAL) ARGUMENT in the field of logic. Here the vagueness and openness of a metaphor can be very helpful, because logical predicates are not necessarily verbs and logical arguments are not necessarily noun phrases, but both stand for a much more abstract way of looking at language.

It is by virtue of this abstractness that it may in fact be difficult to find an alternative explanation for the relationship between a logical predicate and its arguments that has the same explanatory power as the information supplied by the +PREDICATE+ metaphor. So we reach a stage where the metaphor does more than just render an abstract concept more tangible; the metaphor actually seems to make up the abstract concept. Or, as the philosopher Boyd has put it, we arrive at a point where metaphors are 'constitutive of the theories they express rather than merely exegetical' (Boyd 1993: 486).

Metaphors in science: explanatory or constitutive?

As Boyd and others have shown,[16] metaphors are omnipresent in science. Many of them have primarily been introduced for exegetical (i.e. explanatory) purposes. This seems to be especially true of most metaphors used in computer science. Thus many user-friendly programs provide a surface screen which establishes a metaphorical link with the concept OFFICE. The screen is a desktop that can be tidied up, there are folders for filing items, a clipboard where items can be temporarily stored, windows that can be opened and closed, and a trash can into which superfluous items are dropped. It is only when we compare these simple but rich explanations of programming functions with the kind of non-metaphorical, often abbreviated commands employed in specialist programs (e.g. CLS for 'clear screen', MD for 'make directory' or RD for 'remove directory') that the pedagogic value of the metaphor +COMPUTER WORK IS OFFICE WORK+ becomes really obvious.

In addition to metaphors based on the office context, programmes make use of animal and illness metaphors. An example is the concept COMPUTER MOUSE, where the metaphor admirably maps outward appearance and possible movements of the animal onto the concept of this trackball tool (as it was originally called) without actually explaining the abstract principle behind it.

Another area of metaphorical explanation is the malfunctioning of computer programs. Probably the oldest metaphor in this field is the +BUG+ metaphor, which we use quite naturally when something has gone wrong in the program. More complex and also more threatening is the +VIRUS+ metaphor, which has joined the computer vocabulary together with +WORM+. In the case of +VIRUS+ what goes wrong with a computer is linked with the mysterious and invisible spread of viruses which cause an infection in the body of humans or animals. Though ordinary language users will not know much about the organism called virus, they may have a rich if indirect experience of its unpleasant effects on humans and animals, and this source concept is mapped onto the target concept of the computer virus. The result is similar to what we encountered in the case of the +FAMILY+ metaphor (which underlies the family resemblance principle). The metaphorical explanation may ultimately remain vague, but it seems to satisfy the conceptual needs of average computer users, so for them these metaphors do not just fulfil an explanatory function but are constitutive for the conceptualization of computer malfunctioning.

Computer scientists will, of course, look for more precise explanations and will regard the +VIRUS+ metaphor as a helpful tool when confronted with lay audiences. So for them, the +VIRUS+ metaphor and other metaphors in the field of computers are exegetic, not constitutive in Boyd's sense. Yet as Kuhn (1993: 538) claims, there are areas of natural science where metaphors seem to be constitutive not just for popular, but also for scientific models. His example is the orbit model of the atom consisting of nucleus and electrons as developed by the physicist Bohr. For a start, this model can be conveniently explained by comparing the arrangement of nucleus and electrons with the interaction between the sun and the planets, in other words, by making use of the metaphor +THE ATOM IS A (MINIATURE) SOLAR SYSTEM+. This is shown in Figure 3.14, where the metaphorical correspondences are indicated in more detail.

For the layman the situation is probably similar to the case of the +VIRUS+ metaphor in computer science. The +SOLAR SYSTEM+ metaphor provides a helpful explanation and may have contributed substantially to the popular theory about the model of the atom, so for the non-specialist it was (and probably is) both explanatory and constitutive.

In contrast with the popular explanation, Bohr's scientific definition of nucleus and electrons was in terms of bits of charged matter, which were thought to interact under the laws of mechanics and electromagnetic theory. It was the task of the physicists to determine which of these laws applied, and this finally led to the establishment of the quantum theory. However, the physicists did not work non-metaphorically; they also used a model which was ultimately based on a comparison of nucleus and electrons with small pingpong or billiard balls, so it looked pretty much like the one presented in Figure 3.14. The difference from the layman's view was that the scientists did not use the crude metaphor +NUCLEUS AND ELECTRONS ARE PINGPONG BALLS+ as an explanation of the atom. Rather the metaphor was used as a yardstick against which the specific mechanical and electromagnetic behaviour of nucleus and electrons was measured. As far as this yardstick function goes, and this is Kuhn's claim, the +PINGPONG BALL+ metaphor was not just an explanatory tool, but was constitutive to the theory. According to Kuhn, more recent mathematical descriptions of complex atoms and molecules still depend on this model, which integrates these metaphorical elements.

All in all, while the explanatory function of metaphors and their constitutive function in popular scientific theories can be taken for granted,

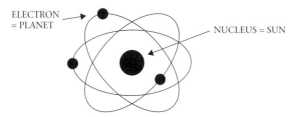

Figure 3.14 The structure of the atom as explained by the metaphor +THE ATOM IS A (MINIATURE) SOLAR SYSTEM+

there is also some evidence that conceptual metaphors may have a constitutive function in more theoretical scientific approaches. We may even speculate whether the central scientific issues of today, such as the big bang theory of the beginnings of the universe, do not incorporate a metaphorical component, or, in plain words, whether the big bang theory does not to some extent make use of the mental concept we have of an EXPLOSION.[17]

Two cognitive linguists and philosophers who would probably support this speculation wholeheartedly are Lakoff and Johnson (1999). In their ambitious and provocative book, they propagate, among other things, the metaphorical explanation of much of traditional philosophy and outline 'embodied philosophy' as an alternative, for which metaphors are clearly constitutive and together with our basic experiences determine our thinking and philosophical thought.[18]

Conceptual metaphors in politics

Much more than science and even philosophy, politics is an area in which we would expect metaphorical expressions to be used. Indeed, political speech is one of the recognized types of classical rhetoric, of which metaphors are an integral part. This rhetorical background is something to keep in mind when we transfer Boyd's distinction of explanatory and constitutive metaphors from science to politics.

Since the purpose of political rhetoric is persuasion, or, more bluntly, the manipulation of the public, the explanatory potential of metaphors is often less important than their emotional impact. Indeed, the metaphors favoured by many politicians combine a very simple explanation with strong emotional effects. Prime candidates are metaphorical links with simple event concepts, such as natural force concepts like WIND, which are reflected in the abundant 'wind-of-change' speeches. Another favourite source concept is ILLNESS; the metaphor +THE COUNTRY IS A PERSON THAT IS ILL+ has been stock-in-trade for politicians since it was used in Gaunt's speech in Shakespeare's *Richard II*. Examples from the past decades are the speeches of Neil Kinnock, former Labour Party leader, who liked to combine the +ILLNESS+ metaphor with the +PART/WHOLE+ metonymy in a way that strangely fits the present situation in many European countries:

> Ailments in a country gradually stain the whole country.
> If limbs are severely damaged the whole body is disabled. If regions are left to rot the whole country is weakened.

Unemployment is a contagious disease. It doesn't stop at the borders of economic regions. It infects the whole economic body.

There is no . . . vaccine to inoculate the country against the spread of shut down.

As Wilson (1990: 128f), who collected these examples, rightly claims, we may not be particularly affected by single examples of these metaphors, but if they are repeated often enough we come to accept their message. In cognitive terminology this means that political audiences and the public in general do tend to submit to powerful metaphors like the +ILLNESS+ metaphor, and after some time will regard these metaphors as constitutive parts of their conceptual framework, especially when faced with complex political, economic and social problems. In other words, just like the computer user the average voter is often happy with a theory based on a rich, though rather vague, metaphor.

But what about the 'specialists', the politicians? Are they also convinced of their own metaphors or do they sharply distinguish between explanatory metaphors and theories based on non-metaphorical factual analysis, as is the rule in science? Surely there cannot be a single answer to this question. If the icily calculating propagandist is not a mere invention (and there is little reason to assume that he is), we must conclude that political metaphors which are designed to structure people's thinking are not necessarily shared by their creators and do not function as constitutive elements in their thinking.

Yet we may assume that there are many politicians (and also administrators and political journalists) whose thinking is in fact influenced by their own or by other people's metaphors. The classic study of the problem is Lakoff's (1992) analysis of metaphors used to justify the Gulf War in 1991.[19] What he found particularly interesting and at the same time highly dangerous is that not only the layman's thinking, but also the argumentation of the specialist, is structured by a set of conceptual metaphors which he calls 'expert metaphors'.

At the centre of this system is a metaphor first coined by the Prussian general Clausewitz, +WAR IS POLITICS PURSUED BY OTHER MEANS+, and closely linked to it, the metaphor +POLITICS IS BUSINESS+. Just by looking at these metaphors it becomes clear that their main effect is to reduce the concept WAR to the level of two quite normal and essentially harmless human activities, politics and business. Like politics, war is a matter of formulating positions, of finding allies and keeping opponents at bay and of convincing the public, and this again presupposes the notions of selling one's ideas, of negotiating the price, of providing the goods, and other aspects of doing business. On a more technical level the +POLITICS+ metaphor and the +BUSINESS+ metaphor fuse into the metaphor +WAR IS A COST/BENEFIT ANALYSIS+, which brings in the notions of accountancy and sober economic evaluation. The impression of normality, harmlessness and accountability which is thus created is further enhanced by a number of additional metaphors. Their purpose is, among other things, to turn problematic actions like enforcing sanctions into an innocent give-and-take and the risks of war into a gamble that can be controlled by mathematical probability calculation and game theory.

Relying on these convenient metaphors, politicians and military commanders do not see, or do not want to see, what these metaphors hide: the reality of pain and death, the long-term health effects for the injured, the psychological effect on veterans, the environmental effects, not to mention the moral aspects of war. A second metaphor, again innocent on the surface, is no less dangerous: the metaphor +THE STATE IS A (SINGLE) PERSON+. While opening up the rich source concept PERSON (or HUMAN BEING) which is healthy, strong, has a home, neighbours, friends and enemies, the metaphor hides the internal diversity of the country, the roles played by ethnic and religious groups, political parties and the big corporations; in other words, it justifies the claim that there is always an overriding unifying national interest which is often pursued at the expense of powerless minorities.

Since the early 1990s Lakoff has widened the scope of his politically oriented cognitive analysis in an attempt to capture the different world-views of American Conservatives and Liberals (Lakoff 2002, 2004). Starting from two contrasting cognitive models of the family, the STRICT FATHER model and the NURTURANT PARENT model, he assembles sets of metaphors to explain Conservative and Liberal morality, which he finds reflected in the stance taken by Conservatives and Liberals towards major political issues. Thus the STRICT FATHER model gives rise to metaphors like +MORALITY IS STRENGTH+, +MORAL AUTHORITY IS PARENTAL AUTHORITY+ and +MORAL ACTION IS A MOVEMENT ALONG PERMISSIBLE PATHS+, while the NURTURANT PARENT model is supported by metaphors like +MORALITY IS EMPATHY+, +MORALITY IS HAPPINESS+ and +MORALITY IS FAIR DISTRIBUTION+. Although Lakoff stresses the objectivity of his analysis in terms of metaphors, the above selection makes it clear where his preferences lie and that he is concerned about the rise of Conservatism in the US during the last decade.[20]

For someone who has followed our essentially positive account of the 'structuring power' of metaphors and metonymies so far, Lakoff's observations may come as a surprise. What was at first celebrated as a rich conceptual contribution to our understanding of the world is now seen as something more ambiguous, creating not only positive but also negative effects. Like their more pleasant counterparts, the negative exploitations of metaphors merely strengthen the view that metaphors are very powerful and natural cognitive processes which help us to understand the complex issues in nature and society via simple and often concrete concepts.

To conclude this discussion of explanatory and constitutive metaphors here is a summary of the main points:

- Conceptual metaphors can aid our thinking in two ways: as explanatory or constitutive metaphors. Explanatory metaphors are used to make it easier for the layman to understand complex scientific, political and social issues. Constitutive metaphors are an integral part of theorizing about these problems.

- While popular theories about natural phenomena tend to rely on constitutive metaphors, scientific theorizing is primarily non-metaphorical, but may also make use of some metaphorical elements.

- In politics, the explanatory function of metaphors is often subjected to the goal of manipulation, which means that metaphors are often primarily selected for their emotional effects.

- Popular political thinking largely depends on constitutive metaphors, which are often consciously created and fostered by politicians and propagandists.

- Political theorizing is also frequently based on constitutive metaphors, and since these metaphors may disguise important aspects of the issue that should have been considered, the effect may be negative and destructive.

Exercises

1. Identify the metaphors underlying the following terms used in word-formation analysis and (traditional) grammatical descriptions:
   clipping, blend, portmanteau word, question tag, cleft sentence, contact clause (for certain types of relative clauses).

2. Collect explanations from science that are based on metaphors, such as *the heart is a pump, mitochondria are the cell's power stations* and *the DNA is the genetic code,* and discuss whether they are mainly used as an explicatory crutch (explanatory metaphors) or actually make up the underlying principle of the scientific problem in question (constitutive metaphors)?

3. Consider how certain metaphors influence our approach towards technological and social problems, e.g. how our view of TRAFFIC differs depending on whether it is based on the metaphor +TRAFFIC IS A RIVER+ or +TRAFFIC LINKS PLACES+ or +TRAFFIC IS A DANGEROUS ANIMAL+. Try to find other examples illustrating the influence of metaphors on our way of thinking.

4. Find examples showing how politicians paraphrase a dangerous or at least negative situation by using harmless metaphors. Pursue the idea in newspapers and TV programmes and collect the metaphors.

5. Study the metaphors in the inaugural addresses of American presidents, starting perhaps with Kennedy's address, and decide which of the metaphors are explanatory and which are constitutive.

3.4 Thinking in metonymies: potential and limitations

Since, just like metaphors, metonymies can be understood as cognitive instruments, or less technically, as a way of thinking, the temptation to use them for explanatory purposes has been great. However, genuine conceptual metonymies are restricted to stand-for links based on a small range of basic experiences and are only effective within a suitable mapping scope, and this seems to limit their explanatory potential.

Like metaphor, metonymy is considered a cognitive process underlying linguistic phenomena and motivating them. Yet while the wealth of attributes mapped in the process of metaphor can form themes that can be exploited and sustained in large sections of texts, the potential of metonymy is more limited. As shown in Section 3.1, the application of contiguity relations or image schemas such as 'part–whole', 'place–person or event', 'cause–effect', 'container–contained' produces a successful stand-for relationship only if the metonymic link is established between concepts supporting a suitable mapping scope (which is prototypically equivalent with a cognitive model; one example was the WHITE HOUSE standing for PRESIDENT in the mapping scope 'US administration').

This should be kept in mind when we go beyond lexical examples of the +WHITE HOUSE+ type, for which metonymies have been traditionally claimed, and consider recent attempts of applying metonymy to a whole range of other linguistic phenomena from such diverse fields as word-formation processes and speech acts.[21]

Metonymy and word-formation

One word-formation type that can be plausibly traced back to a metonymic process are possessive compounds such as *skinhead* or *paperback*. Here a cognitive approach sees the product of the compounding process as describing an interesting feature of a set of entities (that their head is bald or that only paper, and not cloth, is used as material for a book cover). The reason why this particular feature is used to refer to the whole person or object is due to the metonymy +SALIENT FEATURE FOR PERSON/OBJECT+, which can be understood as an application of the 'part–whole' image schema. However, for the metonymy to function properly, the relation between attribute and person/object alone is not sufficient: it is essential that the person or object must be a member of an identifiable and socially accepted concept, which serves as mapping scope for the metonymy. Potential ad-hoc metonymies like *brownhead or *brownhair only work in specific situations but not in general, because there is no socially relevant group of brown-haired people (and therefore no accepted mapping scope). Skinheads, on the other hand, are not only known for their bald heads, but what is more important is the social stereotype about their shared properties (e.g. that they tend to be violent, aggressive and racist). Thus the concept SKINHEAD is motivated by a salient feature standing for a type of person, because both the attribute 'bald head' and the concept PERSON are part of a mapping scope based on the cognitive model SOCIAL GROUP. The concept PAPERBACK is taken to stand for BOOK because both concepts have something to do with the mapping scope focused on print media. Another popular metonymy is +BODILY FEATURE FOR SPECIES+ (e.g. *redbreast, bluethroat, longhorn*) for which the cognitive model ANIMAL functions as mapping scope.

Metonymy is also responsible for another linguistic process that has been traditionally claimed for word-formation: the process of conversion, i.e. occurrence of formally identical words in several word classes such as *mail* (N) – *mail* (V) or *backup* (N) – *backup* (V). Probably the largest group among them are noun–verb conversions like *author* (*a book*), *ski* (*down a hill*), *dust* (*the room*) and the other examples listed in Figure 3.15. As is indicated in the figure and was first suggested by Dirven (1999),[22] conversions of this type also seem to be based on metonymic stand-for relationships: +AGENT FOR ACTION+, +INSTRUMENT FOR ACTION+, +OBJECT FOR ACTION+ and +BODY PART FOR ACTION+. These metonymies, which can be subsumed under the more general metonymy +PARTICIPANTS FOR ACTION/EVENT+, are yet another example of the application of the 'part–whole' relation. They function so effortlessly

Metonymies	Mapping scopes	Examples
+AGENT FOR ACTION+:	'kinship' 'teaching' 'print media'	to *father* a child to *tutor* a student to *author* a new book
+INSTRUMENT FOR ACTION+:	'winter sports' 'workmanship' and 'do-it-yourself'	to *ski* down the hill to *hammer* the nail into the wall to *saw off* a branch
+OBJECT FOR ACTION+:	'household chores' 'food preparation' and 'cooking' or 'seasoning'	to *blanket* the bed to *dust* the room to *scale* the fish to *pepper* the dish
+BODY PART FOR ACTION+:	'careful, sympathizing behaviour' 'rough and ruthless social behaviour'	to *tiptoe* into the room to *elbow* s.o. out of the way

Figure 3.15 Examples of +PARTICIPANT FOR ACTION+ metonymies
extracted from Radden and Kövecses (1999: 37) and Schmid (2005, ch. 10)

because in each case the activated basic relation creates a link between two concepts which are safely anchored in familiar and situationally relevant mapping scopes (see Section 3.1). This can be shown by comparing pairs of suitable and unsuitable mapping scopes:

(1a) Julia peppered the curry. – Julia dropped pepper on the curry.

(1b) ? Julia peppered the table. – Julia dropped pepper on the table.

(2a) Sue has authored two novels. – Sue has written two novels.

(2b) ? Sue has authored a computer program. – Sue has written a computer program.

(3a) He fathered a baby. – He is the father of the baby.

(3b) ? He fathered the project. – He is the father of the project.

Examples (1a) and (1b) show that merely dropping pepper somewhere does not licence a metonymical reading of the substance *pepper* as an activity. What seems to be crucial is that the activity is part of a seasoning context or more generally a mapping scope 'food preparation'. Similarly the verb *author* only lends itself to metonymic uses that are synonymous with the verb *write* within the mapping scope 'print media' (but not necessarily in the mapping scope 'computer work' or 'software engineering'). Kinship seems to be a necessary ingredient of the mapping scope licensing the metonymical use of *father* in (3a), despite the possibility of using the word *baby* metaphorically to refer to a plan or project in (3b) which automatically calls up a different mapping scope (suggesting attributes both of the father and the business context).

This combination of different cognitive models in an overarching or only selective mapping scope is possible and explains cases like *hammer the nail*, which can be interpreted against a background of professional workmanship or amateurish do-it-yourself competence. With examples like *tiptoeing into the room* or *elbowing s.o. out of the way* the mapping scope can no longer be safely tied to a specific cognitive model (a possibility already indicated in Section 3.1). What plays a crucial role in the mapping scope of these metonymies is the motive for the specific way of locomotion, labelled tentatively as 'careful, sympathizing behaviour' or 'rough and ruthless social behaviour' in Figure 3.15. One reason why a metonymic conversion of, say, *heel* does not work (?*she heeled into the room*) is that we cannot think of a plausible motive for such a manner of walking which could serve as an appropriate mapping scope. Of course, the discourse context can provide such a mapping scope licensing an ad-hoc metonymy, e.g. if someone says *the doctor asked me to tiptoe and heel through the room because she wanted to see if my calf muscles were working properly.*

To sum up at this point, conversions can be understood as metonymies supported by mapping scopes which are either identical with a cognitive model or at least related to one or several of these models – all these variants are illustrated in Figure 3.15.

The metonymic background of speech acts

Looking back, the examples of word-formation phenomena discussed so far have still been quite similar to the stock examples of the metonymic use of simple lexical items or names (*hands on deck*, *White House* for *president*) in that they have been restricted to a 'local' application of metonymy within familiar or easily available cognitive models. This is different when we move on to pragmatic phenomena that have also been selected for metonymic treatment.

A good example is Thornburg and Panther's attempt to explain conventionalized indirect speech acts like the classic *Can you pass me the salt?*[23] As claimed by the two authors, these speech acts are to be understood as instantiations of the metonymy +ABILITY FOR ACTION+, which is regarded as an elaboration of the more general metonymy +POTENTIALITY FOR ACTUALITY+. There can be no doubt that the observation is correct: as already noted by Searle (1975: 174), one can use a question concerning the ability to carry out an action (*Can you pass the salt?*) to ask for the performance of the action itself ('pass the salt'). Yet there are two problems: the first is whether one can really claim that the rather abstract relationship +ABILITY FOR ACTION+ fulfils the condition of a prototypical conceptual metonymy. To justify this status one would have to assume a very general mapping scope indeed, something like 'our experience of the world', which could then be said to include both actions and abilities. The second problem is that the metonymic explanation would make it difficult to integrate other speech act conditions, among them intentionality and politeness, which also deserve consideration. Yet even if we are hesitant to subscribe to the far-reaching claims of a metonymic explanation of speech acts, it cannot be doubted that stressing the cognitive link between ability and action con-tributes its share to a better understanding of this pragmatic phenomenon.

In this chapter, then, we have argued that metonymy appears to be involved as a cognitive process in linguistic phenomena that have been treated in diverse ways in different fields of linguistics. Possessive compounds (*skinhead, redbreast*), noun–verb conversions (*to author a book*) and even con-ventionalized speech acts were shown to be at least describable in terms of metonymic mappings. What this discussion has confirmed is that the suc-cess of any metonymy depends on the availability of a cognitive model or some other kind of conceptual background serving as a mapping scope acces-sible to the language users (either by retrieval from long-term memory or by current activation in the discourse situation).

Exercises

1. Which type of stand-for relationship is involved in the following pos-sessive compounds: *greybeard, redskin, redbreast, bluebell, lazy-bones, five-finger, laptop, pick-up, hide-out* and *drop-out*. Suggest mapping scopes in which these items seem to function well as metonymies.

2. It has been claimed (Ungerer 2002: 551–4) that the italicized words in the following expressions should not only be regarded as derivations (*government* 'the act of governing' < *govern* + *-ment, development* 'the pro-cess of developing' < *develop* + *-ment*). In addition these items may involve a metonymy, for example: *government* 'the act of governing' stands for

'a group of people who do the governing', *(housing) development*: 'the process of developing' stands for the result, the housing estate. Analyze the following examples and suggest metonymic links: the meeting of the *management*, the first *detachment of the army*, the *US Administration*, a typed *announcement*, the *introduction* of this book, a valuable *collection* of Impressionists.

3. In the text the metonymic interpretation of conversion is restricted to noun-verb transformations. Find out if it makes sense to extend the analysis to verb–noun conversion as well, e.g. by explaining the noun *(tennis) coach* as an application of the metonymy +ACTION FOR AGENT+.
Apart from +ACTION FOR AGENT+, consider the metonymies +ACTION FOR EVENT+, +ACTION FOR INSTRUMENT+ and +ACTION FOR PLACE+ and try to assign the following nouns to these metonymies:
cheat, cover, divide, drive-in, hit, laugh, lay-by, retreat, rise, shut-down, stand-in, swim, turn, walk-out, wrap.

Suggestions for further reading

Section 3.1

To gain a first impression of the cognitive metaphor analysis, Lakoff and Johnson's seminal book *Metaphors We Live By* (1980/2003) is still the prime choice. The 2003 edition is a reprint of the original book with an afterword summarizing recent developments in the field. Another book in the same vein is Lakoff and Turner (1989). A condensed account of Lakoff's theory combined with a critical review of his findings is offered by Croft and Cruse (2004: 194–204), but is more suitable for advanced students. Kövecses (2002) provides an insightful practical introduction to the cognitive metaphor theory. For an overview of metonymy see Barcelona (2003).

1. For interesting aspects of children's ability and propensity to use metaphorical expressions see Elbers (1988) and Nerlich *et al.* (2002).

2. The earliest discussions of metaphor from a linguistic perspective that we know of are Ullmann (1957, 1st edn 1951) and Leech (1969).

3. Definitions of metonymy in terms of contiguity of referents, and collections of types of metonymies can be found in Ullmann (1962: 218ff), Lakoff and Johnson (1980/2003: 38f), Lipka (1988: 360f).

4. A useful survey of the major theories of metaphor is provided by Gibbs (1994: ch. 6). Applications of the interaction theory can be

found in Ullmann (1962) and Lipka (1988), and especially Leech (1969). For the function of metaphor in literary discourse processing see also Steen (1994, ch. 2).

5. For more information about metaphors arising from body parts in English and other languages, compare Steen (1994). Kövecses (2002, chs 12 and 13) as well as Kövecses (2005) delve deeper into the intriguing question of the universality vs. cultural relativity of conceptual metaphors.

6. Although *mapping scope* is a new term, it takes up and integrates suggestions of early metaphor research and offers easy access to more recent findings. Compare the discussion of the grounding of metaphors in Lakoff and Johnson (1980/2003: 61ff, 117ff) and Lakoff and Turner (1989: 113ff). Also related are the perspectivizing, highlighting and hiding potential of metaphorical mappings discussed in Lakoff and Johnson (1980/2003: 10ff), Lakoff and Turner (1989: 64ff) and Croft (1993) as well as the invariance hypothesis proposed by Brugman (1990) and Lakoff (1990, 1993). See also Croft and Cruse (2004: 204–6) on the 'life story' of a metaphor and Stern (1999: 9ff) on contextual conditions underlying metaphorical mapping.

7. Compare Hampe's (2005: 55) concept of 'experiential correlations'. Other concepts in the cognitive-linguistic literature that are similar to basic experiential correlations but serve different functions in the respective frameworks are Grady's (1997, 1999, Grady and Johnson 2002) 'primary metaphors' and some of Fauconnier and Turner's (2002) 'vital relations' (see Section 6.1).

8. See Ruiz de Mendoza Ibañez (2000) for details of his distinction between one-correspondence and many-correspondence metaphors.

9. Using this limited notion of mapping scope seems more helpful for a first understanding of metonymy than postulating highly abstract domains (such as 'production', 'causation', 'control', 'institution', 'action' or 'whole entity'; Kövecses 2002: 147), and monitoring the production of successful metonymies by a range of general constraints ('human over non-human', 'concrete over abstract', 'good gestalt over poor gestalt', etc.). See Kövecses and Radden 1998 (and later publications of these authors) as well as Barcelona (2000: 12ff; 2003: 243f).

10. The interaction of metaphors and metonymies has been keenly investigated during the last few years. Important research on this

topic is contained in volumes edited by Panther and Radden (1999), Barcelona (2000), and Dirven and Pörings (2002). The latter volume also contains revised versions of well-known earlier publications, for instance Jakobson and Halle's (1956) paper on metaphorical and metonymic poles, Goossens (1990) and Croft (1993). For a concise discussion see Croft and Cruse (2004: 216–20).

Section 3.2

This section is mainly based on publications by Kövecses (1990, 1991, 1995) and on Lakoff's account of ANGER (Lakoff 1987: 380ff). Basically, all of them make good, but sometimes repetitive, reading. See also the overview in Kövecses (2000, ch. 2).

11. For a short overview of various emotion theories see Johnson-Laird and Oatley (1989). Closer to the concerns of cognitive linguistics are Fehr and Russell (1984) and Shaver *et al.* (1987). A more recent account of the research situation is provided by Kövecses (2002) and (2005).

12. While this system was devised for English, universal aspects of physiological effects and the cross-cultural use of the container metaphor are discussed by Kövecses (1995; 2000, ch. 8) and, within her terminology of cultural scripts, by Wierzbicka (1986, 1988); for a recent introduction to cultural scripts see Goddard and Wierzbicka (2004).

13. In view of the introductory character of this book we do not want to give an account of Lakoff's system of ontological and epistemic correspondences between the source and target concepts of ANGER metaphors; see Lakoff (1987: 386ff).

14. For a short (but unnecessarily critical) overview of various approaches to basic emotions see Ortony *et al.* (1988: 25ff). See also Johnson-Laird and Oatley (1989) and the summary in Kövecses (2000, ch. 1).

15. A more recent variant of the scenario conception proposed by Kövecses (2000, chs 5 and 10) is based on Talmy's theory of force dynamics (Talmy 2000/I, ch. 7) and makes use of his terminology of agonist and antagonist to describe the functioning of emotion metaphors, calling force the 'master metaphor' for emotion.

Section 3.3

16. See Boyd (1993) and Kuhn (1993) and also Schön (1993), whose notion of 'generative metaphor' is very similar to Boyd's constitutive metaphor. Gentner (1982) also examines scientific metaphors and,

among other examples, discusses the solar system metaphor described below. See also Gibbs's overview chapter on 'metaphor in thought' (Gibbs 1994, ch. 4).

17. For discussions of the role of metaphors in the history of science and in the teaching of science see Gentner and Jeziorski (1993) and Mayer (1993).

18. Seen from a linguistic angle, chapters 3 to 5 of Lakoff and Johnson (1999) provide an overview of the conceptual tools used in the analysis. Ch. 10 offers a detailed case study of the metaphorical concepts of time. The philosophical provocation is strongest in Part III, where the authors supply sweeping judgements on philosophers from the pre-Socractic thinkers to Chomsky and juxtapose their own metaphor-based 'embodied philosophy'.

19. Lakoff's (1992) article is a committed piece of writing, which he applied to the Gulf War II in a short internet publication (Lakoff 2003). Lakoff (1992) also sparked off other investigations in the field, among them Gibbs (1994, ch. 4) and Sandikcioglu (2000). Compare Musolff's (2001) analysis of +PATH+ and +TRANSPORT+ metaphors used by newspapers to describe the process of European unification.

20. Lakoff (2002, 1st edn 1996) is divided up into an 'objective' first section (Part I to IV), of which Part II contains the linguistically relevant discussion of cognitive models and metaphors, and a second section (Part V), in which (like in his later book, see Lakoff 2004) he openly supports the liberal stance.

Section 3.4

21. Important publications are Kövescses and Radden (1998) and Radden and Kövecsces (1999); a summary is provided by Kövecses (2002, ch. 11).

22. Since Dirven uses this approach to develop a cognitive explanation of the productivity of noun–verb conversions, he excludes the +AGENT FOR ACTION+ metonymy. See Dirven (1999) for more details and Schmid (2005, chs 10.2 and 10.4) for a less restrictive approach and more examples.

23. This approach has been advocated by Panther and Thornburg in several publications: Thornburg and Panther (1997), Panther and Thornburg (1999) and (2003). See also Gibbs (1999).

CHAPTER 4

Figure and ground

4.1 Figure and ground, trajector and landmark: early research into prepositions

> *When we look at an object in our environment, we single it out as a perceptually prominent figure standing out from the ground. The same principle of prominence is valid in the structure of language. For example, in locative relations like in* The book is on the table *the book is conceptualized as the figure.*

In Section 1.2, the notion of gestalt was described as a basis for the categorization of objects. Besides such perceptual principles as the laws of proximity, closure and continuation, the gestalt psychologists were very much interested in how our visual and auditory input is organized in terms of the prominence of the different parts. To take an example from the auditory domain, when we listen to a piano concert we can easily make out the part played by the piano as being more prominent than the accompaniment of the orchestra. Similarly in the visual mode of perception, when we watch someone doing a high jump our eyes will follow the movements of the high-jumper rather than rest on the crossbar or the ground. In this chapter we will have a closer look at how the findings of the gestalt psychologists affect the study of language.

Figure/ground segregation and locative relations

To start with, consider the picture of the well-known face/vase illusion shown in Figure 4.1. You will notice that of the two possibilities of perceiving the picture (as two faces or as a vase) you can only see one at a time. Still, you can easily switch between the two ways of looking at the picture, especially after longer inspection. What lies behind our inability to see both the vase and the faces at the same time is a phenomenon called **figure/ground segregation**. This notion was first introduced into psychology by the Danish psychologist Rubin almost a century ago and later integrated into the more comprehensive framework of perceptual organization by the gestalt psychologists (see also Section 1.2).

Figure 4.1   The face/vase illusion
(after Rubin)

Examining our visual experience when looking at Figure 4.1 more care-fully, we notice that what we single out as figure seems to have special prop-erties. The figure has form or shape whereas the ground is formless and the shared contour seems to belong to the figure. Besides shape and contour the figure seems to have other thing-like qualities such as structure and coher-ence, whereas the ground is unstructured, shapeless and uniform. The figure appears to lie in front of the ground which extends more or less continu-ously behind it. All in all, the figure is perceived as being more prominent than the ground, and psychological research has shown that it is more likely to be identified and remembered, and to be associated with meaning, feeling and aesthetic values.[1]

While a prolonged inspection of Figure 4.1 clearly confirms these aspects of the **perceptual prominence** of the figure, it does not really explain why at one time the vase and at another the two faces assume a figure-like quality. In other words, it would be interesting to know what factors gov-ern the choice of the figure. Since the objective input to our visual system does not change, this choice remains entirely up to the observer; yet it seems not very plausible that it is just a matter of personal taste or whim.

To answer this question one must realize that the face/vase illusion is of course an example of a very special nature, because it allows for what is called a 'figure/ground reversal'. Most visual scenes that we encounter in our everyday lives are of a different kind in that they suggest a particular figure/ground segregation. Thus in the scene depicted in Figure 4.2 the obvi-ous entity to be chosen as figure is the book, while the table will be given

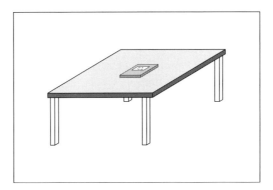

Figure 4.2   Figure and ground: book and table

ground status, unless a special and quite unnatural effort is made to see the table as figure.

According to the gestalt psychologists the principle of *Prägnanz*, which was introduced in Section 1.2, plays a major part in assigning the status of figure to certain parts of a visual scene. Unlike the table, the book in Figure 4.2 readily fulfils such gestalt principles as the principle of closure (its contours are closed) and of continuation (it is an uninterrupted whole). In addition, the relatively small area of dark colour and its balanced proportions attract our attention and make the book a more likely candidate for the figure than the table. Finally, the book seems more likely to be moved around than the table (for example to be picked up), and this may also contribute to our natural choice of figure.[2]

This last aspect is even more important when we turn to examples where an object is depicted in motion as the balloon is in Figure 4.3. Looking at the picture we will not hesitate to regard the balloon as figure and the house as ground because, being conceived as a moving object, the balloon seems to be much more prominent than the house. From a linguistic point of view it is interesting to consider how the selection of figure and ground and the relation the two elements have to each other in our two examples is rendered in words. Describing the situation depicted in Figure 4.2 we would probably say that the book is *on* the table, thus claiming a specific locative relationship for figure and ground. Similarly we would assume that the balloon in Figure 4.3 is *above* the house, or when we think that the balloon must in fact be moving, we might prefer the description *The balloon is flying over the house*. Such a relationship between balloon and house would take into account that the position of the balloon changes in time as suggested by Figure 4.4.

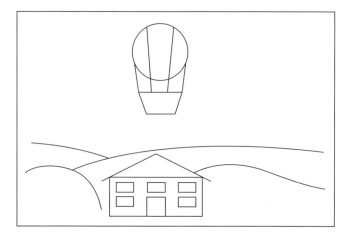

Figure 4.3   Figure and ground: balloon and house

What these two examples show is that the relationship between figure and ground can be seen in terms of locative relations, which are usually rendered by prepositions; or to put it the other way round, the meanings of locative prepositions can be understood as a figure/ground relationship. It is this second view, the prospect of being able to explain linguistic expressions such as prepositions in terms of figure and ground, that has caught the attention of cognitive linguists.

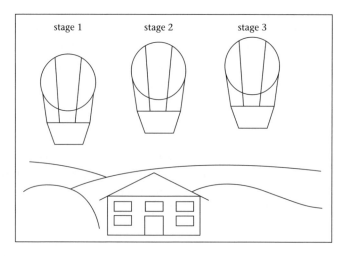

Figure 4.4   Visual representation of *The balloon is flying over the house*

Image schema, trajector, landmark and path: some fundamental notions of prepositional analysis

Before exploring the link between prepositions and the figure/ground contrast more closely let us pick up what was said about locative relations in Section 2.3. There relations like 'over' and 'under', 'up' and 'down', 'in' and 'out' were characterized as image schemas, i.e. simple and basic cognitive structures derived from our bodily interaction with the world, and more specifically, our orientation in the world around us. These **orientational image schemas** are definitely less concrete than the rich prototype categories of specific basic level objects and organisms (see Section 2.1); yet they are not to be understood as abstract principles either, but as mental pictures, which therefore lend themselves quite naturally to pictorial representation.[3]

A good first example is the graphic representation of the image schema of 'over', which underlies our example *The balloon is flying over the house* (Figure 4.5). When comparing Figure 4.5 with Figure 4.4, it is obvious that the representation in Figure 4.5 is less concrete. The balloon (which was identified above as the figure) and the house (the ground) are now represented by symbols. The reason is of course that the image schema 'over' also applies to other objects apart from balloons and houses (e.g. *The bird is flying over the tree* or *The kite is flying over the hill*). The symbol for the figure (the circle) appears several times to indicate that what is represented is

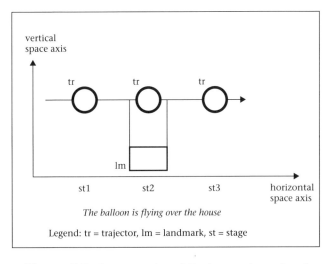

Legend: tr = trajector, lm = landmark, st = stage

Figure 4.5   Representation of the image schema 'over'

a process, something that has a dynamic quality. Each circle stands for a different temporal stage of this process. Moving from stage to stage the figure follows a **path**. Since the path of a bullet or missile can be understood as its trajectory, the figure is called 'trajector'. The ground functions as a reference point for orientation and is therefore called 'landmark'. This means that the notions 'trajector' and 'landmark' are specific manifestations of the more widely applicable notions of 'figure' and 'ground'. This use of trajector and landmark has been generalized in cognitive linguistics, so **trajector** stands for the figure or most prominent element in any relational structure (and is therefore indicated by very bold lines), while **landmark** refers to the other entity in a relation.

Surveying the diagram and the explanations, one might get the impression that this representation is nothing more than a pictorial illustration of our model sentence or a set of closely related sentences. Such a view does not take into account that all the elements involved can be modified in various ways. Trajector and landmark may vary in size and shape, the trajector can be in contact with the landmark or it can even be part of the landmark, as will be illustrated in the following sections. The important thing is that all these variations can be derived from one and the same relationship between trajector and landmark, in our case the 'over' relationship. In other words, the trajector/landmark approach promises to provide a description of the meaning of a preposition revealing the relation between its various senses. Such a unified cognitive description of the various prepositional meanings is in strong contrast with earlier views, which regarded them as an array of unconnected senses.

Unified descriptions need a starting point, a core, a schema that can be regarded as 'central' (we try to avoid the term 'prototypical' because it suggests a rich category structure, which is not characteristic of image schemas). Here we follow Brugman's (1981) analysis of 'over' as summarized by Lakoff (1987)[4] and Lindner's (1982) study of the meaning of 'out' and 'up' in verb-particle constructions.

Over, out and *up*: the central schemas and some elaborations

In accordance with Brugman and Lakoff we accept Figure 4.5 as the central schema for 'over'. It consists of a trajector moving along a path that is above the landmark and goes from one end of the landmark to the other and beyond. As already mentioned, the trajector may stand for a balloon, a plane, a bird, a kite, while the landmark may represent a house, a wall, a tree, a hill, etc.

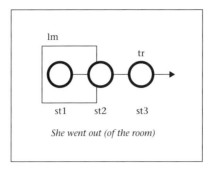

Figure 4.6   Central image schema for 'out'

In addition, there are cases where the landmark is unspecified as in the sentence *The plane flew over*. Here it is the position of the speaker or conceptualizer that functions as a landmark, so the example *The plane flew over* is similar in meaning to *The plane flew over me/us*.

Let us next have a look at the central schemas of the prepositions *out* and *up*. Figure 4.6 provides the graphic representation of this central schema for 'out' as used in the sentence *She went out (of the room)*. As the diagram shows, in the first stage the trajector is included in the space occupied by the landmark, which can represent an object like a room or can remain unspecified, implying 'She went out from where we are'. Viewed in isolation, this initial stage roughly corresponds to what is denoted by the preposition *in* and it can therefore be regarded as the image schema of 'in'.[5] The specific aspect in the schema 'out' is that the trajector moves from being included within the boundaries of the landmark to a location where the two are completely detached from each other. This is indicated in the diagram by the three positions of the trajector.

Compared with 'over' and 'out', the image schema for 'up' (see Figure 4.7), is a more difficult case. Here the path of the trajector has a vertical direction, the landmark is only relevant as far as its vertical extension is concerned. This is why the landmark is only represented by a vertical line in the diagram even where it is specified as in *The boy climbed up the wall*. (After all, when you climb up a wall you do not think of its thickness, but you are only interested in its vertical dimension, in the vertical distance that is involved.) This rather abstract notion of landmark may be more difficult to grasp and to accept than other types of landmark, but it makes it easier to imagine that the landmark is unspecified, as in sentences like *The rocket went up*.

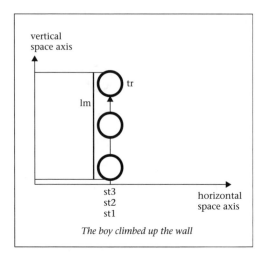

Figure 4.7   Central schema for 'up'

Looking back at this point, we can conclude that all three central schemas represent cognitive configurations consisting of three elements and their interrelations, namely:

a trajector, which moves along

a path, and is seen as being related to

a landmark.

The relationship between these three elements may be sufficient for a rough distinction of the meanings of the three prepositions. To account for more specific meanings or uses, the variations that trajector, path and landmark can undergo have to be taken into consideration. Such variants which only specify certain components of a schema, but do not diverge from its general configuration, are called **elaborations**.

Figure 4.8 illustrates some of the elaborations observed for the image schema 'over'. Variant (a) depicts a very common case, which applies for many verbs of motion, namely contact between trajector and landmark. Variant (b) shows that the trajector can assume a size and shape which is similar to that of the landmark and be located quite close to it so that the trajector actually covers the landmark. Finally, variant (c) illustrates what should probably be regarded as a marginal case – the fusion of trajector and landmark. The fence that collapses (or at least its upper part) is the trajector that is moved along a path and it is at the same time the landmark which acts as reference point for the motion.

Schematic representation	Specification of the schema	Linguistic example
(a)	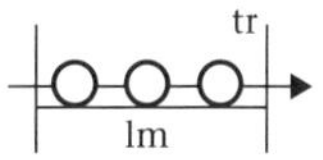 trajector is in contact with landmark	*Sam drove over the bridge.*
(b)	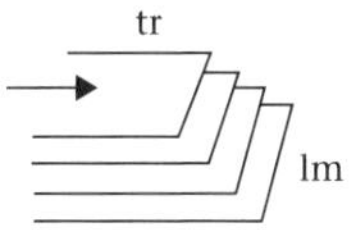 trajector covers landmark	*The city clouded over.*
(c)	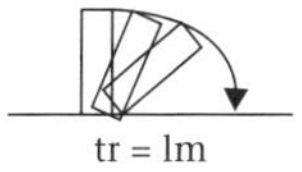 trajector and landmark are identical	*The fence fell over.*

Figure 4.8 Some elaborations of the central schema for 'over'
(based on Lakoff 1987: 419ff)

Figure 4.9 contains another set of elaborations, this time related to the central schema for 'out'. What most of them have in common is that the variation concerns the initial stage, the way the trajector is (or is not) integrated in the landmark. This initial stage is contrasted with the final stage

Schematic representation	Specification of the schema	Linguistic example
(a)	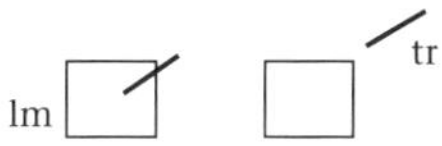 only part of trajector is in landmark in the initial state	*Pluck the feather out.*
(b)	trajector is part of landmark	*Carve out the best piece of meat for yourself.*
(c)	 trajector is a member of a group which functions as landmark	*He picked out two pieces of candy.*
(d)	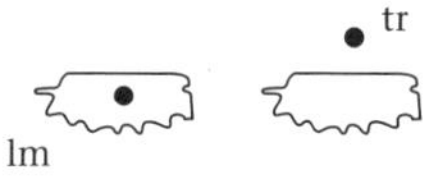 landmark has only one defined boundary; the rest of it may extend indefinitely	*The dog dug the bone out.*

Figure 4.9 Some elaborations of the central schema for 'out'
(based on Lindner 1982: 86ff)

because it is this contrast between the initial and the final stages of the process in which the meaning of 'out' manifests itself; providing the middle
stage would not add any important information.

By directing the attention to selected stages of the image schema, the
analysis of 'out' has pointed the way to how we might approach another
puzzling facet of prepositional use: the fact that essentially dynamic prepositions like *over, out* and *up* are used to render meanings that might at least
superficially be regarded as 'static'.

Compare the following examples:

1. Hang the painting over the chimney.
2. She stays out.
3. She lived three floors up.

To start with the first example, the position of the painting as described in
the sentence can be easily understood as the final stage of a process of moving the picture up into its position. This is represented in Figure 4.10. Similarly,
sentences (2) and (3) can be explained as the final stages of the path of the
'out' and 'up' schemas. See Figure 4.11.

Metaphorical extensions

As it has emerged so far, a fairly general schema of a locative relation can
be employed to explain a considerable variety of uses of prepositions in terms
of elaborations. Yet there are many prepositional meanings that differ from

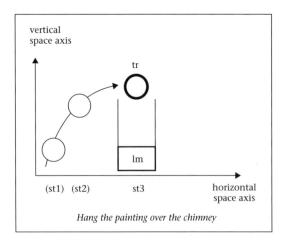

Figure 4.10 Schematic representation of superficially static uses of 'over'

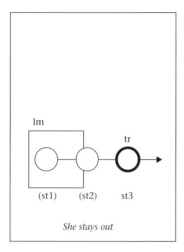
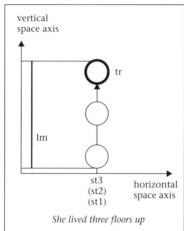

Figure 4.11 Schematic representations of superficially static uses of the 'out' and 'up' schemas

the central schema in such a way that they cannot be explained by reference to the schema alone, but only by assuming a **metaphorical extension**. This is, for instance, true of the following pair of examples taken from Lakoff (1987) – the second example has been slightly adapted.[6]

She has a strange power over me.

The government was overthrown.

In both sentences the use of *over* can be explained by the metaphor +POWER RELATIONS ARE SPATIAL RELATIONS+. This metaphorical link is monitored by a mapping scope based on the image schema 'up–down', which sanctions the upward movement and a position of power as 'up' and the opposites as 'down'. On a more specific level this metaphor can be understood as +CONTROL IS A UPWARD MOVEMENT/UPRIGHT POSITION+, and it is this mapping that quite obviously explains the meaning of *over* in the first example. For the second example the explanation is a little more complex. As Lakoff argues (1987: 439), 'before the event takes place, the government is in control (metaphorically upright), and afterwards it is not in control (metaphorically, it has fallen over)'. One could probably add that another variant of the metaphor which may roughly be characterized as +PROPER FUNCTIONING IS UPRIGHT POSITION+ is also involved. From our everyday experience we know that plants, animals, persons and indeed objects like bookshelves, houses or spires can only fulfil their respective functions in a satisfactory way if they keep their upright position. Lying on the ground, or still worse being scattered around, is a clear sign for an organism or object that it is either currently not active or severely damaged and this may contribute to the rich image evoked by the expression *overthrow the government.*

To add just another example, the sentence *Harry still hasn't got over his divorce* can be seen as a realization of the metaphor +LIFE IS A JOURNEY+, which, as shown in Section 3.1, maps the structure of the event concept JOURNEY onto the abstract concept LIFE, a process monitored by a mapping scope based, among other things, on the 'path' schema. It lies in the nature of journeys that the traveller's progress is sometimes impeded by obstacles such as rivers, gorges and of course hills and mountains, and this is where a more specific variant of the journey metaphor comes into play: +PROBLEMS IN LIFE ARE OBSTACLES IN A JOURNEY+. If bad times, problems or setbacks in one's life are seen as vertical obstacles like mountains in one's life journey, one has to get over them in order to move on in life (cf. also *He is over the hill*). Viewed from the complementary perspective of the schema of 'over' (cf. Figure 4.5) this means that Harry is the trajector, who, in order to pursue his path (= a journey = his life) must get over the landmark (= an obstacle = the divorce).

In conclusion, the discussion in this chapter has given a first glimpse of how the principle of prominence, which underlies the figure/ground distinction, is at work in the structure of language. So far we have confined ourselves to examples from the area of prepositional meanings, which have been described in terms of 'trajector' and 'landmark', 'path', 'central schema' and 'elaboration'. While prepositional meanings are still very much related to the lexical aspects of language, we will now go on to probe a little deeper into the role of prominence in grammatical structures.

Exercises

1. Consider the situations called up by the following sentence pairs:

> The pen is under the table.
> The table is over the pen.

> The lamppost is in front of the house.
> The house is behind the lamppost.

How can the principle of figure and ground be used to explain why only the first sentence in each pair expresses a natural view of the situation?

2. As suggested in the text, the first stage of the image schema for 'out' can be regarded as the image schema of 'in'. Sketch the image schema for 'in' making use of Figure 4.6 ('out' schema).

Look at the following examples and decide which of them render the central schema 'in' and which express elaborations of this schema. Compile diagrams for the elaborations, using Figure 4.9 as a source of information:

The lipstick is in my handbag.

The flowers are in the vase.

There is a hole in your shirt.

Find the mistake in this sentence.

3. Draw diagrams for the image schemas underlying the following sentences:

I met John in the street.

Salesmen spend a lot of time on the road.

How does the difference between the landmarks in the two diagrams explain the contrasting use of *in the street* vs *on the road*.

4. Here are some compound nouns which combine *up* and a verbal element and their definitions in the LDOCE4:

upbringing	'the way that your parents care for you and teach you to behave when you are growing up'
upkeep	'the process of keeping something in good condition'
uproar	'a lot of noise or angry protest about something'
upstart	'someone who behaves as if they were more important than they really are and shows a lack of respect towards people who are more experienced or older'
upturn	'an increase in the level of something, especially in business activity.'

Which of these diverse meanings can be convincingly derived from the image schema 'up'?

5. Draw the diagram for the locative relation 'down', which can be regarded as the reverse of 'up', as shown in Figure 4.7. Show how this schema can be combined with other schemas in order to illustrate the expressions *up and down*, *down and out* ('destitute') and *down under* ('in Australia').

4.2 Figure, ground and two metaphors: a cognitive explanation of simple clause patterns

If the figure/ground distinction could only be used to explain prepositional meanings, it would be of limited importance. However, it has many other applications in linguistics. This section will single out one more of them, the description of clause patterns, which will then be integrated into a larger cognitive framework in the next section.

Traditional grammar holds that a simple clause normally consists of three key elements: a subject, a verb element (or predicate) and a complement (e.g. an object or an adverbial). This standard pattern is illustrated in the following examples (sentences (4) and (8) from Langacker 1991):

1. Susan resembles my sister.
2. Susan is peeling a banana.
3. Susan loves bananas.
4. The hammer breaks the glass.
5. Susan has a large library.
6. Susan received the present.
7. Susan swam the Channel.
8. The garden is swarming with bees.
9. There was a loud bang.

Though all these examples contain the three said elements, a short glance will make it clear that they are in fact rather divergent. The subjects refer to persons, things or places or they are 'empty' (as the *there*–subject in the last example). Persons, things, and places are also eligible as complements. In one case (ex. (1)) subject and object can be exchanged, while this is not possible with the other sentences, and the transformation into passive sentences is also severely restricted. Both traditional grammarians and modern linguistic schools have recognized these differences and have tried to cope with them by proposing different verb classes or case frames (a notion discussed in Section 5.1) or by explaining some of them in terms of transformations of other patterns (e.g. deriving *She swam the Channel* from *She swam across the Channel*).

In contrast with these approaches, Cognitive Grammar, as developed by Langacker (1990; 1991, chs 7, 8), suggests that a unified explanation of this syntactic diversity is possible if one understands the subject–verb–complement pattern as a reflection of the general cognitive principle of figure/ground segregation. Or to put it more pointedly: in a simple transitive clause the subject corresponds to the figure, the object to the ground, and the verb expresses the relationship between figure and ground.

The influence of the figure and ground principle is most plausible in symmetrical constructions, as illustrated by the following sentence pair:

(a) Susan resembles my sister. (= ex. (1))

(b) My sister resembles Susan.

Just as in the case of the face/vase illusion, from which we started out in Section 4.1, the choice of one sentence constituent as the dominant element is up to the speaker. Linguistically, the way to manifest prominence is to put the preferred element into subject position; this is like deciding to regard the face/vase illusion as either two faces or as a vase. Once this decision has been made in favour of *Susan* (sentence (a)) or *my sister* (b), it is clear that in either variant the chosen subject is the figure and is more prominent than the other element (the ground). This means that in (a) it is Susan that is assessed with reference to someone else, while in (b) the situation is reversed. Though less prominent than the figure, the second element is also important as a point of reference.

To account for the degree of prominence that resides in both subject and complement, we will use the terms **syntactic figure** and **syntactic ground** respectively. (Langacker's favourite terms for this distinction are '(clausal) trajector' and '(clausal) landmark', but he also makes use of a number of other terms.)

Like reversible visual scenes such as the face/vase illusion, symmetrical clause structures are exceptional. Normally the choice of syntactic figure is guided and restricted by a number of other cognitive principles. These additional principles and their interaction with figure/ground segregation will be presented in the following sections.

Role archetypes

The most familiar of the cognitive principles evoked by Langacker for the explanation of clause structure is what he calls **role archetypes**. For anyone who has had some grounding in modern linguistics, what lies behind this notion is by no means a novelty, because role archetypes like 'agent', 'patient', 'instrumental' and 'experiencer' will suggest the analysis of sentence elements in terms of 'cases' (or 'actants', 'participants', 'semantic roles', 'theta-roles'), as has been propagated by most linguistic schools current in the last forty years.[7] In fact, two of the roles, agent and patient, have been inherited from traditional grammar. All these attempts to use roles or cases in syntactic analysis have a common aim, which is to establish a list of semantically based roles that permits a satisfactory classification of all non-verbal elements of clause patterns. The result has been a large number of different inventories of roles, but a definitive list has not yet been assembled.

For Langacker this is not surprising. In his view, the roles are not just a linguistic construct, but part of the range of cognitive instruments which we use for linguistic, and also for non-linguistic, mental processing. Role archetypes emerge from our experience of interacting with the world. From this experience we know that we are capable of initiating motion or physical activity in objects or other persons (an approximate definition of the archetypical **agent**). Conversely, we experience that objects or organisms are affected by physical impact from outside and undergo a change of state or are moved to another location. This defines the **patient**, which in this wider definition includes Langacker's separate role of 'mover'. The archetypical role of **instrument** is characterized as the intermediary between agent and patient and the **experiencer** role refers to someone engaged in mental activities, including emotions. Like cognitive categories in general, the role archetypes are not discrete categories, but gradual phenomena; they are, as Langacker puts it, 'not like a row of statues in an art museum, but are instead analogous to the highest peaks in a mountain range' (1991: 285).

However, tracing back clause constituents to cognitive archetypes gives rise to a further problem: how do we know which role is to be put in the subject slot and which in the complement slot? As an analysis of the following examples shows, under certain conditions all role archetypes can occur in subject position:

Susan is peeling a banana. (= ex. (2))	subject = agent
Susan loves bananas. (= ex. (3))	subject = experiencer
The hammer breaks the glass. (= ex. (4))	subject = instrument
The glass broke.	subject = patient

Although it is clear that all four patterns are perfectly acceptable, it turns out that agents are used far more often as syntactic figures than other role archetypes are. The question is why this is so. Again, Langacker offers an explanation which is based on our experience of the interaction between persons and things.

Action chains, energy flow and the billiard-ball metaphor

One of the most elementary kinds of interactions between the objects and organisms of the world is by way of physical contact. In cognitive linguistics

the study of these encounters has given rise to several important theories, notably Talmy's notion of force dynamics[8] and Langacker's conception of energy transmission, which is part of his explanation of sentence
structure.

Theoretically, the simplest case is an interaction of two entities (objects
or organisms) of the following kind: one entity is charged with energy; it is
the source of the energy; this first entity contacts a second one; energy is
transmitted to and consumed by this second entity. This simple interaction
is illustrated in Figure 4.12(a), where the circles represent objects/organisms,
the double arrows symbolize the interaction between them and the squiggly
line indicates where the energy is absorbed.

As shown by Figure 4.12(b), longer interactions involving several instances
of physical contact are possible, indeed they are the rule. (Even a two-element
structure like *Susan is peeling a banana* can be said to imply a third unexpressed
element, i.e. with her hand.) This has led Langacker to talk of action chains.
An **action chain** is characterized by an energetic 'head', an object/organism
which is the source of the energy; from this head the energy is transmitted to
the second entity and so on until an entity is reached which no longer emits,
but consumes the remaining energy; this element is called the 'tail' of the
action chain. To stress the conception of energy flow, Langacker invokes the
metaphor of a river, using the terms 'upstream' (for the head) and 'downstream'
(for the other elements of the action chain).

Though the notion of energy flow is already metaphorical in itself,
Langacker supports this explanation with an even more tangible metaphor,
the +BILLIARD BALL+ metaphor. After being activated by the touch of the
cue, the white ball is pushed against another ball, and if this physical contact has the necessary force, part of the original energy is transmitted to

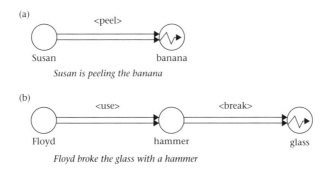

Figure 4.12 Energy transmission in action chains
(partially based on Langacker 1990)

the second ball, which ideally hits a third ball and transmits energy to it and so on. The remaining energy is absorbed by the cushioned edges or, if the balls reach their goals, by the pockets of the billiard table.

In what way do the +ENERGY FLOW+ and the +BILLIARD BALL+ metaphor contribute to our understanding of syntactic patterns? How can they explain the allocation of role archetypes to slots in the clause structure? In a case where only an agent and a patient are expressed (as in *Susan is peeling the banana*), it seems quite obvious that the agent corresponds to the energetic head of the action chain and the patient to the tail. Since an agent is the initiator of the energy flow, he or she is the most prominent element in a situation and is therefore given the status of syntactic figure, i.e. subject. The patient is represented as syntactic ground or object. In short, the result is that, at least in a two-element structure like Figure 4.12(a), agent, head of the action chain and syntactic figure coincide, as do patient, tail of the action chain and syntactic ground. This explains, in cognitive terms, why agents are favoured as subjects and patients as objects.

When we now move on to three-element action chains (Figure 4.12(b)), we can again readily identify the first element as agent and the last element as patient. The element in between represents the instrument role, which serves as the intermediate stage in the transmission of energy. This cognitive structure is linguistically reflected in the sentence *Floyd broke the glass with a hammer*, in which the agent is selected as syntactic figure, followed by the patient as syntactic ground or object, and the instrument (here the cognitive sequence is reversed).

However, as Langacker has shown, this sentence is not the only linguistic realization of this action chain, but other perspectives are possible (see also Section 5.1). Compare Figure 4.13, where it is contrasted with two alternative versions. While sentence (a) provides the overall view of the action chain, sentences (b) and (c) express only a certain portion, as indicated by the boldly printed parts of the diagrams for (b) and (c). In particular, the head of the action chain is not expressed linguistically, which means that the prime candidate for syntactic figure or subject is not available. Figure 4.13 shows how this problem is solved. The status of subject is accorded to the linguistically expressed element of the action chain which is furthest 'upstream'. In 4.13 (b) this is the instrument (the hammer), while in (c) this is actually the last element of the chain, the patient (the glass); in the diagram the subject status is indicated by an extra-bold circle.

With regard to the choice of syntactic ground (or object), sentence (b) is unproblematic because, as with sentence (a), the patient is available for this position (*The hammer broke the glass*; object status is indicated by a

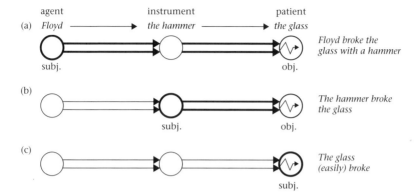

Figure 4.13   Linguistic realizations of a three-element action chain
(adapted from Langacker 1990: 221, examples integrated)

bold circle). This is different in the case of sentence (c), which is limited to a single element of the action chain (the glass), and, as we have just seen, this element functions as syntactic figure. Yet at the same time this element represents the tail of the action chain, the point where the energy is consumed, the archetypal patient. This means that no energy is emitted, no attempt is made to establish physical contact with another object and, consequently, no cognitive ground is established. There is no need for a syntactic object, and this is the cognitive explanation why sentences like *The glass broke* are intransitive.

Summarizing the analysis of the glass-breaking sentences, we find that it yields three results: it confirms the link between agent, head of action chain and syntactic figure or subject, and it supplies a cognitive explanation for the fact, first observed by Fillmore (1968: 33), that the choice of subject is governed by a hierarchy of agent > instrument > patient. Finally, it integrates intransitive uses of verbs like *break* into the paradigm of figure and ground.

However, these findings are only valid for sentences describing concrete situations implying physical contact. It remains to be seen whether the figure/ground interpretation also holds for other kinds of subject–verb–complement structures, for instance sentences expressing a mental activity like *Susan loves bananas* (= ex. (3)) or *She remembered her first bike*.

Mental interactions and clause patterns

Sentences like the examples just quoted do not express physical contact, and therefore they cannot be regarded in terms of action chains, of energy transmission and energy consumption. Instead what 'takes place' has a mental nature and the person that is involved does not produce physical energy, but is a sentient creature engaged in a mental activity. For this role archetype the term **experiencer** rather than agent seems appropriate. The main difference, however, between these mental operations and action chains concerns the second element. While the patient, as the tail of the action chain, receives and consumes physical energy and undergoes a change or is at least moved to another location, the second entity in the mental activity is not really touched or changed by this interaction. To capture this role archetype, Langacker uses the term 'absolute', later replaced by 'theme', but for our restricted discussion the term **(the) experienced**, which is suggested by its relation to the experiencer, seems more helpful. The relationship between experiencer and experienced is schematically represented in Figure 4.14.[9]

In this diagram, the link between the two participants is indicated by a single arrow (as opposed to the double arrow for the strong energy link in action chains). This is to indicate that the mental link is in a sense 'weaker' than the energy link in action chains, but it is nevertheless clearly directional. Its source is the experiencer, which is thus marked as the more prominent active initiator, as figure in this mental interaction, while the experienced functions as ground. This attribution to figure and ground is faithfully reflected in the choice of subject and object, which means that the figure/ground explanation is also applicable to mental activity sentences like *Susan loves bananas*.

An interesting variant of mental operations is provided by situations implying the possession of goods, as in the following two examples:

Susan has a large library. (= ex. (5))

Susan received the present. (= ex. (6))

When one first looks at it, the possessive relationship between Susan and her books in the first example seems to be of a very concrete and physical nature. However, a closer inspection of what the notion of possession implies reveals that the crucial point is that Susan and other people have knowledge

Figure 4.14 Cognitive representation of mental interactions

of the possessive relationship and that she can enjoy its benefits. Since know-
ing and enjoying are of course mental rather than physical activities, it seems
reasonable to apply a role description in terms of experiencer and experienced to this sentence.

For the second example, the interpretation as an essentially mental operation seems even less convincing at first sight, because it involves the physical transfer of goods. The verb *receive* is closely linked with the notion of
giving, which is, of course, most naturally expressed by a sentence with the
verb *give* and two objects, as for example in *Aunt Emily gave Susan the present*. In spite of this parallel to an agentive verb, the subject in *Susan received
the present* should be regarded as an experiencer rather than an agent. This
emerges when we compare the cognitive structures of *give* and *receive* shown
in Figure 4.15. The two diagrams suggest that both *give* and *receive* involve

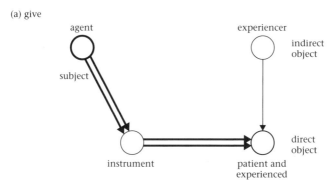

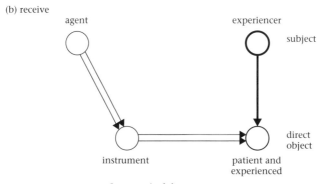

Figure 4.15 Cognitive structure for clause patterns with *give* and *receive*
(adapted from Langacker 1990; 1991: 327)

two cognitive processes, namely an action chain and a mental operation. To start with *give*,[10] the action chain is initiated by the agent (*Aunt Emily* in our example); the agent transmits energy to the patient (*the present*) using the unexpressed instrument (e.g. Aunt Emily's hand) as an intermediary. The experiencer (*Susan*) initiates a mental interaction with the experienced, which is identical with the patient of the action chain. As a result, the experiencer (*Susan*) recognizes that she will be the beneficiary of the action of giving.

If we evaluate the sentence *Aunt Emily gave Susan a present* in terms of figure and ground, we find that the agent is most prominent and the prime candidate for subject; second priority is accorded to the patient, which is expressed as direct object. This distribution of prominence is identical with the figure/ground assignment in action clauses with only one object. The reason why this is so is that the experiencer (which corresponds to the indirect object) is regarded as an external additional element, which does not influence the choice of an agent as subject and patient as direct object.

Turning to *receive* (Figure 4.15(b)), the cognitive structure is largely identical with *give*. Although the same action chain is presupposed, it is not expressed in words, and this is the major difference. What is rendered linguistically is the mental interaction between the experiencer (*Susan*) and the experienced/patient (*the present*). Figure and ground are distributed just like in other mental interactions: the experiencer functions as syntactic figure or subject, the experienced (alias patient) as syntactic ground or object.

Undoubtedly, Langacker's cognitive explanation for the *give* and *receive* paradigms is intriguing, but it is also very radical. One of the things it implies is a complete reappraisal of actions like giving. Instead of regarding the recipient as the endpoint of the physical action of moving something from one person to another, it claims that the physical aspect of motion is restricted to the actor and the thing moved, while the part of the recipient is a matter of the mental acknowledgement of this physical action. If we want to express that something actually reaches the position taken up by the recipient in space, we have to use verbs which permit a locative complement, like *put/place the book in his hand* (this structure will be discussed in the next section).

Compared with *give*, *receive* is, in Langacker's opinion, restricted to the expression of mental operations like control and possession, but does not involve physical contact with the transferred object. Surprising as this view may be at first sight, it becomes much more understandable when we consider that the physical contact between the receiving person and the transferred object can be unequivocally expressed by the verb *take*, which can even be used in conjunction with *give*, as in the following example:

Aunt Emily gave Peter the present. *He took it* and thanked her excessively.

As with *give*, clauses with *take* are based on an action chain. The receiving person is the agent, the person's hand is the unexpressed instrument, and the exchanged present is the patient that is moved. The only thing that is different is the direction of the movement; with *take* it runs towards rather than away from the agent. In terms of the figure/ground segregation in the action chain *give*–clauses and *take*–clauses represent the same pattern: an agent which functions as syntactic figure or subject and a patient which takes the part of the syntactic ground or (direct) object. Where they differ, however, is in the role of the experiencer. While in the case of *give* the experiencer is of course another person, in the case of *take* the agent and experiencer coincide, although the agent role is probably much more dominant than the experiencer role. To illustrate the contrast between *give* and *take*, Figure 4.16 gives the cognitive representation of *take*. In this diagram, the lesser salience of the mental operation as compared to the action chain is indicated by the broken arrow between the experiencer and the experienced.

Participants, setting and the stage metaphor

Action chains and mental interactions, we have found, involve role archetypes like agent, patient, instrument, experiencer and experienced. All of them can be, and often are, chosen as figure and ground in a verbal relation. However, the cognitive intake of a real-world situation also comprises

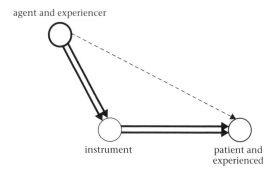

Figure 4.16 Cognitive structure for clause patterns with *take*

many facets which are not selected as figure, but which are nevertheless present in our minds as part of what we will loosely call 'background' (in Langacker's view this 'background' is composed of an array of different domains; see Section 4.3).

To explain the relationship between figure and ground on the one hand and background on the other, Langacker makes use of another metaphor, the +STAGE+ **metaphor**. According to this metaphor, which can already be found in the work of the French linguist Tesnière (1959, ch. 48), the set-up of the constituents in a sentence is similar to what happens in a play on the stage. The background may be compared with the props or setting of the play, while prominence is reserved for the actors that move around on the stage, declaiming, fighting and killing, or alternatively, hugging and embracing each other. Applying the +STAGE+ metaphor to cognitive perception in general, we may distinguish between the **setting** of an event, which is comprehensive and relatively stable, and the **participants** in the event, which are smaller and mobile and engaged in physical contact and mental interaction.

Transferred to linguistic expressions, the distinction between participants and setting seems to be clearly reflected in clause structure. Participants provide subjects and objects, while the setting is expressed by adverbials, in particular by adverbials of space and time, as in the following example:

Susan was eating a banana in the kitchen at nine o'clock in the morning.

However, it would be wrong and quite contrary to the spirit of cognitive explanation to assume that the setting is completely homogeneous. Prominence is by definition a gradual phenomenon, and there is no reason why it should only be relevant for the selection of figure and ground. Indeed, just by looking at locative settings we can easily distinguish degrees of prominence. Compare the following two sentences:[11]

People drink beer in Munich.
Susan lives in Munich.

In the first sentence the place adverbial *in Munich* is a true setting for an action chain involving two participants, an agent (*people*) and a patient (*beer*). Yet in the second sentence the same adverbial is not just a general locative background, but a necessary part of an interaction with the participant *Susan*, which is the syntactic figure. In other words, here the locative setting assumes the functions of the identifiable ground. However, *in Munich* is not a participant because, unlike the patient, it does not undergo a change of state or location. This situation is sketched in Figure 4.17. As the diagram shows,

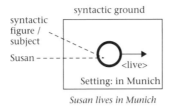

Figure 4.17 Setting as syntactic ground

the circle denoting the syntactic figure is not accompanied by a spatially separated unit denoting the ground. This was the set-up in the previous figures, which illustrated action chains and mental interactions. In Figure 4.17 the circle is placed inside the box denoting the second element; it is as it were 'contained' in the second element, which in this case is the setting. If we understand syntax in terms of image schemas, we may say that the syntactic relation underlying sentences like *Susan lives in Munich* represents a 'be in' or container schema and not a 'path' schema, as is typical of action chains and mental interactions.

A related but more complex case was already mentioned in the last section. Clause patterns with *put/place/set* (e.g. *Susan put the bananas into the basket*) reflect an action chain with an agent–subject and a patient–object, but are also linked with a locative setting of special prominence, which would have to be integrated into the clause pattern as a third element of prominence. It seems that the problem of how this highlighted facet of setting is to be evaluated with respect to the syntactic figure and ground has not been solved so far and thus requires further investigation.

We have seen that the degree of prominence that is given to the setting depends on the choice of the syntactic pattern. For a further illustration of what is gained by treating the prominence of the setting in terms of a gradient, consider the following set of examples:

  a. Susan swam in the Channel.

  b. Susan swam across the Channel.

  c. Susan swam the Channel. (= ex. (7))

In sentence (a) the agent and syntactic figure (*Susan*) initiates an action chain, for which no patient is invoked, but which takes place in a certain setting (*the Channel*); linguistically this is expressed by an intransitive structure with an optional place adverbial. In (b) the setting is more tangible, it has two boundaries and it is fully traversed by the agent/figure. All this is implied by the preposition *across*; as a result this setting is more prominent than in (a). In the last sentence (c) the preposition is dropped. Far from assuming that this is just a formal variant of (b), a cognitive interpretation will claim that *the Channel* has gained in syntactic prominence, that it has moved further away from being a plain setting. It is treated more like a participant in an interaction with the agent-subject, for example an enemy that has to be overcome, and this is reflected in the object-like use of the noun phrase.

While raising settings to the status of objects (as we have discussed so far) seems quite natural, the claim that the setting can also occur as subject is more ambitious. Let us look at the following example (Langacker 1991: 346ff):

The garden is swarming with bees. (= ex. (8))

In this sentence it is not difficult to see the syntactic figure or subject (*the garden*) as locative setting, while the slot of the syntactic ground is occupied by *bees*. The cognitive explanation is documented in Figure 4.18. The basic principle is again a container–contained relationship between syntactic figure and ground. This corresponds to the structure shown in Figure 4.17 for sentences like *Susan lives in Munich*, yet with the decisive difference that the prominence of participant and setting has been reversed. (Compare the reversal of extra-bold and bold lines in the second diagram.) The setting (*the garden*) holds the prominent position in the container–contained relationship, expressing something like 'be the setting for the swarming activity', in which the bees are involved as syntactic ground.

Exceptional as such 'setting–subjects' (as Langacker calls them) may appear because they are not participants, they are still based on an identifiable facet of the setting. This is different with examples like the following:

There was a loud bang. (= ex. (9))

There are at least five Asian takeaways in our town.

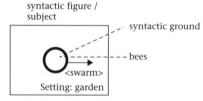

The garden is swarming with bees

Figure 4.18   Setting as syntactic figure (subject)
(adapted from Langacker 1991: 345)

The *there*–element in these well-known structures is normally explained as a dummy element or as a structural or formal subject, yet all these explanations contradict the basic cognitive tenet that all grammatical elements have a conceptual content. This is why Langacker, in agreement with other studies on *there*–constructions (e.g. Lakoff 1987: 462ff), assumes that *there* is used to express a kind of setting, though an 'abstract' or unspecified setting, and that this setting functions as subject. The problem is that as a subject, *there* should be assigned the greatest prominence in the sentence, and this runs counter to our intuition about the two sentences above and similar examples. Another problem, which it seems Langacker has only solved provisionally, is that verbs in *there*–constructions are congruent with the syntactic ground, not with the *there*–subject (see the second example above). Our conclusion is that, for the time being, this interpretation of *there*–sentences should be approached with some caution.[12]

Postscript: schematic subject vs prototypical subject

Langacker's attempt to establish *there* as syntactic figure must be seen in a wider context. The enormous impact that the prototype notion has had on cognitive linguistics has encouraged scholars to use it not only to explain the structure of lexical categories (see Chapters 1 and 2), but also to describe grammatical phenomena. As a result, word classes, sentence types, and clause structure have been analyzed in the prototype paradigm, and more or less convincing attributes have been assembled to distinguish the best example from the lesser examples of nouns, declarative sentences, transitive clauses, etc.[13] For the subject of the clause the result – not unexpectedly – has been that the prototypical subject is the agent in a transitive clause; all other subjects deviate from this definition in certain ways.

Yet while the prototype analysis of clause constituents is satisfied with this description, for Langacker it is only the starting point in his quest for a cognitive definition of subject that is valid for all kinds of subjects, the prototypical and the less prototypical instances. Recapitulating his argument as it has been pursued in this section for active clauses,[14] we can distinguish the following conceptions of the notion of subject:

- subject as realization of the archetypal role of agent (explains agent subjects in transitive action clauses)
- subject as the first expressed element of an action chain, the upstream element in the energy flow characteristic of action chains (adds instrument and intransitive patient subjects in action clauses)

- subject as active participant (adds subjects in mental interactions)
- subject as syntactic figure (adds salient facets of the setting).

The result is (or comes close to) what Langacker regards as a **schematic definition** of subject as opposed to the mere description of a prototype. This notion of schematicity, or general validity, which has, of course, always been one of the goals of science and philosophy, permeates Langacker's whole conception, as we will see in the following section.

Exercises

1. Which of the following sentences express action chains, which render mental interactions, which combine both types of cognitive structures?

    Dad opened the box with a knife.

    Little Sue wants a mountain bike.

    Jack brings along the most recent CDs.

    Tom sold his old Chevy to a friend.

    Diana was sipping her long drink.

    She was dreaming of her Italian boyfriend.

    Sorry, I have forgotten your name.

2. As already mentioned, one could claim that all action chains consist of at least three elements (agent, instrument, patient). Examine the following two-element structures and try to find the instrument that might be added:

    Susan is picking strawberries.

    Susan is reading a book.

    Susan turns the key.

    Susan kicks the ball.

    Susan sings a song.

    Explain why the instrument is not expressed in these sentences.

3. To describe action chains, Langacker does in fact offer two metaphors: the +BILLIARD BALL+ metaphor and what might be called the +RIVER+ metaphor (on which his notion of energy *flow* is based). Which of these two metaphors do you find more helpful?

4. Clause patterns do not only express action chains and mental interactions, they may also reflect a 'container–contained' or a 'part–whole'

relationship. Explain the following examples in terms of these image
schemas:

> The bus holds 40 people.

> Our village consists of a church and three cottages.

> The area abounds with pubs.

> This anthology assembles a lot of unknown poems.

5. For grammatical purposes, verbs are often divided up into dynamic and
   stative verbal meanings (or situation types). Study this classification (e.g.
   in Quirk *et al.* 1985: 200ff or Greenbaum and Quirk 1992: 55f) and discuss where it overlaps with Langacker's distinction of action chains, mental interactions and container–contained structures.

4.3 Other types of prominence and cognitive processing

*Following two sections with exemplary discussions of the figure/ground contrast, the
aim of this section is to complete the survey and to integrate the results into the
framework of Cognitive Grammar developed by Langacker. In view of the
comprehensiveness of this theory, the section will only discuss some of the central
notions: cognitive units and domains, and profiling, on the level of word class, in
clauses and speech events.*

From a cognitive point of view most linguistic expressions are based on
the perception of objects or situations in the real world. Initially this intake
is probably a rather chaotic assembly of perceptual stimuli. Before this
crude cognitive intake can be 'translated' into linguistic expressions, it
needs to be structured into more tangible cognitive units. If we try to
investigate the cognitive processes involved in this translation, the most
pressing questions are:

• How are cognitive units established?

• How are these cognitive units translated into the lexical categories underlying individual words?

• How are the words combined when a more complex situation is conceptualized and verbalized?

In the following we will try to answer these three questions, basing our
account on Langacker's framework.

Cognitive intake, cognitive units and domains[15]

Even if one assumes, as we have just done, that the cognitive intake of a situation consists of a huge number of diverse stimuli, this intake is nevertheless brought under control immediately. One way of explaining this controlling process was presented in Chapters 1 and 2. There we argued that by virtue of their gestalt properties the most salient objects, organisms and persons are readily identified as members of certain basic level categories. Langacker, however, takes a more abstract view, claiming that each stimulus is evaluated with respect to what he calls **domains**. According to him (Langacker 1987a: 147) domains are 'contexts for the characterization of a semantic unit' (i.e. 'cognitive unit' indicated by small italicized caps in the following). The most elementary domains are space and vision, temperature, taste, pressure, pain and colour.

The function of these elementary domains, and of the space domain in particular, is most obvious where geometric figures are involved. Figure 4.19 illustrates this for the cognitive units *CIRCLE* and *ARC*, using boxes to indicate domains and bold lines to symbolize cognitive units. Diagram (a) shows how the cognitive unit *CIRCLE* is characterized in relation to the domain of two-dimensional space. Applying the figure/ground contrast, the circle is the figure or **profile** while the domain functions as ground or **base**. (With 'profile' and 'base' Langacker introduces another metaphor for figure and ground, which seems particularly well suited to capture the contrast involved in these cognitive processes.) Unlike *CIRCLE*, the cognitive unit *ARC* cannot be sufficiently defined only with respect to the space domain. If *ARC* were only profiled in relation to the space domain, it would only represent a curved line and not a segment of a circle. This is why in diagram (b) the domain is not two-dimensional space, but the conception of a circle. In other words, the definition of *ARC* requires two steps, each involving an instance of

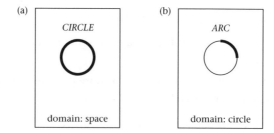

Figure 4.19 Cognitive domains and cognitive units: *CIRCLE* and *ARC*
(Langacker 1987a: 184)

figure/ground segregation. On the first level CIRCLE is profiled as a cognitive unit which, on the second level, provides the domain for ARC. Since 'circle' is the more specific and therefore immediately relevant domain for ARC, it is called its **primary domain**.

ARC is just a simple example of how more specific domains emerge from the elementary domains. To turn to a more elaborate example, which also illustrates how different domains can be evoked simultaneously, let us look at the cognitive unit BODY. This unit is characterized in relation to the basic domain 'space' as far as its shape is concerned; it is also specified in relation to other basic domains like 'colour', 'temperature', etc. These basic domains thus form the matrix for the cognitive unit BODY. The unit BODY in turn provides the domain for ARM, the unit ARM the domain for HAND, ELBOW, etc. The cognitive unit HAND denotes the domain for the more specific cognitive unit FINGER, and finally FINGER can be seen as the (primary) domain for the profiled unit KNUCKLE.

However, there are cognitive units that cannot be defined in terms of the basic domains of 'space', 'temperature' or 'colour'. Langacker's example (1987a: 185) is the unit UNCLE, which is defined with reference to the domains 'person', 'gender', 'birth' and 'life cycle', 'parent/child relationship' and 'sibling relationship'. By considering these we arrive at a more specific primary domain for UNCLE, which is, to put it somewhat loosely, characterized by the notions of person, brother and of mother/father.

From this discussion it emerges that Langacker's conception of domain (or context) is more general than the notion of context developed in Section 1.3. There we defined context as the mental representation of the interaction of related lexical categories, mostly basic level categories like BEACH, SAND, SPADE and TOWEL. For Langacker, context includes domains that are much more elementary or (in the naive sense of the word) 'abstract', such as space, vision, temperature, taste and colour. If several of these domains are applied to the profiling of one and the same cognitive unit, the result is a matrix of elementary domains, which is superficially reminiscent of orthodox linguistic descriptions of meaning in terms of features. The difference is that in Langacker's view these elementary domains are not 'derived' or 'abstracted' from the meaning of individual words, but they are 'basic' in the sense that they represent basic human experiences and are not reducible to other, more fundamental, domains. In other words, they are the cognitive tools with which we approach and master the world.

This matrix of domains is the base (or ground) against which cognitive units are profiled (as figure). The process involved is really pre-linguistic in the sense that in principle it does not determine what kind of linguistic expression will be used to render the cognitive unit. Thus the cognitive unit which was provisionally labelled KNUCKLE above may be expressed by the noun *knuckle*, but in a certain situation it may be subsumed under the verbal action KNOCK and will then be expressed by the verb *knock*. Similarly, the cognitive unit ELBOW can be rendered by the noun *elbow*, but in the phrase *bend one's arm*, it will be expressed by the verb *bend*. As these examples show, the translation of cognitive units into cognitive categories (our second introductory question) is closely linked with the choice of word class. The governing principle is again the principle of prominence, here the selection of what is immediately relevant for the rendering of a certain situation, and this is perhaps the most impressive application of the figure/ground contrast in cognitive processing.

Profiling objects, persons and relations: the emergence of word classes[16]

To study the process of word class selection more closely let us assume that we have profiled a complex cognitive unit consisting of three individuals who somehow belong together. Compare Figure 4.20, where diagram (a) illustrates the cognitive unit (the individuals are symbolized by the small circles, the relation of togetherness by the lines connecting them).

Diagrams (b) and (c) represent the two ways in which this cognitive unit can be turned into a cognitive category. Taking the cognitive unit as base (or ground), it is possible to highlight the relation between the three individuals, as suggested by (b). This profiled relation can be expressed by the adverb *together* (as proposed by Langacker), and also by the adjective *common* or by the verb *share*, as in the following examples:

The three people were together.

The three people have many common views and hobbies.

The group share their views and hobbies.

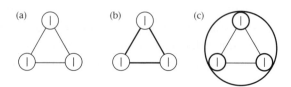

Figure 4.20 Profiling options for the cognitive unit *group*
(adapted from Langacker 1987b: 69)

In more general terms, we may say that the relation of togetherness and other cognitive relations can be rendered by verbs, adjectives, certain adverbs and – to complete the list – by prepositions.

The second profiling option (see diagram (c)) involves the cognitive unit as a whole, including the individuals involved and their relationship; in fact a whole cognitive region with all its components and their interconnections is profiled. This **profiled cognitive region** is rendered by a noun, the lexical item *group*; alternatively it might be expressed by a pronoun or by a more complex nominal phrase like *The Haydn Trio*.

Admittedly, the kind of profiling options observed with cognitive units like GROUP (or KNUCKLE or ELBOW) are not all that frequent. Normally, the facets of a conceived situation are either suited for 'nominal' profiles (i.e. those expressed by nouns and pronouns) or for relational profiles (verbs, adjectives and prepositions). Consider, for example, the situation of cooking a meal: it is fairly clear that the ingredients and the pots, pans and bowls in which the meal is prepared are denoted by nouns; the basic actions of cutting, turning and putting things into the vessels are rendered by verbs, though for more specialized activities there may be a choice between a verb denoting the action or a noun denoting the tool (*mix* vs *mixer*). What is more common than a noun/verb alternative is a choice between two relational profiles, for instance between a verb of motion and a preposition, as in the following examples:

1. (a) She *entered* the room
   (b) *into* the room
2. (a) He *left* the room
   (b) out *of* the room
3. (a) She *climbed* the tree
   (b) *up* the tree

These pairs of motion verbs and directional prepositions are also the prime examples for the fact that relational profiles have an internal figure/ground organization. As discussed in Section 4.1, prepositions like *out* and *up* (and also *into*) denote a relationship between a mobile trajector (the figure) and a stationary landmark (the ground), and this is also true of verbs of motion.

The question is: why are identical trajector/landmark relationships expressed in two ways, by verbs and prepositions? Or, more generally, how can the variation between word classes be explained? Looking for a cognitive explanation, Langacker suggests that the choice of word class is linked to and even determined by our cognitive abilities, in particular our ability to scan the cognitive input.

Scanning and word class distinction[17]

The assumed basic procedure of scanning is the identification of similar and dissimilar items, e.g. of white and black (or coloured) dots (Langacker 1987a: 101ff). Obviously, this is the principle of scanners that record the points of a picture or some other kind of document. After the scanning operation has been carried out, the accumulated information is made available on the computer screen or as a printout. Compared with this technical process, cognitive processing by humans, as it is conceived by Langacker, is more flexible and permits a major distinction between **summary scanning** and **sequential scanning**.

In summary scanning, the facets of a situation, as reflected in a cognitive unit, are examined one after the other, the data are added up, and when the scanning process has been completed, all the relevant aspects of the cognitive unit are assembled in the observer's mind as a whole, as a single 'gestalt' (see Section 1.2). This kind of scanning, which largely corresponds to computer scanning, is suitable for nominal profiles because it is capable of making a whole cognitive region simultaneously available and explains the kind of comprehensiveness of meaning that is typical of nouns. Yet, as we will see, summary scanning can also generate certain relational profiles which are expressed by prepositions or adjectives.

Compared with the summary approach, sequential scanning is more restricted in its application; in fact, it is only used for events (i.e. processes involving change). As with summary scanning, the relevant cognitive units are examined successively, but the data are only added up for a certain stage of the event; when this is done a new set of scanning data is collected for the next stage of the event, and so on. As a result, we are faced with a sequence of episodes that differ from each other, thus representing the change implicit in an event. The effect is similar to watching a film or a video. Just as the speed of the presentation keeps us from distinguishing between the individual pictures of the film, the even greater speed of cognitive processing suggests that the perceived event is an uninterrupted action. As this description suggests, sequential scanning is thus suitable for temporal relations and is predominantly expressed by (finite) verbs. The difference can best be illustrated for examples involving a clear trajector/landmark contrast, and this takes us back to the sets of motion verbs and prepositions listed under (1)–(3). Figure 4.21 illustrates the different types of scanning underlying the first pair, the verb *enter* and the preposition *into*; also included is the related preposition *in*.

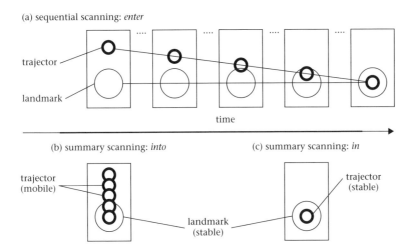

Figure 4.21 Sequential and summary scanning: *enter*, *into* and *in*
(adapted from Langacker 1987a: 144, 245)

This diagrammatic representation seems to be more convincing for sequential scanning. Just as in a film the process is divided up into individual pictures, which stand for an indefinite number of processing stages. Each stage is characterized by a certain relationship of trajector (the person entering) and landmark (the room), which differs slightly from the neighbouring pictures. Seen in sequence, these processing stages reflect the motion of the trajector into the landmark.

Summary scanning is more difficult to render by means of a diagram. Looking at the representation of *into* in diagram (b), we must keep in mind that it reflects the result rather than the individual stages of the scanning process. The various positions of the trajector along the path are, as it were, added up and projected into a single picture. The configuration of small circles stands for a total view of the path followed by the moving trajector. The landmark, though scanned over and over again like the trajector, does not change and is therefore symbolized by a single (larger) circle. In the case of *in* (Figure 4.21(c)) the nature of the scanning operation cannot be deduced from the diagram at all. Since not only the landmark but also the trajector is stable, one might easily get the (wrong) impression that this can be established in a single scanning operation. In fact repeated scanning operations are necessary to ascertain that the trajector is indeed stable. So figure (c) must be understood as a summary view of the relationship between trajector and landmark. Similar results are achieved when adjectival relations are scanned (e.g. *red, large, parallel*). In the case of nouns the scanning operation is much more complex, since the various elements and interconnections of the cognitive region must be scanned.[18]

Syntactic figure and ground revisited

Profiling cognitive regions as nouns and relations as verbs, adjectives and prepositions provides the raw material from which coherent utterances are constructed. This means that we can now go on to the last of our three initial questions and ask ourselves how the words and the underlying concepts combine to form clauses and sentences. This also takes us back to our discussion of clause patterns in Section 4.2. To give an example of what cognitive processing has achieved at this stage, let us imagine that we are dealing with the situation of a girl (Susan) preparing a Greek salad. To recapitulate the major cognitive processes that have already been carried out, we may make the following assumptions: the Greek salad situation has sparked off numerous cognitive stimuli; these stimuli have been profiled in relation to such basic domains as space and taste and with respect to more specific domains like food, vegetable, and vessel (the latter as a base for BOWL); the resulting cognitive units have been sifted for situational relevance (filtering out as irrelevant for SUSAN that she is wearing jeans, for instance, or for OIL that it can be used as fuel); as a final step the cognitive units have been profiled as cognitive regions (nouns) or relations (verbs and prepositions). The result is documented in Figure 4.22.

In this diagram, the background, the kitchen with its furniture and equipment and its additional functions apart from preparing salad, is already marked off as setting and left undifferentiated. The circles indicate the nominal profiles (the person involved, the ingredients, the vessel used, and the actual product, the Greek salad), while the relational profiles are signalled by the lines connecting the circles and the respective verbs and prepositions. If we recall the stage metaphor it is easy to see that the profiled nominal elements may be compared with the actors on the stage and the profiled relations with their interactions or, more generally, that the nouns stand for the participants of the situation and the verbs and prepositions for their interaction. It is with this in mind that Langacker talks of an **interactive network**.

This introduces another metaphor which suggests that there are many paths along which the participants can be connected and from which only some are selected as sentence constituents. This is shown in Figure 4.23. While diagram (a) is a schematic version of Figure 4.22, diagram (b) shows

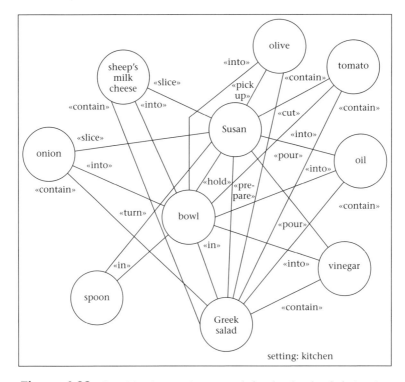

Figure 4.22 Cognitive interactive network for the Greek salad situation

how a certain combination of interrelated participants are chosen as the basis
of the clause pattern. As we know from Section 4.2, this process of selection
is governed by role archetypes, action chains and mental interactions
between participants, with the additional provision that the setting can be

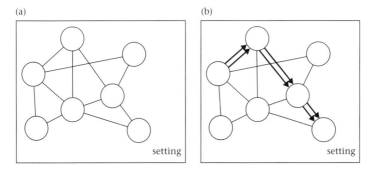

Figure 4.23 Interactive network and the selection of action chains/sentence
constituents

(schematic representation after Langacker 1990: 219)

included as container for a participant. The result is a syntactic structure in which the subject functions as figure, while the object may be, but need not be, added; if it is, it functions as ground. To return to Figure 4.22 and the Greek salad situation, we would expect that the speaker will select either the general action chain comprising an agent–subject as syntactic figure and a patient–object as syntactic ground (example (a) below), or that he will choose a sequence of more specific action chains in which agent/patient chains and agent/patient/locative chains are combined (example (b)); a third possibility is the combination of a setting-subject as syntactic figure (the Greek salad) which is linked to one or several patient roles acting as syntactic ground in a 'container–contained' relation (example (c)):

a. Susan is preparing the Greek salad.
b. Susan puts the oil and the vinegar into the bowl, stirs them, adds onions, tomatoes and olives and puts a large slice of sheep's milk cheese on top.
c. The Greek salad contains onions, tomatoes, olives and sheep's milk cheese.

Now that we have produced some actual sentences related to the Greek salad situation we may leave this subject with the feeling that the principle of prominence has proved helpful in answering our three initial questions. The concluding sections of the chapter will show that the figure/ground contrast can also be applied to pragmatic aspects.

Viewing arrangement

According to Langacker (1995: 9ff) prominence is one of the three principles guiding cognitive processing; the other two, which in a way are dovetailed with it, are specificity and perspective. The principle of **specificity** determines the level at which we interact with the world around us (at the basic, subordinate or superordinate level; see Chapter 2).[19] The second additional principle, perspective, is more often called **viewing arrangement** by Langacker.[20] This notion is best approached via the +STAGE+ metaphor, which has already been mentioned several times, mostly to describe what happens 'onstage', e.g. that participants in the action must be distinguished from the setting (see Section 4.2). However, the +STAGE+ metaphor also takes into account that there is an audience, and it is in this aspect, the relationship between offstage observer and onstage event, that the viewing arrangement manifests itself.

The normal or 'canonical' arrangement is that the relationship between audience (speaker/hearer) and onstage event is not expressed directly. What is expressed in an utterance is the onstage event, and this is why the 'third' person perspective is the norm. An alternative view, which is nevertheless also very frequent, is the egocentric viewing arrangement. Here the relationship between speaker/hearer and event is made explicit and expressed by the use of the deictic first person pronouns to refer to the speaker and second person pronouns for reference to the hearer. Other deictic (or indexical) items, such as *here* and *now*, *this* and other determiners are also understood as expressing reference to the 'viewing position' of the speaker. Compare the following examples where the canonical viewing arrangement is represented by (a), the egocentric variants (b) and (c):

a. (Where is the vinegar?) It is on the table. (relation to speaker/hearer not expressed)
b. I can see the vinegar. (relation to speaker expressed)
c. Have you seen the vinegar? (relation to hearer expressed)

According to Langacker, the viewing arrangement also provides a cognitive explanation of a number of other pragmatic phenomena. Among them are the major speech acts such as assertions (a typical onstage utterance such as *It is on the table* in (a)) and ordering (prototypically a speaker's directive act addressed to the hearer in an egocentric viewing arrangement, as in *Please pass the vinegar*). In addition the viewing arrangement is also assumed to cover what Langacker calls the psychological aspects of speech acts, which encompass the basics of pragmatic description such as Grice's Cooperative Principle and Searle's felicity conditions for successful speech acts.

But how can this diversity of aspects be subsumed under viewing arrangement and more or less be attributed to the speaker's position? Reviewing the argument of the last three chapters the solution will perhaps not come as a surprise. The relationship between onstage event and offstage viewer (i.e. speaker/hearer) is interpreted as an instance of figure and ground. In fact, as Langacker (1991: 498) puts it,

> the ground should be thought of, almost literally as the vantage point from which the speaker and hearer conceptualize the content evoked by a nominal or a finite clause.

In other words, the ground is where the speaker is rooted with not only his geographical, temporal, social, age and gender background, but also his psychological considerations about how to ensure that a speech act will be successful in communication.

COGNITIVE FUNCTION	FIGURE (PROFILE, TRAJECTOR)	GROUND (BASE, LANDMARK)
ORGANIZING PERCEPTUAL STIMULI	cognitive unit	cognitive domain
SELECTION OF WORD CLASS	nominal profile (nouns, pronouns) relational profile (verbs, preposi-tions, adverbs)	cognitive unit
PROFILING IN PREPOSITIONAL RELATIONS	trajector (e.g. 'fly' in: *fly in the soup*); see Section 4.1	landmark
PROFILING PARTICIPANTS IN INTERACTIONS	participants (agent, patient, experiencer); see Section 4.2	setting (location, etc.)
SELECTION OF SUBJECT AND OBJECT	syntactic figure (subject); see Section 4.2	syntactic ground (object, major complement)
PROFILING IN THE SPEECH EVENT	e.g. onstage position of profiled event	e.g. offstage position of speaker/hearer

Figure 4.24 An overview of major applications of the figure/ground segregation in Langacker's Cognitive Grammar

As an attempt to integrate pragmatic considerations into his framework, the link between speaker/hearer and ground is ingenious. It permits Langacker to develop an elaborate conception of 'grounding', i.e. how the relationship between onstage event and ground is established by tense, mood, nominal determiners and indefinite pronouns.[21] Whether it also yields much explanatory detail about speech acts and conversational implicature over and above the well-known pragmatic descriptions is another question.

To conclude this chapter, Figure 4.24 provides an overview which should bring home the pervasiveness of the principle of prominence in Langacker's framework. By extending and refining the notions of figure and ground, he has developed the most comprehensive cognitive conception available so far. Yet in order to give a fair evaluation of where cognitive linguistics stands today we also need to look at other approaches, especially those that stress a notion which is less explicit in Langacker's work, the notion of attention.

Exercises

1. Explain which of the elementary domains (space, temperature, taste, pressure, pain, colour) are called up, when the following cognitive units

are profiled: DOG, CHAIR, BALL, APPLE, ICE CREAM, SOUP, KISS. Which of them are particularly important in each case?

2. Profiling cognitive units normally goes through many stages involving elementary and more specific domains. Which domains contribute to profiling TOE NAIL, KEY HOLE (FRONT DOOR) and WINDSCREEN WIPER?

3. The area between the upper and lower arm can be profiled as the nominal category ELBOW or the verbal concept BEND. Show how, under certain conditions, the parts of the head marked with arrows can be profiled as nominal and verbal categories.

4. Draw an interactive network modelled on Figure 4.22 for one of the following situations: BEACH LIFE (see also Figure 1.14), ROAD ACCIDENT or WEDDING and identify suitable action chains.

5. How can the following sentences be interpreted in terms of viewing arrangement, i.e. onstage/offstage contrast:

> Peter married that beautiful Chinese girl.
>
> Did you attend the wedding?
>
> Then you must have seen her wonderful dress.
>
> It must have cost a fortune.
>
> Like all the other guests, I was fascinated.

Suggestions for further reading

Section 4.1

The study of prepositions was the preoccupation of many first-generation cognitive linguists. In addition to the publications referred to in the notes below we would like to mention Cuyckens (1991), Schulze (1988) and the special issue of *Cognitive Linguistics* edited by Sinha (1995). For an example of a more recent analysis see Taylor (2002, ch. 11).

1. Basic introductions to the main aspects of figure/ground segregation can be found in most textbooks on visual perception, e.g. Yantis (2001) and Gordon (2004).

2. See Talmy (2000/I: 315f) and Schmid (forthcoming) for summaries of typical characteristics of figures and grounds.

3. For literature on image schemas see Chapter 2, reading note 11.

4. Lakoff's summary (1987: 416ff) is more easily accessible than Brugman's MA thesis published in 1988. See also Taylor's (1988) discussion of *over* and other English and Italian prepositions and the discussion in Taylor (2002: 474–9).

5. See Vandeloise (1994) for a very useful survey of research into the preposition *in* and some basic theoretical issues that are at stake in the analysis of locative relations and their extensions.

6. The text in the chapter is based on Lakoff (1987: 435ff), but deviates from his treatment by excluding (bare) image schemas as source concepts of metaphors and establishing them as constituents of the mapping scope. See Section 3.1.

Section 4.2

The most comprehensive view of the issues discussed in this section is provided by Langacker (1991, chs. 7, 8); for a shorter account see Langacker (1990). See also Taylor (2002, ch. 21).

7. For introductions to the notion of valency see the first two chapters of Allerton (1982) and the introduction to Herbst *et al.* (2004: XXIII–XXXIII). For the function of theta-roles in Transformational Grammar see Radford (1988: 372ff, repr. 2004), for an applied view of semantic roles see Quirk *et al.* (1985: 740ff).

8. Talmy's notion of force dynamics can be approached through Talmy (2000/I: 409ff).

9. At this point it might be interesting to draw a comparison with Halliday's approach to transitivity, which also distinguishes between different types of processes with suitable participants: see Halliday (2004: 106ff).

10. Compare also Newman's (1996) book-sized cognitive-linguistic study of the verb *give*.

11. The differing status of locative adverbials is also treated in traditional descriptions (e.g. Quirk *et al.* 1985: 730ff) and has been dealt with in

case and valency grammar; see Fillmore (1968) and Halliday (2004: 149ff) on circumstantial elements.

12. For readers with a knowledge of German or Dutch it may be interesting to study how this explanation can be extended to non-referential German *es*, and Dutch *er* respectively; see Langacker (1991: 351ff). See also Lakoff's cognitive explanation of *there*-constructions (1987: 462ff).

13. The application of the prototype notion to syntactic and other linguistic phenomena is most extensively discussed by Taylor and MacLaury (1995, chs 8–12) and Taylor (2002, ch. 8).

14. To integrate passive sentences into his schematic definition of subjects and clause structure, Langacker postulates that the *-ed* morpheme used to form the passive past participle reverses the figure/ground structure of the active clause, turning the syntactic ground (the direct object) into the syntactic figure (subject) of the passive clause. See Langacker (1991: 200f).

Section 4.3

The most comprehensive account of Langacker's conception is contained in the two volumes of his *Foundations of Cognitive Grammar* (1987a/1991). Two of his articles, (1987b) and (1990), summarize part of the argument of this section, while three more recent papers (1992, 1993, 1995) provide concise surveys of his theory together with applications to specific problems. Further useful sources are Langacker (2000) and (2002), each containing revised versions of 12 articles that had appeared before. Langacker's approach to discourse is developed in Langacker (2001).

In contrast with the reading suggestions for Sections 4.1 and 4.2, the aim of the following notes is to point out passages in Langacker's publications which, in our opinion, might facilitate access to the aspects selected for discussion.

15. Key passages for understanding the notion of domain and the notion of profiling things in relation to domains are Langacker (1987a: 147–50 and 183–6), the notion of scope should be approached through Langacker (1987a: 117–20). See also Taylor (2002: 192–201) and Croft and Cruse (2004: 15–21).

16. For essentials of nominal and relational profiles see Langacker (1987a: 198, 214–22, 244–9). See also Langacker (1987b: 58–63, 68–9) and Taylor (2002, ch.11).

17. The central notions of summary and sequential scanning are introduced in Langacker (1987a: 144–6). The implications of scanning for verbal processes and 'atemporal' relations are summarized in 1987b (70–5). For the respective passages in 1987a, see reading note 16. Interesting technical aspects of the scanning process are discussed in 1987a (101–9, 209–13).

18. Scanning is also thought to be responsible for the distinction between finite verb forms (as discussed above) and non-finite forms. Their status and their interaction with auxiliaries in complex verb forms are investigated in Langacker (1987b: 75–89) and (1991, ch. 5.2).

19. Possible degrees of specificity are illustrated by Langacker for the 'glass-breaking situation' (*Floyd breaks the glass*, etc.). See Langacker (1991: 296ff).

20. The major aspects of the viewing arrangement are presented in Langacker (1987a: 122–32). The topic is taken up in Langacker (1991: 494–506), where he contrasts his position with acknowledged pragmatic thinking.

21. Langacker (1991: 89–91 and 193–7) are suitable as an introduction to the grounding phenomenon, while (1991: 96–125) provides a survey of grounding by means of determiners and (1991, ch. 6) is devoted to the grounding function of auxiliaries. For an interesting parallel see Halliday's interpretation of tense, mood and sentence types as grammatical realizations of the interpersonal language function (Halliday 2004, ch. 4).

CHAPTER 5

Frames and constructions

5.1 Frames and scripts

The necessity of looking at individual linguistic phenomena within their larger cognitive context has emerged in many sections of this book; categories were assembled into cognitive models, emotion concepts were developed into scenarios, and clause patterns were seen in relation to interactive networks. Still another cognitive attempt to widen the scope of lexical and grammatical analysis is provided by the notion of 'frame'.

Frame and perspective

The notion of frame was introduced into linguistics by Charles Fillmore in the middle of the 1970s based on his by now classic example, the so-called 'commercial event' frame.[1] To approach this frame, consider the aspects of a situation which would be described by using the English verb *buy*. In the initial state, a person A owns money and another person or institution D owns some goods that A wants to have. Taking for granted that the two participants come to an agreement on the price of the goods, person A gives a certain sum of money to D, and D surrenders the goods. The final state is that A owns the goods and D owns the money. Leaving the agreement aside as some sort of prerequisite, one could then say that the action category BUY includes a reference to at least four other categories, namely to a BUYER, a SELLER, GOODS and MONEY.

This configuration of interacting categories – the **frame** of BUY – is summarized in Figure 5.1. (Frames will be indicated typographically by small capitals in square brackets.) Postulating a frame for *buy* seems to offer at least two advantages: a single frame can account for various clause patterns, and it can be applied to different (though related) verbs like *sell, cost, pay*

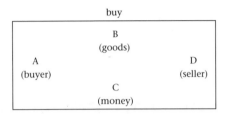

Figure 5.1   The [BUY] frame
(after Fillmore 1977a: 104)

or *charge*. First, consider the following sentence which exemplifies a syntactic pattern in which *buy* may occur:

   1. David bought an old shirt from John for ten pounds.

It is easy to see that in this sentence all four components of the [BUY] frame are rendered linguistically, each in a different syntactic slot: the BUYER (*David*) as subject, the GOODS (*an old shirt*) as direct object, the SELLER (*John*) as the first adverbial and the MONEY (*ten pounds*) as second adverbial. Let us call this assignment of syntactic roles, which is of course to a large extent governed by the choice of the verb *buy*, the **syntactic perspective** of the sentence. (Quite obviously, the notion of perspective relies on the principle of prominence, i.e. on figure/ground segregation, but, as we will see presently, it includes more than that.)

   The perspective of example (1) largely hinges upon the syntax of the verb *buy*. It is of course perfectly possible to put a different syntactic perspective on the same frame, and this takes us back to the other verbs mentioned above, namely *sell, cost, pay* and *charge*. For example, choosing the verb *sell* would allow us to put the categories SELLER and GOODS into perspective as subject and object, with the possibility of referring to the BUYER as an indirect object, as in example (2). The verb *charge* perspectivizes the SELLER and BUYER as subject and object (cf. (3)), and the verb *pay* the BUYER and MONEY, with an option to introduce the SELLER as indirect object (cf. (4)).

   2. John sold an old shirt to David for ten pounds.
   3. John charged David ten pounds for an old shirt.
   4. David paid ten pounds to John for an old shirt.

In short, we see that the [BUY] frame is not just a useful tool for the syntactic description of the verb *buy*, but it can also be applied to the verbs *sell, charge* and *pay*. In terms of the frame notion, the difference between the four verbs is simply a change of perspective within the same frame. Using Figure 5.1 as a basis for a more general [COMMERCIAL EVENT] frame, this difference

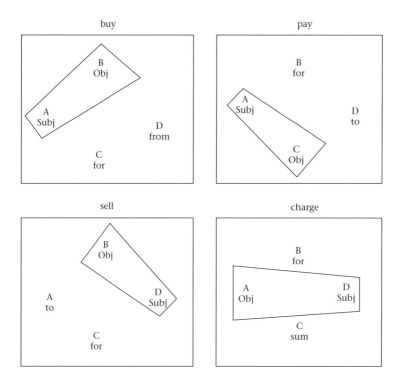

Figure 5.2   The [COMMERCIAL EVENT] frame with the perspectives evoked by the
verbs *buy*, *pay*, *sell* and *charge*
(after Fillmore 1977a: 106ff)

can be indicated by highlighting those components of the frame that make
up the subject and object for each verb. This is illustrated in Figure 5.2.

The four diagrams show that the two verbs *buy* and *pay* describe the commercial event from the BUYER's perspective, while *sell* and *charge* perspectivize
the situation from the SELLER's point of view. In addition to the choice of
subjects and objects, Figure 5.2 includes the prepositions that are used in
the adverbials. This is a first sign that the frame approach goes beyond the
figure and ground approach in that it pays more attention to the less prominent parts of sentences like adverbials.

The frame notion: different conceptions and related concepts

When Fillmore first used the notion of frame he defined it (1975: 124) as
any system of linguistic choices – the easiest cases being collections of words,
but also including choices of grammatical rules or linguistic categories – that
can get associated with prototypical instances of scenes.

This means that at that time, a frame was regarded as an array of linguistic options which were associated with so-called 'scenes', a notion related to our term 'situation' (see Section 1.3). Starting out from this linguistic position, the conception of the frame notion has shifted towards a cognitive interpretation. This becomes clear when we look at later characterizations of the notion of frame, also taken from Fillmore. In 1985 he says that frames are 'specific unified frameworks of knowledge, or coherent schematizations of experience' (1985: 223), in 1992 he views frames as 'cognitive structures [. . .] knowledge of which is presupposed for the concepts encoded by the words' (Fillmore and Atkins 1992: 75). What this collection of definitions and explanations shows is that while frames were originally conceived as linguistic constructs, they have by now received a cognitive reinterpretation.

Such a cognitive interpretation is even more convincing for the notion of perspective. Thus instead of advocating an independent 'syntactic perspective', one may argue that every sentence evokes a certain cognitive perspective on a situation by the choice of the verb and the particular syntactic pattern that it governs.

Accepting that perspective is a cognitive rather than a syntactic notion, one may ask what lies behind it. The basis for perspective is mainly provided by the cognitive ability of directing one's **attention**.[2] Among other things, the perspective from which we view a situation depends on what attracts our attention. Thus we use the verb *buy* in order to describe a commercial event when we want to direct the hearer's attention to the BUYER and the GOODS, and the verb *sell* when the focus of our attention is on the SELLER and the GOODS.

The reader who has followed our account of Langacker's Cognitive Grammar in the last two sections of Chapter 4 will probably be struck by the parallels between the figure and ground approach and the frame and attention approach as it is presented here. Langacker's idea of the profiling of participants in an interactive network as syntactic figure and ground is indeed very similar to the notion of perspectivizing two elements of a frame as subject and object. This parallel, one may well claim, is hardly surprising, given the fact that both approaches strongly rely on Fillmore's early Case Grammar. In addition, both approaches share the belief that clause patterns cannot be seen in isolation but against their cognitive background (i.e. the interactive networks or frames respectively).

However, the two approaches are far from identical. First, researchers working in the frame paradigm are much more interested in problems related to the meaning of the verbs that belong to a frame. Thus the frame notion has already been used for detailed semantic analyses of a number of verbs, and this has developed into the project of a frame-based dictionary.[3] Second, the frame approach presents a unified view of syntactic patterns, while Langacker tackles the problem on various levels of cognitive processing. Third, and perhaps most important, on each level of his analysis Langacker is almost exclusively interested in the two prominent entities, i.e. on the level of clause in the syntactic figure (or subject) and the syntactic ground (or object). Here, the frame notion has a wider scope, because indirect objects and adverbials are also addressed. In other words, the principle of promi-nence – as suggested by its name – applies to those elements in a sentence that attract the main part of our attention and are therefore prominent; the frame notion, however, also has something to say about linguistic items that attract only a small portion of our attention potential. This will become particularly evident when we turn to Talmy's notion of the 'windowing of attention' in 'event-frames' in Section 5.2.[4]

The wider scope of the frame approach also shows up in the fact that the [COMMERCIAL EVENT] frame even captures cognitive categories whose prominence is so low that they are not expressed on the linguistic surface at all. Two verbs where this is the case are *spend* and *cost*, as used in examples (5) and (6).

5. David spent ten pounds on an old shirt.

6. The old shirt cost David ten pounds.

Figure 5.3 shows that both verbs imply a SELLER who cannot be rendered linguistically (and is therefore put in brackets). Instead the perspective directs the attention to the BUYER and the MONEY when *spend* is used, and to the GOODS when the verb *cost* is chosen.

As it has emerged, frames can be conceived as a way of describing the cognitive context which provides the background for and is associated with

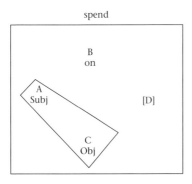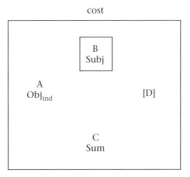

Figure 5.3 The [COMMERCIAL EVENT] frame with the perspective evoked by the verbs *spend* and *cost*
(after Fillmore 1977b: 107f)

cognitive categories. There is thus an obvious similarity with the 'cognitive models' introduced in Section 1.3. The difference is that in our conception cognitive models are of a more general nature than frames, so that frames are just one of a variety of cognitive models which also include the 'scenarios' mentioned in Section 3.2, domains and interactive networks (see Sections 4.2 and 4.3) and the 'scripts' that will be discussed below. Using this terminology, a frame is to be seen as a type of cognitive model which represents the knowledge and beliefs pertaining to specific and frequently recurring situations.[5]

From frames to scripts: flying on a plane

Linguistics is not the only discipline where the frame notion has been applied with quite impressive results (see reading note 1 this section). A second important field of research has been artificial intelligence, i.e. the discipline that researches the potential of computers to copy human behaviour. Here, the frame notion has been used in a more general, though also more technical, way than in linguistics. In this use of the term, the relevance of frames extends over the boundaries of single sentences to much larger linguistic and cognitive units. In order to understand how this wider conception of frames has an impact on linguistic phenomena, consider the following little story:

> Sue caught a plane from London to Madrid. After she had found her seat she checked whether the life vest was beneath it, but she could not find it. So she asked the flight attendant to find one for her.

What should attract attention here are the two occurrences of the definite article *the*. According to the rules of English grammar the definite article is used when one assumes that the hearer knows which specific person or thing one is talking about. If this is not the case the indefinite article is used as in *a plane* in the first sentence. Given these rules, one may ask why the *life vest* and the *flight attendant* are both accompanied by a definite article, although they are neither mentioned previously in the text nor specified later. This question is particularly interesting from the point of view of artificial intelligence, because it touches a notorious problem: even a computer which has been equipped with all the rules of English grammar and an extensive lexicon would have difficulty with our story, because it would look in vain for earlier references that might be helpful in identifying *the life vest* and *the flight attendant*.

Why, then, do the two uses of the definite article sound completely natural, although they cannot be explained with the rules of grammar alone?

The reason is that in order to understand the definite references we need to make **inferences** that are based on our world knowledge, and this is where the computer has a hard time of it. Everybody who has been on a plane knows (among many other things) that airlines provide life vests for all passengers, which are usually stored beneath the seats, and that there are flight attendants whose job it is to help passengers. All this knowledge is activated when *a plane* is mentioned in the first sentence of the text and it is this knowledge which allows us to make the right inferences without effort.

As an attempt to equip computers with the necessary world knowledge, the notion of frame was introduced into artificial intelligence. Thus the computer scientist Marvin Minsky defined a frame as 'a data-structure for representing a stereotyped situation' (Minsky 1975: 212). The idea is that in our plane example the cognitive category PLANE would activate a whole bundle of other categories which belong to the same [FLYING ON A PLANE] frame, for example PILOT, FLIGHT ATTENDANT, LIFE VEST, SAFETY BELT, FIRST CLASS, ECONOMY CLASS, SAFETY INSTRUCTIONS and so on. All these categories and the specific relations that exist between them (e.g. *X has a Y, X is on Y, X is a part of Y*) are part of the frame and must somehow be fed into the computer. In addition to this rather general frame there are many so-called subframes which capture the knowledge of still more specific situations of a flight, e.g. [EATING], [WATCHING THE MOVIE] and [GOING TO THE TOILET]. In view of the complexity of many everyday situations, Minsky suggested that our knowledge should be represented in complex 'frame-systems' (1975: 227ff).

Obviously cognitive categories play a major role within frames. Loosely speaking, categories act both as anchors and as triggers for frames, because it is in the format of categories and their interrelations that frames are designed and it is by the same categories that they are activated. A further function of categories is to provide so-called 'default assignments' (i.e. values for slots in the frame that apply under 'normal' conditions) by supplying context-dependent prototypes (see Section 1.3). For example in the [EATING ON A PLANE] subframe you will not expect to have your meal served on a huge dinner table, set with expensive tableware and a candle. As far as food and drinks are concerned you will presumably not reckon with a gourmet meal accompanied by a vintage wine (unless you are used to flying first class). All these expectations that are based on our experience and stored in our long-term memory are part of the frame-system and influence our ability to produce and understand the language related to it.

To keep matters simple the [FLYING ON A PLANE] frame has so far been presented as if it were a motley collection of categories. But this is of course a somewhat superficial way of looking at it. On more detailed inspection it

1. Pre-flight stage	go to airport → look for check-in counter → check in → go through customs (on international flights) → look for gate → wait for flight to be called
2. The flight	**Pre-take-off stage** board plane → look for seat → stow away hand luggage → sit down and buckle up safety belt → listen to safety instructions → take-off **Flight stage** get drinks → get meal → talk to neighbour, sleep, read, watch movie, etc. → go to toilet → buckle up safety belt → land **Post-landing stage** unbuckle safety belt → get up → get hand luggage
3. Post-flight stage	get off the plane → get luggage → go through customs (on international flights) → get out of airport

Figure 5.4   A rough summary of the [FLYING ON A PLANE] script

turns out that a flight exhibits a very predictable temporal structure in which one stage is often a prerequisite for the next stage. Viewing the flight from such a sequential perspective, we go beyond simple frames and move into the so-called **scripts**, i.e. knowledge structures that are particularly designed for frequently recurring **event sequences**. Before looking at one example of a script in more detail, we will round off our discussion of flights with a rough script-version of their sequential structure (cf. Figure 5.4).

The restaurant script

Although Figure 5.4 may give someone who has never been on a plane a fairly good idea of what happens on a flight, it is clearly insufficient as a thorough instruction for behaviour on a plane. To demonstrate what a more finely grained script would look like let us have a look at what is probably the most famous script in the literature, the [RESTAURANT] script as developed by the computer scientist Roger Schank and the social psychologist Robert Abelson (Schank and Abelson 1977: 42ff).

On a general level the [RESTAURANT] script can be divided into four scenes, namely entering, ordering, eating and exiting. In order for the first, the entering, scene to occur, a number of conditions must be fulfilled, as summarized in Figure 5.5.

It is clear that the main conditions for the application of the [RESTAURANT] script concern the people and the objects that make up the situation. Starting out from these props and roles, we then assume that the entering scene

Props	**Roles**	**Entry conditions**
tables	customer (S)	S is hungry
menu	waiter (W)	S has money
food (F)	cook (C)	
bill	cashier (M)	
money	owner (O)	

Figure 5.5 Preconditions of the
[RESTAURANT] script
(after Schank and Abelson 1977: 43)

can take place: the customer enters the restaurant, looks for a table, decides where to sit, walks to the table and sits down on a chair. Each of these actions is a prerequisite for the next to be performed, and the whole scene taken together is necessary for the ensuing scene to take place in which the meal is ordered. The ordering scene is represented in somewhat greater detail in Figure 5.6. In this figure the actions that are performed by the participants

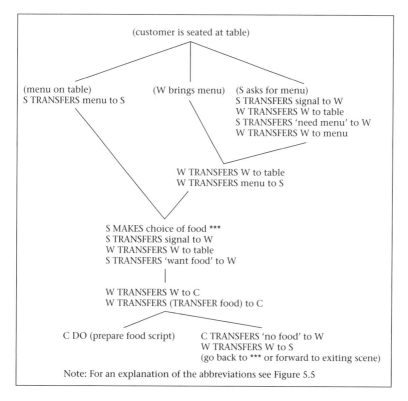

Figure 5.6 Ordering scene of the [RESTAURANT] script
(adapted from Schank and Abelson 1977: 43)

are expressed in a very basic kind of language which is similar to the commands used in a computer program.

How is the ordering scene integrated into the script? Figure 5.6 shows that when the scene begins, three states of affairs are possible: there may be a menu on the table, the waiter may bring the menu or the customer may ask the waiter to bring the menu. Depending on which of these three states applies, the script runs along three different paths, which should however all end with the customer having the menu. Once the customer has the menu in hand, the next step is the choice of food, which is communicated to the waiter, who walks into the kitchen and informs the cook of the order. After that, again two paths are possible: the cook may prepare the food and in so doing create the precondition for the eating scene. Alternatively, the cook may signal the waiter that the desired food is not available. When this happens, there are again two alternative continuations of the script. Either the customer makes another choice of food (this means that the script is resumed at the point indicated by *** in Figure 5.6) or the customer decides to leave the restaurant. In the second case the script jumps to the exiting scene or, more specifically, to the variant of the exiting scene in which the customer leaves the restaurant without paying.

The eating and the exiting scene can also be represented in the script format in a similar way. The reader may now feel that the contents of the [RESTAURANT] script are fairly banal and that the whole business of writing scripts ultimately comes down to translating things that we all know into a special format. Although it is true that we are all familiar with the information stored in scripts, such a view misses the point; it disregards the fact that when we produce or listen to language we unconsciously fill in an incredible amount of information taken from frames and scripts. And what is more, without supplying this information we would certainly not be able to understand even the most simple pieces of discourse. To show that this is true, consider the two stories below, taken in slightly adapted versions from Schank and Abelson (1977: 38f):

1. John went into a restaurant. He asked the waitress for coq au vin. He paid the bill and left.
2. John went into a restaurant. He saw a waitress. He got up and went home.

Although the two stories roughly give the same amount of information, the first is perfectly understandable, while the second does not seem to make sense. The reason for this discrepancy is that the first story fits our internalized script of a meal in a restaurant, and therefore we have no difficulty in filling in the missing parts, e.g. that John presumably looks at the menu before he orders and that he eats his meal before he pays and leaves. Indeed the script may be so powerful that when we form a mental representation of the story we do not even notice that the important eating scene is not expressed linguistically. The potential of scripts, and incidentally also frames, to ensure that the right inferences are made is especially important in face-to-face conversation. Here speakers often rely very much on the hearer's knowledge of a script when they leave out details or whole stages in their description of an event.

In contrast to the first story, the second does not correspond to the script expectations called up by the initial sentence. When they are processed, the three sentences merely describe a collection of situations which do not combine to build a coherent whole. This means that unless links are provided by a script, the events cannot be brought into a meaningful causal chain.[6]

Altogether this section has discussed a number of conceptions and applications of the notions of frame and script. Frames were presented as structured patterns of knowledge related to recurring situations, which are reflected linguistically in the lexical relations between verbs and in the syntax of clauses. To account for knowledge structures that represent larger sequences of events connected by causal chains, the notion of script was introduced. In the next section another conception of the frame notion will be introduced, namely Talmy's universal 'event-frames'.

Exercises

1. Which of the following verbs fit Fillmore's commercial transaction frame and which perspective do they represent?

   leave (to one's heirs), inherit, auction off, pawn, distribute, receive

   Does the frame have to be changed for some of these verbs?

2. Dirven *et al.* (1982) use the notions of scene (i.e. our frames) and perspective to describe the difference between *say, tell* and *talk*. Study our representation for the verb *say* and complete the diagrams for *tell* and *talk*.

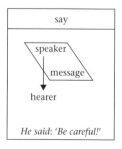

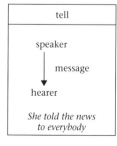

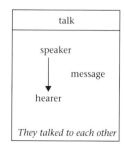

3. Just like other types of cognitive models, frames and especially scripts are culture-dependent. To show this, discuss how your model of a child's birthday party differs from the following one, which is given by Minsky (1975: 243):

dress	Sunday best
present	must please host
	must be bought and gift-wrapped
games	hide and seek, pin tail on donkey
decor	balloons, favours, crepe-paper
party-meal	cake, ice-cream, soda, hot-dogs
cake	candles, blow-out, wish, sing birthday song
ice-cream	standard three-flavour

4. Try to write the scripts [AT THE HAIRDRESSER'S] and [IN THE CINEMA]. What are the obligatory elements of these scripts; which optional aspects (e.g. 'buy popcorn') can be integrated?

5. Here are two little stories which call up the [ORAL EXAM] script. Explain why the first seems to make sense whereas the second does not, although both give roughly the same amount of information:

   (a) Before her oral exam Jane was very nervous. Nevertheless she managed to answer all questions. When the professor told her that she had passed, she jumped in the air.

   (b) Before her oral exam Jane was very nervous. Nevertheless she talked for some time to a professor. When she went home, she was very sad.

5.2 Event-frames and the windowing of attention

As has been shown, frames can provide valuable tools for the linguistic and conceptual analysis of situations like buying and selling, or having a meal in a restaurant. This section will demonstrate how the notion of frame can be extended to describe more general situations, such as event chains linked by temporal sequences or causation.

To a large extent, the explanatory power of the commercial event-frame discussed in the last section lies in the fact that it captures only the more general elements of situations of buying and selling. Thus the frame contains no information as to the people who participate in the commercial event, the kind of goods that are purchased and the particular sum of money that changes hands. Nevertheless, the information provided by the frame is still fairly specific. For example, the everyday practices of paying by credit card or by cheque would require an alteration of the original frame. In cultures where goods are traded for other goods rather than sold for money, the frame would not be valid at all. In more general terms, frames as we have got to know them are cognitive structures that are context- and culture-dependent.

The question is whether the notion of frames is restricted to certain contexts and cultures, or whether it can be conceived of as being a much more basic cognitive phenomenon that underlies a wide variety of real-world situations and is shared by all human beings. Such a universalist–cognitive line of research is pursued by Talmy in his investigation of event types (Talmy 2000/II: 25ff).

Motion events and motion event-frames

To understand Talmy's notion of event, or more specifically, motion event, it is helpful to recapitulate some aspects of situations with moving objects that have already been mentioned in this book. In Section 4.1, the example of a balloon flying over a house was used to illustrate the way in which the perceptual input of a real-world situation is organized in terms of figure (or 'trajector') and ground (or 'landmark'). In this example, there can be no doubt that the moving balloon functions as 'figure' while the stationary house serves as a point of reference or 'ground'. A further component of the situation mentioned in Section 4.1 is the 'path' along which the figure (the balloon) travels. Granted that figure/ground segregation is a universally valid principle of perception, it may well be assumed that these three components, 'figure', 'ground' and 'path', are crucial for a cognitive description of a motion event.

If one takes the conceptual analysis of motion events one step further, it emerges that other aspects of a motion event can be isolated. To start with, motion itself can be regarded as a fourth component of motion events. At first sight this may seem rather trivial, because 'motion' is the property that seems to define the whole event. Yet if one tries to analyze the figure of the event in terms of motion, it becomes clear that the relationship between 'figure' and 'motion' is actually rather complex. Although the concept of motion can hardly be conceived without a figure, the reverse is not true. As the example of a book lying on a table in Figure 4.2 has shown, figures that do not move are perfectly normal. Pursuing this idea a little further, one can include static locative relations between a movable (though unmoving) figure, such as a book, and its ground (e.g. the table) as a special case of motion, i.e. zero-motion or locatedness with a zero-path. The advantages of such an approach have already emerged in Section 4.1, where static uses of prepositions were treated as elaborations of more fundamental dynamic uses. The conclusion is that motion and figure are not inseparably associated with each other, and that MOTION should be added to FIGURE, GROUND and PATH as a component of the event in its own right.

Describing the balloon situation mentioned above, one may perhaps utter a sentence like *A balloon flew over the house*. In this sentence the verb *fly* does not just refer to the fact that something is moving. In addition to the conceptual component 'moving', *fly* also describes the way or MANNER of the movement (as opposed to, e.g., *running* or *crawling*), and this may be regarded as a fifth component to the structure of a motion event. Finally, even if we do not always express it linguistically, we know that for a motion event to take place something must have caused the moving object to start moving or stay in motion; this CAUSE element can also be an important factor in the conceptualization of motion events, but like MANNER it seems to have a less central status.[7]

Altogether, six cognitive components seem to play a role in the conceptual structure of a motion event, namely FIGURE, GROUND, PATH, MOTION, MANNER and CAUSE, and can thus be said to define the motion **event-frame**. Figure 5.7 provides a set of examples used by Talmy to illustrate how all six components can be expressed in fairly simple English sentences.

As the figure suggests, *the pencil* functions as FIGURE and *the table* as GROUND in all four sentences. The MOTION component is expressed in the verbs: *roll* and *blow* refer to a 'true' motion, *lie* and *stick* to the special case of zero-motion, i.e. locatedness. PATH is rendered by prepositions, with *off* denoting a real course through space and *on* denoting a stable location in space. Finally, the reference to the two components MANNER and

	FIGURE MOTION PATH GROUND	FIGURE MOTION PATH GROUND
'GENUINE' MOTION	The pencil rolled off the table.	The pencil blew off the table.
LOCATEDNESS	The pencil lay on the table.	The pencil stuck on the table (after I glued it).
	MANNER	CAUSE

Figure 5.7 Sentences illustrating the six components of motion events (framing event and co-event)
(compiled from Talmy 1985: 61 and 2000/II: 26)

CAUSE is incorporated in the verbs. Here *roll* and *lie* indicate the manner of the movement, while *blow* and *stick* denote the cause.

Generalizing from motion events, Talmy arrives at the following definition of the notion of **event-frame**, which can also be transferred to other types of events:

> A set of conceptual elements and interrelationships that . . . are evoked together or co-evoke each other can be said to lie within or constitute an *event-frame*, while the elements that are conceived of as incidental – whether evoked weakly or not at all – lie outside the event-frame.
>
> (Talmy 2000/I: 259)

Altogether, Talmy identifies the following five types of event-frames: motion event-frames, causation event-frames, cyclic event-frames, participant-interaction event-frames and interrelationship event-frames. To keep matters as simple as possible our discussion will – apart from a short discussion of causal event frames – stick to motion event-frames, which have the most tangible structure of the five types and provide the best examples of what Talmy has called 'windowing of attention'.[8]

Windowing of attention in motion event-frames

Let us start out from a somewhat more elaborate description of a flight situation than the balloon-flying-over-the-house type discussed in Section 4.1:

> On 26 July 1909 Louis Blériot flew across the English Channel from Les Baraques to Dover.

Applying Talmy's motion-event analysis we can readily identify some parts of this sentence as instantiations of the components of the motion event-frame. This is shown in Figure 5.8.

However, this first application leaves important elements of the sentence unaccounted for. Among them are the initial adverbial (*on 26 July 1909*), which provides incidental information about the time at which the event took place, and therefore lies outside the event-frame. The other two adverbials (*from Les Baraques* and *to Dover*) are obviously related to the PATH component, an essential element of the motion event.

FIGURE	MOTION	PATH	GROUND
Louis Blériot	flew	across	the English Channel

Figure 5.8 Realization of major event-frame components

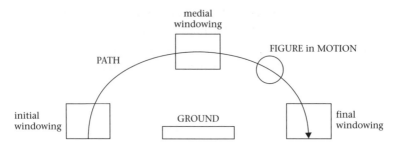

Figure 5.9 Schematic representation of positional types of windowing

Their specific function becomes clearer when we consider all three spatial adverbials contained in this sentence. While the first (*across the Channel*) is seen as evoking the whole PATH component of the motion event-frame, the second and third (*from Les Baraques* and *to Dover*) are regarded as explicit specifications of the PATH component drawing attention to its initial and final points.[9] This cognitive process of foregrounding certain portions of an event-frame is called **windowing of attention** by Talmy (2000/I: 258–309). The reverse process, in which conceptual material that makes up part of an event-frame is backgrounded, is labelled **gapping**. With regard to a motion event-frame, the two processes can be referred to as 'path-windowing' and 'path-gapping' because it is along the PATH component that a number of attentional windows can be 'opened' or 'closed'.

For the purpose of analysis, Talmy distinguishes three positions along the path that can be foregrounded: initial, medial and final windowing. These three forms of path-windowing are schematically represented for the *Louis Blériot* example in Figure 5.9. How all three positional types of windows and their combinations can be expressed on the linguistic surface is illustrated in Figure 5.10 with example sentences taken from Talmy.

The crate that was in the aircraft's cargo bay fell –		
1. Single windows:		
a:	initial windowing	– *out of the airplane.*
b:	medial windowing	– *through the air.*
c:	final windowing	– *into the ocean.*
2. Combined windows:		
a + b:	initial and medial windowing	– *out of the airplane through the air.*
a + c:	initial and final windowing	– *out of the airplane into the ocean.*
b + c:	medial and final windowing	– *through the air into the ocean.*
a + b + c:	maximal windowing over the whole PATH	– *out of the plane through the air into the ocean.*

Figure 5.10 Initial, medial and final path-windowing and combinations
(adapted from Talmy 2000/I: 266)

The sentences in Figure 5.10 show that path-windowing is achieved by explicitly using linguistic expressions that refer to certain portions of the PATH. Conversely, if a conceptual element that is part of the event-frame is not explicitly referred to, it is backgrounded by exclusion, or 'gapped'.

On the hearer's side one may assume that, given sufficient context, the gapped portions of an event-frame can always be reconstructed. This means that no matter how many portions of it are windowed for attention, the PATH is always conceptualized in its entirety. In terms of cognitive processing, the whole path is cognitively represented, but the foregrounded chunks of conceptual content are treated with the increased processing capabilities of the attentional system, and this leads to more elaborated and fine-grained cognitive representations.

As has been shown, one way of looking at the path-windowing process is concerned with the positions of the windows. Another, perhaps even more basic, distinction concerns the types of PATHS that an object, in its function as FIGURE, may follow. Here three types can be distinguished: open paths, closed paths and fictive paths. Both the *Louis Blériot* and the *crate* examples belong to the **open path** type, which is defined as a path whose beginning point and ending point are at different locations in space. Schematically these paths can be imagined as shown in Figure 5.9 as one-way arrows from one point to another.

The paths of the second type, i.e. **closed paths**, are the same as open paths, except that they should be imagined as circular arrows. In other words, the starting and the end point of closed paths coincide at the same location in space. A linguistic illustration of this type of path with windows in different positions is given in Figure 5.11. In this example the figure is not

I need the milk. –		
1. Single windows:		
a:	initial windowing	– **Go.*
b:	medial windowing	– *Get it out of the refrigerator.*
c:	final windowing	– *Bring it here.*
2. Combined windows:		
a + b:	initial and medial windowing	– *Go get it out of the refrigerator.*
a + c:	initial and final windowing	– *Go bring it here.*
b + c:	medial and final windowing	– *Get it out of the refrigerator and bring it here.*
a + b + c:	maximal windowing over the whole PATH	– *Go get it out of the refrigerator and bring it here.*

Figure 5.11 Illustration of closed path-windowing
(after Talmy 2000/I: 268)

explicitly mentioned. It is represented by the person at whom the impera-
tives (*Go and get*, etc.) are directed. This person probably starts out from the
table, moves to the refrigerator and returns to the table, thus completing a
circular path.

With the exception of single initial windowing, all positions and combinations of windows are possible in this example. What Talmy does not
do is provide a reason as to why the initial position of the path cannot be
foregrounded. One possible answer is that the fact of a departure taking place
does not include enough information about the rest of the path to ensure
that the whole motion event is realized. When only the first portion of the
PATH is mentioned, as in the variant *Go* in Figure 5.11, it is not even clear
whether the PATH actually comes to a full circle (and thus qualifies as a closed
PATH) or whether it is an open PATH. Thus the logic behind these unacceptable windowing variants seems to be this: whereas the medial and final portions of paths allow for an inferential conceptualization of the entire path,
the information contained in the initial portions is not sufficient to establish the whole ensuing path.

Fictive paths

The third type of paths in motion events, **fictive paths**, is more clearly
set apart from the other two. The way they are envisaged by Talmy, fictive
paths remind us very much of the static uses of dynamic locative schemas
such as 'over', 'up', and 'out' as discussed in Section 4.1 (e.g. *Hang the painting over the chimney*; cf. Figures 4.10 and 4.11). The analogy is that in both
cases locative relations that are normally understood as unchanged through
time are expressed as involving an imaginary path.

As an example, consider a situation in which a friend asks you to lend
him or her your bike. Imagine further that at the time of your friend's request
you are in a building and the bike is locked up at a certain place in the
street, so that you have to describe its precise location to your friend. One
convenient way of doing this would be to refer to some salient point in
the vicinity of your bike and specify the relation between this point and
the place where your bike can be found. Using this strategy you may perhaps utter a sentence like *My bike is across the street from the bakery* (Talmy's
example). Although the main locative relation in this sentence (*be across*)
has traditionally been regarded as a prime example of a static predicate, it
lends itself to an alternative interpretation in terms of a fictive path
describing the access to the object in question.[10] This can best be seen when
we put ourselves in the position of the language recipient: having taken in

the sentence, the hearer will respond by first directing his or her mind's eye to the reference point (*the bakery*) and then constructing a mental, or fictive, path *across the street*. It is at the end of this path where he or she will think the bike has been placed.

Having accepted that the sentence can actually be analyzed as an instance of the motion event-frame, we can also investigate the way in which the cognitive process of path-windowing is at work. With this goal in mind, we have again integrated the example sentence in a list of possible ways of describing the event (Figure 5.12). Comparing the sentences in Figure 5.12 to the description of the fictive PATH above, one important point must be kept in mind: with fictive PATH windowing the order of the linguistic constituents does not necessarily follow the direction of the PATH. To show this, let us compare the maximal windowing along a fictive PATH (i.e. 2.a + b + c in Figure 5.12) to the maximal windowing order of adverbials along an analogous 'real' PATH, as exemplified by the sentence *Go from the bakery across the street to the lamppost* (see Figure 5.13). While in this sentence the order of the adverbials follows the direction of the PATH, this is not true of the fictive PATH; as is illustrated in Figure 5.13, the final portion of the fictive PATH is rendered by the first adverbial, i.e. *against the lamppost*, and the initial portion of the PATH by the last adverbial (*from the bakery*).

Concluding the discussion of fictive paths, attention should be drawn to the two windowing variants in Figure 5.12, where the main reference point (*the bakery*) is omitted or gapped (1.b: *It is across the street*, and 2.b + c: *It is*

Where is your bike? –		
1. Single windows:		
a:	initial windowing	*It is across from the bakery.*
b:	medial windowing	*It is across the street.*
c:	final windowing	**It is leaning against the lamppost across.*
2. Combined windows:		
a + b:	initial and medial windowing	*It is across the street from the bakery.*
a + c:	initial and final windowing	*It is leaning against the lamppost across from the bakery.*
b + c:	medial and final windowing	*It is leaning against the lamppost across the street.*
a + b + c:	maximal windowing over the whole PATH	*It is leaning against the lamppost across the street from the bakery.*

Figure 5.12 Illustration of fictive path-windowing
(based on Talmy 2000/I: 269)

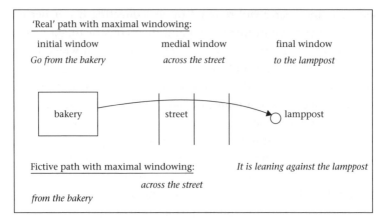

Figure 5.13 'Real' path-windowing and fictive path-windowing

leaning against the lamppost across the street). As Talmy points out, this element can only be gapped when 'its identity is generally provided by the context or by convention' (2000/I: 269). This means that textual and situational factors external to the event-frame have to be taken into account for a proper analysis of such a sentence. In Section 5.3 we will pursue these supra-sentential considerations further and discuss the role of event-frames in texts.

Causal-chain windowing

Apart from motion event-frames and the windowing and gapping options they offer, this section deals with a second type of windowing, which involves causal-chain event-frames. This type of event-frame is particularly interesting because it offers an alternative approach to a familiar, and indeed famous, linguistic example, namely the semantic analysis of the verb *break* (see Section 4.2). However, before we enter this field, a word must be added about the notion of causation and causal chains.

Traditionally, the notion of causation has been treated as a simple yes-or-no category, i.e. a lexical item was either classified as 'non-causative' (e.g. *die, fall*) or 'causative' (*kill, drop*). However, Talmy argued as early as 1976 that different degrees of causation exist. One type are events that are caused by other events which do not involve animate beings (= 'event-causation', e.g. *the vase broke*). These should be distinguished from events whose outcome is caused, but not intended, by a person (= 'author-causation', e.g. *he broke the vase by mistake*). A third type is events whose outcome coincides with the agent's intention (= 'agent-causation', e.g. *he broke the vase to irritate his wife*). In addition to postulating a gradient of causativity Talmy claimed that many events involving causation should be treated as complex sequences of more elementary stages and subevents.[11]

To illustrate the latter point, consider the sentence *John broke the window (with a stone)*, in its agent-causative sense, i.e. with an agent who deliberately initiates the action with a certain goal in mind (example adapted from Talmy 2000/I: 272f). A cognitive analysis of the causative event that is described by this sentence shows that it consists of the following subevents:

1. The agent makes up his mind that he is going to break the window.
2. He bends his knees, moves his hand to the ground to grasp a stone, straightens up and lifts the stone with his hand, swings his arm while holding the stone in his hand, and releases the stone from his hand thus propelling it forward.
3. The stone sails through the air.
4. The stone forcefully makes contact with the window.
5. The window breaks.

Looking at the interrelation between these five subevents one realizes that each subevent is linked to the next by a causal relation, and this motivates Talmy's term 'causal-chain event'. As in the case of motion events, it is now possible to deduce from this example the components of the more generally valid **causal-chain event-frame**. Figure 5.14 gives a rough version

Stages of causal event-frames	Ex. *John broke the window with a stone*
1. Agent intends to act	1. The agent makes up his mind that he is going to break the window.
2. Agent sets parts of his body or his whole body in motion and thereby initiates the causative event	2. He bends his knees, moves his hand to the ground to grasp a stone . . . , releases the stone from his hand thus propelling it forward.
3. Intermediate subevent(s) which are causally related to each other (optional)	3. The stone sails through the air.
4. Penultimate subevent = immediate cause of final result	4. The stone forcefully makes contact with the window.
5. Final resulting subevent = agent's intended goal	5. The window breaks.

Figure 5.14 The stages of causal event-frames
(adapted from Talmy 2000/I: 272)

of the stages of a causal-chain event-frame, which is illustrated by the analysis of the sentence *John broke the window with a stone*, as developed above. Just as in the case of motion event-frames, the most interesting aspect of causal-chain event-frames is again their potential for the windowing of attention. Let us start out from what is probably the standard way of referring to the above situation, from the sentence *John broke the window*. Putting this sentence in relation to the structure of the causal-chain event-frame we realize that stage 1 (the agent) and stage 5 (the final result) are windowed for attention, while the medial stages are gapped. That this kind of 'discontinuous' windowing over agent and result is the most natural way of describing a causal event is not surprising, because it answers the two most important questions 'What happened?' and 'Who initiated the event?' In fact, the link between the intention (stage 1) and its realization (stage 5) in an agent-initiated causal event seems to be so strong that the two stages 'feel seamlessly linked', as Talmy (2000/I: 276) puts it, and the missing parts between them hardly reach the level of awareness. Apart from the initiating agent and the final result, the penultimate event (stage 4) is certainly the most significant aspect in a causal-chain event-frame, because it refers to the immediate cause of the final result. The cognitive significance of stage 4 is reflected in the English language by the fact that one of the main agentive–causative constructions, the *by*-clause, is reserved for the penultimate subevent.

This clearly emerges from Figure 5.15 which lists *by*-phrases expressing the various stages of a causal-chain event-frame. In this collection only the last variant, the phrase *by hitting it with a stone*, is fully acceptable because only this variant represents the penultimate event. As is indicated by the question mark, example (f) is also found acceptable by some speakers who seem to infer from the sentence that the stone actually hits the window. This means that in effect they treat the phrase as referring to the penultimate event.

I broke the window –
    (a) *by grasping a stone with my hand.
    (b) *by lifting a stone with my hand.
    (c) *by swinging a stone with my arm.
    (d) *by propelling a stone through the air.
    (e) *by throwing a stone towards it.
    (f) ?by throwing a stone at it.
    (g) by hitting it with a stone.

Figure 5.15 English *by*-clause reserved for penultimate subevent
(adapted from Talmy 2000/I: 273)

Although many fascinating aspects of event-frames and windowing have not been touched yet, this is as far as we can take their discussion. What this section should have shown is that the frame-based analysis can be extended beyond Fillmore's more 'traditional' position. In this view, the directing of attention is more or less restricted to the choice of subject and object as required by certain verbs. Talmy's notions of event-frames and windowing, however, widen the investigation towards the previously neglected adverbials and other less prominent parts of the clause structure. His approach also takes account of so-called 'blocked complements', i.e. those aspects of event-frames that cannot be expressed on the linguistic surface (e.g. *The book cost ten pounds *to John/*from Sue*).[12] Talmy's approach thus provides a comprehensive cognitive view of how real-world situations are processed in our mind and are rendered linguistically.

In this section frames were approached from a universalist–cognitive point of view, from which event-frames seem to be shared by speakers of all languages. Section 5.3 will deal with some examples of language-specific framing, where the components of frames are expressed by different means in different languages. The concluding section 5.4 will again be devoted to a more general discussion of how frames can be seen as being linked with syntactic structures in constructions.

Exercises

1. Analyze the following sentences as instances of motion event-frames:

   We flew from Strasbourg to London.

   Sir Edmund Hillary climbed to the top of Mount Everest in 1953.

   The train goes from Brussels through the Chunnel to London.

   The Northern Line will take you from Edgware via Charing Cross to Morden.

2. Decide which of the following sentences represent closed and which open paths and describe these paths:

   We are moving to London.

   Could you empty the waste paper basket, please?

   I'll go and get the newspaper from the newsagent's.

   Shall I fetch the dictionary from the study?

   The bus to the City Hall goes via Regency Terrace.

   They arrived from New York last night.

3. Which positional windows are 'opened' in the following sentences?

> The apple fell from the tree to the ground.
>
> The space shuttle was launched from the space centre at Cape Canaveral.
>
> The parachutists glided from the aeroplane through the clouds to the landing place on the airfield.
>
> Amundsen went across the Antarctic to the South Pole.

4. The following examples can all be understood as being based on fictive paths. In each case, give a description which follows the course of the fictive path and contrast it with the arrangement of the elements in the sentence.

> You'll find the matches on the cupboard in the corner behind the kitchen door.
>
> The book on Chinese porcelain is on the third shelf from the top in the white bookcase.
>
> (Are you looking for your car keys?) I think they're among the groceries on the back seat of the car.
>
> I think I parked the car on the third level somewhere to the right of the entrance.
>
> I remember the disco is on the right-hand side just after the second traffic lights down Market Street.

5. Analyze the situation of a hunter shooting a rabbit with his gun as an instance of causal-chain event-frame and decide which of the following *by*-clauses are acceptable.

The rabbit was killed

> by Peter's taking his gun along.
>
> by Peter's raising his gun.
>
> by Peter's aiming at the rabbit.
>
> by Peter's pulling the trigger.
>
> by Peter's shot.
>
> by the bullet.

5.3 Language-specific framing and its use in narrative texts

Keeping the focus on motion events, this section will widen the scope on event-frames in two ways. First, differences in the expression of motion event-frames in various languages will be investigated. Second, it will be shown that the language-specific framing of motion events has consequences for the respective narrative style which seems to be typical of English and Spanish stories and novels.

As shown in Section 5.2, the conceptual representation of motion events seems to involve six components: the four central components FIGURE, GROUND, MOTION and PATH and the two optional ones, MANNER and CAUSE. When they are expressed in an utterance, these components typically occupy specific positions in the clause. This was illustrated by the Blériot sentence in Figure 5.8, which is here repeated as Figure 5.16(a).

To recapitulate, the FIGURE in the English sentence is rendered as the subject (*Blériot*); the PATH and the GROUND are expressed as an adverbial consisting of the preposition *across* and the noun phrase *the Channel*. Finally, the MOTION and MANNER components are incorporated in the meaning of the verb *fly*. Although this arrangement seems to be quite natural for English speakers, it turns out to be true only of the English version of the sentence. If we try to translate the Blériot sentence into French, we cannot imitate the English construction, because the literal translation **Blériot vola par-dessus la Manche* is unacceptable. According to a French style manual for translators of English and French (Vinay and Darbelnet 1975), the closest equivalent is the sentence *Blériot traversa la Manche en avion*, literally 'Blériot traversed the Channel by aeroplane'. Unlike the English sentence, in which the PATH is expressed by the preposition, the French version incorporates the PATH in the verb meaning. The MANNER is expressed in an adverbial construction which is added to the clause. See the analysis in Figure 5.16(b).

It seems, then, that English and French diverge with regard to the syntactic construction and the expressive potential of the two verbs. As demonstrated by Vinay and Darbelnet (1975), such cross-linguistic differences were noticed by translators long before cognitive linguistics came onto the scene. Yet by viewing them from the cognitive perspective of Talmy's event-frames, it is possible to give a more comprehensive and unified account of what used to be treated as unrelated phenomena.

(a)	*Blériot*	*flew*	*across*	*the Channel.*
	FIGURE	MOTION	PATH	GROUND
		MANNER		
(b)	*Blériot*	*traversa*	*la manche*	*en avion.*
	'Blériot	traversed	the Channel	by aeroplane.'
	FIGURE	MOTION	GROUND	MANNER
		PATH		

Figure 5.16 Event-frame analysis for an English sentence and its French translation

Verbs of motion in English, German, French and Spanish: some illustrations

To start with, let us have a look at the expression of the PATH component, this time including German and Spanish in our considerations. In the following set of examples, the linguistic item expressing the PATH component is shown in bold print to make the comparison of the different versions easier. (As above, literal glosses are given below the non-English versions):

E.   *The boy went **out** of the yard.*

G.   *Der Junge ging aus dem Hof **hinaus**.*

      'The boy went from the yard **out**.'

Fr.   *Le garçon **sortit** de la cour.*

      'The boy **exited** from the yard.'

Sp.   *El chico **salió** del patio.*

      'The boy **exited** from the yard.'

These examples show two things. First, the English and the French version suggest that the above contrast between *fly across* and *traverser en avion* is not an isolated example, but seems to reflect the general tendency of English to express the PATH by means of a particle, and of French to incorporate the PATH in the verb meaning. Second, it is evident that German runs parallel to English and Spanish parallel to French. In German the PATH is expressed in a verbal particle (here separated from the complex verb *hinausgehen* and moved to clause-final position), and this is similar to the English particle. In Spanish, on the other hand, the PATH is incorporated in the verb just like in French.

To give an idea of how consistent this difference between French and Spanish on the one hand and English and German on the other actually is, the table in Figure 5.17 lists major verbs expressing motion in space. The pattern in this table fully confirms our impression so far. While French and Spanish motion verbs refer to both MOTION and PATH, the English and German verbs express only MOTION while the PATH is rendered by a particle.

French	Spanish	English	German
entrer	entrar	go in (enter)	hineingehen
sortir	salir	go out (exit)	hinausgehen
ascendre	subir (ascender)	go up (ascend)	hinaufgehen
descendre	bajar (descender)	go down (descend)	hinuntergehen
traverser	traspasar	go over (cross, traverse)	hinübergehen

Figure 5.17 Expression of MOTION and PATH in major verbs of motion in French, Spanish, English and German

For English this is notably true of the combinations with the verb *go*, which is of Germanic origin and belongs to the core vocabulary. As the verbs in brackets show, the 'French' verbs are also available, but they belong to a more formal stylistic level and are therefore less frequent.

Turning to the expression of MANNER in the description of motion events, the four languages pair off exactly in the same way. To show this, we will again first give an example of a whole sentence as rendered in the four languages, where this time the linguistic elements denoting the MANNER component are highlighted:

E.   *The boy **rode** out of the yard.*

G.   *Der Junge **ritt** aus dem Hof hinaus.*
      'The boy **rode** from the yard out.'

Fr.   *Le garçon sortit **à cheval** de la cour.*
      'The boy exited **on horse** from the yard.'

Sp.   *El chico salió **a caballo** del patio.*
      'The boy exited **on horse** from the yard.'

Just as in the Blériot example, in English and German the MANNER of the movement is incorporated in the verb, while in French and Spanish the MANNER is added as a separate adverbial. Again the difference is not just restricted to this particular case but applies to many other verbs as well. Some further examples are listed in the table in Figure 5.18. The table shows that where English verb-particle constructions and German complex verbs express MOTION plus MANNER and PATH, as in section (b) of Figure 5.18, the French and Spanish counterparts become quite elaborate if both elements are to be rendered.

English	German	French	Spanish
(a) MOTION + MANNER			
walk	(zu Fuß) gehen	aller à pied	ir a pie
ride	reiten	aller à cheval	montar caballo (ir a cabballo)
drive	fahren	aller en voiture	ir en coche (conducir)
(b) MOTION + MANNER + PATH			
walk into	hineingehen	entrer en marchant	entrar (caminando)
drive into	hineinfahren	entrer en voiture	entrar conduciendo el coche
ride into	hineinreiten	entrer à cheval	entrar a caballo
fly into	hineinfliegen	entrer en volant	entrar volando
crawl into	hineinkriechen	entrer en rampant	entrar arrastràndose
climb into	hineinklettern	entrer en grimpant	entrar escalando

Figure 5.18 Expression of MOTION, MANNER and PATH in verbs of motion in English, German, French and Spanish

Description of PATH and MANNER: verb-framed vs satellite-framed languages

As confirmed by stylistic manuals like Vinay and Darbelnet (1975),[13] it is certainly possible to describe the cross-linguistic differences in the use of motion verbs in traditional terminology. However, these traditional accounts tend to neglect an important point: when we watch a moving object or person, the path of the movement and the manner in which it is performed are not separate aspects of the situation, but clearly related to each other, at least perceptually. This is why a unifying cognitive view, as is implied in Talmy's event-frames, promises a more convincing explanation.

Although PATH and MANNER are closely linked in the event-frame, this does not cancel out what has been said about the unequal status of these elements. While MANNER is an optional element, a component of the co-event in Talmy's terminology, which can remain unexpressed (as in E. *go out*, Fr. *sortir*, and Sp. *salir*), PATH is one of the central elements of the framing motion-event (see Section 5.2). One way of expressing the framing function of PATH is through the verb, as in Fr. *entrer* and Sp. *entrar*. In view of this, French and Spanish can be called **verb-framed languages** (Talmy 2000/II: 117f, 221ff). Conversely, PATH can be rendered by a particle, as in E. *go into*, or by a verbal particle, as in G. *hineingehen*. To capture the common function of these last two elements, they have been subsumed in one grammatical category by Talmy, labelled 'satellites'. Hence, English and German can be called **satellite-framed languages**.

Talmy (2000/II: 221ff) has argued that probably all languages of the world can be categorized in terms of verb-framing and satellite-framing. The group of verb-framed languages includes all Romance languages, Semitic languages (e.g. Arabic and Hebrew), Japanese and many others. Satellite-framed languages besides English and German are all Indo-European languages (apart from the Romance languages), Finno-Ugric languages and Chinese.

As the examples in the previous section suggest, the cross-linguistic differences in the expression of PATH which gave rise to the distinction between verb-framed and satellite-framed languages seem to coincide with the way the MANNER element is expressed. And indeed, when Talmy (2000/II: 213ff) investigated a range of languages, this impression was confirmed. As a result, we may integrate the contrastive findings on the expression of PATH and MANNER into one general picture. Figure 5.19, which provides such a unified view, is a slightly simplified version of a diagram used by Talmy to summarize his results.

English: satellite-framed

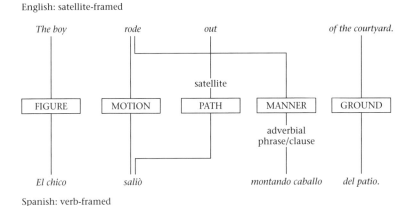

Figure 5.19   Expression of PATH and MANNER in motion events in English and Spanish (based on Talmy 1991)

Figure 5.19 provides us with a concise representation of the strategies the two types of languages follow when it comes to expressing the PATH and the MANNER of a motion event. By looking at the cross-linguistic differences from the cognitive perspective of the event-frame in which they are embedded, the difficulties faced by translators become more transparent. Thus, what seems to be at stake is not just a random collection of 'untranslatable' verbs, but completely different mapping systems of cognitive frame components onto linguistic elements.

While the typological differences discovered by Talmy are interesting in themselves from a syntactic point of view, they also have far-reaching consequences for the narrative style typical of the two groups of languages. In what follows we will have a look at some stylistic differences between English and Spanish focusing on the two major aspects that have emerged, namely that in verb-framed languages the MANNER of a motion event usually has to be added to a clause as a separate adverbial, and that in satellite-framed languages the PATH needs to be expressed in a particle or similar element.

Expression of MANNER and MOTION: a comparative study of novels

Basically, a verb-framed language like Spanish often needs more linguistic material to express the MANNER of a motion event than a satellite-framed language such as English. In order to supply the same quantity and specificity of information that is contained in English motion + manner verbs, Spanish speakers often need an elaborate paraphrase. Verbs like *bolt, dart, scamper, scurry, scuttle, scramble, slither, slide, sidle, slink* (taken from LLCE: 614f) represent just the tip of the iceberg, and all of them are virtually 'unrenderable' in Spanish. When it comes to translating, Spanish translators are thus confronted with the problem of how to cope with this difference.

Working within Talmy's framework, Slobin (1996) addressed precisely this issue in a comparative study of translations of English-language novels into Spanish and vice versa. Slobin took his material from five Spanish-language and five English-language novels by such well-known Latin American, British and North American authors as Isabel Allende, Gabriel García Màrquez and Mario Vargas Llosa, and Daphne du Maurier, Ernest Hemingway and Doris Lessing. All in all he collected 100 descriptions of motion events in both languages. Anticipating his main result, it can be said that

> Spanish translators omit manner information about half of the time, whereas English translators actually **add** manner to the Spanish original in almost a quarter of their translations. (Slobin 1996: 212)

Omission of manner information is often practised by Spanish translators where English motion + manner verbs have no direct Spanish counterpart. Thus, in the following two examples from James Michener's *Chesapeake* and John Fowles's *The French Lieutenant's Woman*, the translator has simply chosen to neglect the manner component which is incorporated in the English verbs *stomp* and *rustle*:

> He stomped from the trim house . . .
> *Salió de la pulcra casa . . .*
> 'He exited from the trim house . . .'
> Mrs Tanter rustled forward, effusive and kind.
> *Mrs Tanter se adelantó, efusiva y amable.*
> 'Mrs Tantler moved forward, effusive and kind.'

As a second strategy, the translator may decide to add an adverbial clause in order to capture the manner component. For an illustration, compare this with another way of translating the verb *rustle* quoted by Slobin from du Maurier's *Rebecca*:

> She rustled out of the room . . .
> *Salió del cuarto, acompañada del susurro siseante de sus ropas . . .*
> 'She exited the room, accompanied by the swishing rustle of her clothing . . .'

Here the translator has made quite an effort to express the manner denoted by the English verb *rustle*. However, the side-effect is that the translation gives the manner of the movement much more prominence than in the original, and therefore the translation can hardly be judged as being more true to the original than the one in the preceding example which is based on what could be called the leave-out strategy.

Reversing the perspective, the first interesting observation concerning English translations of Spanish novels is that sometimes translators seem to avoid English cognates of Spanish verbs. As already mentioned above, this may be due to the fact that English words of Romance origin often have a ring of formality about them. For an illustration consider the following example found by Slobin in Vargas Llosa's *La tía Julia y el escribidor* (*Aunt Julia and the Script-Writer*), where the first line gives the original, the second the literal gloss and the third the translation in the English version of the book:

> *Don Federico avanzó sin apresurarse . . .*
>
> 'Don Federico advanced without hurrying . . .'
>
> *Don Federico walked unhurriedly towards her . . .*

Another example of the same type, this time taken from Allende's *La casa de los espirítús* (*The House of Spirits*), is even more interesting:

> *Se dirigió a la casa, abrió la puerta de un empujón, y entró.*
>
> 'He directed himself to the house, opened the door with a push, and entered.'
>
> *He walked up to the house, gave the door a single forceful push, and went in.*

The first thing we notice is that the two Spanish verbs *dirigir* and *entrar* are not translated with their English cognates *direct* and *enter*, but by the more colloquial verb-particle constructions *walk up to* and *go in*. Second, it is worth having a closer look at the middle portion of the sentence. Here the literal translation *opened the door with a push* is avoided by the translator, although it would certainly have been acceptable. Another translation, *pushed the door open*, is not used either; this would in fact have been rather typical of English because the MANNER of the movement is incorporated in the verb and the PATH and the resultant state are expressed in the satellite *open*. Instead the translator prefers the translation *gave the door a single forceful push*. The reason probably lies in the translator's intention to emphasize the MANNER in which the movement was performed, and this motivates the choice of a construction that permits a more vivid manner description.

Summing up at this point, the data provided by Slobin for the expression of MANNER indicate that the lexico-syntactic differences between English and Spanish seem to have consequences on the level of the rhetorical style of narratives. Perhaps the most spectacular result of the study is that Spanish translators of English narrative texts often have to weigh up descriptive detail against syntactic complexity. This should be kept in mind when we now turn to the expression of PATH in English and Spanish stories.

Expression of PATH in English and Spanish stories and novels

As a second source of material for his article, and also for a book co-edited with R. Berman (Berman and Slobin 1994),[14] Slobin uses authentic stories. Perhaps it is worth noting that material from stories circumvents a potential methodological flaw inherent in the comparison of translations: undoubtedly translators are influenced by the image evoked in the original in their descriptions of events, and this may lead to rather unnatural results. In a story, however, the narrator is free to express his or her own perception and conception of an event. The problem with freely produced stories, on the other hand, is that different stories cannot be compared as easily as translations of the same text. Therefore Slobin and his co-workers elicited stories from Spanish and English speakers in Berkeley and Madrid by means of one and the same wordless picture story called *Frog, Where Are You?* (Mayer 1969). In this way, 60 stories with virtually identical content were collected for each language from 12 narrators in each of the following age groups: 3-, 4-, 5-, 9- year-olds and adult. To give an idea of what the story is about, here is Slobin's own short version of the story:

> The events depicted in *Frog, Where Are You?* invite a rich array of motion
> descriptions: A pet frog escapes from its jar and a boy and his dog go looking
> for the lost frog. Their search involves falling from a window, climbing and
> falling from a tree, climbing a rock and getting entangled in the antlers of a
> deer who throws the boy and dog over a cliff into some water, and finally
> climbing out of the water and over a log to discover the runaway frog.
>
> (Slobin 1996: 197)

To find out how the narrators expressed the PATHS in the many instances of motion descriptions, let us start by looking at the verbs used to describe motion events in the 60 stories in each language. While the Spanish narrators could manage with as few as 27 verb types, the English narrators produced a much greater variety of verbs: counting the verb stems alone, Slobin found 47 verb types; when the combinations with satellites were also taken into account, the number increased to 123 simple and phrasal verb types. In the following list those verbs used by the English narrators which had the largest number of attested satellites are collected:

climb	+*down, on, out, over, up, up in, up on*
come	+*after, down, off, on, out, over, up*
fall	+*down, in, off, out, over*
fly	+*after, away, off, out, over, up*
get	+*away, down, in, off, on, out, over, past, up, up on*
go	+*down, down out, home, in, off, out, outside, over, through, up*
knock	+*down, down out, in, off, out*
run	+*after, along, away, by, from, in, off, out, over, through*
throw	+*down, down in, in, off, over, over in*

Although some of these verbs, e.g. *come* and *fall*, also include at least a hint about the nature of the PATH, it is fairly clear that in the English stories descriptions of PATH are mainly achieved through satellites. Extreme cases are verbs like *get* or *go* which have virtually no meaning over and above the MOTION component, but an enormous potential for PATH descriptions once they are connected with a satellite. As an interim summary, then, one may very well claim that the systematic results from Slobin's study confirm our more or less impressionistic observations from above.

As with MANNER, the difference in the expression of PATH leaves its mark on the narrative style that is typical of the two languages. For one thing, the English narrators seem to devote much more attention to the details of PATHS than the Spanish narrators. A particularly striking aspect of these descriptions is that even young English narrators seem to be proficient in the strategy which was called 'windowing of attention' in Section 5.2. In opening attentional windows, they exploit the resources of their satellite-framed language for detailed descriptions of PATHS. It seems that windowing structures of the type *The deer threw the boy* **over a cliff into a pond**, which include a medial and final window on the PATH, abound in the English stories.

The picture changes when one looks at the Spanish stories. Even when the Spanish data were augmented to 216 stories with narrators from Latin America, not more than three examples could be found where either an initial or a medial window was combined with a final path window. This observation is the more striking because the Spanish language clearly has the linguistic means for path-windowing, as one of those examples shows:

*Se cayó **de la ventana a la calle*** ('[The dog] fell from the window to the street'.) In spite of this structural potential, however, Spanish speakers appear to be much more reluctant to use them than speakers of English.

A look at a more extended example will demonstrate this reluctance more clearly and show how the description of the setting of an event is related to the description of the PATH. First, compare the following Spanish and English descriptions of an episode in *Frog, Where Are You?*, where the boy is carried off by a deer to a cliff, from which he is thrown into a pond.

Sp.   *El ciervo le llevó hasta un sitio, donde debajo habiá un río. Entonces el ciervo tiró al perro y al niño al río. Y después, cayeron.*

'The deer took him until a place, where below there was a river. Then the deer threw the dog and the boy to the river. And then they fell.' [age 9]

E.   *He [the deer] starts running and tips him off over a cliff into the water.* [age 9]

Both the Spanish and the English youngsters supply us with a remarkable amount of information on the PATH that the FIGURE, i.e. the boy (and his dog), follows, and on the setting where the event occurs. But they do it in decidedly different ways. The Spanish child devotes a whole relative clause to relating where the event took place (*un sitio, donde debajo habià un rió* 'a place where below was a river'). Thus the setting is rendered as one event in its own right and described in a rather static way in an extra clause. In the English version, however, such an isolated and static description of the setting does not occur. Instead the setting is incorporated in the motion event. To show how this is done, Figure 5.20 gives an event-frame analysis of the second part of this sentence.

As the analysis in Figure 5.20 shows, a surprising number of cognitive components are expressed in this innocuous-looking clause. Besides the agent and the four components of the main motion event-frame, two additional elements, namely CAUSE and MANNER, are incorporated in it. On top of that, two attentional windows are opened on the medial and the final portions

He	tips	him	off	over a cliff	into the water.
AGENT	MOTION	FIGURE	PATH	medial window	final window
	CAUSE			of attention	of attention
	MANNER			(setting)	(setting)

Figure 5.20   Event-frame analysis of the sentence *He tips him off over a cliff into the water*

of the PATH. In contrast to the Spanish version, these path windows allow for an incorporation of the setting in the motion event, and this results in a more dynamic description of the setting. The English child seems to devote much more attention to the changing relation between the figure and the ground or setting. The Spanish child, on the other hand, leaves some parts of the movement to be inferred from the static description of the setting. For example, the PATH that leads from the boy's being thrown by the deer to his fall into the river must be inferred from the prior information that the river was located below.

To wrap up the discussion let us return once more to the comparison of novels and their translations. Consider the examples below, where the English original from Daphne du Maurier's novel *Rebecca* is given first, followed by the Spanish translation and its literal English translation.

> I . . . climbed up the path over the cliffs towards the rest of the people.
>
> *Tomé el sendero que conducía al lugar donde estaba la gente.*
>
> 'I took the path that led to the place where the people were.'

Du Maurier's original sentence contains a fairly detailed description of an extended motion event which highlights the GROUND (*the path*) and includes attentional windows on the medial (*over the cliffs*) and the final portion (*towards the rest of the people*) of the PATH. As in the examples above, these windows also contain the information on the setting of the event. From the syntactic point of view, it is worth noting that all this is expressed in a single clause. The Spanish translation, however, needs three clauses as opposed to the one in English, and yet it omits two pieces of information contained in the original. First, there is no reference to the vertical directionality of the path, which is expressed in English by the satellite *up*. Second, the medial window on *over the cliffs* is not retained in the translation. Apart from these omissions, the Spanish translation also differs from the original in that it isolates the details about the setting from the movement by expressing it in two separate relative clauses. This slows down the pace of the Spanish description and, compared to the single dynamic picture drawn in the English version, gives it a more static, step-by-step character.

According to Slobin, Spanish translators are apparently well aware of this difference. This can be seen from translations in which locative detail seems to be omitted deliberately for the sake of a more dynamic event-description. In the following two examples from *Rebecca* and J. Fowles's *The French Lieutenant's Woman*, attentional windows that are opened in English are not rendered in Spanish and 'the Spanish reader is simply not informed of the entire journey' (Slobin 1996: 211):

> He strolled across the room to the door . . .
>
> *Se dirigió a la puerta . . .*
>
> 'He went to the door . . .'
>
> . . . she moved out into the sun and across the stony clearing . . .
>
> . . . *la muchacha salió al claro rocoso . . .*
>
> '. . . the girl exited to the stony clearing . . .'

In the first example the medial window of the PATH *across the room* is gapped in the translation. In the second sentence the initial window *into the sun* is omitted and the description of the PATH is rendered somewhat loosely as 'to the stony clearing'.

Altogether, as it has emerged in this section, applying the notion of event-frames to the comparison between different languages and between different narrative texts yields some interesting findings. Apparently, a satellite-framed language such as English is better suited for descriptions of MANNER and elaborate PATH descriptions including dynamic descriptions of locations along the PATH. The reasons are that in satellite-framed languages MANNER is often incorporated in the verb meaning, and the information on the PATH and setting can be expressed in the same clause as the motion event by opening attentional windows. Since Spanish is a verb-framed language, descriptions of motion events tend to be restricted to the motion itself. Often the description of MANNER is only possible at the cost of extended and rather awkward constructions. Similarly, if details of the PATH and the setting are to be given, they are expressed in additional clauses. As this will sometimes slow down the pace of narratives considerably, Spanish speakers may opt for fewer MANNER and PATH details in favour of a more vivid MOTION description.[15]

Exercises

1. Analyze the English sentences and their French counterparts (taken from Vinay and Darbelnet 1975: 106) in terms of the motion event-frame (cf. Figure 5.19):

   > She tiptoed down the stairs.
   >
   > *Elle descendit l'escalier sur la pointe des pieds.*
   >
   > 'She descended the stairs on the tip of the feet.'

He crawled to the other side of the road.

Il gagna en rampant l'autre côté de la route.

'He gained crawling the other side of the road.'

2. Check the etymological origin of the following synonym pairs or near-synonym pairs in a suitable dictionary. How do they mirror the distinction between verb-framed and satellite-framed constructions? Why does English often have both options?

soak through	*percolate*	*run off*	*escape*
get there	*arrive*	*send out*	*emit*
come upon/across	*encounter*	*throw up*	*vomit*
break out	*erupt*		

3. Look up the following English verb + satellite constructions in a bilingual Spanish or French dictionary and discuss how they are rendered. In some cases it may be helpful to counter-check the equivalents that are given.

hop in, squeeze into, creep in, tread in, pour in, flow in, break into

4. Here is an extract from a Turkish version of the frog story (Slobin 2005: 314). Look at the length and number of clauses and the expression of PATH and MANNER and discuss the rhetorical style in relation to the English and Spanish examples in the text.

Geyikla uçurumum kenarina doğru gidiyor. Köpek de yanlarinda koşuyor. Çocuğa aşağiya atiyor, kopek de düşüyor aşağiya. Uçurumum dibinde bir göl varmiş. Göle düşüyorlar.

'With the deer [he] goes straight to the edge of the cliff. The dog runs by their side. [He] throws the boy down, and the dog falls down too. At the bottom of the cliff there was a lake. [They] fell to the lake.'

5. Look at the following English–French examples (taken from Vinay and Darbelnet 1975: 106). Discuss how many clauses are needed for the description of the event and how PATH and MANNER are expressed in the two languages:

Through the wide-open window streamed the sun on to the yellow varnished walls and bare floor.

Par la fenêtre grande ouverte, le soleil entrait à flot et inondait les murs vernissés en jaune et le parquet sans tapis.

'Through the wide-open window, the sun entered floating and inundated the walls varnished in yellow and the parquet without carpet.'

5.4 Construction Grammar

As it emerged in the previous chapters, frames are patterns of knowledge extracted from the experience of recurring situations and events. What is crucial from the linguistic point of view is that frames and the possible perspectives they open up are reflected linguistically in the syntax of clauses or, the other way round, that syntactic patterns may be associated with the conceptual structure of the frame. In this chapter we will look at the theory of Construction Grammar, which claims that this is indeed the case.

From frames to constructions

In Section 5.2, the motion event-frame was introduced to explain the relationship between the conceptual structure of events and their linguistic descriptions. As Talmy suggests, the motion event-frame comprises the central components MOTION, FIGURE, PATH and GROUND, and, in addition, the MANNER and CAUSE components. The more complex variant including the two latter components was illustrated in Section 5.2 by the sentence *The pencil blew off the table*, in which the CAUSE element is integrated in the verb meaning 'moving caused by blowing'. A more explicit way of describing the same situation highlighting the CAUSE element would, for example, be *The draught blew the pencil off the table*. This sentence represents a frame structure that includes elements of both Talmy's motion event-frame (since the pencil is blown off the table) and his causal-chain event-frame (the motion is caused by the draught, an example of event-causation). This combination can be called caused-motion event-frame. Compare Figure 5.21, in which this frame is contrasted with the respective syntactic pattern.

Even if the example may sound a little far-fetched, the caused-motion event-frame is widely used, also with agent-subjects. Other sentences realizing this frame can easily be retrieved from a corpus, and this shows that it is not an ad-hoc decision to postulate such an event-frame. Here are some instantiations taken randomly from the International Corpus of English – Great Britain (ICE-GB):

I [. . .] shoved them into a corner

I brought her out of hospital.

Example	The draught	blew	the pencil	off	the table
Frame structure	CAUSE	MOTION	FIGURE	PATH	GROUND
Syntactic structure	Subject	Verb	Object	Adverbial	

Figure 5.21 Conceptual and syntactic structure of the caused-motion event-frame

They kicked him to the ground.

We can always put a pillow over her head.

The fact that there is a very close correspondence between frame components and syntactic constituents has led cognitive linguists to the idea – which is central to a group of theories subsumed under the term *Construction Grammar* – that the syntactic pattern itself may have a share in the encoding of the particular type of experience. What this means is that we do not simply map frame components onto syntactic constituents guided by the particular perspective that we have in mind, but pick a certain syntactic pattern or **construction** wholesale, so to speak, from long-term memory, where it is stored. However, not only the syntactic make-up of the construction, but also the knowledge about the kinds of scenes and events that the construction typically encodes, is stored in long-term memory. This in turn means that the construction itself conveys some of the conceptual content to be expressed or, in other words, that **the construction carries a meaning of its own** which is related to the corresponding conceptual frame.

But how do we know that the meaning resides in the caused-motion construction and is not just part and parcel of the verb meaning (*blow, shove, bring, kick, put* in the examples above), as maintained for instance in Fillmore's earlier Case Grammar? An argument put forward by Adele Goldberg (1995), one of the protagonists of Construction Grammar, is that we readily identify the caused-motion meaning not only in sentences with fitting verbal meanings (*kick, put, shove*), but also in examples whose verbs, taken by themselves, do not at all suggest a caused-motion meaning. Compare the following pair of examples, where the first sentence represents the prototypical caused-motion arrangement associated with the verb *push*, while the second example contains the verb *sneeze*, which is commonly regarded as intransitive and does not suggest a caused-motion meaning (Goldberg 1995: 152):

Frank pushed the tissue off the table.

Frank sneezed the tissue off the table.

Yet due to the force of the constructional meaning, the second example will also be interpreted in terms of caused motion and may be paraphrased as 'Peter sneezed and thus caused the tissue to be swept off the table'. A similar influence of the caused-motion construction can be observed with other intransitive verbs coupled with an adverbial, especially adverbials used in a figurative sense, as in the following examples:

Barnes [. . .] plays him into trouble.

The police tear-gassed the demonstrators into panic.

In both sentences the goal-orientation is not incorporated in the verbs (*play, tear-gas*), but is derived from the construction as a whole. The constructional approach also provides an interesting interpretation for the whole group of so-called transitive–causative verbs, where the transitive use has tradition-ally been regarded as a special sense to be distinguished from the central intransitive meaning of verbs like *sit* or *stand*:

> And then we'll sit you on your bike.
>
> She stood the flower-pot on the window-sill.

Summarizing what has been shown in this section so far, we will focus on three points:

- There seems to be a close correspondence between certain conceptual structures derived from everyday experience and syntactic structures apparently generated on the spur of the moment.
- Evidence collected by linguists working in the framework of Construction Grammar suggests that constructions may in fact not be generated as we go along but stored in long-term memory just like frames and even individual concepts are.[16]
- Constructions may have meanings of their own independent of the lex-ical items inserted in particular instantiations. Just like words, con-structions are claimed to be pairings of forms and meanings, such that the form automatically evokes the meaning and vice versa.[17]

In the next section we will discuss further examples of constructions, test the claim that constructions are experientially grounded and illustrate their polysemy.

Argument-structure constructions

The caused-motion construction is one of the major argument-structure con-structions (i.e. constructions in which verbs are linked with their obligatory complements or arguments). The other two major constructions discussed by Goldberg (1995) are the cause-receive construction (Goldberg herself sticks to the syntactic label 'ditransitive') and the resultative (i.e. cause-become) construction, which are illustrated in the following examples:

CAUSE-RECEIVE CONSTRUCTION	CAUSE-BECOME CONSTRUCTION (resultative construction)
Joe gave Sally the ball.	*Terry wiped the table clean.*
Joe painted Sally a picture.	*He ate himself sick.*
Bob told Joe a story.	*Terry pushed the door shut.*

Construction	Basic experience	Basic clause structure
Caused-motion construction	Someone causing something else to move	Subject–Verb–Object–Adverbial (SVOA)
Cause-receive construction	Someone causing someone else to receive something	Subject–Verb–Object$_{ind}$–Object$_{dir}$ (SVOO)
Resultative construction	Someone causing something to change state	Subject–Verb–Object–Object complement (SVOC$_O$)

Figure 5.22   The experiential and syntactic basicness of argument-structure constructions
(based on Goldberg 1995: 70)

The conceptual make-up of these constructions is straightforward: the caused-motion construction consists of a cause (expressed by the subject), which initiates the motion directing the patient towards a goal. The CAUSE-RECEIVE construction comprises an agent causing a recipient to receive a patient, and the resultative construction an agent causing a patient to be in a resultant state ('become'). What these three constructions share is that they join basic human experiences with basic syntactic clause patterns. This is shown in Figure 5.22, which is based on Goldberg (1995: 70).

It must be emphasized that such a direct experiential basis seems only plausible for simple and basic clause patterns of the type illustrated. The fact that similar clause patterns can also be found in many other languages of the world reinforces the view that they may be grounded in shared human experience.

However, another caveat must be added here: like most constructions, the three argument-structure constructions can occur in a range of related meanings. This means that just like lexemes **constructions are poly-semous**,[18] and it is only the central and typical senses of argument-structure constructions that may in fact be experientially grounded. As Goldberg puts it: 'Constructions which correspond to basic sentence types encode as *their central senses* event types that are basic to human experience' (Goldberg 1995: 39; our emphasis). To illustrate the polysemy of constructions, Figure 5.23 represents the major senses of the caused-motion construction.

The nature of these semantic variants of the caused-motion construction is reminiscent of Brugman's and Lakoff's attempts (see Section 4.1) to explain the range of meanings of the preposition *over* as interconnected elaborations and extensions of a central sense. Sense (b), for example, differs from the central sense (a) in that the motion is not strictly entailed by verbs like *ask*. If Sam asks someone into the room it is still possible that the person does not comply with Sam's request. Sense (e) is characterized by the rather

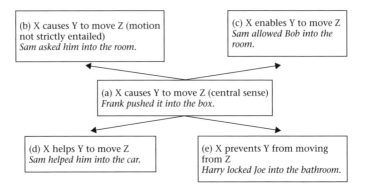

Figure 5.23   The polysemy of the caused-motion construction (adapted from Goldberg 1995: 161ff.)

drastic extension that the agent does *not* cause the patient to move, but prevents him or her from leaving a certain location. Senses (c) and (d) involve weaker variants of the idea of causing, paraphrased by the notions of 'helping' and 'enabling'.

Complex sentence constructions: an example

Although clause patterns probably provide the most convincing examples of constructions, the notion can be extended to complex sentences as well. To illustrate this potential we will focus on what can be labelled '**shell-content construction**' (Schmid 2000) and is linguistically represented by a combination of abstract noun and dependent clause or infinitive; the dependent clause is either directly attached to the nominal (first two examples below) or linked to it by the copula BE (last two examples).

> *The fact that* a conference is taking place is encouraging.
>
> *The chance to* find a cheap hotel room is small.
>
> *The problem is that* hotels don't offer cheap rates.
>
> *The aim is to* open student hostels for guests.

What these structures have in common is their cognitive-pragmatic function: their main job is to make a whole proposition (expressed in the dependent clause) available as a noun-like concept, a process called 'reification' ('turning something into a thing'),[19] and to present it under a certain perspective (i.e. as a fact, aim, goal, etc.). In this process the abstract noun serves as a kind of container or 'shell' for the information contained in the dependent clause and is therefore called 'shell noun'. Figure 5.24 provides a

Semantic structure	*Shell* *reification & perspectivization*	*Link*	*Content*
Syntactic structure	Noun	Ø/BE	*that*-clause/infinitive
Examples	*(The) fact* *(The) aim*	*is*	*that a conference is taking place . . .* *to open student hostels for guests*

Figure 5.24 The structure of the shell-content construction

representation of the shell-content construction modelled on Goldberg's nota-tion of argument-structure constructions.

The claim that the shell-content structure qualifies as a meaningful con-struction is open to similar doubts as the cognitive status of the argument-structure constructions. While with the latter it had to be proved that the meaning does not reside in the verb alone, the shell-content construction has to be defended against the view that its cognitive function exclusively depends on the meaning of the shell noun (*fact, aim, chance, problem*, etc.). As in the case of argument structures, this objection can be overcome when we look at nouns like *idea,* which acquire different meanings depending on whether they are complemented by an infinitive or a *that*-clause – compare Figure 5.25, where *idea* + infinitive is paraphrased as expressing a plan, *idea* + *that*-clause as expressing a thought.

However, this finding does not settle the issue completely because it could still be maintained that the respective meaning is contributed by the com-plement: the future-oriented, volitional meaning by the infinitive, and the factual, thought-related meaning by the *that*-clause.[20] Yet such a simple effect of the clause-types can be ruled out by showing that one clause type can have different effects on different nouns – compare Figure 5.26. Thus the infinitive structure does not always imply 'aim' or 'plan' (as with *idea*, see example above). In the case of *task* it tolerates the perspective of 'obligation',

Construction	*idea* + infinitive structure	*idea* + *that*-clause
Example	*The idea is to open student hostels for guests.*	*The idea that we will open student hostels for guests . . .*
Paraphrase	'What we **plan** to do is to open student hostels for guests.'	'The **thought** that we will open student hostels for guests . . .'
Gloss	'aim', 'plan'	'thought', 'notion'

Figure 5.25 Constructions with *idea* complemented by infinitive and *that*-clause

Construction	*task* + infinitive structure	*solution* + infinitive structure
Example	*The* **task** *is to open student hostels for guests.*	*The* **solution** *is to open student hostels for guests.*
Paraphrase	'What we **have to do** is to open student hostels for guests.'	'The **way** we are going to do it is to open student hostels for guests'
Gloss	'obligation'	'manner'

Figure 5.26 Constructions with *task* and *solution* + infinitive structure

in the case of *solution* the perspective of 'manner'. In particular, the last example makes it clear that the manner meaning ('The **way** we are going to do it . . .') can be derived neither from the meaning of the infinitive structure nor from the lexical meaning of the shell noun.

In other words, one has to posit a special meaning of the construction that cannot be derived from its constituents. This property of non-derivability or non-compositionality seems to be an essential, in fact even defining, attribute of constructions. It is also something that moves constructions in the direction of linguistic phenomena that have traditionally been regarded as idioms.

Idioms as constructions – constructions as idioms[21]

The notion of idiom has been approached in linguistics mainly from two angles, a lexicological and a syntactic one. Lexicologists have used the term for multi-word items like *bite the dust* ('to die'), whose meanings cannot be predicted from the meanings of their parts, thus stressing their semantic non-compositionality. Syntacticians, on the other hand, have been inclined to regard 'formal' idioms like *The bigger they come the higher the fall* or *Why not fix it yourself?* as structural exceptions that are not covered by the system of rules governing 'regular' syntactic structures and may be subject to special pragmatic constraints. For example, syntactically irregular expressions of the type *Him be a doctor?* or *Your brother help me?* (Fillmore, Kay and O'Connor 1988: 511) are only acceptable as markers of strong incredulity in responses to statements made by previous speakers.

Yet far from downgrading these structural idioms as exceptions, Fillmore, Kay and O'Connor focused their attention on them, regarding them as 'syntactic patterns dedicated to semantic and pragmatic purposes not knowable from their form alone' (1988: 505). The object of their seminal study was pairs of sentence elements linked by the conjunction *let alone*. Although superficially comparable to the coordinate conjunctions *and* and *or* in pairing two syntactic elements or clauses of the same type, the *let-alone* structure is characterized by a number of specific syntactic, semantic and pragmatic features. This is illustrated by the following examples adapted from authentic occurrences of *let alone*:

> There are hardly two houses side by side in Shipley, **let alone** five.
>
> The president dropped the pretence that the republics would enjoy greater equality – **let alone** sovereignty.
>
> We have not been able to agree on a negotiating position **let alone** start to negotiate with all the other groups.

Still very much in the syntactic domain, the *let-alone* structure allows for fragments like *let alone five* in the first example, which would be unacceptable if the conjunction *and* were used in the sentence: *There are hardly two houses side by side in Shipley,* **and** *five*. What is more significant is the qualification that the two juxtaposed elements must represent 'points on a scale' (Fillmore, Kay and O'Connor 1988: 513). This is obvious in the example since the two numbers (*two* paired with *five*) are clearly arranged on a semantic scale of quantity. In the second sentence the scale invoked for the evaluation of *equality* and *sovereignty* is something like 'degree of self-determination' and in the last example 'degree of progress in negotiations'. The speakers of sentences based on the *let-alone* structure apparently assume that these scales are feasible, and the hearers must follow the speakers to understand the utterances.

What are the implications of these examples? While formal idioms like *let alone* are both syntactically and semantically idiosyncratic or 'irregular', they still seem to be syntactically productive, in the sense that they serve as syntactic models for new sentences. Like constructions, formal idioms seem to be readily stored syntactic moulds for the expression of highly specific semantic complexes often serving specific pragmatic functions.[22] This is also true of the other formal idioms mentioned above. For example, expressions of the type *Him be a doctor?* are syntactically productive in spite of their idiosyncratic structure, which includes a subject in the object case and a verb in the uninflected stem form – compare expressions like *Your brother help me?* or *Her write a novel about the Spanish Inquisition?* cited by Fillmore, Kay and O'Connor (1988: 511). As a consequence of the irregular syntax, it is impossible to determine the meaning of such expressions solely on the basis of the meanings of the lexical items used. In addition, all occurrences of the formal idiom share the pragmatic force of challenging or questioning an utterance just made by another discourse participant (Fillmore, Kay and O'Connor 1988: 511). Thus *Him be a doctor?* would only be acceptable in response to a proposition like *X is going to/wants to be a doctor* – but in this situation it would be a highly natural reaction produced rapidly and fairly automatically. Therefore, a good case can be made for regarding these idioms as fairly representative examples of constructions.

However, it is also illuminating to reverse the perspective and view constructions as idioms. This has quite a revolutionary effect on how we model the syntactic component of language. Traditionally syntax has been regarded as the regular, rule-governed part of the grammar, while the lexicon and all idioms contained the idiosyncratic pieces of information that have to be stored separately. Now if constructions are indeed responsible for the generation of sentences, and if constructions are stored in long-term memory like words and idioms, then we can do away with the syntactic rules so cherished by transformational and other approaches. In Croft's words: 'The constructional tail has come to wag the syntactic dog' (2001: 17). Constructions can then be imagined as specialized variants or even parts of frames that store all three major types of knowledge together: conceptual-semantic, syntactic and pragmatic knowledge.

In summary, this chapter has introduced some important cognitive-linguistic aspects of grammatical constructions:

- Constructions are pairings of meanings and forms that are stored in long-term memory and specified with regard to their semantic and syntactic structure as well as their pragmatic applicability.

- Verb-based argument-structure constructions provide syntactic moulds for the production of basic clause patterns. Their prototypical meanings are likely to be grounded in frames representing fundamental experiences of recurring types of events.

- Other constructions may not be experientially grounded in the same way, but nevertheless serve as syntactic blueprints for the encoding of specific cognitive functions (like the shell-content construction) and/or specific meanings and contexts (like many formal idioms).

- While formal idioms appear to stand out from the grammar because of their irregularity, they may in fact be just the prominent tip of the hidden iceberg of 'regular' constructions (including the argument-structure constructions) which motivate and sanction all acceptable utterances.

Exercises

1. Assign the following sentences to their underlying construction (caused-motion, cause-receive or resultative construction). Which sentences would you regard as prototypical examples of the construction in question, which as more marginal examples?

> Shall I put your things into your rucksack?
> David has to sleep himself sober.
> I have sent Clarissa to the chemist's.
> Bill cooked his mother a special meal for her birthday.
> Joanna helped her grandmother into the gondola.
> They've painted their garage yellow.

2. Find glosses for the modal meanings in the following examples of shell-content constructions (adapted from Schmid 2000) and discuss the relative contributions of the nouns and the constructions to the overall semantic impact:

> Their mission is to put a military spy satellite into orbit.
> The risk is that the economy goes from bad to worse.
> This is the time to make the right contacts.
> It's a wonderful place to work.
> The fact is that people don't trust politicians.
> The problem is to safeguard the national heritage from decay.
> The danger is that the damage is irreversible.

3. Collect evidence on the polysemy of the cause-receive construction and the resultative construction from Goldberg (1995) and decide which of the three argument-structure constructions discussed in this section is the most polysemous.

4. Go through the following idioms and fixed expressions and decide to what extent they might qualify as meaningful productive constructions especially if you consider their pragmatic function.

> kick the bucket
> null and void, bread and butter
> an apple a day . . .
> boys will be boys
> good morning
> how do you do?
> pay one, take two
> black is beautiful

Suggestions for further reading

Section 5.1

1. References to the origin of the notion of 'frame' in various disciplines can be found in Fillmore (1975: 130; 1976: 9f; 1985: 223).

2. For information on the psychological background of attention see introductions to cognitive psychology, e.g. Eysenck and Keane (2002) or Medin, Ross and Markman (2001, ch. 4).

3. Dirven *et al.* (1982) on *speak, talk, say* and *tell* and Fillmore and Atkins (1992) on *risk* are interesting applications of the frame notion in syntactic and semantic analysis. The latter article also includes some information on the frame-based dictionary which is currently in preparation (see the contributions to the special issue of the *International Journal of Lexicography* edited by Thierry Fontanelle (2003)).

4. Langacker (1987a: 114f) offers a somewhat speculative discussion of the relations between the notions of attention, prominence and perspective.

5. For some useful references to notions related to frames such as 'schemas', 'global patterns' or 'scenes' see Fillmore (1985: 223, fn. 4).

6. The notion of script makes up only a part of the whole system in Schank and Abelson (1977). The other parts of the book deal for example with interferences and distractions of scripts, and with notions like 'plans', 'goals' and 'themes' which are designed for capturing novel situations.

Section 5.2

Most of the following notes have the function of pointing out the many aspects of Talmy's framework that could not be mentioned in the text, and of providing references to the relevant passages in the two volumes of *Toward a Cognitive Semantics* (Talmy 2000), in which almost all his previous publications are assembled in more or less thoroughly revised form.

7. This is why Talmy assigns CAUSE and MANNER to the external 'co-event' (2000/II: 27ff; 220), while the central elements of FIGURE, GROUND, PATH and MOTION constitute the 'framing event' (2000/II: 217).

8. For the remaining types of event-frames see Talmy (2000/I: 271–88).

9. The distinction between the beginning and the end point of a path is similar to the distinction between 'source' and 'goal adjuncts' in

descriptive grammar (see, e.g., Quirk *et al.* 1985: 479, 648). See also Anderson's (1971) detailed and committed localist analysis of clause patterns.

10. Our analysis of the example *My bike is across the street from the bakery* and the windowing options that it offers differs somewhat from Talmy's account. See Talmy (2000/I: 269f) for his own analysis. To get an idea of how extensive and differentiated Talmy's notion of fictive paths is, see Talmy (2000/I: 99–139).

11. For Talmy's view of causation see Talmy (2000/II: 69f).

12. For his idea of 'blocked complements' see Talmy (2000/I: 262–3).

Section 5.3

The theoretical framework of this chapter is based on the notion of event-frame developed in the previous section and used by Talmy (2000/I: 257ff), which means that not all differentiations introduced in Talmy (2000/II) have been considered.

13. See Vinay and Darbelnet (1975: 105ff) and Malblanc (1977: 66ff) on practically oriented accounts of stylistic differences between French and English, and French and German expressions of motion respectively.

14. In Berman and Slobin (1994), frog stories in five languages (English, Spanish, German, Turkish and Hebrew) are analyzed in great detail with regard to comparative and developmental aspects of narrative texts. See also Slobin (1996) and many of his subsequent publications in this field, e.g. Slobin (2004) and Slobin (2005).

15. We have restricted our explanation for the differences in narrative style to the reference to verb-framed and satellite-framed languages. A second explanation for the lack of windowing constructions, especially of final windows, in Spanish is discussed in Slobin (1996) and Aske (1989).

Section 5.4

Construction Grammar is today used as a cover term for a variety of approaches ranging from genuinely cognitive variants such as Goldberg (1995) to somewhat more formalist approaches, as pursued by Fillmore and Kay (e.g. in Fillmore 1999, Kay and Fillmore 1999, Kay 2003) and on to typologically oriented strands, as represented by Croft's *Radical*

Construction Grammar (2001, 2005). Given our cognitive stance and the limitations of an introductory book we will focus on selected aspects of Goldberg's and Fillmore's work. A recent summary of the Fillmorean tradition can be found in Fried and Östman (2004a), a summary of cognitive aspects of Construction Grammar in Östman and Fried (2005a). See also the contributions to Foolen and van der Leek (2000), Fried and Östman (2004b) and Östman and Fried (2005b) as well as the concise overview (in German) by Fischer and Stefanowitsch (2006).

16. The idea that constructions are psychologically real – rather than just theoretical constructs – is pursued in Bencini and Goldberg (2000).

17. Interpreting constructions as pairings of form and meaning is something that Construction Grammar shares with Langacker's Cognitive Grammar (see Chapter 4). Croft and Cruse (2004: 278–83) use these and similar parallels to justify the inclusion of Langacker's approach into their rather wide conception of Construction Grammar.

18. On the polysemy of constructions see Goldberg (1995: 31ff) and Croft (2001: 116ff), who, like Croft and Cruse (2004: 273ff), brings in the notion of prototype (see Chapter 1).

19. Langacker (1991: 34f) uses the notion of reification to explain nominalizations like *Sam's washing of the window*. See also Heyvaert (2003).

20. The most extensive account of constructional meanings of infinitives, *ing*-forms and *that*-clauses used as complementizers has been proposed by Wierzbicka (1988, ch. 1). See also Givón (1990: 515ff), Frajzyngier and Jasperson (1991) and Frajzyngier (1995).

21. Our account of idioms as constructions has mainly exemplary status. The classic, though not the first, paper on the topic is Fillmore, Kay and O'Connor (1988). For a wide-ranging account of idioms in Construction Grammar, including a typology of idioms, see Croft and Cruse (2004, ch. 9).

22. On pragmatic aspects of constructions see Fillmore, Kay and O'Connor (1988: 532f), Goldberg (1995: 92f) and especially Kay (2003), on discourse-related aspects see Lambrecht (2004) and Östman (2005).

Blending and relevance

6.1 Metaphor, metonymy and conceptual blending

In previous chapters we have dealt with linguistic and conceptual structures that have been tacitly assumed to be stored in long-term memory, among them conceptual categories, metaphors and metonymies, image schemas, frames and constructions. To replace this fairly static picture of conceptualization with a more dynamic approach, the cognitive-linguistic view has been extended to include aspects of ongoing language processing, which have traditionally been studied by psycholinguists using experimental methods. The most prominent framework proposed so far is the theory of how mental spaces are constructed and blended during online language processing.

From metaphor and metonymy to conceptual blending

A good way to explain the notion of conceptual blending, which was originally proposed by Gilles Fauconnier and Mark Turner,[1] is to contrast it with the theory of conceptual metaphors discussed in Chapter 3. Consider the following excerpt from an article in *Newsweek*, providing the context leading up to the metaphorical expression *a shot in the arm*, which could be paraphrased as 'something that gives sb/sth the help or encouragement they need' (OALD):[2]

VW's pickup man
Wolfgang Bernhard: Taking on a troubled brand.

He won't start his job until February – and Wolfgang Bernhard has already earned his future employer, German auto giant Volkswagen, many times his salary. When, in October, VW announced the 44-year-old turnaround specialist would become the No. 2 under CEO Bernd Pischetsrieder, investors celebrated by raising VW's market cap by € 1 billion in a single day.
Volkswagen obviously needs a shot in the arm. . . .

Newsweek, December 27/January 3, 2005: 58

Analyzed in terms of conceptual metaphor and metonymy (see Section 3.1) the expression *a shot in the arm* suggests the (specific) metaphor +ECONOMIC WELL-BEING IS HEALTH+, which is supported by the metonymy +SHOT (= INJECTION) STANDS FOR HEALTH+, a cause–effect metonymy. In order to be applicable to *Volkswagen*, the generic metaphor +A COMPANY IS A PERSON+ has to be called up as well, whose source concept PERSON comes with the notion of a body that may receive the shot in the arm. The metaphor +ECONOMIC WELL-BEING IS HEALTH+ is interpreted within the mapping scope rooted in the basic experience of what is good (i.e. feeling healthy) or bad (i.e. feeling ill).

As it stands, this combination of metaphors and metonymy seems to provide a fairly straightforward if complex interpretation of the phrase *a shot in the arm*. Yet it does not agree with our intuitions on how we comprehend the expression on three counts: the interpretation does not consider the specific context in which *a shot in the arm* is used in this text; the analysis only offers a one-way explanation by focusing on what the source concepts contribute to the target concept; finally it suggests that the metaphorical mapping is fully processed to the point where it could be lexicalized as '[giving] the help or encouragement they need' (as suggested by the OALD paraphrase quoted above).

Turning to conceptual blending one finds that it seems to offer a remedy for all three deficiencies. To begin with the first, the preceding context does play an important role in the cognitive processing of the expression *a shot in the arm*. The assumption is that reading the headline, the lead and the first paragraph of the sample text, the reader constructs a **mental space** containing, among other things, the information that Volkswagen has hired a new director. Let us call this mental space a 'hiring space'. This mental space is an online conceptual representation, constructed under the influence of the incoming information but tapping stored cognitive models like VW, PROFIT-MAKING COMPANY, BOARD OF DIRECTORS and HIRING EMPLOYEES. In the words of Fauconnier and Turner (2002: 40, 102):

> Mental spaces are small conceptual packets constructed as we think and talk, for purposes of local understanding and action. . . . [They] operate in working memory but are built up partly by activating structures available from long-term memory.

Along with the hiring space, the incoming metaphorical expression triggers a second mental space, which will be called the 'injection space'. This space taps conceptual structure of a well-known cognitive model, which prototypically features a doctor or a nurse administering a syringe containing medicine intravenously in the arm of the patient. Also included is activated knowledge about the purpose of such an event, the improvement of the patient's health.

According to the conceptual-blending theory, these two mental spaces (the hiring and the injection space, which are called **input spaces**) are brought together and integrated, or 'blended'. The result of this cognitive operation is a new **blended space** containing information projected from both input spaces. However, the blended space does not only draw on the input spaces, but is characterized by a new, emergent conceptual structure in its own right, whose set-up differs from those of the two input spaces. Compare Figure 6.1 for a visual representation in a network model, which makes use of the terminology of participant roles introduced in Section 4.2. (Note that like Mandelblit (2000) and Coulson and Oakley (2003) we have neglected the fourth, so-called 'generic space' proposed by Fauconnier and Turner in this and the later diagrams, because it does not add anything that we regard as essential for understanding the network model.)[3]

According to Fauconnier and Turner (2002: 48f) the projection from the input spaces into the blended space involves three processes: composition, completion and elaboration. **Composition** is always involved when conceptual content from two or more mental spaces is fused in the blended space, e.g. when hiring a director is seen as administering an injection, or raising profits as improving health. The process of **completion** is also required to understand the blend in our example because the sentence

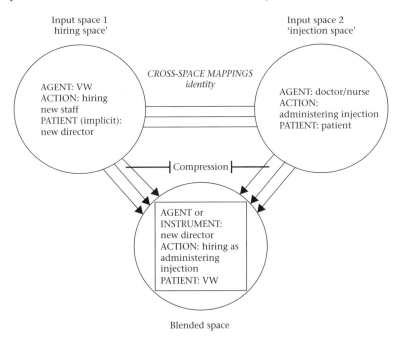

Figure 6.1 Network diagram of the *shot in the arm* blend (the square box indicates the emergent structure of the blend)

Volkswagen obviously needs a shot in the arm underspecifies the situation described: neither the person giving the injection (i.e. the agent) nor the instrument needed for the injection space are mentioned in this sentence. Since these elements are indispensable parts of the injection situation and therefore included in the corresponding frame, they are so to speak 'recommended' for completion by the underspecified sentence. Finally, **elaboration** is envisaged in a highly dynamic fashion, i.e. in terms of 'simulating' or 'running' the blend. The idea behind these explanatory metaphors is that the event construed in the blend is mentally unfolded and taken through its stages like a computer program being tested for correctness and consistency. During this process the blend can be enriched by information deemed necessary, pertinent or even just interesting. What is important is that the depth (and presumably also the duration) of this process of elaboration is in principle open-ended and will vary among readers. Returning to our example, some readers may be satisfied having constructed a blended space that contains the rather general information that the new director will somehow improve the company's economic prospects. Others may actually call up an image of the director giving the injection to the (personified) company.

As illustrated by Figure 6.1, the input spaces not only feed the blended space (by supplying the necessary projections), but are also linked to each other by **cross-space mappings**, which are based on what Fauconnier and Turner (2002: 89–111) call **vital relations**. In the case of metaphor the prominent vital relation is **identity**, in our example the identity relation between the actions of hiring a new director (input space 1) and of administering an injection (input space 2). In order to establish the blend the actions of the two input spaces are projected onto the blended space, largely by means of composition and completion. As a result the actions in the two spaces undergo what Fauconnier and Turner (2002: 92f, 312–25) call **compression**. As will be shown in more detail in the next section, compression is in fact the ultimate goal of the whole blending process. The crucial effect of compression is that the conceptual complexity of the inputs from several sources is reduced considerably. A newly integrated and unified conceptual structure emerges that is cognitively manageable and thus has, as Fauconnier and Turner (2002: 312) put it, 'human scale'. In our example, the result of compression on the identity relation is a new combination of actions, the emergent structure described as the ACTION of 'hiring as injection-administering' in the blended space. Similarly, as we have seen, the goals of the two actions are fused into 'raising profits as improving health'. This shows that both input spaces contribute to the emergent structure of the blend, which is different from the structure of either input space and less complex than their simple addition.

As for the participants of the actions, Volkswagen, the AGENT of the hiring action in input space 1, turns out to be the PATIENT in need of medical treatment in the blended space. Yet what is more interesting is the role of the new director. Although he is not explicitly mentioned in the sentence *Volkswagen obviously needs a shot in the arm*, his role is necessary for its understanding and will be added to the blend by means of completion. His participant role is ambiguous, however. What is clear is that he does not represent the element affected by the action any more, as is the case in the hiring space (input space 1). One possible interpretation is that in the blended space he takes on the AGENT role of the doctor, who is going to administer the syringe to the ailing company. In an alternative understanding, he himself could function as the INSTRUMENT, because even the announcement of his hiring has been a means sufficient to administer the much-needed medicine to VW. Such ambiguities need not be resolved for the blend to 'make sense', they are open to further elaboration. Indeed, they are proof that the blending theory is well suited to capture the kind of conceptual indeterminacy and open-endedness typical of online cognitive processing, and this seems to be much more important for comprehension than more traditional approaches would make us believe.

Summing up at this point, the conceptual blending analysis differs from the metaphor and metonymy analysis in the following ways:

- The conceptual-metaphor approach operates with cognitive models stored in long-term memory, the blending approach with mental spaces constructed during online processing, though often based on cognitive models.
- Unlike cognitive models, mental spaces are context-dependent and include information about specific situations.
- While metaphor is seen as a one-directional mapping from a source to a target model, conceptual blending prototypically involves mappings from two input spaces to a third, blended space, which is characterized by a compressed emergent conceptual structure. This operation involves the cognitive processes of composition, completion and elaboration and can be described in terms of conceptual integration networks.
- The mapping scope, which restrains metaphorical mappings, is to a large extent represented by the vital relations (such as identity), which underlie cross-mappings between input spaces and undergo compression in the blended space.

Further dimensions of compression: space, time, cause–effect and part–whole

Identity may be the most important and most frequent vital relation compressed in blends, but there are other relations that are also affected by this process.[4] One of them is space, which gives rise to **spatial compression**, as can be assumed for the processing of the expression *American-type tornado* in the following sentence:

> Without any warning an American-type tornado hit the sleepy French village of Châtel-les-Bains leaving a trail of destruction behind.

Applying the conceptual blending approach, the reader will call up two mental input spaces. One space will assemble the reader's knowledge of the effects of tornados in the Caribbean or the United States, with huge waves running up beaches, cars being overturned and wooden houses and garages being literally flattened or blown away; a second input space will focus on what normally happens in a thunderstorm in a well-protected European village (torrential rain, perhaps a tree or two uprooted, tiles flying around, a debris of leaves and branches in the streets lined by terraced stone houses). It is obvious that the two input spaces are situated in different locations and it is equally clear that their spatial separation must be overcome for the message to make sense. This is why the two input spaces are compressed to overcome their spatial separation. The result is probably a blended space in which our picture of the French village and the kind of damage normally caused by European thunderstorms is tied up with the devastating effects that are typical of American tornados. But as with the shot-in-the-arm example the exact nature and the details of the damage will not and cannot really be sorted out. What is achieved in this online process and what is obviously quite sufficient for our comprehension is an emergent structure which establishes certain links between the two settings, but leaves the details unresolved.

Closely linked to spatial compression is **compression along the time dimension**. Here is one of Fauconnier and Turner's own examples (2002: 63), the 'regatta blend':

> The clipper ship *Northern Light* sailed in 1853 from San Francisco to Boston in 76 days, 8 hours. That time was still the fastest on record in 1993, when a modern catamaran, *Great American II*, set out on the same course. A few days before the catamaran reached Boston, observers were able to say: at this point *Great American II* is 4.5 days ahead of *Northern Light*.

> (Fauconnier and Turner 2002: 63)

Summarizing the gist of Fauconnier and Turner's argument one can postulate two input spaces, one containing the voyage undertaken by *Northern Light* in 1853 (with as much detail of the trip as we can muster), the other one devoted to the 1993 voyage of the *Great American II* (also equipped with the respective details). Though there are strong identity links between the two input spaces (the two boats involved, their starting point and destination, the course and their positions on the course), which are all projected into the blended space and fused by means of composition, the emergent structure of the blend crucially depends on the compression of the two time periods. This temporal compression is the condition for 'running the blend by imagining the two boats in competition' (Fauconnier and Turner 2002: 63); it provides an immediate grasp of the situation as opposed to mathematical calculations which would have to relate the position of the boats either to the starting point or the end point of the journeys.

Moving on to **cause–effect**, good examples of compression along this vital relation are causation events expressed by verbs like *kill* and *break*, which were traditionally described as conflations of the semantic components 'cause' and 'become'. One cognitive-linguistic approach already discussed in this book (see Section 5.2) was Talmy's notion of the windowing of attention in causal-chain events. Our example in Section 5.2 was *John broke the window*. Analyzed in terms of Talmy's approach, this example opens up an initial and a final window of attention selected from a much larger causal chain of sequential events. The sentence focuses on the agent John and the final result (the fact that the window has been broken), while other events like John's bending down and grasping a stone as well as the actual contact of the stone with the window are backgrounded.

In conceptual-blending theory this 'hiding' of sub events can be explained as a case of compression on the vital relation of cause–effect. The compression mainly concerns the first of two input spaces that must be posited, the space containing John's sequence of actions. The second space contains the result of the action, the broken window. While there is of course a cross-space relation of cause–effect from the first input space to the second, the actual utterance *John broke the window* projects the agent into the blended space, compressing all intermediate stages (bending knees, putting out hand, grasping stone, pulling stone towards the body, and so on) in the single verb *break*. The compression thus substantially reduces the causal complexity of the event, yielding a cognitively manageable conceptual unit.

With the vital relation of **part–whole** we enter the domain of image schemas grounded in our bodily experiences (see Sections 2.5 and 3.1). Normally, the part–whole link between body parts and body (or person) as a whole is as natural as it is unobtrusive. Yet if we react to a portrait with *That's Jane Doe* (Fauconnier and Turner 2002: 97) or – to add another variant – if we say *That's Jim* when hearing someone's voice at the door, it is not all that certain that we automatically call up the person as a whole, although nobody would earnestly claim that we are only conceptualizing the face or the voice of the person in question. Again a blending approach may be helpful in providing a more adequate analysis than either the (improbable) non-metonymic or a fully metonymic interpretation. Assuming the person's face (or the voice backed up by a conversation) as one input space and the person as a whole conceptualized in the other input space, the part–whole relationship between the two input spaces can again be understood as being compressed into a blend with an emergent structure oscillating between face/voice and an image of the whole person.

If one tries to describe the goal achieved by the compression of vital relations in the blended space, it can invariably be understood as a state of unification. This is not only true of the identity relations between hiring a new director and a doctor giving a shot in the arm, from which we started out. It also applies to the compression of spatially and temporally distant elements (the American-type tornado and the regatta boats) or to the compression of the numerous stages of a cause–effect chain (the window-breaking blend) or of parts and wholes (face/person blend).

The unified concept can be conceptualized in the blended space as a person concept (e.g. the new director as doctor), an object concept (the blended regatta boat) or an action concept (window breaking). However, the unified element can also be attached as a property to another concept in the blended space (just as the modifiers *small* or *big* are attached to their heads in phrases like *small boy* or *big house*); this function will be referred to as **blended property**.[5]

Taking the expression *mid-Atlantic English* as a first example, the modifier *mid-Atlantic* can be understood as the compression of a spatial relation involving US and Britain to denote the unification of being an American–British mixture; attached to the concept ENGLISH (as a language) it functions as a blended property to denote a special kind of English found in some British magazines. In the noun phrase *old friend* – the friend may of course be quite young – the property 'old' can be said to result from a compression of the various stages of an acquaintance spread over a long period of time; this is why it qualifies as a blended property while 'old' in *old man* would not. Finally, and this is Fauconnier and Turner's (2002: 100) own example, the modifier *warm* in the noun phrase *warm coat* does not express that the coat has the inherent quality of warmth, but that the coat is something that causes people to be warm if they wear it. 'Warmth' is therefore due to the compression of a cause–effect relation between 'coat' and 'warmth' into a blended property (while the property 'thick' in *thick coat* would not involve a blend).

In surveying this range of conceptual compression and its applications one should take into account that the examples have here been presented in isolation for the sake of clarity. What has been neglected is the fact that compression regularly affects several vital relations, which can be interrelated in various ways. Apart from the well-known symbiosis of spatial and temporal relations, which are often combined in compression, it can be safely assumed that there is always some sort of identity compression involved in blending.

Governing rules of blending and entrenchment

Conceptual blending is, as we have seen, a potentially open-ended cognitive process. This raises the question whether compression based on a few vital relations is sufficient to delimit the emergent structure in the blended space. The wide range of examples considered for conceptual blending ('sexual fantasies, grammar, complex numbers, personal identity, redemption and lottery depression'; Fauconnier and Turner 2002: 309) invites criticism of the type that 'anything goes' (see Gibbs 2000: 349f, Broccias 2004). Reacting to such objections, Fauconnier and Turner (2002: 325–34) have proposed nine governing (or optimality) principles, which determine the degree of compression and unification achieved by a given blend. They have been condensed here into a set of five for the purpose of simplification.[6]

The first principle to be observed in optimizing blending is the **topology principle** – the term takes up the geographical metaphor favoured by cognitive linguists to denote conceptual structure. The topology principle requires the blend to take over and preserve important aspects of the conceptual structure of the input spaces, e.g. the space-internal relations of part–whole when conceptualizing a body and its parts, or the agent–action–patient pattern of events (like a boss hiring a new employee). Considering the importance of vital relations in the blending process, it is not surprising that their strength and intensity both in cross-space mappings between input spaces and in the emergent structure of the blended space should be increased rather than reduced ('principle of promoting vital relations'); as has been shown, the window-breaking blend intensifies the link between the initial stage and the result of the process by compressing all the intermediate stages of the window-breaking action in the single verb *break*.

Moving on to the **principle of integration** (a more pointed term would be 'gestalt principle'), this is what one would expect compression to conform with: the establishment of an emergent structure that has as far as possible the qualities of a conceptual 'gestalt', i.e. holistic conceptualization and easy handling as a unit, qualities that facilitate entrenchment and memorability. In contrast, the **principle of unpacking** ensures that the blend can still prompt the reconstruction of the entire network (Fauconnier and Turner 2002: 332). An extreme case is a blend in which the normal processing direction of the blend is as it were reversed and the input spaces are in fact approached from the angle of the blended space. For instance, in a philosophy lecture the professor may set up a fictive argument between a famous philosopher and himself on the pattern of 'Kant says that X, but I object that Y'. Such a discussion between people living at different times is motivated by a debate frame which defines the structure of the blended space; yet this debate frame unpacks into input frames featuring the philosophers living and teaching at different times ('the debate with Kant', Fauconnier and Turner 2002: 59). What is probably more frequent is a partial unpacking, a return to the input frames and their cross-mappings to reconceptualize parts of the emergent structure that have been temporarily lost. In either case the unpacking principle works for keeping the blend 'open' as an online process and in this way competes with the principle of integration.

Compared with these principles, all of them concerned with regulating the relationship between the spaces in the blend, the **principle of relevance** has a more basic function: by distributing significance to the elements of the blend this principle decides in which direction the blend is developing. Applied to our first example, the shot-in-the-arm blend, this means that relevance is responsible for projecting the new director into the role of doctor (and VW as patient). In other words, relevance is the major motivating force behind blends in their actual contexts. As such it is equally encompassing and omnipresent as the **principle of human scale** mentioned earlier on, which is regarded as the 'overarching goal' by Fauconnier and Turner. While human scale is safely embedded in cognitive thinking – in the notions of prototype, basic level, part–whole hierarchies, the metaphorical derivation of abstract concepts from concrete source concepts – the reason why the principle of relevance should be so important for conceptual blending remains more or less unexplained; this asks for an explanation from a different angle, as it has been proposed by Relevance Theory, which is rooted in pragmatics (see Section 6.4).

Summing up, this is what the last two sections should have added to the preliminary sketch of conceptual blending at the end of the first section:

- The vital relations underlying blends include image schemas (part–whole), basic correlations (cause–effect), place and time and a number of other relations, whose status still awaits critical assessment (Fauconnier and Turner 2002: 98, 100).

- Compression, which is the core of the blending process, normally involves several vital relations.
- The blending process is constrained – and optimized – by a set of governing principles, among them the topology, the integration and the unpacking principles.
- Ideally, the interplay of the governing principles maintains the online quality of indeterminacy and open-endedness and ensures the human scale of the emergent structure.
- Blending is also strongly motivated by the relevance principle, which assigns significance to certain elements of the blend and links the blend with the needs of communicative interaction (see Section 6.3).

Exercises

1. In order to provide a blending representation, which input spaces would you posit for the following metaphors and which emergent structure would you expect in the blended space to occur? Contrast this diagram with a metaphor analysis based on the suggestions made in Section 3.1.

   She lives *at the foot of the mountain.*
   Their *love is a bumpy journey.*
   Prices are still spiralling.

2. The emergent structure may remain vague (for instance by permitting the new director to be seen as a doctor or an instrument in the shot-in-the arm blend). Go back to Chapter 2 and find other examples where we tolerate conceptual alternatives and inconsistencies.

3. Look out for parallel examples of the *American-type tornado, John broke the window, warm coat, that's Jim* and interpret them in terms of spatial, cause–effect, property and part–whole compression respectively.

4. Construct another context in which past and present achievements in sports, science or technology are compared in a similar way as in the regatta blend and provide a blending analysis for your example.

5. Show how the examples you have provided for exercises 3 and 4 contribute to reducing complex conceptualizations to easily handled 'conceptual packages' of 'human scale' (Fauconnier and Turner 2002: 40, 312, 346).

6.2 Conceptual blending in linguistic analysis and description

Applications of the theory of conceptual blending are numerous and wide-ranging. Outside linguistics, they span the gamut from cognitive psychology to mathematics and computing to musicology and archeology.[7] Sticking to our own field we will present in this section some case studies of lexical, grammatical and pragmatic phenomena suitable for analysis in the blending framework.

Conceptual blending and morphological blends

Superficially, the most obvious candidate for an analysis in terms of conceptual blending is its namesake in the area of word-formation, the morphological blend, as represented by items like *smog, brunch, motel, infotainment.* Of course, the fact that all these blends are the result of telescoping two words into a new one suggests that they have all undergone a process of conceptual projection and composition of material from input spaces into a blended space. However, with most accepted morphological blends this process is seen as a stage in the word's history rather than an ongoing or even open-ended conceptual process. When choosing the word *smog,* many language users will not even realize the blending background any longer, so deeply entrenched and lexicalized is the word today. In the case of *brunch* or *motel* the input spaces 'breakfast' and 'lunch', 'motorist' and 'hotel' respectively may be available for processing, but *brunch* and *motel* can also be conceptualized from the emergent structure without 'unpacking' the whole blend. It is only with the last example, *infotainment,* that the blending analysis unfolds some of its explanatory potential. Although the input spaces show considerable similarities – information and entertainment are related abstract principles denoting ways of satisfying an audience – the emergent structure of the blended space is open-ended; it is difficult, and probably not even necessary, to define the mixture represented by *infotainment* in a conclusive way.[8]

The real testing ground for a conceptual blending analysis is two types of morphological blends: those that fail to survive and to be conventionalized and those that are intentionally conceived as a temporary and open-ended phenomenon. Take two candidates that have not really made it as morphological blends, *swimsation* (the name of a New Zealand chain of swim schools) and *sportianity* (Lehrer 1996: 379). Why is it that many people may find it easy to recognize the notion of 'swimming', but difficult to identify the second input space 'sensation' – and the same applies to *sportianity* with regard to 'sports' and 'Christianity'. In either case the cross-space map-pings connecting the first space ('swimming', 'sports') with the second space ('sensation', 'Christianity') do not appear to be very 'vital'; they can-not be grasped as identity, space, time, cause–effect or part–whole rela-tionships. This is why the basic processes of composition and completion do not seem to be applicable. As a result, compression does not lead to an emergent structure that goes beyond the unsatisfactory impression that the blend must have something to do with the content of the first input space, 'swimming' or 'sports'.

A still more interesting application of the blending approach is con-cerned with ad-hoc blends, as they are for instance used in the headlines of popular newspapers to attract attention and entertain the readership (but not really in order to enlarge the vocabulary of the language). Most of these blends presuppose a certain insider knowledge. In the case of *Ballacktisch* ‡ ('Ballacktic'), a front headline of the German popular paper *Bildzeitung* (6 June 2005), the background is that Ballack was the name of a well-known German soccer player of the Bayern Munich team at the time of publica-tion, that he was said to be negotiating a transfer to Real Madrid, another famous soccer team, in fact one that was so highly praised at the time that it had acquired the nickname *galacticos* ('the galactic ones'). Assuming this background knowledge, which the newspaper obviously expected from its readership, one can set up the blend as documented in the simplified net-work representation of Figure 6.2

In the first input space, Ballack is primarily characterized in his role as the soccer player (an 'inner-space' relation in Fauconnier and Turner's ter-minology); he is also tied to the location of Munich as a member of the Bayern Munich team. Input space 2 conceptualizes the Real team, also characterized by its role as soccer team and linked to the location of Madrid. In addition, Real is equipped with the blended property 'galactic/outstanding' – a blended property because it can be understood as the result of a preceding blending process based on the mental space 'stars on the firmament/show-business stars' and another input space devoted to the outstanding qualities of the Real team.

Returning to Figure 6.2, we find that the Ballack space and the Real space are linked by the cross-space mapping of the vital relations of 'iden-tity' with regard to the people involved and their roles as soccer players, while the locations are connected by the relation of 'space' (distance).

‡ This example was pointed out to us by Markus Riedel, Rostock.

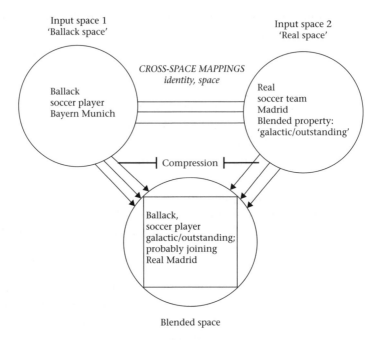

Figure 6.2 Network representation of the morphological blend
Ballacktisch ('Ballacktic')

Now in the blended space the property of 'Real being galactic/outstand-
ing' is projected from input space 2 onto the concept *Ballack*: the identity relation is compressed into the 'unified' message that Ballack can also
be regarded as galactic and therefore as eligible for Real. This message is
supported by the spatial compression which results in the unification of
Ballack's and Real's location. The effect is an emergent structure that suggests, although this is not stated as a fact, that Ballack is going to Madrid
to join the Real team. This condensation of a speculative rumour into
the single word *Ballacktisch* is exactly what the headlines of popular newspapers are aiming at.

In their quest for immediate and short-lived effects the editors of the
Bildzeitung did not care whether the handy label they invented as a headline
was highly context-dependent or not; *Ballacktisch* is surely a poor candidate
for conceptual entrenchment or lexicalization as an independently available
meaning. In fact there is a simple test to assess the online quality of this
blend. You only have to ask yourself if you would have understood it (as
millions of *Bild* readers apparently did at the time of printing) without the
information furnished above.

Compounds and acronyms as conceptual blends

Discussing morphological blends in terms of conceptual blending or integration has led us away from their salient features of telescoped form. In fact, from the conceptual perspective, morphological blends can be understood as a special kind of compound. It is therefore not surprising that they provide a model case of the cognitive processing of compounds at large, in particular nominal compounds based on adjective–noun and noun–noun combinations. Like morphological blends these compounds can all be subjected to a conceptual blending analysis, but this procedure will yield varying degrees of insight over and above what has already been achieved in the concept-based attribute analysis in Section 3.2. Compositional compounds such as *apple juice* can be explained as a set-up of two input spaces ('apple space' and 'juice space'); here the emergent structure in the blended space is characterized by the integration of the core information of the first input space into the second.

More sophisticated types of blending processes can be posited for less compositional compounds like *wheelchair* in order to account for the extra attributes that go beyond the meanings inherent in the constituents *wheel* and *chair*. One way of doing this would be to assume an additional input space 'hospital' or 'invalid' or both; in another interpretation the extra meaning would arise from the blending process as newly emergent conceptual structure. Yet no matter how a more detailed blending analysis will explain these compounds, the compression in these blends has long led to deeply entrenched structures in the blended space – or firmly lexicalized items in more traditional terminology – so the blending process will not be repeated every time these items are used. As observed by Coulson (2001: 142–4) the online quality of the blend only comes to the fore when the entrenched interpretation does not fit a specific context; her rather exotic example is the compound *pet fish*, which normally calls up the context of a fish tank, but might be used by a biologist investigating shark behaviour for her favourite specimen of shark.[9]

A discrepancy between an entrenched meaning and an ad hoc conceptualization is particularly frequent with compounds created in family discourse or in conversation with close friends. Take the example of *cherry jeans*, for which a relatively conventionalized meaning is probably 'jeans of a cherry-like colour'. Yet in specific contexts the conceptual blending of the two input spaces 'jeans' and 'cherry' may produce quite different emergent structures in the blended space. Compare Figure 6.3, where it is clear that the colour interpretation of the blend is the most likely one. It can rely on the cross-space

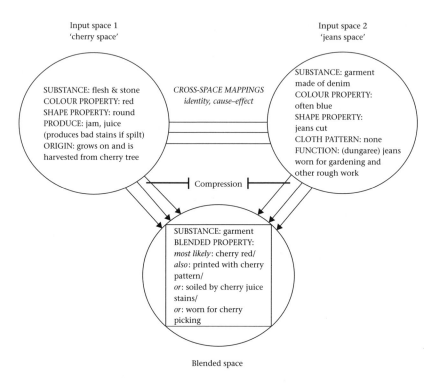

Figure 6.3 Network representation of the **cherry-jeans** blend

mapping involving the vital relation of identity between the colour property of the cherry space and the colour property of the jeans space; both
colour properties are projected into the blended space and compressed into
the blended property of 'cherry red' assigned to *cherry jeans*. A similar (but
more unusual) mapping can be assumed between the (plain) cloth pattern
of jeans and the shape property of cherries to describe a pair of white designer
jeans printed with a cherry pattern; it goes without saying that this conceptualization of the compound *cherry jeans*, which is based on the blended
property 'printed with a cherry pattern', will not be able to compete successfully for entrenchment and lexicalization with 'cherry-coloured jeans'.

For the last two emergent structures documented for *cherry jeans* in the
blended space of Figure 6.3 entrenchment is not really feasible. Conceptualizing *cherry jeans* as 'garment soiled by stains of cherry juice' presupposes
the knowledge that such an accident has in fact happened. Only then will
the cross-space mapping of cause (cherry juice) and effect (colour stain on
jeans) be activated and compressed into the blended property of the jeans
('cherry juice stains on jeans'). More likely than not the blend will be an

ad hoc coinage used for a pair of jeans picked out from the laundry bag for washing and will be discarded when the item has vanished in the washing machine. It is in the improbable case that the stain should persist that the blend 'jeans soiled by cherry juice' might achieve acceptance in the family circle. Just like this version of the blend, the last variant ('jeans used for cherry picking') relies on a cause–effect relation between one traditional FUNCTION of (dungaree) jeans (gardening work, including picking cherries) and the effect of the cherries being harvested (the ORIGIN element of the cherry input space), which is to be compressed into a blended property of the jeans in the blended space. Yet the activation of this link presupposes the context that picking cherries involves climbing cherry trees or dirty ladders requiring special clothing, plus the knowledge that the person in question has worn or intends to wear a certain pair of dungaree jeans for cherry picking. An emergent structure dependent on such a constellation has little or no chance of achieving wider currency, let alone permanence: it is a typical product of context-dependent online conceptualization.

Apart from the prototypical case of the two-element compound there are three-element combinations (*car boot sale, home help service, health care costs, state school heads,* etc.; see Schmid 2005: 212f), which call for a special blending analysis, and this also applies to acronyms (or initialisms) comprising more than two elements.[10] Exploring their blending behaviour would go beyond the range of this introduction, yet there is one aspect of acronym building that will be picked out for discussion because it vividly illustrates our urge for conceptual blending as well as the descriptive potential inherent in blending analysis. Acronyms pronounced like natural words (as opposed to spelling pronunciation) have always shown a tendency to be modelled phonologically and graphically on existing words. If this just means compliance with English syllable structure as in *TAM* (< *Television Audience Measurement*) or *laser* (< *Light Amplification by Stimulated Emission of Radiation*), it is a phonological issue that does not directly affect conceptual blending. However, as soon as existing English words come into play and are used as 'prop words', the governing principle of relevance will motivate us to look for conceptual links between the meaning of the prop word and the acronym, which can be understood as the two input spaces as a conceptual blend. The link can be very obvious, as in the case of the time-hallowed acronym *CARE* (< *Cooperative American Relief to Europe*), where a cause–effect relation can be established between a caring attitude and the execution of this intention; but often it is much less straightforward, as in the well-known example *WASP* (< *White Anglo-Saxon Protestant*) or in the more recent acronym *PISA* (< *Programme for International Student Assessment*). What is typical of acronyms with prop words is that the emergent structure does not boil down to a discrete cognitive meaning, but will retain or even consist of more or less vague and subjective associations quite in line with the indeterminate and open-ended nature of online processing. This is even more noticeable when the 'prop word space' is supported by a pictorial representation. An example is a statistics of the PISA results, which was illustrated with a picture of the leaning tower (*Süddeutsche Zeitung*, 15 July 2005).

This constellation is represented in the network diagram of Figure 6.4, where input space 1 supplies a condensed conceptualization of the acronym meaning (which could be seen as the structure emerging from a separate blending process). Input space 2 provides the conceptualization of the leaning tower of Pisa, a highlight of European culture, which has nevertheless achieved its fame as an architect's nightmare. Yet what is the conceptual link between the two input spaces? If one does not simply deny the existence of any relation, what can be assumed as tentative cross-space mapping is a relation of cause–effect between the educational achievement of the results of input space 1 (cause) and the cultural reputation of the architectural heritage (effect), as suggested both verbally and visually by input

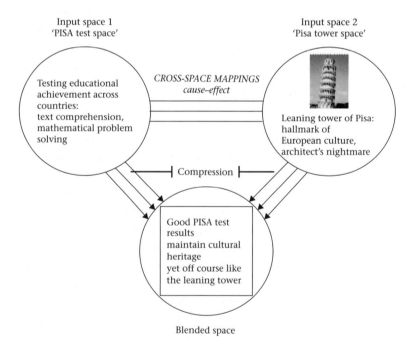

Figure 6.4 Network representation of the PISA blend (PISA test space may also be seen as the result of a preceding blending process)

space 2. This cause–effect relation is compressed in the blended space into an emergent structure that – perhaps rather hazily – indicates that good Pisa results maintain our cultural heritage, but at the same time suggests that education may be off course, just like the leaning tower.

Seen against the background of English word-formation, these acronyms (and especially the combination with pictorial elements like the leaning tower) may appear to be a rather marginal phenomenon. However, the blending processes they give rise to and the type of emergent structure produced for instance in the Pisa blend foreshadow the type of blends that seems to be omnipresent in advertising today (and will be discussed in Section 6.3 below).

Conceptual blending, event structure and constructions

Surveying the mental spaces involved in the creation of morphological blends, compounds and acronyms, we note that most of them will be conceptualized as states or situations. Yet there are also mental spaces qualifying as events (e.g. brunch, swimming, testing students, etc.) that can be described in terms of actions and participant roles, just as our first example in this chapter, the shot-in-the-arm blend (see Figure 6.1). While this blend relies on a single event structure (AGENT/INSTRUMENT – ACTION – PATIENT), which is shared by both input spaces, the more interesting cases are those in which different event structures are involved.

Taking up an example already discussed in Section 5.4 in the context of Construction Grammar, the sentence *Frank sneezed the tissue off the table* can also be explained as an online blend involving three different event schemas – compare Figure 6.5. Two of these event schemas, the causing event (paraphrasable as *Frank sneezed*) and the effected event (paraphrasable as *the tissue fell off the table*), are conceptualized in input space 1 (we mention only in passing that this bipartite input space can be understood as the result of a blending process including compression along the vital relation of cause–effect). The third event schema, the caused-motion event (prototypically paraphrased as *Frank pushed the tissue off the table*) is contained in input space 2. Assuming the participants of the events in the two input spaces are linked by cross-space mappings of identity, which undergo compression, the result is an emergent structure in the blended space combining AGENT, ACTION, PATIENT and (DIRECTIONAL) LOCATIVE.[11] In other words, the two-event pattern of the first input space amalgamates with the construction activated in the second space and the topology of the first space is overruled by the principle of integration.

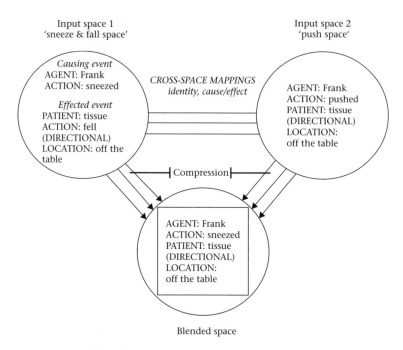

Figure 6.5 Network representation of the blend underlying *Frank sneezed the tissue off the table*

Since the blending analysis provides for the representation of online pro-cesses, it can also be used to describe what may happen in the mind of a language user when confronted with the deviant use of a construction by a foreign language learner. Take the utterance *Susan remembered Tom of Grandma's birthday*. As shown in Figure 6.6 (input space 1), the verb *remember* functions in a construction comprising the elements EXPERIENCER – MENTAL PROCESS – EXPERIENCED OBJECT (a monotransitive pattern in traditional terminology), but this leaves the noun *Tom* unaccounted for.

In order to accommodate the meaning of the verb *remember* as well as the 'loose' element *Tom*, the language user is likely to establish a second input space which takes up the lexical concept REMEMBER and provides for a construction in which the element *Tom* can be placed. These conditions are met by the cause-experience construction (a variant of the cause-receive construction; see Section 5.4). As documented in input space 2 and expressed by the verb *remind*, this construction comprises the elements AGENT – MENTAL ACTION – EXPERIENCER – EXPERIENCED OBJECT. (Since the EXPERIENCED OBJECT

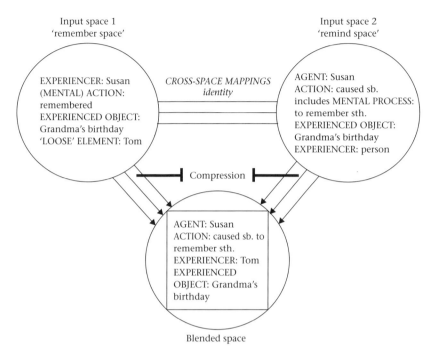

Figure 6.6 Network representation of the blend stimulated by the foreign
learner error *Susan remembered Tom of Grandma's birthday.*

is introduced by the prepositions *of* or *about*, this yields a ditransitive pattern with a prepositional object in traditional terms.)

Assuming that the MENTAL PROCESS ('remembering') and the EXPERIENCED OBJECT
('Grandma's birthday') contained in both input spaces 1 and 2 are linked
by the cross-space relation of identity, it is not difficult to imagine that the
AGENT role ('Susan') of input space 2 is projected onto the mistaken
EXPERIENCER role inherited from input space 1 (also 'Susan'); more importantly,
the EXPERIENCER role of space 2 is projected onto the 'loose' element *Tom* derived
from input space 1. The result is, however, not an immediate replacement
of the verb *remember* by *remind*, but rather an emergent structure best characterized by the paraphrase 'Susan caused Tom to remember Grandma's birthday'. Only when the fact that the blend is due to a learner's error has been
realized by the language user will the replacement of *remember* by *remind*
take place, perhaps accompanied by an utterance like *Oh, you mean 'remind
Tom', not 'remember Tom'*. This is the point when the preposition *of* will
find its place in the expression *Susan reminded Tom of Grandma's birthday*.
The blend has now fulfilled its function and will be discarded.

Blending, counterfactuals and space builders

That counterfactual sentences like *If I were you, I'd apply for the York position just for the experience* (ICE-GB) involve two different 'worlds', a factual and a counterfactual world, is general linguistic knowledge;[12] within the blending approach, sentences of this type take us from the discussion of clause patterns to the pragmatic level of speech events and suggested or imagined actions. Compare Figure 6.7, where input space 1 focuses on the current speech situation, with *I* referring to the speaker and *you* to the hearer. The speaker brings along certain beliefs and dispositions on which his or her advice to the hearer is based, among them the belief expressed in the adverbial *just for the experience*, i.e. that job applications create indispensable experience. Input space 2 represents the suggested ('counterfactual') action of decision-making. The two input spaces are linked by an identity relation between the AGENT roles in the two spaces; its effect is that the speaker is mapped from the first input space onto the hearer slot in the hearer's space so that the blend looks at the hearer's dilemma with the speaker being

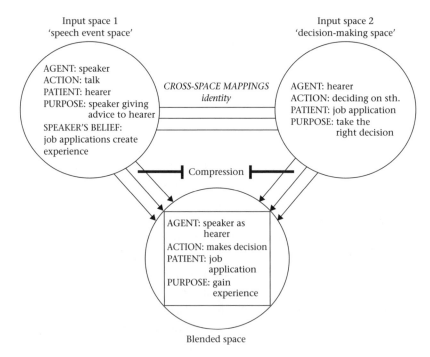

Figure 6.7   Network representation of the York application blend (*If I were you, I'd apply for the York position just for the experience*)

presented as having to make the decision. This shows that despite the explicit assurance by the speaker to construe the basic cross-space relation of 'identity' between his or her own person and the hearer's, the problem of decision-making is still looked at very much from the speaker's point of view. It is perhaps this particular mixture of verbally highlighting the relation of identity while at the same time refusing to go all the way that creates the somewhat patronising tone of expressions of this type.

Hypothetical *if*-clauses may be the prototypical way of establishing counterfactual mental spaces and may thus act as '**space builders**', yet there are many other linguistic elements that fulfil this function. As defined by Fauconnier a space builder is 'a grammatical expression that either opens up a new space or shifts focus to an existing space' (1997: 40). Typical examples are *once upon a time, in that story, in the movie, my daughter thinks that,* or *last night I dreamt that,* and many others. Since the expression *once upon a time* immediately evokes a fairytale space, nobody will be surprised to encounter speaking animals, ghosts, witches and wizards and hear of all kinds of miraculous events. Similarly, by saying *in the movie* or *in the novel* the speaker tells the hearer to build a fictitious space where, just like in the fairytale, the laws of dire reality are temporarily suspended. It is obvious that this view of space builders opens up a huge range of pragmatic and discourse phenomena for a blending analysis.

To sum up, this section has discussed a variety of linguistic examples ranging from lexical blends to compounds, acronyms, argument-structure constructions and counterfactuals. What has emerged is that while fully capable of describing stock examples of lexicalized word-formations or entrenched constructions, the blending analysis can also cope with more marginal but also more interesting examples than the more traditional methods and is therefore well suited to extend the field of linguistic research.

Exercises

1. Discuss the following examples of more or less novel morphological blends (taken from the *Oxford Dictionary of New Words,* Knowles 1997) in terms of conceptual blending and emergent structure:

    edutainment

    < *education* + *entertainment*: 'entertainment with an educational aspect'

    vegelate

    < *vegetable* + *chocolate*: 'chocolate which contains a certain proportion of vegetable fat other than cacao butter'

feminazi

< *feminist* + *nazi*: 'a contemptuous term for a radical feminist'

2. Analyze the following compounds as conceptual blends:

Aga saga

'a form of popular novel typically set in rural location and concerning the domestic and emotional lives of the middle class'; *Aga* stoves are stereotypical of middle-class life and represent a sustained cosiness.

Riot girl

'a young militant feminist'

Discuss how the onomatopoeic impact of the alternative spelling *riot grrl* can be integrated in the analysis.

3. Provide a conceptual-blending analysis for the following acronyms with prop words and discuss the omission of initial letters from the source expression:

FIST < *Federation of Interstate Truckers*

PEN < *International Association of Poets, Playwrights, Editors, Essayists, and Novelists*

WAR < *Women Against Rape*

4. Transfer the blending analyses of *Frank sneezed the tissue off the table,* etc. to the following examples of the resultative construction (cf. Section 5.4):

Terry wiped the table clean.

The pupils chatted the teacher furious.

The crowd shouted the speaker silent.

5. *'I would never borrow Tom a book.*

Provide a blending analysis of this sentence produced by a foreign learner of English modelled on Figure 6.6 and explain the blending process.

6. 'Once upon a time . . .'. Select scenes from fairytales like **Little Red Riding Hood**, or **Puss in Boots**, where animals behave like human beings and discuss how a blending analysis could explain the constantly changing mix of animal and human behaviour in these 'anthropomorphic metaphors'.

6.3 Conceptual blending in advertising texts, riddles and jokes

Conceptual blending can probably be observed in most text types, but there are some where it takes on a special form and achieves a special effect. This seems to be true of advertisements, riddles and jokes, which have been selected for discussion in this section.

Advertising texts as 'forced' blends

Our discussion of advertising texts will be restricted to print ads combining text and pictorial elements. The text/picture constellation has been widely discussed in the literature, particularly in semiotics, where it has led Roland Barthes (1977: 38–41) to postulate a basic distinction between 'anchorage' (text providing disambiguation and deictic support for the picture) and 'relay' (text and image standing in a complementary relationship).[13] Since the second type promises more interesting results, the treatment will focus on it.

The example chosen is a fairly conventional ad taken from the January 2000 UK edition of the magazine *Marie Claire* (Figure 6.8); the blending analysis of this ad is represented in network format in Figure 6.9. To keep the analysis simple, the ad has been documented in two input spaces, a lovers space (picture-based) and a Pantene space (based on both pictures and text, including the headline, which in fact straddles both sections of the ad).

In its pictures as well as in its wording, the ad builds on a rather blatant use of cross-space identity between participants and the spatial relations in which they are involved. There are two lovers and two products (metonymically represented by their bottles) and both pairs are pictured not only close to each other, but, even in the case of the bottles, facing each other. This pictorial effect is supported the verbal messages such as *Don't go it alone* and *used in harmony*. The obvious intention is to create an emergent structure in which the prototypical interaction of the lovers is projected onto the relationship of the hair-care products. What the text stresses in addition is the agenthood of the lifeless products (the shampoo delivering vitamins, the conditioner moisturizing the hair), a tendency culminating in the headline of the ad *Some things just work better together.*

But how do the other elements of the input spaces find their way into the blended space? The SETTING in which the lovers are presented, the sleeping bag and the clear morning light, suggesting that they have spent the night together out in the cornfield, call up associations of nature, freshness, purity and youth (plus all the memories of a romantic meeting, including the 'innocent' whiteness of the underwear). These associations may be even more important for the effectiveness of the ad than the surface relationship between lovers and products. The key question is how the SETTING of the lovers space can be related to the PURPOSE element of the Pantene space (motivating customers to use both the shampoo and the conditioner). While no explicit cross-space mapping offers itself, the ad tries to suggest a loose link, preferably something resembling an identity or a cause–effect relation (indicated in Figure 6.9 in brackets). What is crucial

Figure 6.8   www.pantene.com
Ad for Pantene shampoo and conditioner (from *Marie Claire*, Jan. 2000)

is that the relevance of this cross-space mapping is as it were 'forced upon' the reader (by the size and attractive colours of the picture, the lovers' appeal, etc.). Guided by the relevance principle, the reader will then attempt the compression of the SETTING and the PURPOSE elements of the input spaces, thus creating a new element of PURPOSE in the blended space – based on the notion that the shampoo and the conditioner somehow produce nature, freshness,

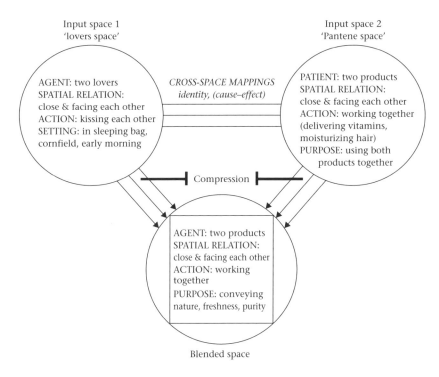

Figure 6.9 Network representation of the Pantene ad blend

purity and youth. Far from trying to spell out the relationship between these hair-care products and the associations of the lovers' kiss, the advertisers will be quite happy to exhaust the indeterminacy of online processing offered by conceptual blending (which was already encountered in the analysis of the PISA acronym above). Even if these positive associations are entrenched as part of the brand image of Pantene, it will remain rather vague because the systematic analysis of the emergent structure is neither attempted nor even desired. In this the Pantene ad joins the range of **forced blends** propagating such powerful, but ultimately undifferentiated images as the Marlboro country of cigarette smokers or the tropical beach life of the happy people drinking Bacardi rum.

Blending in riddles and jokes: using conceptual blending as a problem-solving tool

Compared with advertisements, both riddles and jokes may be more marginal text types, but they are also very interesting from the angle of comprehension and cognitive processing. It is therefore not surprising that Fauconnier and Turner selected a riddle as one of the prime examples of the conceptual-blending analysis, the 'Buddhist monk riddle', which they summarize from Arthur Koestler's *The Act of Creation* (1964: 183f) as follows:

> A Buddhist monk begins at dawn one day walking up a mountain, reaches the top at sunset, meditates at the top for several days until one dawn when he begins to walk back to the foot of the mountain, which he reaches at sunset. Make no assumptions about his starting or stopping or about his pace during the trips. Riddle: Is there a place on the path that the monk occupies at the same hour of the day on the two separate journeys?
>
> (Fauconnier and Turner 2002: 39)

To solve the riddle, Fauconnier and Turner (2002: 39) suggest that one should imagine that the monk is walking up and down the mountain on the same day along the same path. Assuming this, there must be a place where he 'meets himself', i.e. where he passes by on both his journeys even if the exact position of the imaginary meeting point is not clear.

After what has been said about blends, this explanation reads like a paraphrase of the blending process (and is therefore used as an introductory example of the theory by Fauconnier and Turner). By conflating the two journeys we acknowledge that there must be a cross-space identity relation between the two journeys, a link embodied by the monk; in addition, there must be a spatial relation between the paths he follows on both his journeys, and finally and most importantly, there must be a time relation.

All these relations undergo compression in the blend. The person of the monk and the path followed are unified in the blended space without problems, while the compression of time is only carried out to a point: we can compress the days of the two journeys, but not the hour of the imaginary meeting; in this the emergent structure remains vague. Compare Figure 6.10, where the path and direction are represented by lines and arrows, the position of the monk by a bold circle and the person of the monk by the letters a_1 and a_2. Compression in the blended space is indicated by the conflation of the path and the day symbol, while the actual position of the imaginary meeting point is a_1 and a_2 is narrowed down to a stretch between a_1' and a_2', but not really fixed.

While this is the point where the open-endedness and indeterminacy of the emergent structure are made explicit, it is only by means of blending the two journeys into one that the riddle can be solved. This shows that conceptual blending is not only a more or less unconscious process

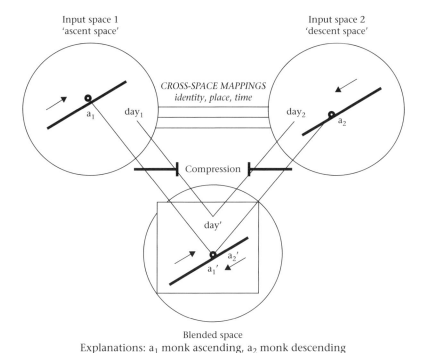

Input space 1
'ascent space'

Input space 2
'descent space'

CROSS-SPACE MAPPINGS
identity, place, time

day_1 day_2

a_1 a_2

Compression

day'

a_2'
a_1'

Blended space
Explanations: a_1 monk ascending, a_2 monk descending

Figure 6.10   Network representation of Buddhist Monk blend
(adapted from Fauconnier and Turner 2002: 45)

involved in interpreting linguistic utterances (and, to some extent, other phenomena), but can also be a deliberately chosen **problem-solving strategy**. Similar types of hypothetical scenarios also need to be blended in weighing the pros and cons of future strategies, say, in business, politics and of course also the private domain. Here several possible future actions are blended and evaluated with respect to their hypothetical outcomes.

The blending approach can also build on earlier explanations, in particular on Arthur Koestler's claim that the principle underlying jokes is

the perceiving of a situation or idea, L, in two self-consistent but habitually incompatible frames of reference, M.1 and M.2 [. . .]. The event L, in which the two intersect, is made to vibrate simultaneously on two different wavelengths, as it were.

(Koestler 1964: 35)

The idea of linking the joke to two different frames of reference (or to two different scripts, as suggested by Raskin 1985) directly leads to the postulation of two input spaces while the 'simultaneous vibrating on two different wavelengths' is aptly captured by the notion of blended space.[14]

To illustrate the potential of the blending approach for the understanding of jokes, here is an example of a type popular with children, where
misdemeanour in school takes an unexpected turn:

Mother: Why were you sent home early, Mary?
Mary: Well, Mum, the boy next to me was smoking.
Mother: But if he was smoking, why were *you* sent home?
Mary: I set him on fire.

As shown in Figure 6.11, the two reference frames or scripts can be represented in terms of participant roles in the two input spaces. Input space 1
documents Mary's first utterance, assigning the role of AGENT to the boy,
who is performing the action of smoking. Since *XY is smoking a
cigarette/pipe* is a well-entrenched construction, the PATIENT role of cigarette
is automatically implied. The figure of Mary is backgrounded and reduced
to the status of BYSTANDER. In addition, this mental space will include the
encyclopaedic knowledge that smoking is a common transgression of
school rules.

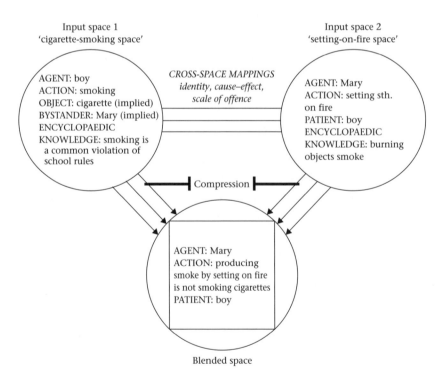

Figure 6.11 Setting-on-fire joke: network representation of the blend

Input space 2 is used to render the contents of the punchline. Here Mary functions as the AGENT engaged in the action of setting fire to the PATIENT, embodied by the boy. So the second input space is a setting-on-fire space including encyclopaedic knowledge that burning objects smoke.

To satisfy the audience's demands for relevance at least three cross-space relations will be established: first an identity relation between the AGENT of input space 1 and the PATIENT of input space 2, both representing the boy, secondly a cause–effect link between the actions of setting on fire and of smoking, and finally a scalar link denoting the seriousness of the offence incurred. In the process of blending, all three cross-space relations undergo compression: in the emergent structure of the blended space the AGENT role is superseded by the PATIENT role while the BYSTANDER role is elevated to the status of AGENT. With regard to the actions involved, the compression of 'producing smoke by setting on fire' and 'smoking cigarettes' proves futile because the two actions are shown to be incompatible and this is also underlined by a compression of the wildly diverging evaluations of the two actions in terms of offensiveness. It is this obvious incompatibility emerging in the structure of the blended space that pinpoints the locus of the joke and the source of its humorous effect. And since the blend also complies with the unpacking principle, it permits the unravelling of the development of the joke and invites the audience to take delight in Mary's verbal skills demonstrated by backgrounding herself as BYSTANDER and highlighting the boy's AGENT role before the genuine relationship is revealed.

To sum up, what all the text types discussed in this section share is a rather blatant exploitation of the online quality of the emergent structure of the blend.

- Advertising texts encourage and even force upon the reader an online compression of the positive effects suggested (often by way of pictures) and the advertised goods. To enhance the effect, they tend to hide the indeterminacy of the blend rather than lay it open to the reader.
- Problem-based riddles (and plans for future actions) are solved by strategically and deliberately blending different event scenarios and assessing their possible outcomes.
- Jokes produce an emergent structure containing at least some elements for which blending is not successful because they are incompatible and this is the source of their humorous effect.

Exercises

1. Many ads try to project associations of luxury, wealth, beauty or fame onto utterly mundane products like chocolates, beer or cosmetics, thus

creating a certain 'image' for a company or brand. Find examples of this type of ad, sketch the mental spaces involved and show to what extent the blend between them is not a 'natural' result of compression but is forced upon the audience.

2. Analyze the following riddles with regard to the mental spaces activated and discuss how the spaces are brought together in the blend. What makes these riddles funny?

Why do cows wear bells?	(Because their horns don't work.)
Why are mosquitoes so annoying?	(Because they get under our skin.)
What did the beach say when the tide came in?	(Long time no sea.)

3. Discuss the following jokes in terms of conceptual blending, trying to locate the incompatibility in the blend:

After swallowing a (wind) surfer, the shark pensively looks at the empty board and sail. 'Nicely served, with breakfast tray and napkin.'

Everyone had so much fun diving from the tree into the swimming pool, we decided to put in a little water. (Coulson 2001: 3)

A: Do you know the way to the station?

B: No, I don't!

A: Listen, you take a right turn at the next corner, then straight ahead . . .

Everybody likes the torero. I don't. I'm the bull.

6.4 Relevance: a cognitive-pragmatic phenomenon

As we have seen, relevance has been proposed as one of the governing principles of conceptual blending by Fauconnier and Turner. Originally conceived as a pragmatic principle of interaction, the notion of relevance has been given a cognitive turn by Sperber and Wilson (1995). This section looks at their approach, selecting (and simplifying) some aspects that seem to be akin to cognitive-linguistic thinking and from which cognitive linguistics might benefit.

The search for relevance and the notion of cognitive environment

Human understanding of verbal and non-verbal communicative events seems to be controlled and dominated by the search for relevance. Confronted with an apparently incoherent contribution to an ongoing piece of discourse, we still cannot help but pursue the question *Why was this said to me here and now?* For example, as suggested in the previous section, if two pieces of information, such as the text and the picture of an advertisement, are presented to us on one page, we automatically assume that there must be some reason why they occur together and look for some plausible relation between them. Similarly, participants in discourse will generally look for the relevance of an utterance in the context of previous ones; and even if they do not immediately recognize how a contribution could tie in, they often go to great lengths to construct a satisfying link.

Picking up one of Sperber and Wilson's examples (1995: 34), here is a short dialogue which might have been uttered at the end of a dinner and in which Peter's question obviously does not receive a straightforward answer from Mary:

Peter: Do you want some coffee?
Mary: Coffee would keep me awake.

Yet although no direct answer is provided, Peter will try to make sense of this answer, probably concluding that Mary does not want coffee in order to ensure a good night's rest. To a large extent Mary's utterance will be understood by Peter because they share the situational information that it is late in the evening and the encyclopaedic knowledge about the effects of caffeine on sleep. Both pieces of knowledge are, in Sperber and Wilson's words, part of Peter's and Mary's '**cognitive environment**'. This is defined as the set of all assumptions that are manifest to Peter and Mary because they can perceive them in their physical environment or infer them using such cognitive abilities as memory and reasoning (1995: 39). In short, the cognitive environment is made up of **assumptions** that are either stored in memory, currently perceived or currently inferred.

The stored knowledge acquired by a person is obviously equivalent to the sum of all the cognitive models (frames, scripts, scenarios) he or she has internalized. However, while many cognitive linguists tend to focus on 'idealized' cognitive models shared by groups of people, Sperber and Wilson – working as they are in a largely pragmatic framework – emphasize that the cognitive environments differ from one person to another and from one situation to another. In particular, like the conceptual-blending approach presented in the previous sections, Sperber and Wilson are interested in the ongoing meaning construction and therefore stress that cognitive abilities also include the ability to become aware of further facts and thus to generate **new assumptions and inferences**.

To pick up the coffee-offering example quoted above (and using it for our own interpretation), Mary's cryptic answer *Coffee would keep me awake* could also stimulate Peter to develop new inferences, which might generate different assumptions. One of them might be that Mary perhaps wants to stay awake to take an active share in the conversation with the other party guests, another one that she is afraid that without the coffee she might fall asleep on her drive back home. But how should Peter know that one of these additional inferences is also part of Mary's cognitive environment, is shared by her and can therefore be assumed to be part of the intended message?

Ostensive–inferential behaviour, figure/ground segregation and communicative relevance

The key to Peter's understanding of what Mary means is of course what she actually said. What she did say, together with her gestures, facial expression and other non-verbal cues, is called her **'ostensive–inferential behaviour'** in Relevance Theory. From a cognitive-linguistic point of view this can be understood in terms of figure/ground segregation: the ostensive–inferential *stimulus* (as it is called) stands out as figure from the conceptual (back)ground of all the potential assumptions that are not explicitly encoded, be it verbally or non-verbally. The most explicit realization of ostensive–inferential behaviour in our case would be a clarifying linguistic utterance: compare the following pair, where the first version unequivocally supports the sleep-robbing assumption while the second version would fit the car-driving assumption:

No, thank you, coffee would keep me awake.
Yes, please, coffee would keep me awake.

Less unambiguous but still helpful would be the employment of different intonation patterns, a falling intonation to indicate the rejection of the offer and a rise to signal its acceptance.

Ostensive behaviour can also be expressed by body posture, body movement and eye contact. Sperber and Wilson's own example is the park bench situation (Sperber and Wilson 1995: 48–9): Peter, who is sitting on the bench together with Mary, indicates by a rigid act of leaning back that he does not just want to take up a more comfortable position: rather he wants to draw Mary's attention to a phenomenon that had been hidden from her view before his movement. Mary realizes how this ostensive–inferential act changes their shared cognitive environment, gives prominence to different assumptions and this may well spark off a new set of assumptions on her part (which will be sketched out in the next subsection). While the cognitive operation of providing prominence to certain assumptions can be easily captured in terms of profiling (see Chapter 4), the notion that change is initiated by an intentional act of the conversational partner brings the interactional component to the fore, which is rather neglected in cognitive-linguistic thinking. As stressed by Wilson and Sperber (2003: 611f),[15] Peter's ostensive act conveys not just one, but two intentions: the intention to inform Mary of something and, more importantly, the intention to inform her of his informative intention; this second 'communicative intention' is a clear sign of the **communicative relevance** attributed to ostensive–inferential acts.

Relevance: cognitive effectiveness, cognitive efficiency and cognitive economy

Assuming that Peter's ostensive behaviour has achieved the intended effect, this is what Sperber and Wilson think might happen to Mary's cognitive environment:

> Imagine, for instance, that as a result of Peter's leaning back she can see, among other things, three people: an ice-cream vendor who she had noticed before when she sat down on the bench, an ordinary stroller who she has never seen before, and her acquaintance William, who is coming towards them and is a dreadful bore. Many assumptions about each of these characters are more or less manifest to her. She may already have considered the implications of the presence of the ice-cream vendor when she first noticed him; if so, it would be a waste of processing resources to pay further attention to him now. The presence of the unknown stroller is new information to her, but little or nothing follows from it; so there again, what she can perceive and infer about him is not likely to be of much relevance to her. By contrast, from the fact that William is coming her way, she can draw many conclusions from which many more conclusions will follow. This, then, is the only true relevant change in her cognitive environment; this is the particular phenomenon she should pay attention to.
>
> (Sperber and Wilson 1995: 48f)

Reading the account it becomes clear that relevance is to be understood in terms of **effects** on a person's cognitive environment and **efficiency** of short-term information processing. From this angle, assumptions about the ice-cream vendor are a waste of processing resources, and the same applies to the second person involved, the stroller. Instead, considering how large the memories of terribly boring meetings loom in Mary's cognitive environment, William is the only individual triggering significant contextual effects and worth the cognitive effort (even if it is only to develop strategies of how to get rid of him again). And since so much has already been stored about him in the cognitive environment, the effort needed to develop these strategies should not be too great. In short, the sight of William has a positive cognitive effect on Mary's cognitive environment without costing her too much effort.

Abstracting from this description one could say that the assumptions concerning William meet the two extent conditions of relevance to individuals postulated by Sperber and Wilson:

CONDITION 1:
An assumption is relevant to an individual to the extent that the positive cognitive effects achieved when it is optimally processed are large.

CONDITION 2:
An assumption is relevant to an individual to the extent that the effort required to achieve these positive cognitive effects is small.

(Sperber and Wilson 1995: 265f)

Relevance is thus tied to two complementary claims: on the one hand relevance depends on the positive cognitive effects that an optimally processed assumption will exert on a participant of an interaction. On the other hand relevance is linked to cognitive efficiency which demands an **economic** use of processing resources. For cognitive linguists the term cognitive efficiency is strongly reminiscent of the notion of *cognitive economy* developed by Rosch (1978) to justify the dominance of the basic level categories in the conceptualization of the world – her definition of cognitive economy was that the largest amount of information about an item can be obtained with the least cognitive effort (see Section 2.1). Undoubtedly, Sperber and Wilson's conception of cognitive efficiency is much more comprehensive than Rosch's characterization of basic level conceptualization, and this is exactly where cognitive-linguistic thinking might again be stimulated by Relevance Theory. It could well be worth examining how cognitive efficiency is involved with other elements and operations investigated by cognitive linguists apart from basic level categories. An interesting candidate might be holistic or gestalt perception, which was explained as a short-cut approach that precedes and often replaces the detailed conceptualization in terms of attributes (see Section 1.2). As for metonymies, there are also many examples promising economic processing by way of easily accessible source concepts – think of *a glass (of beer)*, *drive a Ford*, *wait for a White House decision* (see Section 3.1). Even the use of meaningful syntactic constructions (see Section 5.4) could be investigated from this angle. Finally, as already mentioned, conceptual blending explicitly integrates relevance – and thus by definition includes cognitive efficiency – as one of its governing principles.

Assumptions, vital relations and compression

Both Relevance Theory and Conceptual-Blending Theory address online aspects of cognitive processing, but they approach the problem in different ways. In Relevance Theory the change in the cognitive environment is thought to be initiated by an act of ostensive–inferential behaviour that sparks off various types of assumptions – assumptions based on the fact that a series of sounds has been uttered as well as assumptions based on the semantic content of this sound chain. Following the philosophical tradition of pragmatic reasoning, Sperber and Wilson cast these assumptions in the shape of statements, as shown in Figure 6.12 for the 'dinner is ready' example. The utterance of the sound sequence [ɪtlgetkəʊld] by Mary changes Peter's cognitive environment even if the semantic content of the utterance is disregarded. This is reflected in the assumptions of set {A}. If Peter regards some of these assumptions as relevant and selects them for processing, e.g. assumptions (3) – (5), the ostensive act of producing *It will get cold* achieves about the same effect as if Mary had cleared her throat. Only if he decides

---

ACT OF OSTENSIVE BEHAVIOUR:
Sound sequence [ɪtlgetkəʊld] (*It will get cold*)
produced by Mary in the presence of Peter:

ASSUMPTIONS MADE MANIFEST TO PETER BY MARY'S OSTENSIVE BEHAVIOUR:

Set {A}
(1) Someone has made a sound.
(2) There is someone in the house.
(3) Mary is at home.
(4) Mary has spoken.
(5) Mary has a sore throat.
(6) Mary has said to Peter: 'It will get cold.'
(7) There is a set of assumptions {I} which Mary intends to make manifest to Peter by saying to him 'It will get cold.'

Set {I}
(8) Mary's utterance is optimally relevant to Peter.
(9) Mary has said that the dinner will get cold.
(10) The dinner will get cold very soon.
(11) Mary wants Peter to come and eat dinner at once.

Figure 6.12 Assumptions generated for the 'dinner is ready' example
(selected from Sperber and Wilson 1995: 176–82)

to process assumptions (6) – (7), because they promise the largest cognitive gains without requiring too much processing effort, will this lead on to the assumptions assembled in set {I}.

This second set of assumptions first states the general principle of communicative relevance (8) and then opens up a choice between a reported statement (9), a plain assertion (10) and the more complex evaluation *Mary wants Peter to come and eat dinner at once* (11). This last variant is definitely more than a mere logical deduction from the previous assumptions because it also draws on Peter's memorized experience of the whole scenario 'dinner at home' and Mary's part in it. It is indeed highly relevant for Peter and well worth the processing effort if only for the sake of domestic peace.

On a more technical level, an ostensive act like the sound sequence [ɪtlgetkəʊld] is, of course, a stimulus of a very indirect kind; it is clear that all assumptions it sparks off can only be inferred, including the final variant *Mary wants Peter to come and eat dinner at once*, and can therefore be regarded as **implicatures**.[16] However, even if Mary had chosen the explicit utterance *Peter, you must come at once to eat dinner because it's getting cold*, this simple example of an **explicature** (Sperber and Wilson 1995:180–3) could not be safely processed by just considering the word meaning of the utterance and neglecting the inferences to be drawn from the cognitive environment in which the utterance is placed. Just to call up the 'dinner at home' scenario once more, its knowledge is definitely necessary to evaluate the urgency of Mary's request and the consequences of a delayed reaction on Peter's part.

How does this system of inferential assumptions and its realization as implicatures and explicatures compare with the toolkit proposed by Conceptual-Blending Theory for online processing?[17] Rooted in the tradition of pragmatic reasoning, the format of assumptions seems to provide a fairly systematic and logical approach to the treatment of cognitive input. Compare again Figure 6.12, where a first set of 'preparative' assumptions (set {A} concerning Mary's physical presence, the state of her voice and the realization of the utterance) paves the way for the second set of more central assumptions (set {I}), from which – after the consideration of memorized experience – the most relevant is selected. No matter what is said about the consideration of non-verbal ostensive acts, the system works best when these acts contain a linguistic element and when the cognitive environment as a whole lends itself to the establishment of 'chains' of assumptions.

By contrast, the treatment of cognitive material in Conceptual-Blending Theory seems to be much more liberal, but also much vaguer. Cognitive input, whose sources are often not really explored, but which include linguistic, visual and aural stimuli, is assembled in mental input spaces and is supported by material drawn from long-term memory in the form of cognitive models, and also by additional contextual material. As discussed in Section 6.1, the structuring of the material in the input spaces as well as the cross-space mappings between them rely on vital relations, in particular on the relations of identity, space and time, property, cause–effect and part–whole. The crucial point is that these relations do not form a coherent system and the same applies to compression, on which the emergent structure in the blended space is based. This lack of hierarchy and systematic sequence has given rise to the criticism that 'anything goes' in conceptual blending and has led to the postulation of governing principles by Fauconnier and Turner, among them the principle of relevance (other governing principles are topography, integration, unpacking; see Section 6.1). Yet like the vital relations (and perhaps for the same reasons) these principles have not been organized in a systematic hierarchy, but actually counteract and cancel out each other in certain blends.

In short, Relevance Theory is clearly positioned more on the logical–deductive side typical of pragmatic work inspired by the philosophical tradition, while Conceptual-Blending Theory has a much richer and multi-faceted view of cognition, which is, however, also more hazy and intuitive. In addition, like other cognitive-linguistic theories discussed in this book conceptual blending favours a holistic view of cognition which sees language structure and use as intertwined with general cognitive abilities like perception, attention and problem-solving. Relevance Theory, on the other hand, postulates a separate inferential module which is only loosely related to general cognition.[18]

The question that can only be asked here but not answered is if the two theories could profit from a closer cooperation with each other – assuming that the rather fundamental ideological differences could be reconciled. For instance, could vital relations and the process of compression benefit from the more systematic organization underlying the response to the cognitive environment and to ostensive acts in Relevance Theory? Or could the disregard of the interactional component, which is widespread in cognitive linguistics, but particularly regrettable in a theory of online processing, be overcome by relevance-theoretic suggestions? Or, from the complementary perspective, could Relevance Theory enrich the cognitive complexity of its explanations by letting in more 'soft' cognition?

Since our concern is the development of cognitive linguistics, we will conclude this short and introductory sketch of Relevance Theory by recapitulating the other suggestions for the development of cognitive linguistics the discussion has yielded:[19]

- The notion of idealized cognitive models (frames, scripts, scenarios) should be extended to individualized cognitive environments.
- The notion of figure and ground should be given a speaker- and hearer-oriented interpretation to cope with the cognitive aspects of relevance.
- The related notions of cognitive economy and cognitive efficiency should gain wider currency in cognitive linguistics (e.g. in the analysis of gestalt, metonymies, etc.).

Exercises

1. Imagine driving down a busy one-way street in a car with your partner in the passenger seat.

   The street is lined by trees and shops with sales announced in the shop windows, young mothers with toddlers in buggies, important-looking executives passing by on the pavement, a group of little children playing ball close to the kerb, cars parked along the other kerb and reversing into empty lots.

   Suddenly your partner shouts *Watch out!* in an agitated voice. Describe your and your partner's cognitive environments and your partner's ostensive behaviour and discuss what types of assumptions you could infer from it. What could a description in terms of figure and ground contribute to this analysis?

2. Look at the following sentence pairs and decide which member of each pair promises greater efficiency of cognitive processing. Which member involves a metonymy, and if this applies, which metonymy?

   I'd like to have another half pint of White Label, please.
   I'd like to have another glass, please.

   Nine-eleven changed our view of the world.
   The terrorist attack against the World Trade Center in September 2001 changed our view of the world.

   If we take the car, we'll need a tankful of petrol for the journey.
   If we take the car, we'd better fill her up for the trip.

   You see the whole medical staff, doctors and nurses and all, are working to rule.
   You see the whole hospital is on strike.

3. Imagine Susan reading the entertainment guide in the local newspaper in the presence of Tom, pointing at a picture of the Rooftop Band, drumming a rhythm on the table and uttering the sound sequence [ðəɪl bɪ ˌsəʊldˈaʊt baɪ naʊ].

Show how this utterance can spark off a sequence of assumptions in Tom along the lines of the example illustrated in Figure 6.12.

Suggestions for further reading

Section 6.1

This section and the following sections are based on Fauconnier and Turner's work (esp. Fauconnier and Turner 2002). In trying to provide a first impression, the complexity of their approach has been reduced to arrive at an easily manageable set of analytic tools.

1. See Turner and Fauconnier (1995), Fauconnier and Turner (1996), Fauconnier (1997, ch. 6).

2. Grady, Oakley and Coulson (1999) discuss the relationship between metaphor and blending. See Givón (2005) for a critical account of the conceptual metaphor theory from the point of view of online activation of metaphors and Grady (2005) on basic 'primary' metaphors as inputs to, rather than results of, blending processes. Coulson and Oakley (2005) look at the traditional distinction between literal and figurative meaning from a conceptual-blending perspective.

3. The network model is summarized and illustrated e.g. in Fauconnier and Turner (1998: 142ff), Coulson and Oakley (2000: 178ff) and (2003: 54ff).

4. A more detailed discussion of vital relations than we are able to present can be found in Fauconnier and Turner (2002: 89–111 and 312–27).

5. This interpretation is in line with Fauconnier and Turner's (2002: 99f) idea of 'property' as an 'inner space relation', i.e. a vital relation structuring mental spaces. Note that there is a parallel between simple (inner-space) properties vs blended properties, on the one hand, and so-called inherent vs non-inherent adjectives in descriptive grammar on the other (see e.g. Quirk *et al.* 1985: 428f, 435f).

6. Optimality principles (whose name is inspired by phonological 'Optimality Theory', see e.g. Kager (1999) for an introduction) were

first sketched very briefly in Fauconnier (1997: 185f), expounded by Fauconnier and Turner (1998) and later revised and partly renamed in Fauconnier and Turner (2002), where they are referred to as 'governing principles'.

Section 6.2

7. The easiest way of getting an idea of the broad range of issues addressed by blending theorists is to look at the conceptual blending website at http://markturner.org/blending.html.

8. For other cognitive-linguistic approaches to lexical blends see Lehrer (1996) and Kemmer (2003), and in terms of isomorphism between word form and concept Ungerer (1999).

9. Coulson (2001: 128–33) has further analyses of interesting nominal compounds, among them rather exotic ones, but does not sufficiently emphasize their online quality. See Sweetser (1999) for an application of blending theory to adjective–noun combinations and a discussion of their compositionality.

10. Depending on the match between input spaces and the relative dominance of them in the blended space, different types of networks such as 'mirror networks', 'simplex', 'single-scope' and 'double-scope networks' can be distinguished. See Fauconnier and Turner (2002: 119ff) for a survey of these types.

11. See Mandelblit (2000: 199–203), who postulates a blending process between an input space containing the causing and effected events (providing the lexical information) and a second input space, which contains the caused-motion construction (providing the structural information), and also analyzes other motion-event constructions mentioned in Section 5.4 in this way.

12. For studies on conditionals and counterfactual blends see Fauconnier (1996) and (1997: 99ff), Sweetser (1996), Dancygier and Sweetser (1997), and Fauconnier and Turner (2002: 217ff). See Lakoff (1996: 94–8) for a discussion of the *if-I-were-you* construction.

Section 6.3

13. For a study of pictorial metaphors see Forceville (1998), and for an alternative interpretation of the relation between text and picture in terms of metaphors and metonymies see Ungerer (2000a).

14. Koestler's (1964) classic model is known as the 'bisociation theory' of

joking. Raskin and Attardo now call their approach the 'general theory of verbal humour' (see Attardo 2001: 1–29 for a historical survey). See also the papers in Attardo (2003) on pragmatic and cognitive theories of humour. Coulson (2001) investigates online jokes and Coulson (in press) cartoons from a conceptual-blending perspective.

Section 6.4

This introductory account of Relevance Theory from an experientialist cognitive angle is based on Sperber and Wilson's own account, integrating the modifications suggested by the authors in the postface of the 2nd edition of *Relevance* (Sperber and Wilson 1995; 1st edn 1986) and in their more recent paper (Wilson and Sperber 2003). Relevance Theory is now accessible through a large number of introductory books, among them Blakemore (1992). For a first overview of the overwhelming literature that has been published on Relevance Theory in pragmatics see Sperber and Wilson (1995: 255–60) and Wilson and Sperber (2003).

15. For a concise account of the current version of the communicative principle of relevance and its role in understanding and cognition, see Wilson and Sperber (2003).

16. The notion of implicatures was of course first introduced into the philosophy of language and pragmatics by Grice (1975) in the context of his Cooperative Principle, from one of whose maxims (the maxim of relation) Sperber and Wilson have derived Relevance Theory.

17. See Fauconnier (2003) for a discussion of pragmatic aspects of conceptual-blending theory.

18. See Wilson and Sperber (2003: 623–5) for arguments in favour of a modular architecture of cognition including a specialized inferential device – a view largely incompatible with the experientialist cognitive-linguistic approach. Earlier in their paper, Wilson and Sperber (2003: 618) express their scepticism towards the prototype theory of categorization.

19. Another source of inspiration on how to include the interactional component might be Givón's 'context as other minds', which means that successful online processing of cognitive input always includes the systematic online construction of mental models of the interlocutor's belief and intention states (Givón 2005: xiv; see also chs 1.1 and 4).

CHAPTER 7

Other issues in cognitive linguistics

7.1 Iconicity

The study of iconicity, or more tangibly, of language miming the world, ranks prominently among those lines of research that have not been initiated by cognitive linguists, but have much earlier beginnings. Originally a topic of philosophical discussion and later claimed by semiotics as an important parameter for the description of signs, iconicity has benefited a great deal from being put on a cognitive basis.

Iconic and arbitrary linguistic signs

The question why words have the sound shape they have and whether they may be regarded as 'icons' (or imitations) of real objects and organisms has occupied philosophers throughout the ages. Plato, in his Cratylos dialogue,[1] distinguished between items for which form and content are determined by nature, as in *bow-wow, cuckoo* or *splash,* and those items where the relationship between form and content is based on agreement in a speech community, as in *bread* or *chair.* This distinction was taken up at the beginning of the twentieth century by the founder of modern linguistics, Ferdinand de Saussure, who maintained that the form of most words (or linguistic signs) is linked to what they signify only by convention, that the relationship between form and meaning is in fact arbitrary. In his conception, sound-symbolic expressions like *bow-wow* are at best regarded as exceptions.[2]

More recently, however, this rigid view of the linguistic sign has come under increasing criticism. In this context the ideas of C.S. Peirce, a nineteenth-century American philosopher, have been revived and have become the backbone of modern semiotics.[3] According to Peirce, only one type of sign, which he calls '**symbol**', represents a conventionalized relationship with an object, and therefore comes close to Saussure's standard interpretation of the arbitrary sign. The other two major sign categories postulated by Peirce, the 'index' and the 'icon', are characterized by their 'natural' grounding, as already discussed by Plato. The **index** basically has a pointing function, which is often realized by expressing the positioning of an object in space and time. This indexical function is fulfilled by personal and demonstrative pronouns as well as deictic adverbs of place and time, such as *here*, *there*, *now* and *then*. However, the notion of index also transcends the level of linguistic expression and is often rendered non-verbally, for instance when the direction of the wind is indicated by a weather vane or when a fire is signalled by smoke.

Yet it is the third type of sign proposed by Peirce (**the icon**) that is most relevant for the issue of iconicity and its cognitive interpretation. Peirce uses the term for those signs that convey a certain similarity with an object. The important thing is that he does not restrict the use of *icon* to the more or less realistic non-verbal imitation of an object (e.g. the signs used on a computer screen for files and documents) or – on the linguistic level – to sound-symbolic expressions. Apart from this type of icon (which he calls '**image**'), he also includes similarities between the structure of language and the structure of events (and other phenomena) encountered in reality; his term for this type of icon is '**diagram**'.

Talking about structural similarities takes us into the domain of grammar and raises the question of the arrangement of linguistic elements. The iconic principles that have been proposed for this area are **iconic sequencing**, **iconic proximity** and the **iconic quantity** of linguistic material.[4] To start with iconic sequencing, consider the following two pairs of sentences:

He opened the bottle and poured himself a glass of wine.

*He poured himself a glass of wine and opened the bottle.

He jumped onto his horse and rode out into the sunset.

*He rode out into the sunset and jumped onto his horse.

It is evident that in the first version of both sentence pairs, the sequence of the two clauses corresponds to the natural temporal order of events. In contrast, the second versions are odd to say the least, because they do not comply with this natural sequence. As far as the rules of syntax proper are concerned, nothing is wrong with the second versions. Nevertheless, the sentences are unacceptable because the order in which the clauses are arranged violates the principle of iconic sequencing.

The second type of iconicity, iconic proximity, is perhaps less obvious because the similarity relation between language and the extra-linguistic world is less obtrusive. Compare the following examples (based on Radden 1992: 515f):

the famous delicious Italian pepperoni pizza
*the Italian delicious famous pepperoni pizza
*the famous pepperoni delicious Italian pizza
*the pepperoni delicious famous Italian pizza

As the example shows, only the first version is acceptable while the other three (and all other possible combinations) are not. The reason is that only the first sentence follows the principle of iconic proximity, which states that elements that have a close relationship must be placed close together. Since *pepperoni* is an inherent component of this kind of pizza, this word must precede the noun directly; *Italian*, which denotes the place of origin, deserves the second closest position, while the characterization of the pizza as *delicious* and its evaluation as *famous* take the positions which are more distant from the noun. The problem is that while the linguistic description consists of a linear sequence of elements, in the real world all the characteristics of the pizza are integrated in one single object.

Before pursuing this problem further, let us take a look at the third type of iconicity, iconic quantity or quantitative iconicity (Givón 1990: 966ff). Consider the following example:

This guy is getting on my nerves.
This aggressively impertinent egghead is getting on my nerves.

Obviously, there is a marked difference in the length of the subject noun phrase between the two sentences. This difference corresponds to the amount of information provided for the description of the person referred to, and this has been regarded as a manifestation of iconic quantity. However, this view brings with it a serious problem: no matter how much information is supplied, the person in the real world that is referred to stays the same. In other words, the view that iconic quantity establishes a relation between linguistic expressions and the person (or object) in the real world cannot be upheld in such a simple form, and this is the point where cognitive linguistics comes into play.

Putting iconicity on a cognitive footing: examples of diagrammatic iconicity

If one recalls that cognitive linguists do not claim to make statements about the real world of objects and organisms, but deal with the categories and cognitive models we have about the real world, this provides a new reference point for the iconicity relation. Instead of comparing words and grammatical structures with real objects and events, we may now compare them with our categories and cognitive models of the real world, and this makes the diagrammatic comparison much easier and much more plausible. This means that in our example, iconic quantity is a relationship between the length of the linguistic expression and the complexity of the cognitive model evoked for the description of the impertinent egghead. Returning to our pizza example, we find that iconic proximity is now a matter of the mental proximity of associated object categories (PIZZA, PEPPERONI, ITALY) and the adjectival category GOOD (which underlies both *delicious* and *famous*). And of course, the iconic sequence in the first examples (pouring a glass of wine, riding out into the sunset) can also be understood as a similarity relation between the sequence of linguistic elements and the sequence of the respective event categories.

There can be no doubt that the cognitive reinterpretation of iconicity has boosted research in this field. One fascinating aspect of this work is that linguistic facts which used to be taken for granted but were in fact unexplained can now be interpreted as manifestations of the principle of iconicity. Investigations of verb morphology[5] have shown that in many languages, aspect markers are closer to the verb stem than tense markers, and tense markers in turn are closer to the verb stem than modality markers. To a certain extent this is also reflected in the English verb phrase, as illustrated by the following set of examples:

She was **working** at that time.
She **worked** a lot at that time.
She **could swim** when she was three.
*She **swim-could** when she was three.

In the first sentence the aspect marker *-ing* is closest to the lexical verb stem because it is used as a suffix, while the tense marker is part of the preceding auxiliary and therefore less closely linked with the verb stem. However, the tense marker can be attached to the verb stem when aspect is not expressed, as in the second example, which proves that the link is still very strong. This is not the case with the modality marker 'can' contained in the *could* form of the third sentence (the other grammatical component of *could* is the tense marker). As shown by the ungrammatical fourth sentence, the modality marker cannot be moved into a closer position to the verb stem, for instance by being turned into a suffix.

For the cognitive linguist, the proximity between the aspect marker and the verb stem reflects the close relationship between the grammatically specified notions of DURATION and PROGRESSION and the 'verbal' action category WORK. In contrast, the relationship between the notion of TEMPORAL LOCATION (underlying tense markers) and the category WORK seems to be less intimate. Yet the link is still stronger than the affinity between the modality notion ABILITY and the lexical category SWIM.

Turning to noun morphology, we find that the relative positions of plural markers and case markers (e.g. dative and genitive markers) can be explained in a similar way. Most concrete objects and persons are conceived as entities that can be easily counted, so the concepts expressing them combine well with the notion of QUANTITY, which underlies plural markers, and this is why plural markers are directly attached to the noun stem. Case markers (which are, for instance, expressed as prepositions and suffixes) also have their conceptual background. Dative markers (as in *give something to the girl*) are probably based on orientational image schemas (see Section 2.4) while genitive markers (as in *Peter's pen*) can be related to the 'part–whole' schema. These schemas are also very elementary parts of our experience, but seem to be less closely related to object and person categories than the plural category QUANTITY. This difference is duly mirrored in noun morphology, where case markers are normally placed in the second closest position if a plural marker is present.

Since English has lost most of its noun morphology, it is not a good testing ground. One of the few examples it provides is the genitive plural form *children's* (as in *children's books*). Here the 'irregular' plural marker *-ren* is closer to the noun stem than the genitive marker *-s*, and this sequence cannot be reversed.

Like iconic proximity, quantitative iconicity has also been given a wider interpretation in cognitive studies. Starting from the principle that longer linguistic expressions reflect a larger amount of conceptual information, Givón (1990) suggests that the amount of linguistic material corresponds to the importance and the degree of predictability of the information processed. This applies to the egghead sentence discussed above, but it is perhaps more obvious in the following examples:

> On the Brighton train from Victoria I met **her**.
>
> On the Brighton train from Victoria I met **the girl from next door**.
>
> Just imagine! Last night on the Brighton train from Victoria I met **this fair-haired, fragile, just unbelievably beautiful creature**.

It is evident that the pronoun *her* (first sentence) is normally only justified if the person referred to is neither particularly important nor unknown and the reference is not unexpected. *The girl from next door* (second sentence) indicates a larger degree of conceptual importance and unexpectedness, but this sentence is easily beaten by the last version, where the singular conceptual importance of the information and its unexpectedness are matched by an exploding linguistic expression. On a more general level, the principle of quantitative iconicity explains why personal pronouns are usually shorter than full noun phrases and why the standard forms of pronouns tend to be shorter than contrastive forms (which are stressed to signal importance). Compare the unstressed French first person pronoun *je* (in *je sais* and *j'aime*) with the contrastive form *moi*.

A cognitive view of onomatopoeia (sound symbolism)

The claim of cognitive linguists that the iconic relationship is established between a linguistic item and the conceptualization of the object in question (and not the object itself) is also helpful for a better understanding of sound-symbolic or onomatopoeic words (Peirce's images).[6] To start with what is conventionally regarded as prototypical sound symbolism ('**imagic iconicity**' in Peirce's terminology), the imitation of movements or of 'natural' animal noises, it is not surprising that onomatopoeic words differ from language to language, as illustrated in Figure 7.1. This is not just a matter of the divergent phonological development languages have undergone since a sound-symbolic word was accepted in the vocabulary – an example of this would be the different pronunciations (and spellings) of the initial labial sounds in English *bow-wow* and German *wauwau*. As our perception of the world is determined by cultural models, speakers of different languages will tend to highlight different aspects of animal sounds in the process of conceptualization – compare this to Arabic *haphap*, which is much closer to English *woof-woof* and French *oauf ouaf* than to *bow-wow*. Similarly, sound

English *bow-wow* *woof-woof*	French *ouah ouah* *ouaf ouaf*	Bulgarian *bau-bau*
German *wauwau*	Spanish *guau*	Yoruba *waw-waw*
English *miaow*	French *miaou*	Bulgarian *miau*
German *miau*	Spanish (*moullar*)	Yoruba *miu*
English *cock-a-doodle-do*	French *cocorico*	Bulgarian *kukuriguu*
German *kikeriki*	Spanish *quiquiriquí*	Yoruba *kokorookoo*
English *moo*	French *meuh*	Bulgarian *muu*
German *muh*	Spanish (*mugir*)	Yoruba *broo*

Figure 7.1 Onomatopoeic rendering of animal sounds in selected languages

clusters like /kr/ in *crash, creak, crush, Crunchies* can either convey harsh unpleasant conceptualization of a creaking sound or the pleasant impression of crunchiness experienced when eating a breakfast cereal.

The cognitive approach also explains the effectiveness of 'secondary' sound-symbolic clusters, which develop from an accumulation of words containing a certain sound cluster and expressing related meanings. A case in point are English words introduced by the cluster /sw/, such as *swing, sway, sweep, swirl, swagger*. Since all of them express the notion of swinging, they have created the impression that /sw/ iconically reflects the motion and sound of swinging.

Finally, a cognitive interpretation may also throw some light on the most puzzling type of onomatopoeia, evocative or associative sound symbolism, which claims, among other things, that the front vowel /i/ stands for smallness, brightness and pleasant feelings and the back vowels /u/ and /o/ suggest large size, strength and unpleasant feelings. A similar but less pronounced tendency of positive and negative associations has been observed for the distinction between voiceless and voiced consonants (Masuda 2002). These associations have been repeatedly confirmed in experiments, starting with Sapir's study in 1929, in which informants were asked to assign minimal nonsense utterances like [mil] and [mal] to large and small objects.

The good/bad association has also been used by authors in choosing names for fictional characters and creating artificial languages for them. In these cases, the cognitive view of iconicity is particularly convincing since the referents of these names do not 'live' in reality, but only in the readers' imaginations. A good example is Tolkien's classic *Lord of the Rings*, from which the following names of characters are taken (Podhorodecka, forthcoming):[7]

> Aegnor, Carcharoth, Draugluin, Earendil, Gorthaur, Idril, Celebrindal, Lúthien Tinúviel, Míriel Serinde, Morgoth, Túrin Turambar

When informants (most of them unfamiliar with Tolkien's work) were asked which of these names they thought suitable for a positive and which for a negative character, the majority agreed with Tolkien's assignment, based on the dominance of front vowels for positive and of back vowels for negative characters:

Positive characters:	Aegnor, Earendil, Idril, Celebrindal, Lúthien Tinúviel, Míriel Serinde
Negative characters:	Carcharoth, Draugluin, Gorthaur, Morgoth
Intermediate:	Túrin Turambar

Language	/iː/	/e/	/u/	other vowels	C per V
Sindarin	22.5 %	35.5 %	2 %	40 %	1.22
Quenya	28 %	23 %	10 %	39 %	1.08
Black Speech	14 %	0 %	40 %	46 %	1.7

Figure 7.2   Distribution of vowels, ration of consonants and vowels in Tolkien's artificial languages (selected from Podhorodecka, forthcoming)

A similar relationship was observed for the distribution of the front vowels /i/ and /e/ and the back vowel /u/ in the three artificial languages invented by Tolkien: the two 'positive' Elves' languages, Sindarin and Quenya, and the 'negative' Black Speech of the Orks: this distribution was also accompanied by a significant difference in the rate of consonant per vowel, as shown in Figure 7.2.

Tolkien's use of evocative sound symbolism is just an extreme case of what can be observed in many literary texts, especially in lyrical poems, as shown by Leech (1969) for Tennyson's 'Oenone' – see Figure 7.3. Reading the poem one cannot deny that the many front vowels (contained in ll. 1–4) contribute to creating a pleasant atmosphere, while the back vowels (in ll. 7–8) are likely to evoke its sombre counterpart.[8]

What is different is that unlike the Tolkien examples the words of these poems are not invented, but part of a natural language and carry a lexical meaning which is supported by the sound-symbolic effects.

Problems arise when one tries to transfer the evocative sound symbolism observed in poems to language as a whole. What is skillfully merged in the poem into a symbiosis of lexical and sound symbolic 'meaning' by the artist falls apart when it is tested in ordinary language use. However much we would have it, there is no sound-symbolic principle underlying

```
                        Oenone
[1] There lies a vale in Ida, lovelier
[2] Than all the valleys of Ionian hills.
[3] The swimming vapour slopes athwart the glen,
[4] Puts forth an arm, and creeps from pine to pine,
[5] And loiters, slowly drawn. On either hand
[6] The lawns and meadow-ledges midway down
[7] Hang rich in flowers, and far below them roars
[8] The long brook falling thro' the clov'n ravine
[9] In cataract after cataract to the sea.
                                          Alfred Tennyson
```

Figure 7.3   Tennyson's poem 'Oenone'

the phonological form of lexical words. Somewhat ironically, the small/big and the good/bad associations of front and back vowels respectively are cancelled out by the sound shapes of the two adjective pairs expressing these notions in English, and the same is true for many other languages.

It is not surprising that, faced with this contradiction between lexical and sound-symbolic meaning, traditional linguists have had difficulties accepting the existence and relevance of evocative sound symbolism. Semioticians working in the tradition of Peirce have found it easier because they will attribute lexical signs like *big* and *small* to the category of 'symbol', while the contradictory sound-symbolic effects will be regarded as iconic images. Yet it is only a cognitive-linguistic explanation that really comes to terms with the problem. First, the most central of the associations, the small/big contrast, can be related to bodily experiences of the small and large resonance room created in the oral cavity for the articulation of the /i/ and /u/ sound respectively (Masuda 2002). Secondly and more importantly, empirical research has shown that human conceptualization tolerates differing and even contradictory concepts and can deal easily with competing linguistic expressions. Considering for instance how effortlessly we alternate between onomatopoeic *bow-wow* or *miaow* and the lexical forms *dog* or *cat* using each in its appropriate context, it is understandable that we have no problem in tolerating the coexistence of non-iconic lexical symbols such as *small* and *big* with the iconic use of the /i/ sound denoting smallness, etc.

Iconic explanation of text strategies

On the linguistic level, imagic iconicity tends to affect individual words, while diagrammatic iconicity, as discussed before, seems to be concerned with the quantity of the linguistic output and the arrangements of linguistic elements in phrases and sentences. Yet there is no reason to keep us from extending the iconic interpretation to more comprehensive text structures and to relate them to the complex action patterns used in the conceptualization of the world.[9]

The most obvious example is the **path strategy**, which can be observed in many text-types and is at the same time firmly rooted in our conceptualization. As discussed in previous chapters, the notion of path is not only regarded as one of the basic image schemas that reflect our bodily experiences (Section 2.3), it is also an integral part of the figure/ground contrast, supplying as it does the notion of trajectory on which the dynamic interpretation of figure is based (Section 4.1). Path is also at the core of the motion event schema (Section 5.1), with its different options of windowing (Section 5.2), and as part of the motion event it is reflected in different ways in different languages (Section 5.3), not to mention that it supports important syntactic constructions (Section 5.4).

In transferring the notion of path to the understanding of texts, we must take into consideration that – at least in readable and user-friendly texts – readers are not left to their own devices and forced to 'find their own way' through the text but are gently guided by the writer. So a more appropriate and tangible way of imagining the path strategy is a situation where someone guides another person along a path, for example a local guiding foreign visitors to a new destination or a tourist guide taking groups round a castle, garden or park. From this perspective the path strategy comprises much more than a simple A-leads-to-B relationship. It includes the action of walking along a certain path, in itself a complex action. Other elements of the action pattern are opening rituals that climax in inviting someone to follow, deciding between alternative routes, pointing out objects of interest encountered during the tour, explaining them, and finally the appropriate closing rituals. All this is something authors of prototypical travel guidebooks and brochures describing a guided tour through a building, town, etc. will incorporate in their work, something that readers will expect to find in these texts because they automatically transfer their notion of path and guiding from their own cognitive experiences to their text comprehension. Yet this does not mean that the iconic relationship supporting the travel book will rely on a detailed transfer of individual attributes of the path strategy, a kind of checklist approach. What is much more likely is a **holistic transfer** of the comprehensive action pattern developed within a certain cultural model, a cognitive process that may be compared with the holistic or gestalt perception of concrete objects (Section 1.2). Read the short extract from a tourist brochure for a Welsh manor house, which shows how general motion verbs like *step over* and *enter* and the 'path verb' *guide* combine with the imperative form of address, greeting rituals and descriptive detail (*dressed in period costume,* etc.) to create a rich and vivid impression of being shown around the building.

Step over the threshold of Llancaiach (pronounced glan kayack) Fawr and travel back over 350 years to a time of great unrest and Civil War in Wales. As you enter the manor house you are greeted by the servants of 'Colonel' Edward Prichard, dressed in period costume and speaking in the style of the 17th century, who guide you around the manor's many beautiful rooms with fascinating tales of life in a Civil War gentry household.

(From: *Llancaiach Fawr Manor. Where History Comes Alive!;* tourist brochure)

Admittedly, the textual path strategy would not merit so much attention if it were restricted to travel guidebooks. The important thing is that the prototypical strategy serves as a reference point for a huge variety of text structures ranging from instructions and procedural texts (cookery books, do-it-yourself manuals, etc.) to chronological accounts (non-fictional documentations, historical novels, biographies, etc.). Another advantage of assuming a holistically transferred conception of path and guiding is that it is effective beyond the linguistic medium, i.e. it invites a combined dynamic interpretation of linguistic, visual and auditory elements and their interplay, and this is essential for the understanding of advertising spots and other television genres.

Faced with this situation one might ask whether there are any alternatives to the path strategy or whether it is the only iconically supported text strategy available. Surveying text-types as far apart as phone books (or dictionaries) and news stories, it is difficult to understand them as being based on a strategy of leading the reader from one item to the next. There is no real guiding quality in an alphabetical arrangement of items, and if one looks at prototypical news stories, they follow the top–down principle of placing items in the order of decreasing importance, which is often at odds with the notions of spatial path or chronological sequence. Yet, looking for a reason why we accept these textual arrangements so effortlessly, it emerges that these text-types can also rely on iconic support.

A starting point could be the observation that one of the abilities already exhibited by small children and available for us all through our lives is the aptitude (and even urge) to arrange objects in certain patterns. Though perhaps not obvious at first sight, this **sorting strategy** is also a rich strategy, which includes the assembly of the material as well as exploring sorting parameters (size, shape, colour and value), selecting the most suitable sorting principles (sorting into pairs, triads, quartets, dozens), dividing the sorting process up into suitable stages and finally deciding on the display of the sorting result (linear, circular presentation, etc.). More often than not, the sorting strategy is combined with a **weighting strategy** that suggests an upward or downward arrangement of items along the sorting parameters and this supplies either an initial or an end focus for the weighting process. One linguistic application is that the sorting-and-weighting strategy can provide the conceptual underpinning for the role assigned to thematic prominence (or initial focus) and to end focus in the analysis of linguistic information units. More importantly, assuming again the holistic iconic transfer of a comprehensive cognitive strategy, the

sorting-and-weighting strategy can be used to explain the universal acceptance of alphabetical sorting in directories, but also the success of the
top–down structure of news stories or the end-focus strategies, as employed
for instance in rhetorical speeches, anecdotes or jokes.

Summing up at this point, it appears that the cognitive-linguistic
approach of understanding iconicity as a relationship between the linguistic (and also visual, auditory) level[10] and the level of conceptualization offers
a number of advantages:

- Onomatopoeic words (iconic images) denoting natural noises (wind,
  waves) and animal calls (*bow-wow, miaow*) need not be objectively compared with their models in reality. Like secondary sound-symbolic
  effects (/sw/ expressing a swinging motion) they convey our culture-
  dependent conceptualizations. This is also true of evocative sound
  symbolism (/i/ sound for smallness), which is tolerated side by side with
  phonologically conflicting lexical items.
- Diagrammatic iconicity should be conceived as a relationship between
  the linguistic level and its underlying conceptualization rather than
  as a link connecting linguistic expressions and objects in reality. The
  comparison is possible in terms of quantity of information, of proximity and sequence, and this permits the iconic explanation of a range
  of morphological phenomena and syntactic structures.
- Holistically experienced iconic text structures take the notion of
  iconicity on yet a higher level by providing a conceptualist background
  for many of the major text strategies and their combinations.

Exercises

1. The following examples might be said to violate the principles of
   iconic sequencing. Why are they nevertheless acceptable?

   Before he found a new position he gave up his job at the local super-
   market.

   We moved to Canada as soon as we sold our house in England.

   Last night we had dinner with Sue and Jack. We met them on holiday a couple of years ago.

   The photographs in this book remind me of what life was like when
   I was a child.

2. Why are the following sentences odd? How should the modifiers be rearranged to make them more acceptable? What kind of iconicity is involved?

> *He bought a blue-and-yellow cotton striped oversize shirt.

> *I was led into a poorly furnished, crowded, dirty, run-down, repulsive basement two-room flat.

3. In the text, certain claims are made about the proximity of noun stem, plural and case markers and of verb stem, aspect, tense and mood markers. Show how these claims are supported by the following examples taken from Turkish:

ev	'house', singular (nominative case unmarked)
ev + ler	'house' + plural (nominative case unmarked)
ev + ler + im	'house' + plural + dative

ev + e	*git + mek*	*isti +*	*yor + um*
'house'/dative	'go' + infinitive	'want' + present +	1st person
'home'		prog.	singular

'I am wanting (= I want) to go home.'

4. Select names chosen for the characters of another bestseller, *Harry Potter* (Hermione, Dumbledore, Voldemort, Sirius Black, Hagrid, Malfoy, Severus Snape, Sybill Trelawney, Quirrell, etc.) and find out to what extent their positive or negative connotations rely on evocative sound-symbolic associations described in this section. What other aspects seem to have been relevant for the choice of these names?

5. Find more lyrical poems from English literature or the literature of your own country in which evocative sound symbolism is important and discuss its effect.

6. Choose a short technical instruction and show to what extent it follows a path strategy (sequential arrangements of individual steps, additional elements of guidance). Apply the top–down sorting-and-weighting strategy to a short news story, e.g. the report of an accident.

7.2 Lexical change and prototypicality

While iconicity is rooted in language philosophy and has only recently attracted the attention of linguists on a larger scale, the study of language change has been a focal concern of linguistics since its very beginnings around 1800. Yet in spite of its long research tradition and the infinite effort that has gone into exploring, for instance, the history of the English vocabulary, it seems that the cognitive approach is capable of throwing new light on some crucial aspects of lexical change.

Traditionally, changes in word meaning have been described in terms of generalization, specialization, figurative use, and to mention the most radical change last, in terms of substitution or semantic shift. Some stock examples of these processes are assembled in Figure 7.4.

As these examples show, the impact of lexical change on the meaning of words can be quite strong. But somehow the vocabulary of English (and of other languages) has never been in danger of being overwhelmed by these changes. Languages seem to have a kind of inbuilt stability, a core of meanings the speakers can rely on. At the same time languages seem to be flexible enough to permit substantial lexical change.

The development of the lexical category BIRD

According to Geeraerts (1992, 1997),[11] the coexistence of stability and flexibility in lexical development can best be explained if we take a cognitive stance and understand lexical meaning in terms of prototype categories. This means that what was said about prototype categories in Chapter 1 is also relevant for the historical perspective of lexical change. Since we cannot attempt to present Geeraerts's comprehensive system in full, we will select a few key aspects and illustrate them with the examples that have accompanied us through the book, starting with the category BIRD.

Figure 7.5 documents the first three types of lexical change listed in Figure 7.4, specialization, generalization and metaphor, and shows how they affect the category structure of BIRD. The central portion of the diagram is

SPECIALIZATION	Old Engl.:	*fugol* ['any bird']	→	Mod. E.: *fowl* ['cocks, hens, chickens']
GENERALIZATION	Old Engl.:	*bryd* ['young bird']	→	Mod. E.: *bird* ['any bird']
FIGURATIVE USE (METAPHOR)	Middle E. and Mod. E.:	*bird*	→	17th cent.: *bird* ['prisoner', additional meaning]
SUBSTITUTION (SEMANTIC SHIFT)	17th cent.:	*coach* ['horse drawn - carriage']	→	20th cent.: *coach* ['motor coach']

Figure 7.4 Traditional view of major processes of lexical change

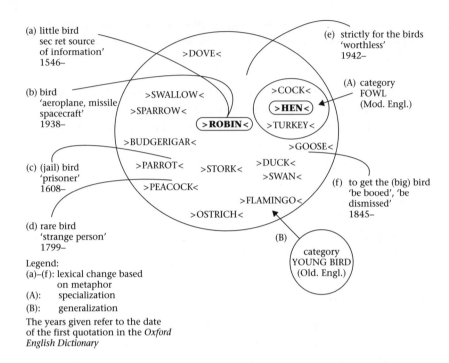

(a) little bird
    sec ret source
    of information'
    1546–

(b) bird
    'aeroplane, missile,
    spacecraft'
    1938–

(c) (jail) bird
    'prisoner'
    1608–

(d) rare bird
    'strange person'
    1799–

(e) strictly for the birds
    'worthless'
    1942–

(A) category
    FOWL
    (Mod. Engl.)

>DOVE<

>SWALLOW<
>SPARROW<

>ROBIN<

>COCK<
>HEN<
>TURKEY<

>BUDGERIGAR<

>GOOSE<

>PARROT<   >STORK<   >DUCK<
                       >SWAN<
    >PEACOCK<

(f) to get the (big) bird
    'be booed', 'be
    dismissed'
    1845–

>FLAMINGO<
>OSTRICH<

(B)

category
YOUNG BIRD
(Old. Engl.)

Legend:
(a)–(f): lexical change based
        on metaphor
(A):   specialization
(B):   generalization
The years given refer to the date
of the first quotation in the *Oxford
English Dictionary*

Figure 7.5   Examples of lexical change involving the category BIRD

a simplified version of Figure 1.8 in Chapter 1, which assembled category members, or rather subcategories, of BIRD and the attributes linking them. Since the attributes are not shown in the present figure, we should perhaps recapitulate that typical attributes of BIRD are most numerous for the central members of the category (e.g. >ROBIN<, >SPARROW<, >BLACKBIRD<), while more peripheral members (e.g. >OSTRICH<, >FLAMINGO<) have fewer typical attributes and rely on family resemblances with other less central members (for instance, ostriches and flamingoes share their long necks with swans and storks). Considering the fact that lexical change has traditionally been seen as involving the meaning of a word as a whole, one might assume that it also affects the underlying category as a whole including the category centre. Looking at Figure 7.5 one finds that this is not the case.

To start with metaphorical change, there are of course examples where the mapping is based on the attributes of the prototype BIRD, such as 'chirps or sings', 'small and lightweight', 'can fly' and 'has wings'. Thus the 'little bird supplying secret information' (example (a)) focuses on the first three of these attributes (chirps/lightweight/can fly), while the metaphorical use 'aeroplane' (b) relies predominantly on the last two (can fly/has wings).

The majority of the metaphorical uses, however, seem to spring from family resemblances uniting the periphery of the BIRD category rather than from its centre. Take the use of *bird* for prisoner (c), which is dominated by the attribute 'locked in a cage'. Though this metaphor also calls up various other aspects of birds, among them the central attributes 'can fly' and 'has wings', the idea of being locked up is typical of parrots, budgerigars and other cage birds, but not of birds in general. The use of *bird* to denote 'strange or queer persons' (d) seems to focus on the peripheral attribute 'exotic appearance', which applies to ostriches, flamingoes, peacocks and again to parrots and budgerigars rather than to central category members. The examples listed on the right-hand side of the figure are even more extreme. According to a quotation from *American Speech* given in the OED, the use of *strictly for the birds* (e), meaning 'completely worthless', is related to 'birds eating droppings from horses and cattle'. Although apparently many types of birds look for grain and insect larvae in droppings and dunghills, this is certainly not among the most salient attributes connected with the category BIRD. Finally, the use of *get the big bird* in the sense of 'booing an actor' or 'dismissing a person from a job' (f) is derived from the hissing sound produced by geese (but not by birds in general).

Reviewing these examples of metaphorical mappings, it is easy to see that they do not really affect the category structure of BIRD, let alone change it. But what is the outcome when a whole section is, as it were, carved out of a category? This process occurred in the case of the BIRD category when hens and other birds raised for their meat, eggs and feathers were collected in a separate category. To complicate matters, the orginal name of the category BIRD, Old English *fugol* (Mod. Engl. *fowl*), was used for this new category (see (A) in Figure 7.5).

In Old English the word *fugol* referred to all kinds of birds. Now we do not really know what the BIRD category was like in Anglo-Saxon times because the major descriptive tools of category structure, i.e. goodness-of-example ratings and attribute listing by informants, are obviously not available. Yet apart from exotic birds like ostriches and flamingoes, most birds are mentioned in extant Old English texts, and therefore we may assume that the category structure was not totally different from what it is today. Even if we cannot safely pinpoint the Anglo-Saxon prototype, the major attributes of good examples of the BIRD category were probably similar to what they are today.

How, then, did this category structure survive the transfer of the category name to the peripheral members of the BIRD category denoted by Modern English *fowl*? The traditional explanation would point out that *fugol* was replaced by the word *bird*, whose meaning underwent the process of generalization (Figure 7.4). The background is that its Old English version *bryd* was already used for the closely related category YOUNG BIRD (see (B) in Figure 7.5). This means that even in Anglo-Saxon times the category structure underlying *bryd* included all the major attributes of the BIRD category (as expressed by Old Engl. *fugol*). As a result, the focal area of the category remained intact. Its stability ensured that the transition from *fugol* to *bird*, which extended over several centuries, was smooth. It was made even smoother by the fact that for some time there was a tendency to use *bird* for smaller birds while *fugol* (or Middle Engl. *foule*) was increasingly reserved for larger birds. In cognitive terms, this can be seen as a way of using an important attribute of young birds, their smallness, as a crutch to facilitate the switch of the word *bird* from the category YOUNG BIRD to the category BIRD.

Summing up our diachronic discussion of the category BIRD, the stability shown by the category structure across centuries is indeed impressive. The main reason seems to be that the focal area of the category and the prototype in particular remain largely unaffected by metaphorical change and even by the processes of specialization and generalization in which the category BIRD has been involved.

Prototype shift and prototype split: the categories COACH and IDEA

Even if this does not apply to BIRD, there are cases where central attributes of a category are replaced, normally as a result of extra-linguistic changes. Traditionally called substitution or semantic shift (Figure 7.4), the appropriate cognitive term is **prototype shift**. A fairly straightforward illustration of this process is provided by the history of the category COACH, as documented in Figure 7.6.[12]

The word *coach* was introduced into English in the sixteenth century to denote a large closed carriage with four wheels and seats inside and outside, which was drawn by horses. In the sixteenth and seventeenth centuries such carriages were mainly used by the Royal Family and other officials. This situation is illustrated in Figure 7.6(a), where the category prototype >STATE CARRIAGE< is circled by a bold line. Yet as indicated by the circle round >STAGE COACH<, this second use was gaining ground as coaches were increasingly used for regular cross-country services for ordinary citizens. In diagram (b) of the figure, which sketches the situation in the nineteenth century, >STAGE COACH< has superseded >STATE CARRIAGE< as prototypical subcategory,

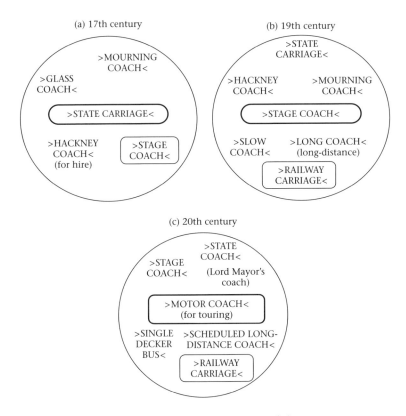

Figure 7.6 Prototype shift: the development of the category COACH

but new competition has arisen through the use of *coach* for the techno-logical innovation of railway carriages. Finally, in diagram (c) >STAGE COACH< has been pushed towards the category periphery in favour of >MOTOR COACH< as a new prototype, and this again reflects technological developments.

From a cognitive point of view, the main reason is that most of the impor-tant attributes are carried over from the old into the new category proto-type, for example 'is used for transporting people', 'large closed carriage', 'has four wheels' and 'has seats inside'. Among these attributes the crucial one is the functional attribute 'used for transporting people'. This attribute seems to have held the category members together even though attributes

Faced with these massive changes in the conceptual content of the pro-totype, especially the change from >STAGE COACH< to >MOTOR COACH<, it is sur-prising how little language users are disturbed by them. It seems as if the category structure remained intact in spite of the shift of the prototype. How can this remarkable stability be explained?

on other dimensions changed dramatically. An example of such a change is the development on the dimension 'power source' where the attributes changed from 'horse drawn' for >STAGE COACH<, through 'drawn by an engine' for >RAILWAY CARRIAGE<, to 'self-powered' for >MOTOR COACH<. The development of the attributes on this dimension is indeed striking. But it has not led to a dissolution of the category integrity because the uniting power of the functional attribute 'used for transporting people', and of the other attributes mentioned above, has prevailed.

Yet there is one exception. Although, as we have seen, the use of *coach* for railway carriages may have fulfilled a transitional function between >STAGE COACH< and >MOTOR COACH<, it represents a new departure in another respect. Unlike all other types of coaches, a railway carriage cannot be used as a single unit, and it does not run on roads but on rails. In spite of their shared function, then, today the distinction between motor coaches and railway carriages is so clear-cut that the use of *coach* for >RAILWAY CARRIAGE< could be regarded as involving the splitting off of a second prototype.

Such **prototype splits** are not very common in the domain of concrete objects, but are much more frequent among abstract categories. This can be demonstrated by looking at the development of the category IDEA, which was already discussed in the context of metaphors in Chapter 3.1. There we tried to show how certain metaphors (the +CONTAINER+ metaphor, the +OBJECT+ metaphor, etc.) contribute to an overall conceptualization of the category IDEA, which could be roughly glossed as 'thought'. To arrive at the finer conceptual distinctions that are also historically relevant we should first look at the sample sentences in Figure 7.7.

A short glimpse at the examples and the semantic labels attached to them makes it clear that version (a) has received the most general label, while versions (b) to (d) have been given more specific paraphrases. In a cognitive context the labels could be regarded as a rough indication of prototypes, and we would expect each of them to be representative of less clearly defined instances (or lesser category members; Schmid 1993: 188ff). To introduce the historical perspective it must be pointed out that, though the sentences are all taken from present-day English for convenience, they do in

---

(a) **The idea of** truth is hard to grasp.　　　　　　　IDEA = CONCEPT, MENTAL PICTURE
(b) **The idea that** the earth is a disc has been refuted.　　IDEA = BELIEF
(c) **The idea is to** put all cards on the table.　　　　　IDEA = AIM, PLAN
(d) And then he **had a brilliant idea**.　　　　　　　IDEA = SUDDEN INSPIRATION

Figure 7.7　The category IDEA: sample sentences and semantic labels

fact reflect the sequence of stages in which the category IDEA has unfolded since the word *idea* entered the English language in the fifteenth century. If we consider that this implies a change from one global prototype to more specific 'local' ones, we can understand this development as an example of prototype split. Compare the diagrams in Figure 7.8, which is based on an analysis of the examples contained in the *Oxford English Dictionary* (Schmid 1996b).

If one contrasts Figure 7.8 with Figures 7.5 and 7.6 (dealing with the categories BIRD and COACH respectively), it is evident that any statement about the structure of abstract categories will be much more general than descriptions of concrete object categories. Faced with the absence of tangible attributes and the vagueness of most conceptual metaphors, there are no reliable semantic criteria that a historical description of the category IDEA might be based on, let alone an evaluation of its stability.

The only available parameter seems to be the syntactic environment in which abstract terms like *idea* occur. The oldest prototype in the history of the category IDEA, the prototype >CONCEPT<, is closely linked to the syntactic structure *the idea of*. The prototype >BELIEF< is connected with the construction *the idea that*, the prototype >AIM< with *the idea is to*, and finally the prototype >SUDDEN INSPIRATION< is coupled with the structure *have/get an idea*. (See also Figure 7.7 where these structures are shown in bold print.) As the analysis of the examples for IDEA in the *Oxford English Dictionary* has shown, such a 'contextual approach' to abstract categories is feasible and helpful in describing lexical change and can also explain the emergence of certain constructions (see Section 5.4 on the shell-content construction).

If at the end of this section, one looks back at the traditional classification from which the discussion started out, it should have become clear that, on the whole, cognitive linguistics offers a richer description of lexical change and opens up a line of research which could profitably be further pursued.[13]

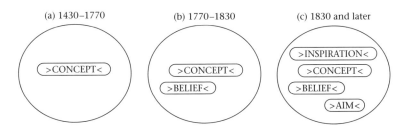

(a) 1430–1770   (b) 1770–1830   (c) 1830 and later

>INSPIRATION<

>CONCEPT<   >CONCEPT<   >CONCEPT<

>BELIEF<   >BELIEF<

>AIM<

Figure 7.8 Prototype split: the development of the category IDEA (Schmid 1996b)

Exercises

1. As Geeraerts (1997: 33–41) has shown, the stability of lexical development can also be illustrated in 'quick motion' for recent additions to the lexicon. His example is the Dutch concept LEGGING, which since its introduction in 1988 has kept the prototype relatively fixed while adding additional non-prototypical category members representing for instance different types of material. Transfer this method to the concept MOBILE PHONE and find out if the core meaning also remains stable while additional meanings are added due to changes in size, shape and colour, additional electronic functions and equipment, battery support, etc.

2. In Old English the word *man* referred to human beings while 'male human being' was normally expressed by another word (Old Engl. *wer*). Compare the present usage of *man* and discuss the semantic change involved in terms of prototype categories. A comparison with the development of *fugol/fowl* might be helpful.

   Discuss whether the sexist use of *man*, which is much criticized today, has been in the language since Anglo-Saxon times or whether it is a more modern development.

3. Here is an extract from the entry for *car* in the *Oxford English Dictionary:*

   1. A wheeled vehicle or conveyance
      a. *generally* – a carriage, chariot, cart, wagon, truck, etc.
         (quotations from the fourteenth to the eighteenth century)
      b. From sixteenth to nineteenth century, chiefly poetic with associations of dignity, solemnity and splendour. Applied also to the fabled chariot of Phaeton or the sun . . .
      d. *transf.* a miniature carriage or truck used in experiments, etc.
         (quotation from the nineteenth century)
      e. = motor car
         (quotations from the late nineteenth and the twentieth century)
   4. a. The part of a balloon in which aeronauts sit
         (quotations from the eighteenth and the nineteenth century)
      b. The cage of a lift. Chiefly US
         (quotations from the nineteenth and the twentieth century)

   Try to sketch the development of the category structure on the basis of this information.

4. Sketch the development of the concept underlying the nouns *liquor* and *sensation* by analyzing the entries in the OED. Can you see evidence of a prototype shift (in the case of *liquor*) or of a prototype split (in the case of *sensation*)?

7.3 Cognitive aspects of grammaticalization

Apart from lexical change, the origin and development of grammatical forms (tense markers, plural and case markers, etc.) has been a long-standing concern of linguistics. Here a cognitive approach has proved helpful in explaining the development of individual grammatical forms, but it also seems capable of providing a framework for a whole range of grammaticalization processes.

In the nineteenth century the study of the development of grammatical forms was motivated by the general interest in the etymological roots of languages. The term 'grammaticalization' was probably first used by the French linguist Meillet. According to Meillet (1912), the aim of studying grammaticalization is to investigate 'the transition of autonomous words into the role of grammatical elements' (1912: 133), or to add a more recent definition, to show 'where a lexical unit . . . assumes a grammatical function, or where a grammatical unit assumes a more grammatical function' (Heine *et al.* 1991: 2).[14] It is the first of these two stages, the transition from a lexical unit to a grammatical form, for which an explanation from the perspective of cognitive linguistics seems to be most rewarding.

Motion events, metaphor and metonymy in grammaticalization

Our test case is one of the best-known instances of grammaticalization in English, the development of the lexical verb *go* into an auxiliary used to express the future tense.[15] The suitable starting point of a cognitive analysis is the notion of motion event developed by Talmy (2000). As shown in Sections 4.1 and 5.2, a motion event can be basically conceived as the path of a figure in motion over a ground. Assuming an open path leading from A to B, the motion of the figure (or trajector) is always directed towards the destination B, in other words it is characterized by goal orientation. At the same time the destination or goal can only be reached if the position of the trajector along the path keeps changing, an observation that supports the basic correlation 'action/change<>motion' (see Section 3.1). The figure and its path are contrasted with the ground, which functions as a reference point or 'landmark' for orientation and is normally tied to what the speaker regards as the present state of the world; this can be captured in the correlation '(present) viewpoint<>landmark'.

Analyzing the motion event in this way, we have already assembled the three aspects, goal orientation, change and viewpoint, which will play an important role in the grammaticalization of the so-called *going-to* future. To complete the picture we should consider that the path of the trajector can be accessed conceptually through different windows of attention. Talmy's own example of path-windowing is:

> The crate that was in the aircraft's cargo bay fell out of the plane through the air into the ocean (see Figure 5.10).

In this example all three possibilities of path-windowing are assembled: initial windowing (*out of the cargo bay*), medial windowing (*through the air*), final windowing (*into the ocean*), but it is fairly clear that the last possibility is normally preferred. This is even more so for the motion verb *go*, which is most likely combined with an adverbial of direction denoting a concrete destination while the initial and medial windows are gapped, as in example (1).

> Susan**'s going** to London next month.
>
> She**'s going** to hospital/college/prison.
>
> She**'s going** to London to work at our office.
>
> She**'s going** to work at our office.
>
> You**'re going** to like her.
>
> You**'re going** to be friends.
>
> You**'re gonna** like her.
>
> You **gonna** like her. (non-standard)

In terms of grammaticalization, example (1) represents stage 1 of the process- compare Figure 7.9, where 'final windowing' is selected and 'destination' of the path is singled out as foregrounded. Examples (2) and (3) show how this foregrounded aspect of the motion event invites a conceptual extension: the concrete destination can be 'specified for the purpose associated with it' (OALD) (as in the 'destinations' *hospital*, *college* or *prison* in (2)); the second type of extension occurs if an adverbial of purpose (such as *to work at our office* in (3)) is added that is more or less closely linked to the direction adverbial. Both examples stress the goal orientation of the motion event and thus indicate in which direction the notion of destination can be extended in stage 2 of the grammaticalization process. As shown in Figure 7.9, stage 2 can be understood as a metonymic transfer based on the relationship +GOAL-ORIENTED MOVEMENT STANDS FOR INTENDED ACTION+, for which the 'part–whole' image schema and the basic experiential relation of 'purpose<>goal' (see Section 3.1) determine the mapping scope. Monitored by this mapping scope the source concept GOAL-ORIENTED MOVEMENT is metonymically related to the wider target concept PURPOSEFUL OR INTENDED

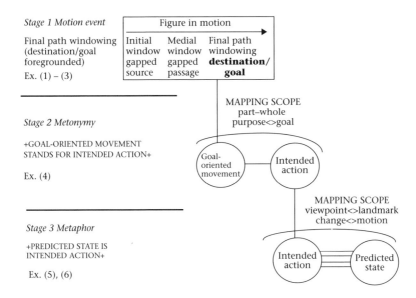

Figure 7.9 Cognitive view of the grammaticalization of the *going-to* future:
stages 1–3

ACTION (e.g. *going to work at our office* in example (4)). Since the notion of purposeful or intended action comes with the expectation of future enactment, the verb form *is going* acquires an aspect of futurity in this construction. Futurity in turn is, like other tenses, normally expressed by auxiliaries in English and so it is not surprising that the reduction of the *going-to* future to the status of an auxiliary is initiated.

Building on this level of grammaticalization, a metaphorical extension develops (stage 3 in Figure 7.9), in which the source concept INTENDED FUTURE ACTION is carried over to the target concept PREDICTED FUTURE STATE – or in the usual format of metaphor labelling +PREDICTED STATE IS INTENDED ACTION+. Compare examples (5) and (6), where the attitude of affection or the state of friendship are predictions based on the speaker's evaluation. This metaphorical mapping is again monitored by a mapping scope based on the underlying motion event (a topic addressed in more detail below).

Compared with stage 2 and 3, the final stage (stage 4, represented in examples (7) and (8), but not in Figure 7.9) does not change the meaning any more, but documents the phonological and graphic changes that accompany the final reduction to auxiliary status.

What is the advantage of this cognitive explanation compared with the traditional description, which characterizes stage 2 as syntactic reanalysis (instead of metonymy) and stage 3 as analogy (rather than metaphor)? As it appears, the cognitive explanation not only throws light on the semantic changes involved in the grammaticalization of *going to*, it is particularly helpful in describing the limitations of the process.

Looking at the representation of the motion event in Figure 7.9 again, it is evident why the motion verb *go* is selected for this grammaticalization process and not other verbs of motion such as *leave* (which focuses on the initial windowing or source of the motion), *pass* (stressing the medial window or passage) or *stagger, ride* and *fly* (with their strong emphasis on the manner-of-motion component). It is only a verb focused on the final path window like *go* that has the goal orientation that permits the infinitive, with its inherent intentional potential, to be added (but not participles or gerunds). Finally and perhaps more interestingly, the motion event is also responsible for the way in which the mapping scope of the metaphor +PREDICTED STATE IS INTENDED ACTION+ captures the limitations that competent speakers of English still feel when using the *going-to* future. As shown at the beginning of this section, the basic correlation '(present) viewpoint<>landmark (of the motion event)' suggests that there must be some reference point in present time for establishing a prediction, either some present evaluation (as in examples (5) and (6)) or some present observations or evidence, such as the ominous clouds supporting *It's going to rain*. Secondly, the correlation 'change<> motion', which is based on our conceptualization of a trajector moving along the path, limits the predictive use of the *going-to* future to human attitudes such as likes or dislikes (inherently non-permanent and liable to change; see (5)) and to states that do not exclude the notion of change. This mapping constraint explains for instance why *You are going to be friends* (6) is fully acceptable while *The earth is going to be round for ever* is not.

Although the emergence of the *going-to* future is probably the best example, other grammaticalization processes like the development of the verbal participles *given, provided* and *granted* and of the imperative *suppose* into conditional conjunctions could also benefit from a cognitive analysis (see also Exercise 1 below). Yet, as has been claimed, the real explanatory power of the cognitive view only becomes apparent when it is used as a unifying framework for a whole range of grammaticalization processes. This is what Heine attempts in his description of the development of tense, aspect and mood markers (Heine 1993).

A cognitive framework for grammaticalization

Heine's starting point is a system of so-called **propositional schemas**,[16] which represent processes and events and consist of three elements, a set-up

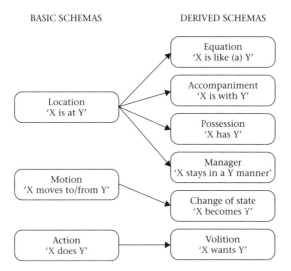

BASIC SCHEMAS   DERIVED SCHEMAS

Figure 7.10 Major propositional schemas underlying the grammatical categories
of aspect and tense
(adapted from Heine's event schemas, Heine 1993: Table 2.1)

well known from traditional clause patterns and Construction Grammar (see
Section 5.4). While many processes and their propositional schemas are fairly
specific (e.g. X EAT Y or X WRITE Y), some of them, for instance X GO Y, X
COME Y, X BE AT Y, are much more general, and it is from these general propositional schemas that grammatical categories have developed.

Figure 7.10 assembles the major propositional schemas underlying
aspect and tense in many languages. As the figure shows, the schemas can
be divided into two groups: three basic schemas (Location, Motion, Action)
and a number of schemas that have been derived from these basic schemas
(Equation, Accompaniment, Possession, Manner, Change of state, Volition).
What is particularly striking is the role attributed to the location schema
as the main source of derived schemas; this judgement is supported by a
long-standing non-cognitivist tradition of localist thought and it is also in
agreement with the everyday observation that space is our primary sphere
of experience.

Turning to the kind of grammaticalization process sparked off by the individual propositional schemas (cf. Figure 7.11), we find that some of them are
quite obvious: volition generates future tense (the *will*-future in English) and
so does change of state (*werden* (='become')-future in German); accompaniment develops into a progressive marker documented for many African languages. With other propositional schemas, especially the basic schemas, the
grammaticalization potential is more ambiguous. Thus the motion schema

326 AN INTRODUCTION TO COGNITIVE LINGUISTICS

PROPOSITIONAL SCHEMA	GRAMMATICALIZATION	EXAMPLE
Location	progressive, ingressive	Dutch: *Hij is een boek aan het lezen.* 'He is a book at the reading.'
	continuous	Germ.: *Er ist beim Lesen.* 'He is at the reading.'
Motion	ingressive, future, perfect, past	Engl.: *going-to* future Fr.: *venir-de* past
Action	progressive, continuous, ingressive, completive, perfect	African languages
Equation	resultative, progressive, perfect, future	Fr.: *être* perfect
Accompaniment	progressive	African languages
Possession	resultant, perfect, future	Engl.: *have* perfect
Manner	progressive	Ital.: *sto mangiando* 'I stay eating' (I'm eating)
Change of state	ingressive, future	Germ.: *werden* future
Volition	ingressive, future	Engl.: *will* future

Figure 7.11 Propositional schemas and possible grammaticalizations
(adapted from Heine 1993: 47)

can be used for looking both forwards and backwards, resulting in future or perfect and past tenses, while the action schema may be used to express ingressiveness (the beginning of an action) as well as its completion. Considering these conflicting types of grammaticalizations it is not surprising that languages have developed quite different tense/aspect systems from a common conceptual basis.[17]

To conclude this section, we will add a note on an issue that has been hotly debated in recent years: the question of whether or not grammaticalization should be seen as a unidirectional process from lexical units to units with grammatical functions and from grammatical functions to still more grammatical functions. As far as we can see, for the first stage, on which we have concentrated in this section, a cognitive analysis seems to provide evidence for the unidirectional evolution from lexical to grammatical units. Whether the switch from one type of grammatical function to another one (e.g. from adverbs linking main clauses to subordinators) is not reversible in some cases is another matter. Yet what can be said from our point of view is that even if examples of the reverse development of 'de-grammaticalization' from grammatical into lexical items should be uncovered, cognitive linguists should be well equipped to tackle these linguistic phenomena as well.

Exercises

1. How do the conceptual meanings of GIVE and GRANT differ in the following examples? Try to interpret these conceptual and functional changes in terms of grammaticalization.

   Aunt Mable gave me a piece of cake.

   We waited for him at the given place and time, but he didn't come.

   Given her youth, she is quite experienced in the field.

   Given that he has lost all his money gambling, he is still surprisingly optimistic.

   Regrettably, the bank didn't grant me the loan.

   It's an ingenious project, I grant you, but will it work?

   Granted, it's not a perfect cake, but it should be edible.

   Granted (that) your grandfather was rich, why didn't he pay for your education?

2. Both the English suffixes -ly and -like are based on a common Germanic root word meaning 'appearance', 'form', 'body'. Compare pairs like *fishlike/fishy*, *foxlike/foxy* and *roomlike/roomy* and decide where the original category is still more vivid and what this means in terms of grammaticalization.

3. Pidgin English, a kind of elementary language spoken in contact situations in various parts of the world, is said to represent an early stage of grammaticalization, in which the source categories of grammatical markers are still easily recognizable. Try to find out which English words (and underlying categories) the following grammatical markers in Cameroon Pidgin are based on:

go	(future marker)
don	(positive perfect marker)
neva	(negative perfect marker)
sei	(element introducing indirect speech)
fit	(modal auxiliary 'can')
mek	(element introducing polite imperatives)

4. If your native language is not English, find out which tense forms, modal forms and ways of expressing possession are based on motion and action schemas in your own language (see also Figure 7.11.).

7.4 Effects on foreign language teaching

Since many more people are engaged in teaching English than in linguistic analysis, it is only natural that each new linguistic approach is soon examined for practical applications, especially for foreign language teaching. This chapter tries to show how some of the major aspects of cognitive linguistics discussed in this book either give support to existing teaching methods or provide new ideas in the field of language learning.

Surveying the cognitive-linguistic literature addressing aspects of foreign language teaching, one gets the impression that cognitive linguistics makes a twofold contribution to the field: it suggests new forms of **cognitive-experiential access** to a foreign language through basic level, metonymy and metaphor, figure and ground as well as gestalt, and it provides **insights into cognitive networks** based on these approaches. This section draws together examples from various fields of language teaching to support this claim. The first example is vocabulary acquisition, where cognitive linguistics lends theoretical support to long-standing, empirically developed teaching approaches.

Prototypes, basic level, conceptual hierarchies, metaphor and the structure of lexical fields

It has always been a golden rule for teachers and textbook writers that the vocabulary of a foreign language must be introduced gradually and with an eye to the usefulness of the individual item. This has led to the establishment of 'frequency lists' or 'pedagogical vocabularies', which are widely taken into account by the authors of textbooks, readers and dictionaries for foreign learners and are now even indicated in general dictionaries, as the 'Oxford 3000' are in the OALD (2005). The systematic work on these frequency lists goes back to the *Interim Report on Vocabulary Selection*, published in 1936, but is more easily accessible in Michael West's revised version *A General Service List of English Words* (1953). Though the list was based on a frequency count of word meanings in a collection of written texts, West was fully aware of the fact that frequency alone was an insufficient yardstick for the vocabulary he had in mind. This judgement is fully supported by the frequency lists culled from present-day computer corpora, which are invariably headed by function words like *the, of* or *and* as well as general lexical items used in high-frequency grammatical constructions (e.g. *time, place* and *way*). To forestall these distortions, West used a number of other criteria which, together with later additions from other sources, are assembled in the following list:

- cover
- value for definitions and word-formation
- degree of stylistic neutrality
- availability (what first comes to mind)
- ease or difficulty of learning

For the cognitive linguist, most of these criteria are familiar; indeed, the list reads like a description of the basic level categories discussed in Chapter 2. Though West's definition of our term 'cover' ('covers a certain range of necessary ideas'; West 1953: ix) still shows a certain weakness for superordinate terms, the notion has since been overwhelmingly interpreted as referring to basic level categories. The second criterion mirrors what we have found out about the word-formation potential of basic level categories (cf. Schmid 1996a). Stylistic neutrality, the third principle, often goes hand in hand with morphological simplicity, while availability is the major psychological criterion of basic level categories, and ease of learning is related to the observation that words for basic level categories are first acquired by children. All in all, one may claim that what the compilers of frequency lists are after are, on the whole, words for basic level items, or to put it the other way round, basic level categories seem to provide the preferred access to a frequency vocabulary.

While the basic level of categorization may guide teachers and textbook writers to choose the right kind of vocabulary, the prototype idea may be helpful for decisions on how to introduce lexical items and their meanings. The long-standing intuition that word meanings are easier to grasp if they are illustrated with typical rather than exotic examples is confirmed by the prototype theory of categorization. Undoubtedly, children learning English will grasp the meaning of a lexeme like *bird* more quickly when they can connect it to the corresponding prototype in their own language and culture. On the other hand, differences between the prototypes underlying superficially corresponding words such as English *bread*, French *pain* and German *Brot*, provide a good opportunity for raising the level of intercultural awareness. The salience of prototypes is also reflected in the long-standing practice in textbooks to prefer prototypical examples of categories for illustrations with pictures or simple line-drawings.[18]

A third aspect which is also fully accepted in language teaching is that words should not be learned in isolation, but embedded in context as they are used in natural communication. Yet introducing and practising every word in a natural context is a very time-consuming procedure. This is why there has been a long tradition of assembling words in lexical fields of related meanings, based on the practical experience that this is a good base for memorizing vocabulary items. After what has been said about cognitive networks in this book it is quite obvious that lexical fields are successfully employed because they reflect the way our mental lexicon is structured. A condition is that word fields are not restricted to specific word classes (nouns, verbs, adjectives), as it was advocated by many structuralist linguists, but cut across word classes drawing together all items that are semantically related.

However, cognitive linguistics does not only provide justification for the use of lexical fields, but it can also explain how they should be structured. Scrutinizing the vocabulary in a current textbook of English for foreign learners and trying to arrange it in lexical fields, it is helpful to think in terms of part–whole organization rather than taxonomic type-of hierarchies (see Section 2.4). Compare Figure 7.12, which assembles the frequency-filtered vocabulary items found in the first volume of *Green Line* (so-called 'classroom vocabulary' like *desk* and *blackboard* has been excluded).[19] At a first glance, there seems to be a near-balance of lexical fields based on the type-of and part–whole relationship, but this impression is deceptive. The reason is that the taxonomic models ANIMAL, CLOTHES, FURNITURE and SPORTS (marked by an asterisk in Figure 7.12) could also qualify as candidates of partonymic models. Most of the animals introduced belong to a farmyard, clothes consist of various individual clothing items,

Taxonomic models (type-of relation)		Partonymic models (part–whole relation)	
ANIMAL	12*	BODY	11
FOOD	17	HOUSE	8
CLOTHES	4*	NEIGHBOURHOOD	9
MEALS	2	PARTY	5
FURNITURE	6*	HOLIDAY	17
UTENSILS	3	TRANSPORT	15
SPORTS	10*	SHOPPING & SERVICES	12
PROFESSION	?	AUDIO & VISUAL MEDIA	15

Figure 7.12 Taxonomic and partonymic lexical fields on a textbook vocabulary (Function words and 'classroom vocabulary' are not considered)

furniture can be seen as an assembly of tables, chairs, beds, etc., sports as a realization of physical exercise with individual sporting activities as its parts. In fact, this is why experienced textbook authors introduce the vocabulary by exhausting the possibilities of part–whole links (as described in Section 2.4) before moving on to type-of relations. From a cognitive-linguistic angle this preference for part–whole links is not surprising; it only reflects the status of image schema assigned to the part–whole relationship (which also plays a key role as metonymy and one of the vital relations of the blending theory; see Sections 3.4 and 6.1). What is also striking is that the words for the superordinate concepts used as category labels (*animal, body, house*) are already available for the partonymic models (apart from transport) in the first year of teaching, while only a few type-of superordinates are introduced that early, e.g. *fruit, vegetable* and *toy*. Other superordinates, especially abstract concepts, only crop up when the possibilities of basic level vocabulary have been exhausted. Concepts like IDEA, FACT, ASPECT, ISSUE or PROBLEM will be introduced at a later stage together with the discourse strategies in which they are used.

Subordinate categories may be regarded as supplementary for the ordinary learner, but they will be crucial in teaching English for Special Purposes. The important thing is to find out whether specialists still start out from what is usually regarded as basic level, or whether they have already established a certain subordinate level as a new basic level to which the teacher has to adapt his or her teaching. Quite obviously, a vocabulary training course for foreign botanists or zoologists, for example, should not be concerned with basic level terms like *tree, flower, horse* or *bug*, but employ a much finer grid of terminological distinctions.

When it comes to facilitating access to abstract lexical items denoting, for example, emotion concepts, the cognitive-linguistic insight that many of them are rooted in conceptual metaphors can be exploited for language teaching purposes. As claimed by Kövecses (2001: 93ff), pointing out the underlying metaphors to students can facilitate access to idioms; the assembly of idioms expressing a related metaphor can help us to imagine the structure of our conceptual system. The 'networks' constructed in this way also include metaphorical expressions consisting of one word, which help to support the conceptualization of the target concept. Compare the list of +FIRE+ metaphors in Figure 7.13, which conceptualize a wide range of target concepts including ANGER, LOVE, IMAGINATION, CONFLICT and ENTHUSIASM. Although this is an interesting approach, it is yet somewhat difficult to assess the learning effects of this form of presentation.[20]

+ANGER IS FIRE+ After the row he was spitting fire. He was doing a slow burn. *He's smoldering with anger.* +LOVE IS FIRE+ She carries a torch for him. The flames are gone from their relationship. *I'm burning with love.* +IMAGINATION IS FIRE+ The painting set fire to the composer's imagination. His imagination caught fire. *The story kindled the boy's imagination.*	+CONFLICT IS FIRE+ The killings sparked off the riot. The flames of war spread quickly. The country was consumed by the inferno of war. They extinguished the last sparks of the uprising. +ENTHUSIASM IS FIRE+ The speaker fanned the flames of the crowd's enthusiasm. Don't be a wet blanket. *Her enthusiasm was ignited by the new teacher.*

Figure 7.13 A 'network' of idiomatic expressions and one-word items (in italics) based on the +FIRE+ metaphor (after Kövecses 2001: 93ff)

Figure, ground and the teaching of prepositions and phrasal verbs

Just like prototypes, basic level, metonymy and metaphor, the notions of figure and ground have always been essential components of cognitive-linguistic thinking, and from the very beginning they have been linked to the study of prepositions, in particular of prepositions expressing direction such as *in*, *out*, *up* and *down* or *across*, *over* and *under* (compare Section 4.1). From a teaching perspective the cognitive description of prepositions (and their use as particles in phrasal verbs and idioms) can be instrumental for facilitating both access to the wide variety of seemingly unrelated meanings and the construction of corresponding networks. The juxtaposition of figure and ground, or in Langacker's terminology of trajector and landmark, provides a tangible access to the topic, which can be supported by a wealth of visualizations (see Figures 4.5 to 4.11 in Section 4.1); the network representation of prepositional senses should have a beneficial effect in an area of language use regarded as notoriously unordered.

Based on earlier cognitive research on prepositions, this network idea was the background of a first cognitive-linguistic workbook on phrasal verbs compiled in the 1990s by Rudzka-Ostyn;[21] compare Figure 7.14, which illustrates her approach by way of an exemplary diagram covering the major uses of *across*. A quick glimpse at the diagram already shows that it is probably not always easy to transfer this array of prepositional senses into a communicatively oriented teaching unit. The network of senses (and other more

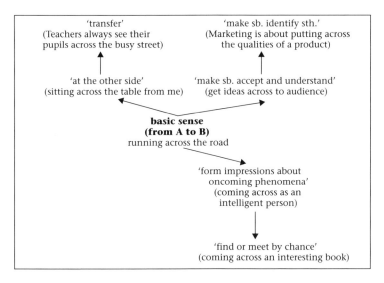

Figure 7.14   A network for *(walk/get/put/come) across*
based on Dirven (2001:19f)

specific networks proposed by cognitive linguists)[22] may be helpful for the
design of pedagogical grammars (Dirven 2001: 20) and may provide insights
into the conceptual model underlying the diverse uses of prepositions and
particles. Yet in order to increase the practical value for language learners
on an intermediate level, the short-hand labels used in Figure 7.14 like 'transfer' and 'at the other side' will have to be extended to the other senses, as
proposed by Tyler and Evans (2004). In addition, the descriptive labels should
be supported by specific visual representations of the trajector/landmark
contrast and equipped with iconic images like the oversize dot (compare
Figure 7.15) to indicate completion.

As Tyler and Evans (2004: 273) rightly claim, these representations
reflect 'the gestalt-like conceptualizations of situations or scenes'. Holistic
conceptualization is further strengthened by a series of exercises, which they
suggest for the 'normal interpretation' and the completion sense of *over*. In
order to familiarize the learner with the A–B–C trajectory (see Figure 7.15,
box (a)) of the default sense, they propose to use a flip book or clips of
movies or cartoons depicting a cat jumping over a wall and to arrest the
sequence of pictures at various points to convey the different stages of the
movement expressed by *over*. By highlighting the final stage C of the jump
or of any other action, the completion sense of *over* can be introduced in
a natural way.

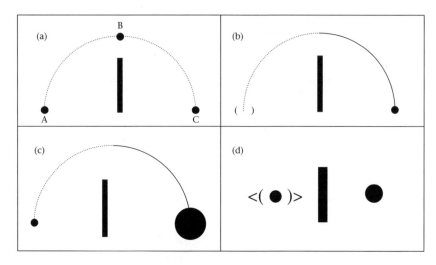

Figure 7.15 Diagrams of major senses of the preposition *over*
(Tyler and Evans 2004: 267ff) (a) normal interpretation, (b) transfer sense (with empty
source element), (c) completion sense (with inflated target element), (d) on-the-other-side sense (with
left-hand symbol of eye)

Although it may be difficult to agree with Tyler and Evans's judgement that this method is suitable for intermediate-level learners of English, who might well find it a little primitive, this highly iconic visualization could be profitably used in teaching Modern Languages at Primary Schools (MLPS).

The gestalt approach to grammatical issues and pre-grammatical learning

If the conceptualization of prepositions suggests a gestalt approach, there are other areas of grammar where this holistic view could also be helpful. One is the area of noun classes. Although it is common in English grammars to distinguish between count and mass nouns, and assign nouns to these rather abstract categories,[23] the question is whether it is not much more natural to approach nouns in terms of person and object concepts, which can be experienced holistically as gestalts. Figure 7.16 provides a sketch of this gestalt approach to noun grammar, indicating the types of concepts to be distinguished and the grammatical features involved.

Like many other conceptual phenomena discussed in this book, the access to noun grammar through person and object concepts is perhaps less satisfactory intellectually than a clear-cut binary contrast, but it seems to reflect the conceptual priorities guiding the native language user. This means that the distinction between countable and uncountable items is only relevant

Person concept		Object concept		
MALE PERSON uncle, waiter (male, sg. & pl.)	FEMALE PERSON aunt, waitress (female, sg. & pl.)	INDIVIDUAL OBJECTS car, house (sg. & pl.)	SUBSTANCES milk, bread (only sg.)	'ABSTRACT SUBSTANCES' anger, advice information (only sg.)
BOTH SEXES friend, doctor, coach (male & female, sg. & pl.)	GROUPS family, police (sg. + neuter & pl. + male/female; or: only pl. + male/female)	'PAIR' OBJECTS shorts, scissors (only plural)	COLLECTIONS OF THINGS furniture, luggage, clothes (only sg./only pl.)	

Figure 7.16   An approach to noun classification based on the distinction
between person and object categories
(Ungerer 2000b: 9ff, Ungerer et al. 2004: 7ff)

for object concepts (and there are borderline cases such as 'collections of things'), while person concepts are primarily subcategorized in terms of gender. Another advantage is that the person/object approach has no problems in accommodating group concepts (FAMILY, GOVERNMENT), where the two grammatical criteria of countability and gender overlap. What remains a little hazy, however, is how these subordinate concepts are related to each other (e.g. both-sex concepts and groups, 'pair' objects and collections of things'), but this indeterminacy of relationship is again a problem for linguists rather than for the ordinary language user.

Turning to verb grammar, gestalt access might be claimed for a number of grammatical phenomena often collected under the label of 'signal grammar' in foreign language teaching. One of the best-known examples is the British Standard use of past tense and present perfect, where the past tense is said to be signalled by temporal concepts, as expressed in *yesterday* or 'noun phrase + *ago*'. Similarly, the use of the simple form is said to be sparked off by habitual concepts (*always*, *often*), whereas the progressive form is frequently supported by the concept of simultaneity (*at this moment, at present*). Admittedly, grammarians will quickly point at counterexamples for each of these uses, but this does not cancel out the function fulfilled by these signals as marking prototypes and therefore reference points for the use of the respective tense and aspectual forms.

The question is whether the gestalt access can be transferred from these rather simple phenomena to the more intractable areas of English grammar. A good test case is the use of non-finite forms, which is dominated by isolated attempts to provide semantic explanations in traditional grammar. Compare the following examples:

He wants **to write** a book about college dropouts.	'intention'
I would like **to take** the weekend off.	'concrete event'
I like **to spend** Sunday mornings in bed.	'habit'
He is engaged in **writing** a book about college dropouts.	'ongoing activity'
He remembers with some horror **losing** half his manuscript in a computer breakdown.	'past activity'
I like **spending** Sunday mornings in bed.	'general statement'

Looking at the examples and the labels, one may indeed accept some of them as signals for individual uses, yet this leaves the links between the individual uses unexplained. What, one might ask, is the relationship between 'intention' and 'concrete event', which are both offered for the infinitive, or between 'past' and 'ongoing activity' and 'general statement', all of them used for the gerund? And to take the argument one step further, how is 'habit' (infinitive) to be distinguished from 'general statement' (gerund)?

It is against this background that Dirven (1989) developed a unified system based on what he regarded as two closely related cognitive 'schemas' (see Section 4.2 for the notion of schema); a simplified version, on which our account partly relies, is provided by Taylor (1993: 210).[24] As shown in Figure 7.17, the various uses of the infinitive are subsumed under the meaning that a situation is perceived in terms of individual instances. According to Dirven and Taylor, this definition includes specific events as well as an 'indefinite number of instances', which is equivalent to the label 'habit' in the introductory examples, while 'intention' is represented in Dirven and Taylor's account as 'bringing about a new situation'. By extending this interpretation the authors are able to include certain causative verbs (*ask, tell, persuade*) and verbs of accomplishment (*manage, try*), which are not very well covered by traditional explanations. The schema for the *gerund* (= 'situation as such detached from single events') may appear somewhat vague at first sight, but it permits the inclusion of such diverse traditional notions as 'general' and 'ongoing activity' ('psychological experience of a situation').

Yet how can this system be distinguished from the many attempts to find umbrella terms for the disparate uses of infinitive and gerund constructions? This becomes more obvious when Dirven and Taylor's schemas are approached with the cognitive notion of gestalt in mind. Starting with the definition of the gerund meaning ('situation as such detached from single

to-infinitive complement	*gerundial complement*
SCHEMATIC MEANING	SCHEMATIC MEANING
to denote instances, or series of instances, of a situation	to denote a situation as such detached from single events
THIS INCLUDES	THIS INCLUDES

– specific particular event
  propose/be keen to jump from Tower Bridge
	– a situation in general
	  propose/be keen on swimming

– indefinite number of events
  like to eat hamburgers
	– a situation that is considered a fact
	  like eating hamburgers

FURTHER APPLICATIONS	FURTHER APPLICATIONS
– bringing about a new situation	–'near reality', i.e. an activity is due but not realized
want/intend to buy a dishwasher	*avoid/postpone doing the dishes*

– effort leading to an accomplishment
  manage/try to find a flat
	– object of a mental activity
	  consider/imagine being homeless

– influence and indirect causation
  *advise/invite/permit someone to play
  a piece on the piano*
	– psychological experience of a situation
	  enjoy/hate singing

Figure 7.17 *To-infinitive* and *gerund*: schematic meaning and selected applications (based on Dirven (1989) and Taylor (1993: 210); examples added)

events'), the 'detachment' need not be seen as an abstraction from the constituent events of the situation, but can be understood as a claim that the 'situation' is grasped holistically as a gestalt, as an intermediate stage between what is expressed by a verb and a noun. Compared with this prototypical embodiment of gestalt, the infinitive meaning ('instances or a series of instances of a situation') seems more specific, but does not really require an analytic decomposition of a situation. In fact, the distinction between a situation as a whole and the instance of a situation can still be experienced holistically, and this is probably what happens in a native speaker's mind when confronted with the decision to choose a gerund or an infinitive construction.

Yet how can this conceptual distinction between a situation as a whole and the instance of a situation be acquired by a foreign learner, in whose native language this conceptual contrast is perhaps not grammatically relevant (as is for instance the case in German)? What the foreign learner would have to develop is this specifically 'English' holistic sensitivity for the situation/instance contrast as part of their learning strategies; to design suitable teaching material would obviously be a challenge for textbook writers and teachers, but one that might be worth the effort.

Summing up, there seem to be quite a number of grammatical decisions that are facilitated by assuming a gestalt conceptualization. This is true for grammatically relevant noun classes, and also for certain temporal and aspectual concepts governing the use of verb forms. Whether this gestalt approach works largely depends on how well the holistic conceptualization underlying the foreign language use is already entrenched in the learner's 'native' conceptualization. While a good 'native' grounding in many cultures may be assumed for PERSON and OBJECT concepts, this is more doubtful with regard to the SITUATION/INSTANCE contrast underlying the use of non-finite verb forms, for which a conceptual sensitivity would have to be developed in foreign language teaching.

However, gestalt conceptualization does not only apply to the way in which grammatically relevant concepts are experienced. In fact, gestalt perception can be seen as a condition for any non-analytical processing of linguistic input. This is not just a matter of conceptualizing the meaning of non-transparent phraseologisms (*kick the bucket, white elephant,* etc.), which are experienced as single conceptual units. Quite ordinary sentences that could easily be analyzed in terms of lexical constituents and grammatical functions seem to be conceptualized holistically as 'chunks', i.e. in a pre-grammatical mode. This type of conceptualization is typical in young children, who are better used to gestalts than to analytical segmentation and composition. The extending of foreign language teaching into these age groups means that gestalt perception has to be considered as the major access route to the foreign language.

One consequence is that gestalt conceptualization can and should be used as a yardstick to evaluate the extensive range of text-types proposed for teaching primary-school English (simple role-plays and slapstick sketches, ABC rhymes, counting-out rhymes, lullabies, riddles, proverbs, jokes, fairytales and fables, etc.).[25] In addition, the other cognitive criteria discussed, in particular the preference for basic level vocabulary and simple cognitive models based on part–whole relationships, should be taken into account, and the same goes for the easy approach offered to children by identifiable figures (in the cognitive sense of the word), i.e. situations with prominent persons, animals and objects.

Access, method and goal in foreign language learning

Returning to the two aspects of cognitive-experiential access and cognitive network representation mentioned at the beginning of this section, it should have become clear in the course of the discussion that **cognitive network representations**, especially those connecting prepositional senses and senses of non-finite structures, are more helpful for the curriculum designer, the textbook author, or the teacher planning his teaching units than for the learner involved in one of those units. By contrast, **conceptual access** to the foreign language, for instance through basic level vocabulary, through

the figure and ground view of prepositional senses and through gestalt conceptualization of temporal and aspectual concepts, seems to be geared to certain kinds of learning processes and also certain kinds of learning ages. How
does this fit into current theories of foreign language learning?

It is widely accepted that language teaching should focus on learning goals
(preferably the goals of communicative and intercultural competence) and
on learning strategies and teaching methods (with a clear bias for action-
oriented and learner-centred methods). What seems to be somewhat neglected
in this conception is that learning strategies promise to be more successful
if they are backed up by suitable cognitive access routes, as they can be investigated and described with the tools of cognitive linguistics. Considering this,
a modern theory of foreign language teaching that takes into account the
findings of cognitive linguistics could be constructed along the following lines:

- Goal: communicative, and ultimately, intercultural competence
- Method/strategy: action-oriented, learner-centred
- Access: cognitive-experiential access routes to the foreign language
  through prototype, basic level, figure and ground, and gestalt.

Combining these three elements in the learning paradigm might prove fruitful for foreign language teaching in general, but, as it has been suggested
in this chapter, it may well yield the most interesting results in the field of
primary-school English.

Exercises

1. Study the vocabulary list of an introductory textbook for English as a
   foreign language (or part of it), arrange the items in part–whole lexical
   fields and type-of fields and compare the results with Figure 7.12. If
   there are differences, try to explain them.
2. Assemble idioms based on specific body parts and try to find situations
   in which several of them can be used in natural communication. Ask
   learners if they feel that this method reduced the learning effort.
3. Go through the illustrations of the prepositional meanings in Figures
   4.5–4.12 (Section 4.1) and decide which of them might be helpful for
   teaching purposes, which less so.
4. Some pedagogical grammars are organized in terms of syntactic patterns
   (clauses consisting of subject, predicate and object expressed by nouns
   and verbs, of main clauses and subordinate clauses, sentence types). Other
   grammars are based on a grid of word classes, their meanings and their

functions (nouns, verbs, adjectives, adverbs, prepositions, conjunctions). Which structure is more convincing from a cognitive-linguistic perspective?

5. Compare the following classification (based on Ungerer 2000b: 216ff) with Dirven and Taylor's proposal illustrated in Figure 7.17.

Major verb + infinitive constructions

1. Verb expressing intention/willingness/wish/request/order/permission + infinitive with future-oriented meaning

2. Verb expressing opinion/supposition/probability + infinitive expressing probability

Major verb + gerund constructions

1. Verb expressing general/mental occupation + gerund expressing that an action is taking place/has taken place

2. Verb expressing prevention/reaction/relation + gerund expressing that something is regarded as a fact

Do you find the two approaches helpful for teaching and learning purposes and which approach do you prefer?

6. Consider typical counting-out rhymes, lullabies, riddles, proverbs, jokes, limericks, fairytales, fables, comics and examine them in terms of basic level vocabulary items, 'part–whole' links between these items, simple utterances that can be taken in as gestalts, a plot with clearly identifiable (conceptual) figures. Decide which text types are most suitable for teaching English at primary-school level.

Suggestions for further reading

Section 7.1

1. The issue is discussed in Plato's Cratylos dialogue (1998), which still makes very good reading today, also for the non-philosopher.

2. See also Saussure (1985 [1913]) and Holdcroft's (1991) discussion of Saussure's conception.

3. For a short overview of Peirce's system see Nänny and Fischer (1999: xxiff), for a more thorough account see Nöth (2000: 59–70). For the basic distinction of icon, index and symbol see also Dirven and Verspoor (2004, ch. 1).

4. For a discussion of diagrammatic iconicity and its subcategories see Givón (1990: 968ff), who offers some very imaginative suggestions for a

wide range of applications of the iconicity principle. He also proposes psychological and biological explanations of the major types of iconicity.

5. For the iconic interpretation of inflections see Bybee (1985) and Bybee *et al.* (1994). For an overview of current research issues in the domain of iconicity, see Nänny and Fischer (1999), Fischer and Nänny (2001), Müller and Fischer (2003) and Maeder *et al.* (2005).

6. For an overview of sound symbolism, see Masuda (2002).

7. See Podhorodecka (forthcoming) for a discussion of sound symbolism in children's books.

8. For a more thorough analysis of Tennyson's poem see Leech (1969: 98).

9. For more details on the path and the sorting-and-weighting strategy discussed in the following, see Ungerer (forthcoming (b)), who also proposes a third text strategy dubbed 'kaleidoscope' strategy.

10. Good examples of this 'multimodal iconicity' are performances, combining, i.e. computer-animated motion sequences, dance performances and rhythmically spoken text. See Moser (forthcoming).

Section 7.2

11. Geeraerts (1992) provides a concise view of what is discussed in more detail in Geeraerts and Grondelaers (1995). In particular Geeraerts distinguishes between the intensional level of analysis focusing on the senses of the lexical item (which are related to our use of attribute) and the extensional level focusing on what we describe as internal category structure. See Geeraerts (1997: 17–26) for an introduction to his conception.

12. For other examples of this type of analysis see Schneider (1998: 29–48) on the development of HARVEST, GRASP and GLAD.

13. For the much rarer case of prototype merger see Geeraerts (1992). Another cognitive issue that cannot be treated adequately is the interpretation of a set of etymological roots in terms of metaphors. Sweetser's (1990, ch. 2) study of Indo-European verbs of perception is a good example of this approach.

Section 7.3

14. See similar definitions of grammaticalization in Hopper and Traugott (2003: xv). Generally this textbook provides an excellent overview of the important aspects of the subject.

AN INTRODUCTION TO COGNITIVE LINGUISTICS

15. To choose just two of the many discussions of the topic, see Fischer and Rosenbach (2000: 3f) and also Hopper and Traugott (2003: 1ff), who advocate an analysis of the *going-to* grammaticalization in terms of metonymy and metaphor, but also offer alternative explanations (reanalysis and analogy, problem-solving explanation).

16. Heine's earlier term was 'proposition', which was replaced in Heine (1993) by 'event schema'. However, following Talmy (see Sections 5.2 and 5.3) the same term is used in a different (and more cognitive) way, and we have therefore opted for 'propositional schema'. See Heine (1993: 30f) for further details.

17. Heine's conception also covers modal auxiliaries, which he derives from more complex schemas. See Heine (1993: 27ff).

Section 7.4

For an overview of recent research in the field see the two collections edited by Pütz *et al.* (2001) and Achard and Niemeier (2004).

18. On the use of visual elements in language teaching see for instance Wright (2001) and Wright and Haleem (1995).

19. See Ungerer (2001) for methodological aspects and more details of the study.

20. The experiment summarized by Kövecses to test the success of his method is devoted to phrasal verbs with the particles *up* and *down* and is based on 'up–down' metaphors (which we would regard as image schemas). See Kövecses (2001: 102ff).

21. Rudzka-Ostyn died before the workbook was completed for publication. For a detailed account of its contents see Kurtyka (2001), for a cognitive-linguistic evaluation see Dirven (2001: 17ff).

22. See Tyler and Evans (2004) on *over*, as well as Queller (2001) for the uses of *all over*, and Chapter 4, reading note 4.

23. This distinction is also taken up by Langacker (1987a: 203f), who regards the count/ mass contrast as a schema. Taylor (1993) also sticks to this distinction, but introduces a more holistic view by assuming the gestalt-like prototypes 'thing' and 'substance' for count and mass nouns respectively.

24. The text provides only a selective account of Dirven's (1989) comprehensive description of verb complementation, which also covers other non-finite constructions and finite clauses.

25. See the extensive list of text types in Schmid-Schönbein (2001: 86).

Conclusion

As it should have emerged in the course of this book, cognitive linguistics is not a unified and monolithic theory, but rather a cluster of linguistic approaches sharing underlying assumptions about the essence of language. Given the interdisciplinary nature of most strands within cognitive linguistics it is not surprising that there are ongoing endeavours to put linguistic theorizing on a safer psychological and neurological footing. This final section summarizes some of these developments, which cut across the chapters of this book, and relates them to current trends.

Originating in experimental work in cognitive psychology, as pursued by Eleanor Rosch and others, prototype theory (including basic level theory) has always had a psychological basis. Fundamental cognitive abilities like **perception** and **memory** are undoubtedly involved in the selection of prototypes, the gradation from good to bad category members (e.g. from >ROBIN<, >SWALLOW< to >OSTRICH< and >PENGUIN< in the category BIRD) and the fuzziness of category boundaries (e.g. between CUP and BOWL). While the theoretical status of prototypes is still somewhat contentious, hovering as it does between the status of best example and cognitive reference point (see Section 1.2), there seems to be little controversy about the psychological salience and importance of the basic level, as long as its dependence on context and cultural models is acknowledged. What must be questioned, however, is the strong traditional focus on type-of (or taxonomic) conceptual hierarchies (e.g. JEEP – CAR – VEHICLE – MOVABLE OBJECT). As we have shown in Section 2.3, part–whole relations, such as TYRE – WHEEL – BODY – CAR – TRAFFIC, are probably equally important; they are often more tangible than taxonomic relationships and seem to play a more decisive role in structuring cognitive models in our memory. The primacy of part–whole relations is also noticeable in the formation of perceptual and conceptual gestalts and in language acquisition and should also be reflected in foreign language learning (see Section 7.4).

While gestalt psychology is of course not a particularly recent invention, its central claims concerning gestalt perception and figure/ground distribution are still widely accepted in cognitive psychology. The notion of **gestalt** has been successfully applied in a variety of areas ranging from prototype formation, where for instance a prototype chair is characterized by the presence of its part in optimally functional proportions (see Section 1.3), to image schemas and to prepositional meanings, which have been shown to reflect diverse constellations of figure and ground (see Section 4.1). The basic principle behind these phenomena seems to be the urge to produce holistic, rather than decomposed, analytical, experiences that reduce the cognitive effort and thus contribute to cognitive economy and efficiency of conceptual processing, including conceptual blending. Gestalt properties can also be attributed to the units posited by Construction Grammar, which range in size from short idioms (*let alone, him be a doctor?*) to whole clause patterns, such as the caused-motion and cause-receive constructions (see Section 5.4). Fundamental clause patterns like these have been claimed to be based on experiential event-frames and to be stored as ready-made chunks in long-term memory alongside the latter. In this context it is interesting to note that there is a growing body of work indicating that constructions also play a crucial role in language acquisition (Tomasello 2003).

Figure/ground effects and the distribution of attention in perception and language are also the key to the notion of **perspective**, which lies at the heart of the prominence approach and the frame-and-attention approach (outlined in Chapters 4 and 5 respectively) and is involved in the categorization of organisms, objects and events in the world around us. It is a long-standing truism that for any 'objectively' given situation, speakers have a basically unlimited choice of options both on the lexical and the grammatical level – compare, for example, the sentences *The dog chased a rabbit* and *The rabbit tried to escape our terrier through a small hole in the fence* describing the same event. What cognitive-linguistic work has brought to the fore, however, is that decisions concerning the specificity of categories (e.g. DOG vs TERRIER), the allocation of syntactic figure and ground (*the dog* vs *the rabbit* as subject) or the opening of 'windows' of attention (*through a small hole in the fence*) may result in dissimilar conceptions of the scene described.

Event-frames and image schemas are not only based on figure/ground segregation and other principles of perception and attention, but are assumed to have a grounding in our bodily experience. In fact the **embodiment-of-language** thesis pervades a number of approaches in cognitive linguistics, most prominently in the area of conceptual metaphor theory. The starting point was the relatively modest claims of early cognitive metaphor research (Lakoff 1987: 380ff, esp. 406–8) that emotion concepts are tied to certain physiological symptoms by way of metonymy (+BODY HEAT STANDS FOR ANGER+) and that meaning in general may be rooted in bodily experienced image schemas like 'up' and 'down' or 'in and 'out' (Johnson 1987; see Section 3.2). This explains, among other things, the striking similarity of figurative expression in this domain in totally unrelated languages and cultures.

In Lakoff and Johnson's *Philosophy in the Flesh* (1999), and in many more recent publications and statements, bodily roots have been claimed for large parts of our conceptual system and abstract thinking. In line with the slogan in neuroscience 'neurons that fire together wire together' (Lakoff and Johnson 2003: 256) the 'neural theory of metaphor' claims that when an abstract concept is understood metaphorically, two sets of neurons are activated in the brain (Gallese and Lakoff 2005, Kövecses 2005: 23–6). What is more, when two neural structures are repeatedly activated together, the connections tend to grow stronger – which gives us an assumed neurological correlate of the entrenchment of conceptual metaphors.

Not only metaphors but also **conceptual blends** (see Sections 6.1 to 6.3) are said to have a neurological foundation. Indeed, Fauconnier and Turner (2002: V) argue that it was the emerging ability for blending different mental spaces that allowed humans to gain the upper hand over competing species from the Upper Paleolithic onwards, since this ability gave them the imagination required to invent new concepts, tools and means of communication (among them language). Undoubtedly, hypothetical reasoning, as expressed in *if*-clauses, presupposes the capacity to compare imagined possible future events to previously experienced ones and arrive at possible outcomes by blending aspects like cause and effect. Conceptual blending has a close counterpart in neurological theory in the notion of *binding*, which refers to a basic neurological process necessary even for the most mundane perceptual tasks. While there are different types and groups of receptors and brain areas involved in the perception of, for example, lines, corners, colours, shades of brightness or texture, it is in the process of binding that these diverse inputs are integrated to form a holistic perceptual experience of, say, a baseball cap (see Kolb and Wishaw 2003: 239ff).

Essentially, 'traditional' cognitive-linguistic work is concerned with cognitive aspects of the system of a language and its speakers' competence. However, since the increasing recognition of conceptual-blending theory in the late 1990s, more attention has been devoted to the procedural and contextual aspects of language use (see the interpretation of *Ballacktic, cherry jeans, Pisa* and also of ads, riddles and jokes in Sections 6.2 and 6.3). This focus on **on-going language processing** and its open-ended nature in actual language use has brought cognitive linguistics closer to **pragmatic approaches** which stress the context-dependence and indeterminacy of understanding. As was made clear in our short survey of Relevance Theory in Section 6.4, we believe that there could be a fruitful exchange of ideas between cognitively minded pragmatics and cognitive thinking.

Like all interdisciplinary undertakings, the cognitive-linguistic enterprise is undoubtedly enriched and strengthened by constantly widening its scope and joining forces with neighbouring fields within the cognitive sciences – and even with evolutionary biology (Givón 2005). But it also faces the pitfalls of most interdisciplinary work, among them, for example, the danger that the full complexity of psychological, neurological and biological issues and debates gets lost in the unavoidably selective borrowing of insights from these fields. No matter how cognitive linguists will manage to deal with this dilemma in the future, what seems uncontroversial at this stage is that the cognitive approach to language is definitely here to stay and will have a lasting impact on how linguists theorize about language.

References

Achard, Michel and Susanne Niemeier, eds (2004), *Cognitive Linguistics, Second Language Acquisition, and Foreign Language Teaching,* Berlin; New York: Mouton de Gruyter.

Aitchison, Jean (2003), *Words in the Mind: An Introduction to the Mental Lexicon,* 3rd edn, Oxford: Basil Blackwell.

Akman, Varol, Paolo Bouquet, Richmond Thomason, Roger A. Young, eds (2001), *Modeling and Using Context.* Third International and Interdisciplinary Conference, CONTEXT 2001, Dundee, UK, July 2001: Proceedings, Berlin: Springer.

Allerton, David (1982), *Valency and the English Verb,* London: Academic Press.

Anderson, John (1971), *The Grammar of Case: Towards a Localist Theory,* London.

Armstrong, Sharon L., Lila R. Gleitman and Henry Gleitman (1983), 'What some concepts might not be', *Cognition* **13**, 263–308.

Aske, Jon (1989), 'Path predicates in English and Spanish: a closer look', *Proceedings of the Fifteenth Annual Meeting of the Berkeley Linguistics Society,* Berkeley, CA: Berkeley Linguistics Society, 1–14.

Attardo, Salvatore, ed. (2003), 'The Pragmatics of Humor'. Special issue of *Journal of Pragmatics,* **35.**

Attardo, Salvatore (2001), *Humorous Texts: A Semantic and Pragmatic Analysis,* Berlin; New York: Mouton de Gruyter.

Barcelona, Antonio (2003), 'Metonymy in cognitive linguistics: an analysis and a few modest proposals' in Cuyckens *et al.* (2003), 223–55.

Barcelona, Antonio, ed. (2000), *Metaphor and Metonymy at the Crossroads. A Cognitive Perspective,* Berlin; New York: Mouton de Gruyter.

Barsalou, Lawrence W. (1982), 'Context-independent and context-dependent information in concepts', *Memory and Cognition* **10**, 82–93.

Barsalou, Lawrence W. (1987), 'The instability of graded structure: implications for the nature of concepts' in Ulric Neisser, ed., *Concepts and Conceptual Development: Ecological and Intellectual Factors in Categorization,* Cambridge: Cambridge University Press, 101–40.

Barthes, Roland (1977), *Image Music Text,* London: Fontana Press.

Bauer, Laurie (1983), *English Word-Formation,* Cambridge: Cambridge University Press.

Bechtel, William and Adele Abrahamsen (2002), *Connectionism and the Mind: An Introduction to Parallel Processing in Networks,* 2nd edn, Oxford: Blackwell.

Bencini, Giulia and Adele E. Goldberg (2000), 'The contribution of argument structure constructions to sentence meaning', *Journal of Memory and Language* **43**, 640–51.

Berlin, Brent and Paul Kay (1969), *Basic Color Terms: Their universality and evolution,* Berkeley, Los Angeles: University of California Press.

Berlin, Brent, Dennis Breedlove and Peter Raven (1973), 'General principles of classification and nomenclature in folk biology', *American Anthropologist* **75**, 214–42.

Berlin, Brent, Dennis Breedlove and Peter Raven (1974), *Principles of Tzeltal Plant Classification,* New York: Academic Press.

Berman, Ruth and Dan I. Slobin (1994), *Relating Events in Narrative: A Crosslinguistic Developmental Study,* Hillsdale, NJ: Lawrence Erlbaum Associates.

Black, Max (1949), *Language and Philosophy,* Ithaca: Cornell University Press.

Black, Max (1962), *Models and Metaphors,* Ithaca: Cornell University Press.

Black, Max (1993), 'More about metaphor' in Ortony (1993), 19–41.

Blakemore, Diane (1992), *Understanding Utterances,* Oxford: Blackwell.

Bouquet, Paolo, Luciano Serafini, Patrick Brézillon, Massimo Benerecetti and Francesca Castellani, eds (1999), *Modeling and Using Context.* Second International and Interdisciplinary Conference, CONTEXT '99, Trento, Italy, September 1999: Proceedings, Berlin: Springer.

Boyd, Richard (1993), 'Metaphor and theory change: What is "metaphor" a metaphor for?' in Ortony (1993), 481–532.

Broccias, Cristiano (2004), Review of Fauconnier and Turner (2002), *Cognitive Linguistics* **15**, 575–88.

Brown, Cecil H. (1990), 'A survey of category types in natural language' in Tsohatzidis (1990), 17–47.

Brown, Roger (1958), 'How shall a thing be called?', *Psychological Review* **65**, 14–21.

Brown, Roger (1965), *Social Psychology,* New York: Free Press.

Brown, Roger and Eric H. Lenneberg (1954), 'A study in language and cognition', *Journal of Abnormal and Social Psychology* **49**, 454–62.

Brugman, Claudia M. (1981), *The story of Over,* Trier: LAUT.

Brugman, Claudia M. (1988), *The story of Over: Polysemy, Semantics, and the Structure of the Lexicon,* New York; London: Garland.

Brugman, Claudia M. (1990), 'What is the invariance hypothesis?', *Cognitive Linguistics* **1**, 257–66.

Bybee, Joan (1985), 'Diagrammatic iconicity in stem-inflection relations' in Hàiman (1985), 11–48.

Bybee, Joan, Evere Perkins and William Pagliuca (1994), *The Evolution of Grammar: Tense, Aspect, and Modality in the Languages of the World,* Chicago: Chicago University Press.

Cain, A.J. (1958), 'Logic and memory in Linnaeus's system of taxonomy', *Proceedings of the Linnaen Society of London* **169**, 144–63.

Clark, Herbert H. and Eve H. Clark (1977), *Psychology and Language: An Introduction to Psycholinguistics,* New York: Harcourt Brace.

COBUILD Sinclair, John M. *et al.* (1987), *Collins COBUILD English Language Dictionary,* Landen: Collins.

COD Pearsall, Judy, ed. (1999), *The Concise Oxford Dictionary of Current English,* 10th edn, Oxford: Clarendon Press.

Coleman, Linda and Paul Kay (1981), 'Prototype semantics: the English word LIE', *Language* **57**, 26–44.

Coulson, Seana (2001), *Semantic Leaps: Frame Shifting and Conceptual Blending in Meaning Construction,* Cambridge; New York: Cambridge University Press.

Coulson, Seana (in press), 'What's so funny?: conceptual blending in humorous examples' in Vimala Herman, ed., *The Poetics of Cognition: Studies of Cognitive Linguistics and the Verbal Arts,* Cambridge; New York: Cambridge University Press.

Coulson, Seana and Todd Oakley (2000), 'Blending basics', *Cognitive Linguistics* **11**, 175–96.

Coulson, Seana and Todd Oakley (2003), 'Metonymy and conceptual blending' in Panther and Thornburg (2003), 51–79.

Coulson, Seana and Todd Oakley (2005), 'Blended and coded meaning: literal and figurative meaning in cognitive semantics', *Journal of Pragmatics* **37**, 1510–36.

Craig, Collette, ed. (1986), *Noun Classes and Categorization,* Amsterdam; Philadelphia: John Benjamins.

Croft, William (1993), 'The role of domains in the interpretation of metaphors and metonymies', *Cognitive Linguistics* **4**, 335–70.

Croft, William (2001), *Radical Construction Grammar: Syntactic Theory in Typological Perspective,* Oxford: Oxford University Press.

Croft, William (2005), 'Logical and typological arguments for radical construction grammar' in Östman and Fried (2005b), 273–314.

Croft, William and D. Allan Cruse (2004), *Cognitive Linguistics,* Cambridge; New York: Cambridge University Press.

Cruse, D. Allan (1986), *Lexical Semantics,* Cambridge: Cambridge University Press.

Cruse, D. Allan (2000), *Meaning in Language,* Oxford: Oxford University Press.

Cuyckens, Hubert (1991), *The Semantics of Spatial Prepositions in Dutch: A Cognitive-Linguistic Exercise,* Ph.D. Dissertation, University of Antwerp.

Cuyckens, Hubert, Thomas Berg, René Dirven and Klaus-Uwe Panther, eds (2003), *Motivation in Language: Studies in Honor of Günter Radden,* Amsterdam: John Benjamins.

Dancygier, Barbara and Eve Sweetser (1997), '*Then* in conditional constructions', *Cognitive Linguistics* **8**, 109–36.

Davitz, Joel (1969), *The Language of Emotion,* New York: Academic Press.

Dirven, René (1989), 'A cognitive perspective on complementation' in Dany Jaspers, Wim Klooster, Yvan Putseys and Peter Seuren, eds, *Sentential Complementation and the Lexicon: Studies in honour of Wim de Geest,* Dordrecht: Foris, 113–39.

Dirven, René (1999), 'Conversion as a conceptual metonymy of event schemata' in Panther and Radden (1999), 275–87.

Dirven, René (2001), 'English phrasal verbs; theory and didactic applications' in Pütz *et al.* (2001), 3–27.

Dirven, René and John Taylor (1988), 'The conceptualization of vertical space in English: the case of *Tall*' in Rudzka-Ostyn (1988), 379–407.

Dirven, René, Louis Goossens, Yvan Putseys and Emma Vorlat (1982), *The Scene of Linguistic Action and its Perspective by* SPEAK, TALK, SAY *and* TELL, Amsterdam; Philadelphia: John Benjamins.

Dirven, René, Roslyn Frank and Martin Pütz, eds (2003), *Cognitive Models in Language and Thought: Ideology, Metaphors and Meanings,* Berlin: Mouton de Gruyter.

Dirven, René and Ralf Pörings, eds (2002), *Metaphor and Metonymy in Comparison and Contrast,* Berlin: Mouton de Gruyter.

Dirven, René and Johan Vanparys, eds (1995), *Current Approaches to the Lexicon.* A Selection of Papers presented at the 18th LAUD Symposium, Duisburg, March 1993, Frankfurt: Peter Lang.

Dirven, René and Marjolijn Verspoor, eds (2004), *Cognitive Explorations in Language and Linguistics,* 2nd edn, Amsterdam: John Benjamins.

Dixon, Robert M.W. (1977), 'Where have all the adjectives gone?', *Studies in Language* **1**, 19–80.

Elbers, Loekie (1988), 'New names from old words: related aspects of children's metaphors and word compounds', *Journal of Child Language* **15**, 591–617.

Eysenck, Michael W. and Mark Keane (2002), *Cognitive Psychology: A Student's Handbook,* 4th edn, Hove: Psychology Press.

Fauconnier, Gilles (1996), 'Analogical counterfactuals' in Fauconnier and Sweetser (1996), 57–90.

Fauconnier, Gilles (1997), *Mappings in Thought and Language,* Cambridge: Cambridge University Press.

Fauconnier, Gilles (2003), 'Pragmatics and cognitive linguistics' in Horn and Ward (2003), 657–74.

Fauconnier, Gilles and Mark Turner (1996), 'Blending as a central process of grammar' in Adele Goldberg, ed. *Conceptual Structure, Discourse, and Language,* Stanford: Center for the Study of Language and Information, 113–29.

Fauconnier, Gilles and Mark Turner (1998), 'Conceptual integration networks', *Cognitive Science* **22** (2), 133–87.

Fauconnier, Gilles and Mark Turner (2002), *The Way We Think: Conceptual Blending and the Mind's Hidden Complexities*, New York: Basic Books.

Fauconnier, Gilles and Eve Sweetser, eds (1996), *Spaces, Worlds and Grammars*, Chicago: University of Chicago Press.

Fehr, Beverley and James A. Russell (1984), 'Concept of emotion viewed from a prototype perspective', *Journal of Experimental Psychology: General* **113**, 464–86.

Fillmore, Charles C. (1968), 'The case for case' in E. Bach and R.T. Harms, eds, *Universals in Linguistic Theory*, London: Holt, Rinehart and Winston, 1–88.

Fillmore, Charles C. (1975), 'An alternative to checklist theories of meaning' in C. Cogen, H. Thompson, G. Thurgood and K. Whistler, eds, *Proceedings of the Berkeley Linguistic Society*, Berkeley: Berkeley Linguistics Society, 123–31.

Fillmore, Charles C. (1976), 'The need for a frame semantics within linguistics', *Statistical Methods in Linguistics,* 5–29.

Fillmore, Charles C. (1977a), 'Topics in lexical semantics' in R.W. Cole, ed., *Current Issues in Linguistic Theory*, Bloomington; London: Indiana University Press, 76–138.

Fillmore, Charles C. (1977b), 'The case for case reopened' in P. Cole and J.M. Sadock, eds, *Syntax and Semantics, Vol. 8: Grammatical Relations*, New York; San Francisco; London: Academic Press, 59–81.

Fillmore, Charles C. (1982), 'Towards a descriptive framework for spatial deixis' in R.J. Jarvella and W. Klein, eds, *Speech, Place and Action*, Chichester: John Wiley and Sons, 31–59.

Fillmore, Charles C. (1985), 'Frames and the semantics of understanding', *Quaderni di Semantica* VI, 222–54.

Fillmore, Charles C. (1999), 'Inversion and constructional inheritance' in Gert Webelhuth, Jean-Pierre Koenig and Andreas Kathol, eds, *Lexical and Constructional Aspects of Linguistic Explanations*, Stanford, CA: Stanford University, 113–28.

Fillmore, Charles C. and Beryl T. Atkins (1992), 'Toward a frame-based lexicon: the semantics of RISK and its neighbors' in Adrienne Lehrer and Eva Kittay, eds, *Frames, Fields, and Contrasts*, Hillsdale, NJ: Lawrence Erlbaum Assoc., 75–102.

Fillmore, Charles J., Paul Kay and Mary Catherine O'Connor (1988),

'Regularity and idiomaticity in grammatical constructions: the case of *let alone*', *Language* **64**, 501–38.

Fischer, Kerstin and Anatol Stefanowitsch (2006), 'Konstruktionsgrammatik: Ein überblick' in Kerstin Fischer and Anatol Stefanowitsch, eds, *Konstruktionsgrammatik. Van der Anwendung zur Theorie*, Tübingen: Stauffenberg.

Fischer, Olga and Anette Rosenbach (2000), 'Introduction' in Olga Fischer, Anette Rosenbach and Dieter Stein, eds, *Pathways of Change: Grammaticalization in English*, Amsterdam: John Benjamins, 1–37.

Fischer, Olga and Max Nänny, eds (2001), *The Motivated Sign. Iconicity in Language and Literature*, Vol. 2, Amsterdam: John Benjamins.

Fontanelle, Thierry, ed. (2003), 'FrameNet and frame semantics', *International Journal of Lexicography* **16** (3).

Foolen, Ad and Frederike van der Leek, eds (2000), *Constructions in Cognitive Linguistics*. Selected Papers from the Fifth International Cognitive Linguistic Conference, Amsterdam 1997, Amsterdam: John Benjamins.

Forceville, Charles (1998), *Pictorial Metaphor in Advertising*, London: Routledge.

Frajzyngier, Zygmunt (1995), 'A functional theory of complementizers' in Joan Bybee, and Suzanne Fleischman, eds, *Modality in Grammar and Discourse*, Amsterdam; Philadelphia: John Benjamins, 473–502.

Frajzyngier, Zygmunt and Robert Jasperson (1991), '*That*-clauses and other complements', *Lingua* **83**, 133–53.

Fried, Mirjiam and Jan-Ola Östman, (2004a), 'Construction grammar: a thumbnail sketch' in Fried and Östman (2004b), 11–86.

Fried, Mirjiam and Jan-Ola Östman, eds (2004b), *Construction Grammar in a Cross-Linguistic Perspective*, Amsterdam; Philadelphia: John Benjamins.

Gallese, Vittorio and George Lakoff (2005), 'The brain's concepts: the role of the sensory-motor system in conceptual knowledge', *Cognitive Neuropsychology* **2**,455–79.

Geeraerts, Dirk (1988a), 'Prototypicality as a prototypical notion', *Communication and Cognition* **21**, 343–55.

Geeraerts, Dirk (1988b), 'Where does prototypicality come from?' in Rudzka-Ostyn (1988), 207–29.

Geeraerts, Dirk (1990), 'The lexicographical treatment of prototypical polysemy' in Tsohatzidis (1990), 195–210.

Geeraerts, Dirk (1992), 'Prototypicality effects in diachronic semantics: a round-up' in Günter Kellermann and Michael D. Morrissey, eds (1992), *Diachrony within Synchrony: Language History and Cognition.* Papers from the International Symposium at the University of Duisburg, 26–28 March 1990, Frankfurt, Main: Peter Lang, 183–205.

Geeraerts, Dirk (1993), 'Vagueness's puzzles, polysemy's vagaries', *Cognitive Linguistics* **4**, 223–72.

Geeraerts, Dirk (1997), *Diachronic Prototype Semantics: A Contribution to Historical Lexicology,* Oxford: Clarendon Press.

Geeraerts, Dirk and Stefan Grondelaers (1995), 'Looking back in anger: cultural traditions and metaphorical patterns' in Taylor and MacLaury (1995), 153–79.

Geeraerts, Dirk, Stefan Grondelaers and Peter Bakema (1994), *The Structure of Lexical Variation: A Descriptive Framework for Cognitive Lexicology,* Berlin: Mouton de Gruyter.

Geiger, Richard A. and Barbara Rudzka-Ostyn, eds (1993), *Conceptualization and Mental Processing in Language,* Berlin; New York: Mouton de Gruyter.

Gentner, Dedre (1982), 'Are scientific analogies metaphors?' in David S. Miall, ed., *Metaphor: Problems and Perspectives,* Sussex: The Harvester Press.

Gentner, Dedre and Michael Jeziorski (1993), 'The shift from metaphor to analogy in Western science' in Ortony (1993), 447–80.

Gentner, Dedre and Albert. L. Stevens, eds (1983), *Mental Models,* Hillsdale, NJ: Lawrence Erlbaum Assoc.

Gibbs, Raymond W. Jr. (1994), *The Poetics of Mind: Figurative Thought, Language, and Understanding,* Cambridge: Cambridge University Press.

Gibbs, Raymond W. Jr (1999), 'Speaking and thinking with metonymy' in Panther and Radden (1999), 61–76.

Gibbs, Raymond W. Jr (2000), 'Making good psychology out of blending theory', *Cognitive Linguistics* **11**, 347–58.

Gibbs, Raymond W. Jr and Herbert L. Colston (1995), 'The cognitive psychological reality of image schemas and their transformations', *Cognitive Linguistics* **6**, 347–78.

Gibbs, Raymond W. Jr and Gerald Steen, eds (1999), *Metaphor in Cognitive Linguistics.* Selected Papers from the 5th International Cognitive Linguistics Conference. Amsterdam, July 1997. Amsterdam: John Benjamins.

Givón, Talmy (1990), *Syntax: A Functional-Typological Introduction,* Vol. 2, Amsterdam: John Benjamins.

Givón, Talmy (2005), *Context as Other Minds,* Amsterdam: John Benjamins.

Goddard, Cliff and Anna Wierzbicka, (2004), 'Cultural scripts: what are they and what are they good for?', *Intercultural Pragmatics* **1–2**, 153–66.

Goldberg, Adele E. (1995), *Constructions: A Construction Grammar Approach to Argument Structure,* Chicago: University of Chicago Press.

Goossens, L. (1990), 'Metaphthonymy: the interaction of metaphor and metonymy in expressions for linguistic action', *Cognitive Linguistics* **1**, 322–40.

Gordon, Ian E. (2004), *Theories of Visual Perception,* 3rd edn, Hove: Psychology Press.

Grady, Joseph E. (1997), 'THEORIES ARE BUILDINGS Revisited', *Cognitive Linguistics* **8**, 267–90.

Grady, Joseph E. (1999) 'Typology and motivation for conceptual metaphor: correlations vs. resemblance' in Gibbs and Steen (1999), 79–100.

Grady, Joseph E. (2005), 'Primary metaphors as inputs to conceptual integration', *Journal of Pragmatics* **37**, 1595–614.

Grady, Joseph E. and Ch. Johnson (2002), 'Converging evidence for the notions of subscene and primary scene' in Dirven and Pörings (2002), 533–54.

Grady, Joseph E., Todd Oakley and Seana Coulson (1999), 'Blending and metaphor' in Gibbs and Steen (1999), 101–24.

Greenbaum, Sidney and Randolph Quirk (1992), *A Student's Grammar of the English Language,* London: Longman.

Grice, H. P. (1975), 'Logic and conversation' in Peter Cole and Jerry L. Morgan, eds, *Syntax and Semantics, Vol. 3: Speech Acts,* New York: Academic Press, 41–58.

Haiman, John, ed. (1985), *Iconicity in Syntax,* Amsterdam: John Benjamins.

Halliday, Michael A.K. (2004), *An Introduction to Functional Grammar,* 3rd edn, London: Edward Arnold.

Halliday, Michael A.K. and Ruqaiya Hasan (1989), *Language, Context, and Text: Aspects of Language in a Social-Semiotic Perspective,* 2nd edn, Oxford: Oxford University Press.

Hampe, Beate (2005), 'On the role of iconic motivation in conceptual metaphor: has metaphor theory come full circle?' in Maeder *et al.* (2005), 39–66.

Hampton, James A. (1979), 'Polymorphous concepts in semantic memory', *Journal of Verbal Learning and Verbal Behavior* **18**, 441–61.

Heider, Eleanor R. (1971), ' "Focal" color areas and the development of color names', *Developmental Psychology* **4**, 447–55.

Heider, Eleanor R. (1972), 'Universals in color naming and memory', *Journal of Experimental Psychology* **93**, 10–20.

Heider, Eleanor R. and D.C. Oliver (1972), 'The structure of the color space in naming and memory for two languages', *Cognitive Psychology* **3**, 337–45.

Heine, Bernd (1993), *Auxiliaries. Cognitive Forces and Grammaticalization*, New York; Oxford: Oxford University Press.

Heine, Bernd, Ulrike Claudi and Friederike Hünnemeyer (1991), *Grammaticalization: A Conceptual Framework*, Chicago; London: University of Chicago Press.

Herbst, Thomas, David Heath, Ian F. Roe and Dieter Götz (2004), *A Valency Dictionary of English: A Corpus-based Analysis of the Complementation Patterns of English Verbs, Nouns and Adjectives*, Berlin; New York: Mouton de Gruyter.

Heyvaert, Liesbet (2003), *A Cognitive–Functional Approach to Nominalization in English*, Berlin: Mouton de Gruyter.

Holdcroft, David (1991), *Saussure. Signs, System, and Arbitrariness*, Cambridge: Cambridge University Press.

Holland, Dorothy and Naomi Quinn, eds (1987), *Cultural Models in Language and Thought*, Cambridge: Cambridge University Press.

Hopper, Paul J. and Elizabeth C. Traugott (2003), *Grammaticalization*, 2nd edn, Cambridge: Cambridge University Press.

Horn, Laurence R. and Gregory Ward, eds (2003), *Handbook of Pragmatics*, Oxford: Blackwell.

Hüllen, Werner and Rainer Schulze, eds (1988), *Understanding the Lexicon: Meaning, Sense and World Knowledge in Lexical Semantics*, Tübingen: Niemeyer.

Hunn, Eugene S. (1975), 'A measure of degree of correspondence of folk to scientific biological classification', *American Ethnologist* **2**, 309–27.

Hunn, Eugene S. (1977), *Tzeltal Folk Zoology: The Classification of Discontinuities in Nature,* New York: Academic Press.

Johnson, Mark (1987), *The Body in the Mind: The Bodily Basis of Meaning, Imagination, and Reason,* Chicago; London: University of Chicago Press.

Johnson-Laird, Philip N. (1983), *Mental Models,* Cambridge: Cambridge University Press.

Johnson-Laird, Philip N. and Keith Oatley (1989), 'The language of emotions: an analysis of a semantic field', *Cognition and Emotion* **3**, 81–123.

Johnson-Laird, Philip N. and Keith Oatley (1992), 'Basic emotions, rationality and folk theory', *Cognition and Emotion* **6**, 201–23.

Kager, René (1999), *Optimality Theory,* Cambridge: Cambridge University Press.

Katz, Jerrold and Paul Postal (1964), *An Integrated Theory of Linguistic Descriptions,* Cambridge: MIT Press.

Kay, Paul (1971), 'Taxonomy and semantic contrast', *Language* **47**, 866–87.

Kay, Paul (1999), 'Color appearance and the emergence and evolution of basic color lexicons', *American Anthropologist* **101**, 743–60.

Kay, Paul (2003), 'Pragmatic aspects of grammatical constructions' in Horn and Ward (2003), 675–700.

Kay, Paul and Charles J. Fillmore (1999), 'Grammatical constructions and linguistic generalizations: the *What's X doing Y?* construction', *Language* **75**, 1–33.

Kay, Paul and Chad K. McDaniel (1978), 'The linguistic significance of the meanings of basic color terms', *Language* **54**, 610–46.

Kemmer, Suzanne (2003), 'Schemas and lexical blends' in Cuyckens *et al.* (2003), 69–97.

Kempton, Willett (1987), 'Two theories of home control' in Holland and Quinn (1987), 222–42.

Kerrigan, John (1986), *The Sonnets and a Lover's Complaint,* London: The New Penguin Shakespeare.

King, D. Brett and Michael Wertheimer (2005), *Max Wertheimer and Gestalt Theory,* New Brunswick: Transaction Publisher.

Kirkpatrick, Betty (1852; 1987), *Roget's Thesaurus of English Words and Phrases,* London: Longman.

Kleiber, Georges (1998), *La sémantique du prototype: Catégories et sens lexical,* 2ème ed., Paris: Presses Universitaires de France.

Knowles, Elizabeth, ed. (1997), *The Oxford Dictionary of New Words,* Oxford; New York: Oxford University Press.

Koestler, Arthur (1964), *The Act of Creation,* New York: Macmillan.

Koffka, Kurt (2002 [1935]), *Principles of Gestalt Psychology,* reprint, London: Routledge.

Köhler, Wolfgang (1992), *Gestalt Psychology: An Introduction to New Concepts in Modern Psychology,* reissued, New York: Liveright.

Kolb, Brian and Ian Q. Wishaw (2003), *Fundamentals of Human Neuropsychology,* 5th edn, New York: Worth Publishers.

Kövecses, Zoltán (1990), *Emotion Concepts,* New York: Springer.

Kövecses, Zoltán (1991), 'Happiness: a definitional effort', *Metaphor and Symbolic Activity* **6**: 29–46.

Kövecses, Zoltán (1995), 'Anger: its language, conceptualization, and physiology in the light of cross-cultural evidence' in Taylor and MacLaury (1995), 181–96.

Kövecses, Zoltán (2000), *Metaphor and Emotion: Language, Culture, and Body in Human Feeling,* Cambridge: Cambridge University Press.

Kövecses, Zoltán (2001), 'A cognitive linguistic view of learning idioms in an FLT context' in Pütz *et al.* (2001), 87–115.

Kövecses, Zoltán (2002), *Metaphor. A Practical Introduction,* Oxford: Oxford University Press.

Kövecses, Zoltán (2005), *Metaphor in Culture: Universality and Variation,* Cambridge; New York: Cambridge University Press.

Kövecses, Zoltán and Günter Radden (1998), 'Metonymy: developing a cognitive linguistic view', *Cognitive Linguistics* **9**, 37–77.

Kuhn, Thomas S. (1993), 'Metaphor in science' in Ortony (1993), 533–42.

Kurtyka, Andrzej, (2001), 'Teaching English phrasal verbs: a cognitive approach' in Pütz *et al.* (2001), 29–54.

Labov, William (1973), 'The boundaries of words and their meaning' in Charles-James N. Bailey and Roger W. Shuy, eds, *New ways of Analyzing Variation in English,* Washington DC: Georgetown University Press, 340–73.

Labov, William (1978), 'Denotational structure' in Donka Farkas, Wesley M.

Jacobsen and Karol W. Todrys, eds, *Papers from the Parasession on the Lexicon,* Chicago: Chicago Linguistics Society, 220–60.

Lakoff, George (1986), 'Classifiers as a reflection of mind' in Craig (1986), 13–51.

Lakoff, George (1987), *Women, Fire, and Dangerous Things. What Categories Reveal About the Mind,* Chicago; London: University of Chicago Press.

Lakoff, George (1990), 'The Invariance Hypothesis: is abstract reason based on image-schemas?', *Cognitive Linguistics* **1**, 39–74.

Lakoff, George (1992) 'Metaphor and war: the metaphor system used to justify war in the gulf' in Pütz (1992), 463–81.

Lakoff, George (1993), 'The contemporary theory of metaphor' in Ortony (1993), 202–51.

Lakoff, George (1996), 'Sorry, I'm not myself today: the metaphor system for conceptualizing the self' in Fauconnier and Sweetser (1996), 91–123.

Lakoff, George (2002), *Moral Politics: How Liberals and Conservatives Think,* 2nd edn, Chicago: University of Chicago Press.

Lakoff, George (2003), 'Metaphor and war, again'. *Alter Net.* Available at http://www.alternet.org/story/15414/, posted 18 March, 2003.

Lakoff, George (2004), *Don't Think of a White Elephant: Know Your Values and Frame the Debate,* White River Junction, Vermont: Chelsea Green Publishing.

Lakoff, George and Mark Johnson (1980/2003), *Metaphors We Live By,* 2nd edn with a new afterword, Chicago; London: University of Chicago Press.

Lakoff, George and Mark Johnson (1999), *Philosophy in the Flesh: The Embodied Mind and its Challenge to Western Thought,* New York: Basic Books.

Lakoff, George and Mark Turner (1989), *More Than Cool Reason: A Field Guide to Poetic Metaphor,* Chicago: Chicago University Press.

Lambrecht, Knud (2004), 'On the interaction of information structure and formal structure in constructions: the case of French right-detached *comme*-N' in Fried and Östman (2004b), 157–99.

Langacker, Ronald W. (1987a), *Foundations of Cognitive Grammar, Vol. I: Theoretical Prerequisites,* Stanford, California: Stanford University Press.

Langacker, Ronald W. (1987b), 'Nouns and verbs', *Language* **63**, 53–94.

Langacker, Ronald W. (1990), 'Settings, participants, and grammatical relations' in Tsohatzidis (1990), 213–38.

Langacker, Ronald W. (1991), *Foundations of Cognitive Grammar, Vol. II: Descriptive Application,* Stanford, California: Stanford University Press.

Langacker, Ronald W. (1992), 'The symbolic nature of cognitive grammar: the meaning of *of* and of *of*-periphrasis' in Pütz (1992), 483–502.

Langacker, Ronald W. (1993), 'Reference-point constructions', *Cognitive Linguistics* **4**, 1–38.

Langacker, Ronald W. (1995), 'Raising and transparency', *Language* **71**, 1–62.

Langacker, Ronald W. (2000), *Grammar and Conceptualization,* Berlin: Mouton de Gruyter.

Langacker, Ronald W. (2001), 'Discourse in cognitive grammar', *Cognitive Linguistics* **12**, 143–88.

Langacker, Ronald W. (2002), *Concept, Image, and Symbol: The Cognitive Basis of Grammar,* 2nd edn, Berlin: Mouton de Gruyter.

LDOCE2 Summers, Della *et al.* (1987), *Longman Dictionary of Contemporary English,* 2nd edn, London: Longman.

LDOCE4 Summers, Della *et al.* (2005), *Longman Dictionary of Contemporary English,* 4th edn, London: Longman.

Leech, Geoffrey N. (1969), *A Linguistic Guide to English Poetry,* London: Longman.

Leech, Geoffrey N. (1981), *Semantics: The study of Meaning,* 2nd edn, Harmondsworth: Penguin.

Lehrer, Adrienne (1996), 'Identifying and interpreting blends: an experimental approach', *Cognitive Linguistics* **7**, 359–90.

Leisi, Ernst (1985), *Praxis der englischen Semantik,* 2. Aufl., Heidelberg: Winter.

Lenneberg, Eric H. (1967), *Biological Foundations of Language,* New York: Wiley.

Lindner, Susan J. (1982), 'A lexico-semantic analysis of English verb particle constructions with *out* and *up*', PhD Dissertation, San Diego, University of California.

Lipka, Leonhard (1987), 'Prototype semantics or feature semantics: an alternative?' in W. Lörscher and R. Schulze, eds, *Perspectives on Language in Performance: Studies in Linguistics, Literary Criticism, and Language Teaching and Learning,* Tübingen: Narr, 282–98.

Lipka, Leonhard (1988), 'A rose is a rose is a rose: on simple and dual categorization in natural languages' in Hüllen and Schulze (1988), 355–66.

Lipka, Leonhard (1995), 'Lexicology and lexicography: poor relations, competition, or co-operation?' in Dirven and Vanparys (1995), 381–403.

Lipka, Leonhard (2002), *English Lexicology: Lexical Structure, Word Semantics and Word-Formation*, Tübingen: Narr.

LLCE McArthur, Tom, (1981), *Longman Lexicon of Contemporary English*, Harlow: Longman.

Lyons, John (1977), *Semantics*, 2 vols, Cambridge: Cambridge University Press.

Lyons, John (1981), *Language, Meaning and Context*, Bungay, Suffolk: Fontana.

Maeder, Costantino, Olga Fischer and William J. Herlofsky, eds (2005), *Outside-in – inside-out. Iconicity in Language and Literature*, Vol. 4, Amsterdam: John Benjamins.

Malblanc, Alfred (1977), *Stylistique comparée du français et de l'allemand*, 5ème edn, Paris: Didier.

Mandelblit, Nili (2000), 'The grammatical marking of conceptual integration: from syntax to morphology', *Cognitive Linguistics* **11**, 197–251.

Masuda, Keiko (2002), 'A phonetic study of sound symbolism'. Unpublished PhD dissertation, Cambridge University.

Mayer, Mercer (1969), *Frog, Where Are You?*, New York: Dial Press.

Mayer, Richard E. (1993), 'The instructive metaphor: metaphoric aids to students' understanding of science' in Ortony (1993), 561–78.

McArthur, Tom (1981), *Longman Lexicon of Contemporary English*, London: Longman (= LLCE).

McArthur, Tom (1986), *Worlds of Reference*, Cambridge: Cambridge University Press.

McCloskey, Michael (1983), 'Naive theories of motion' in Gentner and Stevens (1983), 299–324.

Medin, Douglas L. Brian H. Ross and Arthur B. Markman (2001), *Cognitive Psychology*, 3rd edn, Hoboken: Wiley.

Meillet, Antoine (1912; 1921), *Linguistique historique et linguistique générale*, Paris: Champion.

Mervis, Caroline B. and Eleanor Rosch (1981), 'Categorization of natural objects', *Annual Review of Psychology* **32**, 89–115.

Minsky, Marvin (1975), 'A framework for representing knowledge' in P. H. Winston, ed., *The Psychology of Computer Vision*, New York: McGraw-Hill, 211–7.

Moser, Sibylle (forthcoming), 'Iconicity in multimedia performance' to appear in: Elsbieta Tabakowska and Christina Ljungberg, eds, *Iconicity in Language and Literature*, Vol. 5, Amsterdam: John Benjamins.

Müller, Wolfgang G. and Olga Fischer, eds (2003), *From Sign to Signing. Iconicity in Language and Literature*, Vol. 3, Amsterdam: John Benjamins.

Murphy, Gregory L. (1988), 'Comprehending complex concepts', *Cognitive Science* **12**, 529–62.

Musolff, Andreas (2001), 'The metaphorization of European politics: movement on the road to Europe' in Musolff, Andreas, Colin Good, Petra Points and Ruth Wittlinger, eds, *Attitudes towards Europe: Language in the Unification Process*, Aldershot: Ashgate, 179–200.

Nänny, Max and Olga Fischer, eds (1999), *Form Miming Meaning. Iconicity in Language and Literature*, Vol. 1, Amsterdam: John Benjamins.

Nerlich, Brigitte, David D. Clarke and Zazie Todd (2002), ' "Mummy, I like being a sandwich". Metonymy in language acquisition' in Dirven and Pörings (2002), 361–83.

Newman, John (1996), Give: *A Cognitive-Linguistic Study*, Berlin; New York: Mouton de Gruyter.

Niemeier, Susanne (1998), 'Colourless green ideas metonymise furiously'. *Rostocker Beiträge zu Sprachwissenschaft* **5**, 119–46.

Niemeier, Susanne und René Dirven, eds (2000), *Evidence for Linguistic Relativity*, Vol. I, Amsterdam: John Benjamins.

Nöth, Winfried (2000), *Handbuch der Semiotik*, 2nd edn, Stuttgart: Metzler.

OALD Wehmeier, Sally, ed. (2005), *The Oxford Advanced Learner's Dictionary of Current English*, 7th edn, Oxford University Press.

OED Simpson, J.A. and E.S.C. Weiner, eds (1991), *The Oxford English Dictionary*, 2nd edn, Oxford: clarendon Press.

Ortony, Andrew, ed. (1993), *Metaphor and Thought*, 2nd edn, Cambridge: Cambridge University Press.

Ortony, Andrew, Gerald L. Clore and Allan Collins (1988), *The Cognitive Structure of Emotions*, Cambridge: Cambridge University Press.

Östman, Jan-Ola (2005), 'Construction discourse: a prolegomenon' in Östman and Fried (2005b), 121–44.

Östman, Jan-Ola and Mirjam Fried (2005a), 'The cognitive grounding of construction grammar' in Östman and Fried (2005b), 1–13.

Östman, Jan-Ola and Mirjam Fried, eds (2005b), *Construction Grammars: Cognitive Grounding and Theoretical Extensions,* Amsterdam; Philadelphia: John Benjamins.

Panther, Klaus-Uwe and Günter Radden, eds (1999), *Metonymy in Language and Thought,* Amsterdam; Philadelphia: John Benjamins.

Panther, Klaus-Uwe and Linda Thornburg (1999), 'The potentiality for actuality metonymy in English and Hungarian' in Panther and Radden (1999), 333–57.

Panther, Klaus-Uwe and Linda Thornburg, eds (2003), *Metonymy and Pragmatic Inferencing,* Amsterdam; Philadelphia: John Benjamins.

Plato (1998) *Cratylus,* transl. by C.D.C. Reeves, Indianapolis: Hackett.

Podhorodecka, Joanna (forthcoming), 'Is lámatyáve a lingustic heresy? Iconicity in J.R.R. Tolkien's invented languages' to appear in Elsbieta Tabakowska and Christina Ljungberg, eds, *Iconicity in Language and Literature,* Vol. 5, Amsterdam: John Benjamins. ·

Putnam, Hilary (1981), *Reason, Truth and History,* Cambridge: Cambridge University Press.

Pütz, Martin, ed. (1992), *Thirty Years of Linguistic Evolution,* Amsterdam; Philadelphia: John Benjamins.

Pütz, Martin ed. (2000), *Evidence for Linguistic Relativity,* Vol. II, Amsterdam: John Benjamins.

Pütz, Martin, Susanne Niemeier, and René Dirven, eds (2001), *Applied Cognitive Lingustics II: Language Pedagogy,* Berlin: Mouton de Gruyter.

Queller, Kurt (2001) 'A usage-based approach to modeling and teaching the phrasal lexicon' in Pütz *et al.* (2001), 55–83.

Quine, Willard V.O. (1960), *Word and Object,* Cambridge, MA: MIT Press.

Quinn, Naomi (1987), 'Convergent models for a cultural model of American marriage' in Holland and Quinn (1987), 173–92.

Quirk, Randolph, Sidney Greenbaum, Geoffrey Leech and Jan Svartvik (1985), *A Comprehensive Grammar of the English Language,* London; New York: Longman.

Radden, Günter (1989), 'Figurative use of prepositions' in René, Dirven, Wolfgang Zydatiss and Willis J. Edmondson., eds (1989), *A User's Grammar of English,* Frankfurt: Lang, 551–76.

Radden, Günter (1992), 'The cognitive approach to natural language' in Pütz (1992), 513–41.

Radden, Günter and Zoltán Kövecses (1999), 'Towards a theory of metonymy' in Panther and Radden (1999), 17–59.

Radford, A. (1988), *Transformational Grammar,* Cambridge: Cambridge University Press.

Raskin, Victor (1985), *Semantic Mechanisms of Humor,* Dordrecht: D. Reidel.

Richards, Ivor A. (1936), *The Philosophy of Rhetoric,* Oxford: Oxford University Press.

Rifkin, Anthony (1985), 'Evidence for a basic level in event taxonomies', *Memory and Cognition* **13**, 538–56.

Rosch, Eleanor (1973), 'On the internal structure of perceptual and semantic categories' in Timothy E. Moore, ed., *Cognitive Development and the Acquisition of Language,* New York; San Francisco; London: Academic Press, 111–44.

Rosch, Eleanor (1975), 'Cognitive representations of semantic categories', *Journal of Experimental Psychology: General* **104**, 193–233.

Rosch, Eleanor (1977), 'Human categorization' in Neil Warren, ed., *Studies in Cross-Cultural Psychology, Vol. I,* London: Academic Press, 1–49.

Rosch, Eleanor (1978), 'Principles of categorization' in Eleanor Rosch and Barbara B. Lloyd, eds, *Cognition and Categorization,* Hillsdale, NJ; NY: Lawrence Erlbaum, 27–48.

Rosch, Eleanor (1988), 'Coherence and categorization: a historical view' in F.S. Kessel, ed., *The Development of Language and Language Researchers. Essays in Honor of Roger Brown,* Hillsdale, NJ; NY: Lawrence Erlbaum, 373–92.

Rosch, Eleanor and Caroline B. Mervis (1975), 'Family resemblances: studies in the internal structure of categories', *Cognitive Psychology* **7**, 573–605.

Rosch, Eleanor, Caroline B. Mervis, Wayne D. Gray, David M. Johnson and Penny Boyes-Braem (1976), 'Basic objects in natural categories', *Cognitive Psychology* **8**, 382–439.

Roth, Emilie M. and Edward J. Shoben (1983), 'The effect of context on the structure of categories', *Cognitive Psychology* **15**, 346–78.

Rudzka-Ostyn, Brygida, ed. (1988), *Topics in Cognitive Linguistics,* Amsterdam; Philadelphia: John Benjamins.

Ruiz de Mendoza Ibañez, Francisco José (2000), 'The role of mappings and domains in understanding metonymy' in Barcelona (2000), 109–32.

Sandikcioglu, Esra (2000), 'More metaphorical warfare in the gulf: orientalist frames in news coverage' in Barcelona (2000), 299–320.

Saussure, Ferdinand de (1985 [1913]), *Cours de linguistique générale.* Paris: Edition Payot.

Schank, Roger C. and Roger P. Abelson (1977), *Scripts, Plans, Goals and Understanding,* Hillsdale, NJ; NY: Lawrence Erlbaum.

Schmid, Hans-Jörg (1993), *Cottage and Co., Idea, Start vs. Begin: Die Kategorisierung als Grundprinzip einer differenzierten Bedeutungsbeschreibung,* Tübingen: Niemeyer.

Schmid, Hans-Jörg (1996a), 'Basic level categories as basic cognitive and linguistic building blocks' in Edda Weigand and Franz Hundsnurscher, eds, *Lexical Structure and Language Use.* Proceedings of the International Conference on 'Lexicology and Lexical Semantics', Münster 1994, Tübingen: Niemeyer, 285–95.

Schmid, Hans-Jörg (1996b), 'The historical development and present-day use of the noun *idea* as documented in the OED and other corpora', *Poetica* **47**, 87–128.

Schmid, Hans-Jörg (1996c), Review of Geeraerts *et al.* (1994), *Lexicology* **2**, 78–84.

Schmid, Hans-Jörg (2000), *English Abstract Nouns as Conceptual Shells: From Corpus to Cognition,* Berlin: Mouton de Gruyter.

Schmid, Hans-Jörg (2003), 'Introduction: context and cognition – a concern shared by the cognitive sciences' in Ewald Mengel, Hans-Jörg Schmid and Michael Steppat, eds, *Anglistentag 2002 Bayreuth: Proceedings,* Trier: Wissenschaftlicher Verlag Trier, 363–7.

Schmid, Hans-Jörg (2005), *Englische Morphologie und Wortbildung: Eine Einführung,* Berlin: Erich Schmidt.

Schmid, Hans-Jörg (forthcoming), 'Entrenchment, salience and basic levels' in Dirk Geeraerts and Hubert Cuyckens, eds, *Handbook of Cognitive Linguistics,* Oxford: Oxford University Press.

Schmid, Hans-Jörg and Karina Kopatsch (forthcoming), 'Alienation or adaptation? A cognitive-semantic study of Nigerian English words in comparison with American English, Hausa and Fulfulde'.

Schmid-Schönbein, Gisela (2001), *Didaktik: Grundschulenglisch*. Berlin: Cornelsen.

Schneider, Kristina (1998), 'Prototypentheorie und Bedeutungswandel: die Entwicklung von HARVEST, GRASP und GLAD', *Rostocker Beiträge zur Sprachwissenschaft* **5**, 29–48.

Schön, Donald (1993), 'Generative metaphor: a perspective on problem solving social policy' in Ortony (1993), 137–63.

Schulze, Rainer (1988), 'A short story of *down*' in Hüllen and Schulze (1988), 395–414.

Searle, John R. (1979), *Expression and Meaning*, Cambridge: Cambridge University Press.

Searle, John R. (1975), 'Indirect speech acts' in Peter Cole and Jerry L. Morgan, eds, *Syntax and Semantics. Volume 3*, 59–82.

Seto, Ken-ichi (1999), 'Distinguishing metonymy from synecdoche' in Panther and Radden (1999), 91–120.

Shaver, Phillip, Judith Schwartz, Donald Kirson and Cary O'Connor (1987), 'Emotion knowledge: further exploration of a prototype approach', *Journal of Personality and Social Psychology* **52**, 1061–86.

Sinha, Chris, ed. (1995), 'Special issues on spatial language and cognition', *Cognitive Linguistics* **6**, 1–3.

Slobin, Dan I. (1996), 'Typology and rhetoric: verbs of motion in English and Spanish' in Masayoshi Shibatani and Sandra A. Thompson, eds, *Grammatical Constructions: Their Form and Meaning*, Oxford: Oxford University Press.

Slobin, Dan I. (2004), 'The many ways to search for a frog: linguistic typology and the expression of motion events' in Strömquist, S and I. Verhoeven, eds, *Relating Events in Narrative: Typological and Contextual Perspectives*. Mahwah, NJ: Erlbaum, 219–57.

Slobin, Dan I. (2005), 'Linguistic representation of motion events: what is signifier and what is signified?' in Maeder *et al.* (2005), 307–22.

Smith, Edward E. (1978), 'Theories of semantic memory' in W.K. Esters, ed., *Handbook of Learning and Cognitive Processes, Vol. 6*, Potomac, MD.

Smith, Edward E. and Douglas L. Medin (1981), *Categories and Concepts*, Cambridge, MA; London: Harvard University Press.

Smith, Edward E., Daniel N. Osherson, Lance J. Rips and Margaret Keane

(1988), 'Combining prototypes: a selective modification model', *Cognitive Science* **12**, 485–527.

Sperber, Dan and Deirdre Wilson (1995), *Relevance. Communication and Cognition,* 2nd edn, Oxford: Blackwell.

Springer, Ken and Gregory Murphy (1992), 'Feature availability in conceptual combinations', *Psychological Science* **3**, 111–17.

Steen Gerard, (1994), *Understanding Metaphor in Literature: An Empirical Approach,* London: Longman.

Stein, Gabriele (1991), 'Illustrations in dictionaries', *International Journal of Lexicography* **4**, 99–127.

Stern, Joseph (1999), *Metaphor in Context,* Cambridge, MA; London: MIT Press.

Stuessy, Tod F. (1990), *Plant Taxonomy: The Systematic Evaluation of Comparative Data,* New York: Columbia University Press.

Sweetser, Eve E. (1990), *From Etymology to Pragmatics: Metaphorical and Cultural Aspects of Semantic Structure,* Cambridge: Cambridge University Press.

Sweetser, Eve E. (1996), 'Mental spaces and the grammar of conditional constructions' in Fauconnier and Sweetser (1996), 318–33.

Sweetser, Eve E. (1999), 'Compositionality and blending: semantic composition in a cognitively realistic framework' in Theo Janssen and Gisela Redeker, eds (1999), *Cognitive Linguistics: Foundations, Scope and Methodology,* Berlin; New York: Mouton de Gruyter, 129–62.

Talmy, Leonard (1985), 'Lexicalization patterns: Semantic structure in lexical forms' in Timothy Shoper, ed., *Language typology and syntactic description,* vol. 3, Cambridge: Cambridge University Press, 36–149.

Talmy, Leonard (1991), 'Path to realization: a typology of event conflation', Proceedings of the Seventeenth Annual Meeting of the Berkeley Linguistics Society, Berkeley: Berkeley Linguistic Society, 480–519.

Talmy, Leonard (2000), *Toward a Cognitive Semantics,* 2 vols., Cambridge, MA; London: MIT Press.

Taylor, John R. (1988), 'Contrasting prepositional categories: English and Italian' in Rudzka-Ostyn (1988), 299–326.

Taylor, John R. (1993), 'Some pedagogical implications of cognitive grammar' in Geiger and Rudzka-Ostyn (1993), 201–26.

Taylor, John R. (2002), *Cognitive Grammar,* Oxford: Oxford University Press.

Taylor, John R. (2003), *Linguistic Categorization,* 3rd edn, Oxford: Oxford University Press.

Taylor, John R. and Robert E. MacLaury, eds (1995), *Language and the Cognitive Construal of the World,* Berlin: Mouton de Gruyter.

Tesnière, Lucien (1959), *Eléments de syntaxe structurale,* Paris: Librairie C Klincksieck.

Thornburg, Linda and Klaus-Uwe Panther (1997), 'Speech act metonymies' in Wolf Andreas Liebert, Gisela Redeker and Linda Waugh, eds, *Discourse and Perspectives in Cognitive Linguistics,* Amsterdam: John Benjamins, 205–19.

Tomasello, Michael (2003), *Constructing a Language: A Usage-Based Theory of Language Acquisition,* Cambridge, MA: Harvard University Press.

Tsohatzidis, Savas L., ed. (1990), *Meanings and Prototypes: Studies on Linguistic Categorization,* Oxford: Routledge.

Tuggy, David (1993), 'Ambiguity, polysemy, and vagueness', *Cognitive Linguistics* **4**, 273–90.

Turner, Mark (1993), 'An image-schematic constraint on metaphor' in Geiger and Rudzka-Ostyn (1993), 291–306.

Turner, Mark and Gilles Fauconnier (1995), 'Conceptual integration and formal expression', *Journal of Metaphor and Symbolic Activity* **10** (3), 183–204.

Tversky, Barbara (1990), 'Where partonomies and taxonomies meet' in Tsohatzidis (1990), 334–44.

Tversky, Barbara and Kathleen Hemenway (1984), 'Objects, parts, and categories', *Journal of Experimental Psychology: General* **113**, 169–93.

Tyler, Andrea and Vyvyan Evans (2004), 'Applying cognitive linguistics to pedagogical grammar: the case of *over'* in Achard and Niemeier (2004), 257–80.

Ullmann, Stephen (1957), *The Principles of Semantics,* 2nd edn, Oxford; Glasgow: Basil Blackwell.

Ullmann, Stephen (1962), *Semantics: An Introduction to the Science of Meaning,* Oxford: Basil Blackwell.

Ungerer, Friedrich (1994), 'Basic level concepts and parasitic categorization: an alternative to conventional semantic hierarchies', *Zeitschrift für Anglistik und Amerikanistik* **42**, 148–62.

Ungerer, Friedrich (1995), 'The linguistic and cognitive relevance of basic emotions' in René Dirven and Johan Vanparys, eds, *Current Approaches to the Lexicon,* Frankfurt Main: Peter Lang, 185–209.

Ungerer, Friedrich (1999), 'Iconicity in word-formation' in Nänny and Fischer (1999), 307–24.

Ungerer, Friedrich (2000a), 'Muted metaphors and the activation of metonymies in advertising' in Barcelona (2000), 321–40.

Ungerer, Friedrich (2000b), *Englische Grammatik heute,* Stuttgart: Klett.

Ungerer, Friedrich (2001), 'Basicness and conceptual hierarchies in foreign language learning' in Pütz *et al.* (2001), 201–21.

Ungerer, Friedrich (2002), 'The conceptual function of derivational word-formation in English', *Anglia* **120**, 534–67

Ungerer, Friedrich (forthcoming (a)),'Derivational morphology and word-formation' in Dirk Geeraerts and Hubert Cuyckens, eds, *Handbook of Cognitive Linguistics,* Oxford: Oxford University Press.

Ungerer, Friedrich (forthcoming (b)), 'Iconic text strategies: path, sorting & weighting, kaleidoscope' to appear in Elsbieta Tabakowska and Christina Ljungberg, eds, *Iconicity in Language and Literature,* Vol. 5. Amsterdam: John Benjamins.

Ungerer, Friedrich and Hans-Jörg Schmid (1998), 'Englische Komposita und Kategorisierung', *Rostocker Beiträge zur Sprachwissenschaft* **5**, 77–98.

Ungerer, Friedrich, Peter Pasch, Peter Lampater and Rosemary Hellyer-Jones (2004), *A Guide to Grammar,* new edn, Stuttgart: Klett.

van Dijk, Teun (1981), *Studies in the Pragmatics of Discourse,* The Hague: Mouton.

van Dijk, Teun (1999), 'Context models in discourse processing' in Herre van Oostendorp and Susan R. Goldman, eds, *The Construction of Mental Representations during Reading,* Mahwah, NJ: Lawrence Erlbaum Associates, 123–48.

Vandeloise, Claude (1994), 'Methodology and analyses of the preposition *in', Cognitive Linguistics* **5,** 157–84.

Verschueren, Jef (1985), *What People Say They Do with Words: Prolegomena to an Empirical–Conceptual Approach to Linguistic Action,* Norwood, NJ: Ablex.

Vinay, J.-P. and J. Darbelnet (1975), *Stylistique comparée du français et de l'anglais,* nouvelle édition, Paris: Didier.

West, Michael (1953), *A General Service List of English Words,* London: Longman.

Wierzbicka, Anna (1985), *Lexicography and Conceptual Analysis,* Ann Arbor: Karoma.

Wierzbicka, Anna (1986), 'Human emotions: universal or culture specific?', *American Anthropologist* **88**, 584–94.

Wierzbicka, Anna (1988), 'The semantics of emotions: *fear* and its relatives in English,' *Australian Journal of Linguistics* **10**, 359–75.

Wilkinson, Peter R. (1993), *Thesaurus of Traditional English Metaphors*, London; New York: Routledge.

Wilson, Deirdre and Dan Sperber (2003), 'Relevance theory' in Horn and Ward (2003), 607–32.

Wilson, John (1990), *Politically Speaking: The Pragmatic Analysis of Political Language*, Oxford: Blackwell.

Wittgenstein, Ludwig (1958), *Philosophical Investigations*, transl. by G.E.M. Anscobe, 2nd edn, Oxford: Blackwell.

Wright Andrew (2001), *Pictures for Language Learning*. Cambridge: Cambridge University Press.

Wright Andrew and Safia Haleem (1995), *Visuals for the Language Classroom*, London: Longman.

Yantis, Steven, ed. (2001), *Visual Perception: Essential Readings*, Philadelphia: Psychology Press.

Index of persons

Abelson, R.P. 214–16, 254
Abrahamsen, A. 63
Achard, M. 342
Aitchison, J. 45, 60, 62, 90, 113, 132
Akman, V. 62
Allerton, D.J. 204
Anderson, J. 255
Armstrong, S.L. 42, 44
Aske, J. 255
Atkins, B.T. 210, 254
Attardo, S. 299

Barcelona, A. 130, 159–61
Barsalou, L.W. 11, 63
Barthes, R. 281
Bauer, L. 112
Bechtel, W. 63
Bencini, G. 256
Berlin, B. 8–10, 12f, 60, 67, 69f, 73,
    102, 111
Berman, R, 238, 255
Black, M. 19–21, 116, 118, 253,
    307, 312
Blakemore, D. 299
Bouquet, P. 62
Boyd, R. 147f, 150, 161
Breedlove, D. 67
Broccias, C. 265
Brown, C. 41, 80, 110f
Brown, R. 8, 67, 70, 72
Brugman, C.M. 160, 168, 204, 247
Bybee, J. 341

Cain, A.J. 110
Clark, E.H. 60
Clark, H.H. 60
Coleman, L. 42, 101f
Colston, H.L. 112

Coulson, S. 112, 259, 271, 288,
    297–9
Croft, W. 59–62, 89, 111f, 159–61, 205,
    252, 255f
Cruse, D.A. 59–62, 88f, 111–13, 159–61,
    205, 256
Cuyckens, H. 203

Dancygier, B. 298
Darbelnet, J. 231, 234, 242f, 255
Davitz, J. 134
Dirven, R. 60, 63, 107, 155, 161f, 217,
    254, 333, 336f, 340, 342
Dixon, R.M.W. 113

Elbers, L. 159
Evans, V. 333f, 342
Eysenck, M.W. 254

Fauconnier, G. 5, 160, 257–60, 262–7,
    269, 279, 283–5, 288, 295,
    297–9, 345
Fehr, B. 42, 140, 161
Fillmore, C.C. 5, 113, 181, 204, 207–11,
    217, 229, 245, 250–2, 254–6
Fischer, O. 340, 342
Fontanelle, T. 254
Foolen, A. 256
Forceville, C. 298
Frajzyngier, Z. 256
Frank, R. 63, 245, 275f, 280
Fried, M. 256

Gallese, V. 345
Geeraerts, D. 59–62, 111, 113, 138,
    313, 320, 341
Gentner, D. 63, 161f
Gibbs, R.W. Jr. 112, 159, 162, 265

Givón, T. 256, 299, 302, 304, 346
Goddard, C. 161
Goldberg, A.E. 5, 245–9, 253, 255f
Goossens, L. 161
Gordon, I.E. 61, 204
Grady, J.E. 160, 297
Greenbaum, S. 191
Grice, H.P. 201, 299
Grondelaers, S. 138

Haleem, S. 342
Halliday, M.A.K. 47, 204, 206
Hampe, B. 160
Hampton, J.A. 26
Hasan, R. 47
Heider, E.R. 12f, 60
Heine, B. 321, 324–6, 342
Hemenway, K. 112
Herbst, T. 204
Heyvaert, L. 256
Holdcroft, D. 340
Holland, D. 63
Hopper, P.J. 341f
Hunn, E.S. 111

Jakobson, R. 161
Jasperson, R. 256
Jeziorski, M. 162
Johnson, M. 4, 60, 63, 104, 112, 118,
    121–4, 138f, 150, 159–62, 345
Johnson–Laird, P.N. 63, 138f, 161

Kager, R. 297
Katz, J. 61
Kay, P. 8–10, 12–14, 42, 60, 70, 101f,
    250–2, 255f
Keane, M. 254
Kemmer, S. 298
Kempton, W. 57
King, D.B. 61
Kirkpatrick, B. 66
Kleiber, G. 59, 62, 110f
Koestler, A. 284f, 298
Koffka, K. 61
Köhler, W. 61
Kolb, B. 345
Kopatsch, K. 54f, 59
Kövecses, Z. 133–6, 141–3, 156, 159–62,
    331f, 342, 345

Kuhn, T.S. 148f, 161
Kurtyka, A. 342

Labov, W. 20–2, 33–6, 60, 101f
Lakoff , G. 4, 41f, 59–63, 104, 109f,
    112f, 117–19, 121–4, 128, 133,
    135f, 142f, 150–2, 159–62, 168,
    171, 173, 189, 204f, 247, 298, 345
Lambrecht, K. 256
Langacker, R.W. 5, 48, 61–3, 98, 112f,
    118, 139, 145f, 176–84, 186,
    188–202, 204–6, 210f, 254, 256,
    332, 342
Leech, G.N. 61, 112, 115f, 159f, 307, 341
Lehrer, A. 268, 298
Leisi, E. 63
Lenneberg, E.H. 8, 10
Lindner, S.J. 168, 171
Lipka, L. 53, 61f, 111–13, 159f
Lyons, J. 58, 60f, 111

Malblanc, A. 255
Mandelblit, N. 259, 298
Markman, A.B. 60, 62, 254
Masuda, K. 306, 308, 341
Mayer, M. 238
Mayer, R. 162
McArthur, T. 110f
McCloskey, M. 56
McDaniel, C.K. 14, 60
Medin, D.L. 60–2, 254
Meillet, A. 321
Mervis, C.B. 29, 31, 33f, 42, 61,
    111, 146
Minsky, M. 213, 218
Moser, S. 341
Murphy, G.L. 112
Musolff , A. 162

Nänny, M. 340
Nerlich, B. 159
Newman, J. 204
Niemeier, S. 60, 132, 342
Nöth, W. 340

Oakley, T. 259, 297
Oliver, D.C. 60
Ortony, A. 161
Östman, J.-O. 256

Panther, K.-U. 157, 161f
Plato 300f, 340
Podhorodecka, J. 306f, 341
Pörings, R. 161
Postal, P. 61
Putnam, H. 60
Pütz, M. 60, 63, 342

Queller, K. 342
Quine, W.V.O. 20, 59
Quinn, N. 63, 131
Quirk, R. 191, 204, 255, 297

Radden, G. 156, 160–2, 302
Radford, A. 204
Raskin, V. 285, 299
Raven, P. 67
Richards, I.A. 116
Rifkin, A. 106, 113
Rosch, E. 4, 11–18, 26, 29, 31, 33f, 41f,
    54, 59–62, 72, 74–7, 80, 84, 102,
    107, 111f, 146, 292, 343
Rosenbach, A. 342
Ross, B.H. 60, 62, 254
Roth, E.M. 62
Rudzka–Ostyn, B. 332, 342
Ruiz de Mendoza Ibañez, F.J. 126,
    131, 160

Sandikcioglu, E. 162
Saussure, F. de 300f, 340
Schank, R.C. 214–16, 254
Schmid, H.-J. 35, 54f, 59, 62, 93, 110,
    112f, 124, 156, 162, 204, 248,
    253, 273, 318f, 329, 342
Schmid-Schönbein, G. 342
Schneider, K. 341
Schön, D. 161
Schulze, R. 203
Searle, J. 47, 158, 201
Seto, K. 112
Shaver, P. 134, 161
Shoben, E.J. 62
Sinha, C. 203
Slobin, D.I. 5, 236–9, 241–3, 255
Smith, E.E. 44, 60–2, 112

Sperber, D. 5, 288–94, 299
Springer, K. 112
Steen, G. 160
Stein, G. 62
Stern, J. 160
Stevens, A.L. 63
Stuessy, T.F. 110
Sweetser, E.E. 112, 298, 341

Talmy, L. 5, 161, 179, 204, 211, 217,
    219–29, 231, 234–6, 244, 254f,
    263, 321f, 342
Taylor, J.R. 59f, 107, 110f, 113, 203–5,
    336f, 340, 342
Tesnière, L. 186
Thornburg, L. 157, 162
Traugott, E.C. 341f
Tuggy, D. 60
Turner, M. 5, 112, 117–19, 121, 128,
    159f, 257–60, 262–7, 269, 284f,
    288, 295, 297f, 345
Tversky, B. 41, 112
Tyler, Andrea 333f, 342

Ullmann, S. 59, 159f
Ungerer, F. 93, 98, 110–13, 139, 158,
    298, 335, 340–2

van der Leek, F. 256
van Dijk, T. 62
Vandeloise, C. 204
Verschueren, J. 102
Verspoor, M. 340
Vinay, J.-P. 231, 234, 242f, 255

Wertheimer, M. 61
West, M. 328f
Wierzbicka, A. 44, 61, 111, 138, 161, 256
Wilkinson, P.R. 117
Wilson, D. 5, 288–94, 299
Wilson, J. 151
Wishaw, I.Q. 345
Wittgenstein, L. 28f, 79, 146
Wright, A. 342

Yantis, S. 204

Index of subject

References to the main passages are indicated by bold page numbers.

abstract categories 2, 4, 40, 318f, 334

abstract noun 248

acronym 271, 273–5, 279f

actants 177

action categories 101–10, 122, 125

action chain 179–91, 199f, 203

ad-hoc blends 269

adjective 68, 106–8, 113, 140, 194–8, 297, 308

advertisement 289

advertising 3, 275, 280f, 310

agent (as a semantic role) 58, 155f, 159, 162, **177–90**, 200, 202, 226–8, 240, 244, 247f, 260f, 263, 265, 275–8, 286f

Alsatian 45f

American English 18, 54f

analogy 122, 323, 342

anchorage 281

anger 2, 121, 126, 132–44, 161, 331f, 345

animal 4, 64, 66, 70, 86f, 100, 111, 330f

anthropological linguistics 52

apple juice 92f, 95, 97–9, 104, 145, 271

Arabic 58, 234, 305

archetype *see* role archtetype

argument 121–8

argument structure 249, 279

aspect 312, 324–6, 335, 337, 339

associations 1–3, 43, 58, 79, 86, 90, 120, 274, 281, 283, 287, 306, 308, 312, 320

assumptions 289–97

atom (as a solar system) 148f

attention 3, 5f, 11f, 14, 66, 172, 202, **210f**, 218, 221–5, 228f, 239, 241, 254, 263, 269, 295, 322, 344f

attentional view (in cognitive linguistics) 3, 5

attribute listing **31–3**, 55, 77, 93, 95, 315

attribute-based typicality ratings **31**, 34, 40, 47, 61

attributes 1, 4, **24–8**
  and action categories 104f
  and basic-level categories 70
  and cognitive economy 71
  and dimensions 33f
  and essential features 25f
  and family resemblances 28–31, 42f
  and gestalt perception 34–6
  and lexical change 314–19
  and types of metaphorical mapping 124f
  and subordinate categories (salient specific attribute) 81
  and superordinate categories (salient general attribute) 82–4, 123
  category-wide attributes 29, 43f, 77, 79, 146
  cognitive status of 42f
  distinctive attributes 25, 32
  evaluative attributes 120
  functional attributes 37f
  non-derived attributes 95, 97, 112
  salient attributes 91, 125, 140, 315
  weight of 27, 33, 47, 58, 94
  see also essential features

bad examples of categories 16–18, **23–7**, 29, 32f, 40, 42, 92, 105

ballacktisch 69f

base (of comparison) 116, 119

base (in profiling) **192–4**, 198, 202

basic colour terms 10–13, 23, 101f, 108, 132

basic correlation **120**, 126, 131, 160, 321, 324

basic domain 113, 193, 198

basic emotion categories **138–41**, 144

basic emotions 138–41, 161

basic level categories 4, 6, **64**, **70–5**, 266, 292

and cognitive economy 71, 76, 292

and domains 192f

and image schemas 167

and prototypes 75f

in foreign language teaching 328–32, 338, 343

sources for conceptual metaphors 123, 125, 135, 137, 139f, 143f,

sources for subordinate categories 79–81

sources for superordinate categories 77–9

emergence of new basic level categories 95–8

see also cognitive efficiency

battle 122f, 125, 129

beach 49, 50, 57, 129, 193, 203, 283, 288

bean 68f, 76, 85, 92

beneficiary 184 *see also* role archetype

best examples 10f

billiard-ball metaphor 178

birds 7, 18, 24–8, 30, 38, 64, 75, 78, 122, 315f

bisociation 298

black bean 92, 99

blackbird 92, 100, 314

blended property 264, 269, 272f

blended space **259–282**, 284f, 287, 295, 298

blending *see* conceptual blending

bodily interaction 167

boundaries *see* categories, boundaries of

bowl 21–4, 34f, 42, 44, 77, 198, 343

break 2, 181, 226f, 243, 263, 265

breakfast 52f, 57, 106, 268, 288, 306

Buddhist monk (riddle of the) 284

building 36, 39, 48f, 85, 100, 105, 112, 121–6, 145f, 224, 273, 309

building-block metaphor 112

Bulgarian 305

bungalow 39

bus 32, 44, 55, 73, 77, 82f, 103, 191, 229

buy 207–10, 218

by-clause 228, 230

car 1–4, 29–32, 44, 58, 64, 67, 73f, 77, 83, 88, 90, 97f, 127, 230, 273, 290, 296, 320, 343

Case Grammar 210, 245

castle 43, 123, 125, 309

categorical view of categorization 25 *see also* classical view of categorization

categories (cognitive) **7f**, 22f.

and family resemblances 28–31

and foreign language teaching 328–32

and lexical change 316–19

boundaries of 7f, 11, 18–23, 26, 33, 41, 45, 57, 77, 99, 169, 187, 212, 343 *see also* fuzziness

cognitive status of 40–3

internal structure of 24–8

see also abstract categories; action categories; basic-level categories; category member; cognitive categories; colour categories; lexical categories; object categories; organism categories; prototype categories; shape categories; subordinate categories; superordinate categories

categorization 4, **8f**

and attributes 24–26

everyday 76, 80, 86, 91

levels of 64ff, 70, 72, 89, 101

of colours 12–14

of concrete objects 19, 23f, 35, 38–43, 64, 76, 140, 304, 309, 318

of shapes 14–16

of organisms and objects 16–18

of plants (in Tzeltal) 67–9

prototype view of 7–45

scientific 65–7, 85–7

see also categories; children; parasitic categorisation

categorization task 35

category member 16, 18, 26, 29–33, 41–43, 46, 49, 62, 72f, 77–80, 146, 155, 269, 296, 314–18, 320, 343

category membership 18, 31, 41f, 62, 78, 146
category structure 24, 34, 42–7, 57, 62, 76, 79, 92, 106f, 124, 168, 313–17, 320, 341
causal-chain 226–230, 244, 263
causal-chain windowing 226–9
causation 104, 139, 160, 218, 221, 226f, 244, 255, 263
causation event-frame 221
cause
  as component of an event-frame 220f, 228, 231, 240, 244–8, 253f, 258,
  as semantic primitive 103f
  in metonymies 133f, 142f.
  see also cause-effect
cause-effect 120, 129, 131, 133, 154, 258, 262–75, 281, 286f, 295, 344f
central schema 168–75
cereal 85, 306
chair 2, 19–23, 29–31, 37f, 42, 53, 70f, 74–81, 84, 88, 95f, 106, 112, 138, 145f, 203, 215, 271, 300, 344
chair museum 19–21
charge 208f
cherry jeans 271–3
children
  and metaphor 114, 140, 159
  as test persons 12–14
  and language/category acquisition 79, 89f, 103f, 140, 159, 328ff
church 44, 110, 191
class inclusion 64f, 69, 91
classical model of categorization 41
classical view of categories 25, 27, 29f, 42, 61
classification 8, 11f, 19f, 87, 110
  plant classification 67–9
  of semantic roles 78
  scientific classification 42, 62, 65–7, 76, 86, 91, 111
clause patterns 2, 176, 178, 181, 183, 185, 198, 207, 210, 247f, 252, 255, 278, 325, 344
clothing 17, 23, 31, 73f, 85, 111, 113, 236, 273, 330
coach 159, 316–19
coat 94–97, 264, 267

coat collar 94, 97
COBUILD 25
cognitive categories 4, 8, 11, 19, 22–6, 32, 45, 48, 52, 58, 62–66, 71, 76–9, 83, 96–101, 108, 110, 141, 178, 194, 211–13 see also categories; categorization
cognitive economy 71, 76, 111, 291f, 296, 344
cognitive effect 291f
cognitive effectiveness 291
cognitive efficiency 291–3, 296
cognitive environment 288–96
Cognitive Grammar 118, 176, 191, 202, 205, 210, 256
cognitive intake 185, 191, 192
cognitive model 47–58, 63, 95–101, 106, 118, 129f, 142, 302f, 338, 343
  and conceptual hierarchies 90–2
  and emotion metaphors 144f, 152f–8, 162
  and frames/scripts 207, 212, 218
  and mental spaces 258, 261, 289, 295f.
  naive model 56, 59
cognitive network 328, 330
cognitive network representation 338
cognitive processing 5, 11, 191, 194, 196, 198, 200, 211, 223, 258, 261, 271, 283, 293, 296
cognitive region 195–8
cognitive unit 99, 191–8, 202f, 212
cognitive-experiential access 328, 338f
collecting function 83–5
colour 8–16, 19, 23, 25, 37, 41f, 60, 80–4, 92f, 99, 106–108, 132, 165, 192f, 202, 271f, 310, 320
colour categories 8, 10–14, 41f
commercial event 207–11, 218
communicative relevance 290–4
completion (as a blending process) 259–261, 269
composite term 86, 99, 104
composition
  as a blending process 259–63, 268f
  as a word-formation process 94–107, 112, 145, 271, 328
compound 19, 94–107, 145f, 175, 271–273

compression **260–71**, 275–7, 282–4, 287f, 293, 295 *see also* conceptual blending
concept 4, **8**, 48
  as source in metaphors 115-60
conceptual blending 5, 112, **257–99**
  and acronyms 273–5
  and advertising 281–3
  and metaphor 257–61
  and compounds 271–3
  and constructions 275–7
  and morphological blends 268–71
  governing rules of 265–7
  see also compression; forced blend; governing principles
conceptual metaphor 4, **114–60**, 257f, 297, 319, 331, 345
conceptual metonymy 115, **127–44**, **154–9**
consistency profile 21, 34
constitutive metaphor 150, 153, 161
construction 5, **245–50**
  and conceptual blending 275–7
  argument-structure construction 246–8
  caused-motion construction 244–8
  cause-receive construction 246f, 253, 276, 344
  idioms as constructions 250–2
  resultative construction 246f, 253, 280
  shell-content construction 248–50
Construction Grammar **244ff**, 255f, 275, 344
container schema 119, 121–4, 127, 135, 137, 141–3, 154, 161, 187–91, 200, 248
context 4, 21f, 335, **42–52**, 57f,
  and metaphors 115–18
  and metonymies 128f
  and word-formation 156f
  in conceptual blending 257–61, 267, 270–5
  of culture 47, 52
context-dependence 22, 45, 58, 62, 99, 346
contiguity 88, 115, 128f, 154, 159
conventionalization 121, 130f
conventionalized metaphor 131

conversion 155–9
copulative compounds 100
corn 69, 76, 85
corpora 124, 138, 244, 278, 329
correlation *see* basic correlation
cost 207f, 211, 229
cottage 36, 39, 43
colour *see* focal colours
countability 335
counterfactuals 278f
creature 86, 111
cross-space mapping 260, 265, 269–75, 281f, 295
cross-space relation 263, 277–81, 284, 287
cultural model 4, 45, **51–9**, 63, 73, 76, 85, 99, 106, 118, 305, 309, 343
culture 12, 47, 51, 54, 67f, 120, 144, 218f, 274, 311, 329
culture-dependent evaluation 120
cup 20–2, 33–5, 42, 44f, 77, 99, 106, 343
cutlery 4, 52, 84

daisy 80f, 98–101
dandelion 80–2, 98–100, 104
Dani 12–16
desk 53f, 90, 330
diachronic 59, 316
dictionary 24–6, 28, 32, 39, 132, 211, 229, 243, 254, 279
derived metaphor 135
dime 80, 98f
dimension 22, **33f**, 43, 84, 101, 108, 110
  of compression in conceptual blending 262–5
direct object 184, 205, 208
discourse 47, 205
  discourse context 157
  discourse participant 252, 289
  discourse situation 158
  literary discourse 160
  scientific discourse 86
discourse space 62
ditransitive 246, 277
domain 3f, 48f, 51, 63, 113, 160, 186, **191–3**, 202, 205
  basic 198
  elementary 192f, 198, 202
double-scope network 298

eat 11, 52, 103, 105f, 110, 120, 293f, 325
efficiency 75, 291f, 296, 344
elaboration
    as blending process 259–61
    of image schemas 158, 174
elevator 31
embodiment 337, 344 *see also* bodily experience; bodily interaction
emotion concepts 4, 132, **138–44**
emotion scenarios 141–3
emotion words 133, 138f
English 5, 8–13, 23, 39, 52–5, 65, 68, 76, 84, 86f, 103, 105, 110f, 118, 131, 133, 138f, 144, 160f, 204, 207, 212, 220f, 228, 231–44, 255, 264, 273, 275, 280, 303–8, 312–40
enter 196f, 237, 309
entrenched 117, 120f, 268, 271, 279, 283, 286, 338
entrenchment 110, 121, 130, 265f, 270, 272, 345
essential features 25f, 30, 41, 61
estate car 32, 67, 73, 74
evaluation *see* culture-dependent evaluation
event
    and viewing arrangement 200–2
    commercial event 211f
    social event 129
event categories/concepts 105f, 110, 113, 125, 135, 150, 154, 303
event schema 275, 309, 325, 342
event sequence 214
event-frame 211, **218–43**, 254, 344
    causal-chain 227–9
    closed-path 223f
    cyclic 221
    interrelationship 221
    motion 5, **219–30**, 240–4
    participant-interaction 221
experience
    basic **76**, 88, 90, **101**, 106, 108–10, 139, 150, 154, 258
    bodily experience 4, 91, 108f, 119f, 263, 308, 344f
    collective 51, 55f, 58
        in emotion metaphors 133, 137, 139

everyday 51, 57
    see also embodiment; experiential view of language; image schema
experienced (as semantic role) **182–5**, 276f
experiencer (as semantic role) **177f**, 182–5, 202, 276f
experiential
    access to foreign language learning 328, 338f
    attribute 95, 97
    correlations 160
    grounding of constructions 246f, 252
    prototype 26, 41
    view of language 2, 4, 299
experimental evidence 40
expert model 55f, 59
explanatory metaphor 146, 151, 153, 260
explicature 294
extension
    metaphorical 172f
    of senses 247f, 322f
eye 101, 114–6

family resemblances 4, 24, **28–30**, 40–5, 77–9, 314f
fear 132–44
figure **163–6**, 174, 176, 191–210
    syntactic **177–90**, 200, 202, 205, 210f, 344
figure/ground 5, **163–7**, 174–7, 181–5, 191–5, 200–5, 208, 219, 290, 308, 344
figure/ground segregation 5, **163f**, 177, 185, 193, 202, 204, 208, 219, 290, 344
flower 24, 80f, 98–101, 246, 331
focal colours 9, 11–15, 41, 67
folk taxonomies 64, **67–70**, 76, 84f, 87, 91, 99f
food 54, 63, 85, 91f, 120, 137, 330
forced blend 283 *see also* conceptual blending
foreign language teaching 328–42
frame 5, 49, 63, 106, 142, 176, **207–18** *see also* event-frame
framing function (of event-frame components) 234

French 5, 52f, 98, 186, 231–6, 241–3, 255, 262, 305, 321, 329
frog story 243
fruit 17f, 29, 31f, 59, 73, 77, 85, 331
function
  assembling 88
  collecting 84–6
  explanatory function (of metaphors) 148–50, 153
  highlighting 81–5, 104, 131, 140, 160, 209, 244, 279, 287, 333
  of types of metaphors 127f
  referential function (of metonymies) 131
functionally relevant parts 37–40, 43
furniture 17, 29–31, 73–81, 84, 198, 330f
fuzziness 19–24, 60, 77, 343

game 12, 28f, 44, 51, 79, 152
gapping 222, 226 *see also* windowing
gender 193, 201, 335
generalization 313, 316
generic level 67–70, 76, 125
generic metaphor 125f, 135, 258
generic space 259 *see also* conceptual blending
German 5, 9, 16, 51, 63, 205, 232–4, 255, 257, 269, 305, 325, 329, 337
gerund 336f, 340
gestalt 5f, 15, 24, **34–44**, 61, 72–7, 80, 88, 90, 99, 102–5, 110, 113, 139, 145, 160, 163, 165, 192, 196, 265f, 292, 296, 309, 328, 333–9, 342, 344
gestalt principles 36f, 43, 61, 165
gestalt psychology 15, 37, 40, 44, 61
give 18, 24, 183–5, 204, 304
going-to future 321–324
goodness-of-example 17f, 24, 31–6, 45–7, 51, 54f, 58, 62, 70, 140, 315
governing principles 267, 288, 295, 298
grammaticalization 5, **321–42**
ground *see* figure; figure/ground; figure/ground-segregation
  in traditional metaphor theory 115f, 119
  syntactic ground 177, 180, 184–9, 200, 202, 205, 211

grounding
  in basic experiences 90, 160, 344
  in cognitive grammar 202, 206
Gulf War 151, 162

height 8, 33–36
hierarchy 9, **64–9**, 85–91, 99f, 105, 109–12, 181, 266, 295, 328, 330, 343
  multi-level hierarchy 86
highlighting *see* function, highlighting
holistic
  conceptualisation 266, 292, 295, 309f, 334, 337f, 342, 344f
  perception 36, 43, 75, 80, 292
  transfer 309f.
house 4, 36, 39, 44, 57, 77, 81, 88–92, 100, 123, 125, 129, 132, 145, 154, 165–8, 174, 219–21, 236f, 264, 293, 309, 311f, 330f
house in the country 36
human scale 260, 266f *see also* conceptual blending
humour 299

ICE-GB 244, 278
icon 301, 340
iconic proximity 301–4
iconic quantity 301–3
iconic sequencing 301, 311
iconicity 5, **300–12**, 340f
  imagic 305, 308
idea 124, 127, 249, 319
identification 11f, 74, 99, 196
identity (as a vital relation) **260–5**, 269–72, 275–81, 284, 287, 295
idiom 5, **250–3**, 256, 331, 339, 344
if-clause 279, 345
image-schema 4, 109, 112, 119, 122, 124, 130, 134f, 154, 169–75, 187, 191, 204, 233, 266, 304, 308, 322, 331, 342, 344
implicature 202
indirect speech act 157
inference 213, 217, 289f, 294
infinitive 248–50, 312, 324, 336f, 340
infotainment 268
input space 259–78, 281–7, 295, 298
  see also conceptual blending

insect 72, 86, 315
instrument (as semantic role) 155–9,
    178, 180–5, 189f, 260f, 267, 275
interaction theory of metaphor 116, 159
interactive network 198f, 203, 207, 210,
    212
intercultural awareness 329

joke 285–7
journey 118–22, 126, 129, 131, 174, 267,
    296
joy 133–44

kill 47, 103, 104, 113, 226, 263
knowledge of the world 65, 67, 95

lamp 29, 84
landmark 122, 163, **167–71**, 174, 177,
    195–7, 202, 219, 321, 324, 332f
language acquisition 344
language processing 257, 346
language-specific framing 229
LDOCE 25, 39, 117, 175
lean mapping 125f
let alone 251, 344
lexical change 5, 100, 313f, 319, 321,
    341
lexical field 328, 330, 339
lexicalization 86, 98, 112, 117, 258,
    268–72, 279
lie 102, 220f
living being 86f
location 169, 178, 182, 186, 202,
    220–4, 248, 269f, 280, 304, 325
locative relation 5, 108f, 163–7, 172,
    175, 204, 219, 224
logical hierarchies 87
logical view of language 25f, 34, 44, 97
    see also experiential view
long-term memory 13f, 49, 158, 213,
    245f, 252, 257–61, 295, 344
love 121, 133–44, 267, 331f
lower animal 86f

mammal 64, 66, 72, 86–9
manner (as a component of
    event-frames) 220f, 231–44, 250,
    254, 324
mapping

metaphorical 4, 118–32, 154–60,
    173f, 204
of event-frame components 235
cross-space 258, 261, 269, 272, 274,
    281f
mapping scope 4, **119–32**, 154–60,
    173f, 204, 258, 261, 322–4
mass noun 334, 342
meal 53, 92, 106, 330
measure of family resemblances 31, 146
member *see* category member
memory 11–14, 245, 258, 289, 343 *see
    also* long-term memory
mental interactions 182–7, 190f, 199
mental lexicon 4, 40, 42, 60, 62, 330
mental operation 182–5
mental processing 3, 178
mental space 3, 5, **257–61**, 269, 275,
    279, 286, 288, 297, 345 *see also*
    conceptual blending
metaphor 6, 98, 101, **114–25**, 159–62,
    345
    and conceptual blending 257–61
    and emotion concepts 132–44
    and foreign language teaching 331f
    and image schemas 172–4
    and grammaticalization 321–3
    and lexical change 314–16, 318
    and metonymy 114–16, 127f, 135–8
    and the description of linguistic
        phenomena 145–7
    as a figure of speech 114–16
    as a way of thinking 118, 144
    as cognitive instruments 117–21, 154
    in politics 150–3
    in science 145–50
    structuring power of 121–5
    traditional view of 116f
    see also conceptual metaphor;
        conventionalized metaphor;
        constitutive metaphor; derived
        metaphor; explanatory metaphor;
        mapping scope; primary
        metaphor; source concept;
        specific metaphor; target concept
metaphorical extensions 116, 172f
metonymy 6, 99, 101, **114-16**, **127f**,
    158–62, 342, 345
    and cognitive economy 296

and compounding 155
and conceptual blending 257–61
and conversion 155–7
and emotion concepts 132–44
and foreign language teaching 331f
and grammaticalization 321–3
and indirect speech acts 157f
and metaphor 114–16, 127f, 135–8
and part-whole relations 88, 91
and word-formation 155–7
as cognitive instrument 127f, 154
as a figure of speech 114–16
as a way of thinking 154–9
see also mapping scope
mirror network 298 *see also* conceptual
    blending
Modern Languages at Primary Schools
    334
modifier-head compounds 100
morphological blend 268–71, 275, 279
morphology 304
mosquito 86
mother 42, 86, 193, 253
motion
    and iconicity 306–11
    as a component of caused-motion
        constructions 275, 298
    as a component of event-frames
        219–48, 253–5
    in action chains 184,
    in image schemas 165, 170, 178
    verbs of 195–7
motion event 5, 219–44
    and caused-motion construction 275,
        298
    and iconicity 309
    and grammaticalization 321–4
motion event-frame *see* event-frame
motor movements 72, 74
motorcycle 32, 73f
mug 21, 34, 42, 44
Munsell colour chips 9f

naming 1, 8, 14, 21, 24, 35, 67, 69
narrative 230f, 235, 238f, 242, 255
narrative texts 230, 238, 242, 255
network 29, 50, 89, 92, 199, 259,
        266, 269, 274, 281, 286, 297,
        332f, 338

network model 259, 297
neural agitation 138
neural theory of metaphor 345
newspaper 84, 97, 146,
newspaper texts 154, 229, 269, 297
Nigerian English 55
noun 2, 92, 107f, 147, 155, 158f, 162,
        188, 194f, 231, 248, 264, 271,
        276, 298, 302–5, 312, 334–337
nurturant parent model 152

OALD 24, 257f, 322, 328
object (in a clause) 176f, 180–4, 186–8
object categories 20–4, 74, 96, 103–6,
        109, 135, 138, 303, 319, 335
objects
    and word class 191, 194f, 338f,
    concrete objects 19, 23, 35, 38f, 41,
        43, 64, 76, 140, 304, 309, 318
    moving objects 219
odd number 42
Old English 315f, 320
olive 31f, 107, 132
online processing 3, 5, 6, 257f, 261f,
        266f, 270–6, 283, 287, 293–9
onomatopoeia 305 *see also* sound
        symbolism
open path 223f, 229, 321
optimality 265
ostensive-inferential behaviour 290–6
ostrich 25–31, 33, 343

parasitic categorization 77–80, 84f, 96,
        104, 111, 139, 141
parrot 17, 25, 27
participants
    discourse 58, 122
    in metonymies 155
    in Cognitive Grammar 177, 182, 186,
        188, **198–204**, 207, 210, 215,
        261, 275, 281, 289
particle 168, 232–5, 237
partonomy 88–91, 106, 108, 112
part-whole
    compound 94, 97
    in conceptual blending 262–9
    relation 4, 61, 85, 88–92, 94–100,
        103, 111f, 119, 128f, 154f, 190,
        304, 322, 330f, 338, 340, 343

path
    as component of image schema
        167–74
    as component of motion-event
        219–44, 254
    fictive path 223–6, 230, 255
    see also windowing, path
path schema 119, 122, 162, 174, 187,
    197
path strategy 308–12
patient (as semantic role) 177–90, 200,
    202, 247f, 258, 261, 265f, 275,
    286f
pay 207–9, 291, 327
perception 5, 9, 14, 36f, 40–4, 62, 72,
    75, 80, 88, 90, 102, 105, 108,
    139, 163, 186, 191, 204, 219,
    238, 292, 295, 305, 309, 338,
    341–5
perceptual prominence 164
perspective 344
    frame and perspective 207–11, 214,
        217
    in Cognitive Grammar 200f
pet 100, 238, 271
phrasal verbs 239, 332, 342
phraseologisms 338
physiological
    aspects of perception 14, 40f, 108
    metonymy 133–7, 143, 161, 345
pictograms 39, 85
pine 68, 76, 85, 307
PISA 273–5
politics 144, 150–3, 285
polysemy 23, 61, 246–8, 253, 256
poodle 46, 79, 98–100
pragmatic aspects
    of Cognitive Grammar 200–6
    of cognitive linguistics 5f, 346
    of conceptual blending 268, 278f
    of Construction Grammar 248–56
    of context 49
    of Relevance Theory 288f, 293–5, 299
pragmatics 58, 266, 299, 346
Prägnanz 37, 61, 165
preposition 108, 167–75, 187f, 195f,
    204, 231, 247, 277, 334
pride 133, 144
primary domain 193

primary metaphor 160
priming 18
principle of integration 265f, 275
principle of promoting vital relations
    265
principle of relevance 266f, 273, 282,
    287f, 295, 299
principle of unpacking 266
principle of topology 266
problem-solving 283, 285, 295
profile 192, 202
    consistency profile 21f
profiled cognitive region 195
profiled relation 194, 198
profiling 191–195, 202–5, 210, 291
prominence 2–6, 163, 174, 177,
        184–191, 194, 200, 202, 208,
        211, 237, 254, 290f, 310, 344
prominence view 3, 5
properties 106–9
propositional schema 324f, 342
prototype 4, 9f, 15f, 20, 23, 59–62, 92
    and action categories 103–5
    and attributes 26–8, 31–3, 42
    and basic-level categories 72, 75f, 102
    and cultural models 51–5
    and event categories 105f
    and family resemblances 28–31
    and foreign language teaching 339,
        341, 343f
    and gestalt 34–40, 43
    and lexical change 313–20
    and properties 106–8
    cognitive status of 41f
    context-dependence of 45–7
prototype categories 20, 26, 32, 42f, 75,
        102, 105–10, 167, 313, 320
prototype shift 46, 316, 320
prototype split 316–20
prototypical subject 189
prototypicality 17, 40, 62, 103, 111,
        141, 143, 312
pub 39

raincoat 95, 97, 100
re-analysis 323
receive 183f, 217 *see also* construction,
        cause-receive
recognition task 13

regatta blend 262f
reification 248f, 256
relay 281
relevance 5
  see also principle of relevance
relevance theory 289–96
reptile 72, 86
restaurant script 214
retriever 16, 46
rich mapping in metaphors 126f
riddle 284
robin 24–8, 30, 75, 314, 343
role archetypes 177f, 180, 182, 185, 199
rose 79–81, 99f, 105

sadness 133, 135, 140–4
saloon 32, 73
satellite 234–43, 253–5
satellite-framed language 234f, 239,
    242, 255
scanning 196–8, 206
scenario 142–4, 161, 294
scotch terrier 66
script 49, 214–18, 254
sell 207–10
semantic primitive 103, 113
semantic roles 177, 204 see also role
    archetype
semiotics 281, 300
sequential scanning 196f, 206
setter 46
setting 198–202, 240–2, 281f, 287
  and the stage metaphor 185–90
  unspecified 189
shell noun 248–50
shell-content constructions 253
short-term memory 13f
shot in the arm 257–9
signal grammar 335
similarity
  and iconicity 301, 303
  and metaphor 115
  gestalt principle of similarity 36f
  of category members 43, 70, 72, 89,
    345
simplex network 298 see also
    conceptual blending
single-scope network 298 see also
    conceptual blending

situation 48f, 58
solar system metaphor 149, 162
sorting strategy 310
sound symbolism 305, 311f, 341
source category (of compounds) 94, 97,
    100f, 105
source concept (of metaphors) 4, 118f,
    121, 125–32, 135, 144–7, 152,
    161, 204, 258, 261, 266, 293f,
    322f, 331
source model 118
space builder 278f
Spanish 5, 231–43, 251, 255, 305
sparrow 17, 26, 59, 73, 314
spatial compression 262, 270
specialization 313, 316
specific attribute 35, 80f, 93, 98, 104, 120
specific metaphor 125
specificity 200, 206, 235, 344
speech act 154, 157f, 201f
speech event 49, 58, 191, 202, 278
sport 17, 23
sports car 73f
stability of category strcucture 313,
    316–20
stage metaphor 185, 198
stationery 85
stories (used in experiments) 102, 142,
    216, 218, 231, 238f, 255, 310f
strict father model 152
structuring power of metaphor 4, 121,
    124, 152
style 114, 231, 235, 238f, 243, 255, 309
subject 1–3, 5, 147, 176–90, 200, 202,
    205, 208–11, 229, 231, 247, 250f,
    302, 339, 341, 344
  prototypical vs schematic 189f
subordinate category 4, 73, 76f, 79–86,
    92–4, 98–100, 104–6, 109f
subordinate clause 339
subordinate level of categorization 64,
    70, 72, 74, 84, 200, 331, 335
summary scanning 196f
superordinate categories 4, 29f, 64, 67,
    69–74, 77–88, 90, 92, 100, 103–6,
    111, 123, 125, 140f, 329, 331
superordinate level of categorization 72,
    77, 105, 200
symbol 167, 284, 300, 308, 334, 340

syntactic figure *see* figure
syntactic ground *see* ground

take 185
tall 107–9
target concept (of metaphors) 4, 118f, 121–32, 147, 258, 322f, 331
target model 118, 261
taxonomy 65, 67, 69f, 84f, 91, 95, 112
telephone 31, 44
tenor 115f, 119
tense 1, 202, 206, 303f, 312, 321, 324–6, 328, 335
text strategies 308, 311
that-clause 249, 256
toiletries 85
tool 17, 73, 92
toy 17, 79, 82–4, 103, 145, 331
trajector 163, **167–71**, 174, 177, 195–7, 202, 219, 321–4, 332f
translation 191, 194, 231, 236–8, 241f
truck 29, 32, 67, 73, 83, 320
tulip 81, 99
Turkish 243, 255, 312
type-of relationship 4, 64–5, 69, 83–5, **88–95**, 97, 99f, 104, 106, 330f, 339, 343
typicality 16, 18, 23, 31, 34, 41f, 46, 54, 62, 107, 109
typicality ratings 31, 34, 54
Tzeltal 67–9, 73, 76, 84f, 111
Tzeltal plant classification 67–9, 111

uncle 42, 61, 193

vagueness 8, **19f**, 24, 59f, 133, 146f, 319
varieties of English 55
vase 21, 24, 44,

vegetable 17, 31, 59, 198, 279, 331
vehicle 3, 17f, 29–31, 39, 73f, 77, 79, 82f, 88, 103, 115f, 119, 320, 343
verb 1, 102, 155f, 158f, 162, 168, 176f, 181, 183, 185, 194–6, 204, 206–11, 217, 220, 226, 231–9, 242–5, 249, 251, 255, 263, 265, 276f, 303, 309, 312, 321–4, 335, 337f, 340, 342
verb morphology 303
verb of motion 195
verb-framed language 234f, 242f, 255
viewing arrangement 200–3, 206
villa 36
vital relation 160, **260–9**, 272, 275, 293, 295, 297, 331
vocabulary 9, 138f, 148, 233, 269, 305, 313, 328–31, 338–40

walk 104f, 113, 159, 215f, 237, 284, 333
war 115, 121, 123, 137, 151f, 332
weapon 17, 31, 103
weight (of attributes) 27, 33, 47, 58, 94
weighting strategy 310–12, 341
wheelchair 95f, 98, 101, 145, 146, 271
windowing 211, 218, **221–9**, 239, 255, 263, 309
  final 222, 322
  initial 224, 322, 324
  medial 322
  path 223–6, 239, 322
word class 189, 191, 194–6, 202, 330, 339
word-formation 92, 97, 100, 112, 153–5, 157, 268, 275, 279, 329

Yoruba 305